One Who Almost Made it Back

One Who Almost Made it Back

The Remarkable Story of one of World War Two's Unsung Heroes, Squadron Leader Edward 'Teddy' Blenkinsop, DFC, CdeG (Belge), RCAF

Peter Celis

GRUB STREET · LONDON

Published by
Grub Street Publishing
4 Rainham Close
London
SW11 6SS

British Library Cataloguing in Publication Data
Celis, Peter
One who almost made it back: the remarkable story of one of World War Two's unsung heroes, Sqn Ldr Edward 'Teddy' Blenkinsop, DFC, CdeG (Belge), RCAF
1. Blenkinsop, Teddy 2. World War, 1939-1945 – Prisoners and prisons, German 3. Bomber pilots – Canada – Biography 4. Belgium – History – German occupation, 1940-1945
I. Title
940.5′47243′092

ISBN-13: 9781906502164

Typeset by Pearl Graphics, Hemel Hempstead

Printed and bound by MPG Ltd, Bodmin, Cornwall

Grub Street Publishing uses only FSC
(Forest Stewardship Council) paper for its books.

Contents

Acknowledgements

The author received the generous assistance of many people in the preparation of this story of Squadron Leader Ted Blenkinsop. Without it this project could not have been undertaken, and to them a great debt of gratitude is owed.

The lion's share of the credit for this book must go to J.R.W. Wynne, himself a retired RCAF colonel and amateur historian, who provided much-needed assistance in various ways. In 1989, Dick generously volunteered to analyse the Blenkinsop files held by the Provincial Archives of British Columbia, after which he selected for microfilming the relevant records for use in this project, provided countless other documents and leads, and led the way in assisting the search for 'lost' documents and persons who were related to Ted Blenkinsop. In addition to his invaluable material help, his constant enthusiasm and encouragement went a long way in seeing this book through to completion. Much to my grief, Dick passed away on January 6, 2006, when I was just about ready to show him the first version of the manuscript.

Ted Blenkinsop's flying school classmates, Jim Grant and Bob McRae, helped me by providing an insight into a substantial part of Ted's life, his flying training. Jim also helped trace many of the individuals who had crossed Ted's path in the RCAF. I am greatly obliged to both of them.

I want to thank the late Air Marshal 'Larry' Dunlap and the late Lieutenant General 'Reg' Lane, both former commanding officers of Teddy's, in addition to being his friends. Larry Dunlap kindly volunteered, at an early stage, to copy large parts of Ted Blenkinsop's files kept in the Provincial Archives of British Columbia and sent me countless pages of his carefully handwritten copy notes. Reg Lane gave me a sense of a pathfinder's duties and a feeling for the events surrounding that fateful night when Ted's Lancaster bomber was shot down. Both these noted men of Canadian aviation agreed to write the foreword to this book.

I must acknowledge John Neroutsos, a retired air force brigadier general, who furnished many of Teddy's insightful letters written to his family around which I moulded this incredible story. It was also John to whom I turned to discuss the quandaries associated with putting together this manuscript. His wise counsel, together with the sharing of his considerable aviation knowledge, is ultimately reflected in the quality of this project.

I'm grateful for the help of Philip Neroutsos, also a first cousin of Teddy's, who was my first contact with Ted's direct descendants. Philip, together with Teddy's friend Yvonne Jukes, was my greatest supporter. Right from the start of this project they were convinced this story had to be told and recorded. Yvonne, although aging and infirm, provided many of the anecdotes associated with Ted's early life.

The late Wilfried Roels, a Belgian, provided illustrations, maps, artwork and technical insight. He was undoubtedly one of the most erudite aviation and aeronautical devotees I ever had the pleasure to meet.

I am beholden to Faith Gildenhuys, a retired professor of English literature at Ottawa's Carleton University, who undertook the final edit. Finally, I am very indebted to John Davies of Grub Street, who has proved to be the most understanding and considerate of publishers.

I would like to thank again the many people from around the world, many who have now passed on, who gathered the pieces for this amazing life story. Without all their effort in providing their recollections, their wartime letters, aiding in research, or sharing their photos this book would never have come to fruition. Their names can be found in the Bibliography and Sources section at the back of this book.

Finally, I must express my deepest appreciation to my beloved late grandfather, Albert Stas, for suggesting that I research Ted Blenkinsop's life, and to my wife Hilde and children Frederik and Kaat, for their patience and understanding.

Introduction

Brave men are not fearless. Brave men are ordinary men with normal fears who accomplish their dangerous duties or missions in spite of their fears. This is the story of one such man.

I must have been nine or ten years old when I first asked my grandfather about the stranger who was being remembered amidst the victims of the August 1944 raids on our hometown Meensel-Kiezegem, Belgium. Every year in August, this tiny village remembers the brutal crimes committed on August 1 and 11 by armed German troops and Flemish collaborators who encircled the community and let loose atrocious brutalities on its innocent inhabitants.

My late grandfather, who had lost some of his best friends in these raids, visited the memorial cemetery in Meensel regularly. While walking and holding his hand, I became intrigued by the many faces on the individual headstones, in particular the one with a different flag below the face. When my grandfather explained to me that this man was a Canadian pilot, my interest was aroused and I never gave up asking questions about 'the Canadian pilot'. Nobody in the village seemed to be able to provide any answers. Several years later, when I was in high school, my grandfather became a bit tired by my incessant cross-examination, and asked me, 'Why don't you find out about him yourself?' I did, and this is the story.

In 1984, I started writing letters to archives and institutions in England and Canada. Little by little the story came together, and before long it became apparent that Edward Blenkinsop had been a remarkable person. Supported by his cousins, I accepted the task of sorting the story out so I might write this book. The resulting manuscript – originally written in Dutch – of Teddy Blenkinsop's story was essentially completed in the mid-nineties. The unsuccessful and frustrating search for a publisher, as well as rewarding but time-consuming matters, such as starting a family and pursuing an air force career that included countless assignments away from home, caused my interest to temporarily wane. Teddy's first cousin, John Neroutsos, deserves the credit for motivating me to translate the story from my native language into English.

This is the life story of Edward Weyman Blenkinsop. The reader will notice that I occasionally take the liberty of interpreting what Teddy might have been thinking. I venture to do this for the following reasons; first, my background of 20 years in the air force allowed me to step quite easily into Teddy's psyche. Furthermore, in-depth research into his life provided me with a very clear picture of his personality. It is almost as if I had known him in person. Third, I have made a great effort to find as many testimonies as possible, including written reports of people who knew him during the war and even those who were with him right up to the point of his demise. Finally, having read many accounts of the air war over Europe, one is able to construct a somewhat clearer picture of what a crewmember's thoughts might have been during his moments of distress.

Although this book is about the life of a 'pathfinder', a specialised elite airborne soldier, I do not intend to discuss the merits of a strategy of war but rather to paint a picture of the war as seen through the eyes of a single crew. The crews were doing their job as military aviators, which was to execute orders directed towards ending the aggression of a rogue nation-state while attempting to stay alive. I leave the questioning of strategy and morality to others.

Additionally, I never intended to pass judgement on any of those concerned in the atrocious events of August 1944 in Meensel-Kiezegem. I have endeavoured to patch together the bare facts that led to the demise of 67 men in that ill-fated town, including Teddy Blenkinsop, based on available and reliable sources. If I have offended anyone with my writings, I sincerely apologise.

I have attempted to develop and connect the events that I have uncovered which I believe moulded and nurtured this future pathfinder, into what one could only judge to be, a most remarkable individual. Speaking as a Belgian, I can only say, Canada, you must be proud to have this man as your native son.

Peter Celis
Belgium 2008

Foreword

Air Marshal Clarence R. 'Larry' Dunlap CBE, CD, DCL, DEng, BSc

Teddy Blenkinsop arrived in North Africa in July 1943 while my wing left there in October. The overlap was brief but quite long enough for me to recognise his talents as a pilot as well as those of his crew. Indeed his worth as an operational pilot was so quickly established that he and his crew were selected as 'target illuminators' – illuminators are a sort of pathfinder – on six separate occasions during the month of September, an assignment reserved for the best crews.

When Peter Celis contacted me in 1987 to seek my help with his commendable undertaking of writing Teddy Blenkinsop's life story, I was delighted to offer my assistance. What I was able to do by way of archival research I found both stimulating and nostalgic. What little work was involved was the very least I could do in memory of a gallant young man who served me well during the critical days of war. So, if what I did could in any way be described as working, I would say I was doing so for Teddy Blenkinsop, for his late mother, and for my very esteemed friend Cyril Neroutsos, his uncle.

Lastly, may I say that I regard it as a privilege to have been able to help Peter Celis in his efforts to record the story of this outstanding young man who, like so many others, sacrificed his life to the fight against Nazi tyranny.

Victoria, October 1987

Air Marshal Clarence R. (Larry) Dunlap, born January 1, 1908, in Sydney Mines, Nova Scotia, died in Victoria, British Columbia, October 20, 2003, at the age of 95. The Air Marshal, a former Chief of the Air Staff, was inducted into Canada's Aviation Hall of Fame in May 2002.

Foreword

Lieutenant-General Reginald John Lane, DSO, DFC, CD

Teddy Blenkinsop was a remarkable man, whose loyalty, dedication and devotion was brought to light through a dreadful war in which he played a significant part.

Teddy and I were both from the same city, Victoria, British Columbia, and it was sheer coincidence that we should have come together in the same squadron. Our paths had crossed before the war, but we, at that time, were not close friends. I was the commanding officer of 405 (PFF) Squadron, RCAF, when he volunteered to come to pathfinders to start a second tour of operations. This was indicative of this man's dedication to his country.

He was a first-class pilot and crew captain and quickly established himself as a leader. I was, at that time, looking for someone to replace me as the squadron commander when my own tour of operations was completed, and Teddy was the obvious choice.

It was with horror and shock that I watched him shot down while returning from an attack on Montzen, April 27-28, 1944. I was the master bomber for that raid. Teddy was my deputy and would have taken over control of the attack had anything happened to me. The attack came to an end and I released him to return home. It was shortly thereafter that he was shot down, and I was able to identify his plane by the colour of the pyrotechnics that blew up as his plane exploded. His and my airplanes were the only two carrying that colour.

Not until after the war did I hear the rest of his incredible story, starting with his miraculous escape from his airplane.

This book by Captain Celis relates the whole story of a man who can only be described as exceptional. One wonders what he might have accomplished after the war had he survived. He had much to offer and made the supreme sacrifice for his country and the allies. I had hoped that someone might write his biography, because what he did with the RCAF and after his capture is a remarkable tale and needed to be recorded. I am delighted that Peter Celis has taken on the task of bringing this fascinating story of Edward Blenkinsop to light.

Victoria, August 1991

Lieutenant-General Reginald John Lane, born January 4, 1920, in Victoria, British Columbia, passed away peacefully there, October 2, 2003, at the age of 83. General Lane is one of Canada's legendary pathfinders, who are celebrated at the Lancaster Society Air Museum, Nanton, Alberta. He was inducted into Canada's Aviation Hall of Fame in May 2000.

Preface

Edward 'Teddy' Weyman Blenkinsop was the product of a transplanted English gentleman-turned-rancher from the Chilcotin area in the British Columbia interior and a mother whose enthusiasm as a rancher's wife belied her sheltered, cultured upbringing. Teddy's childhood of hardship with the ranching life, interspersed with periods of learning, and warm, loving attention provided by his grandparents in Victoria, produced a young man with all the skills of leadership and attributes he would need to face the challenges brought on by a world in conflict.

Those who knew Teddy at that time were impressed by the dedication of this young man, mature beyond his years, who possessed all the gallant and virtuous traits of the Victorian era. It would be difficult for today's younger, post-heroic era generation to fully comprehend his idealism but, nevertheless, one cannot help but be drawn to this man by virtue of his exemplary strength of personality, his intellect, his intense professionalism and courage.

This story recounts the short life of a master pilot and his crew, as told from the perspective of a young Belgian air force officer and pilot, Peter Celis. It has a sad ending, but it is an uplifting story, which needed to be told after 50 years being dormant. It is also the story of 67 brave Belgians from Meensel-Kiezegem, whose fates were intertwined with that of Teddy. This account records the experiences and impressions of a young Canadian airman, drawn by the imperial call of duty into a global war and its fast-moving series of events. He, in the space of four short years, experienced circumstances and events, sufficient to say, one would never experience in a lifetime.

The family never fully recovered from the loss and the unknown events surrounding Teddy's final months in the infamous concentration camp at Bergen-Belsen. We thank Peter Celis for his dedication and persistence in determining the details to write this portrait of an air force officer and, more particularly, a story that gives a glimpse into the lives of those Canadian youth who chose voluntary service during that tremulous era, the Second World War, the greatest human event of the twentieth century.

John Rolf Neroutsos
Montreal, January 1991

CHAPTER ONE

Roots

It was August 15, 1901, when the steamship SS *Islander* struck an iceberg off Douglas Island, near Juneau, Alaska. The ship's mate, Cyril Demetrius Neroutsos, who was asleep in his cabin at that instance, quickly jumped up, grabbed a pair of trousers, his captain's certificate and life insurance policy and rushed through the ship knocking on the cabin doors. When he eventually got on deck, the last lifeboat was pulling away. A woman rushed to him, saying, 'Save my baby'. Cyril yelled to the lifeboat below and dropped the baby overboard into the arms of a survivor. He then picked up the woman and heaved her into the water. He watched to see that both were rescued by the lifeboat and then jumped into the water just as the ship made its final plunge to the ocean floor. It took only 20 minutes for the ship to disappear beneath the waves. A powerful swimmer, Cyril kept afloat in the frigid waters. Swimming around in the fog, he found a man with a broken leg and supported him for some time until he found a cabin door from the wreckage and put him on it. Rescue crafts arrived and discovered Cyril, exhausted by the cold, reportedly still supporting on his shoulders the unconscious body of a small girl. Only 43 people on board the *Islander* were saved; 142 souls were lost at sea that night. Cyril Neroutsos was the only surviving deck officer.

About 25 years later, when Cyril was walking down Granville Street in Vancouver, a man stopped him and said, 'I believe you are Captain Neroutsos'. He then went on: 'You won't know me, but I'm the man you put on the door after the *Islander* went down. I want to thank you and let you know I'm still alive.' Apparently, the Chamber of Commerce at Juneau still have a pamphlet telling the story of that fateful night, stating the hero of the sinking of the *Islander* was Cyril Neroutsos, the ship's mate.

Cyril Demetrius Neroutsos was the youngest surviving son of George Demetrius Neroutsos, an Athenian aristocrat who had left Greece and settled in Bowden, near Liverpool. There he established himself in the shipping business and ultimately became a mill owner. George had been educated in America at Princeton in the late 1830s where one of his visiting professors was the poet Henry Wadsworth Longfellow. In 1856, George

Neroutsos married Mary Elizabeth Jones, the granddaughter of a Welsh lord of the Barony of Dinorben. The couple had nine surviving children. Cyril, born in 1868, was orphaned at the age of 13 after his parents and a younger brother succumbed to a plague epidemic while in Marrakech, Morocco, where his father, George, had financial interests. The surviving children in England went from extreme wealth to financial insecurity when their father's company assets ended up in the hands of his business partner.

Still, most of the Neroutsos descendants found their way in life. George, the eldest, became a British diplomat. While in Morocco on a routine trip into Bedouin territory, he disappeared one day and was never heard from again. It is assumed tribesmen did him in. Another brother, Arthur, after having been a successful sheep rancher in Australia, gambled his fortune away. After that indiscretion he returned to England, joined the Royal Navy and rose to the rank of chief petty officer. He died in the Battle of Jutland in the clash of the dreadnoughts, during the First World War. One of the daughters, Florence, spent her entire adult life as governess to generations of the family of the dukes of Sutherland. After her death, she was buried at Dunrobin Castle in Golspie, Scotland, an honour normally reserved for the Sutherland family alone. Her sister Catherine married a wealthy British officer attached to the Indian army. Another sister Corinne took vows in a religious order, while yet another one started a Montessori school in Kensington. They all managed to live successful and meaningful lives.

Cyril's uncle, Tassos Neroutsos-Bey, MD and PhD, was another family role model. He was a renowned Munich-educated physician who attended Egypt's ruling Khedives of the Muhammad Ali dynasty having emigrated from Athens to Alexandria. He was also one of Egypt's pre-eminent Egyptologists and a well-published archaeologist. In 1874, he was instrumental in locating what was thought to be the tomb of Alexander the Great. He also undertook the preliminary research which ultimately led to the finding of the ruins of Cleopatra's lost palace and the Lighthouse of Alexandria at Pharos, one of the Seven Wonders of the Ancient World.

As for Cyril Demetrius, the sea was in his blood and, at the age of 14 he went 'before the mast' as a midshipman. He apprenticed in full-rigged sailing ships operating the Australian, South American and East Indian trade where he experienced all the excitements and discomforts of that time. By the age of 18 he had rounded Cape Horn five times under sail. After qualification and for the next ten years, his initial assignment was as a deck officer in the clipper ship *Taranaka*. This ship carried tea to England and, as was the custom of the time, resulted in many thrilling races from New Zealand to the port of London. When steam came of age, he passed his papers for deep sea captain. During this period he met and married a vivacious young English woman from Somerset, Ada Sarah Buchanan Houlton, whose family were landed gentry, the Houltons of

Farleigh Hungerford Castle near Bath.

Cyril's job as a deck officer at the famed British India Steam Navigation Company did not offer him enough excitement and, after serving the company for eight years, he changed to the perishable produce business, sailing out of London to Morocco and the Canary and Madeira islands. In 1898 Cyril left the secure life in England and sailed with his new wife around Cape Horn to Tacoma near Seattle on the SS *Garonne*. During the 1890s Gold Rush in the Yukon Territory ships were crammed with gold and fortune seekers. Because of his marine experience, Cyril was appointed the port captain for Frank Waterhouse out of Seattle, but that did not last long, as he refused to send men to sea in ships that he thought were in a questionable condition. Thus came a period of worry and unemployment, until he was offered a marine survey assignment in the Hawaiian Islands. He spent many months surveying the harbours with a plumb bob for sounding. Some of the maps he made of Hawaiian harbours were so accurate that elements of his charts are still in use today.

In 1899, Cyril's wife, Ada, gave birth to a daughter, Winsome Hazel. Shortly thereafter, Cyril yearned to be back under the Union Jack, so he took his family to nearby Victoria on Vancouver Island. There he joined the Navigation Company shortly before it was taken over by the Canadian Pacific Railway to become known as the British Columbia Coastal Service (BCCS). After the SS *Islander* disaster, Captain Neroutsos served on the SS *Princess May* and ultimately took command of the SS *Queen City* and later the SS *Princess Royal*, all crack steamers sailing between Victoria and Vancouver and Skagway, Alaska.

In those early days before wireless, radar and global positioning, shipping along Canada's west coast was an extremely hazardous business. Dense fogs, fierce gales and blinding blizzards, particularly north of Prince Rupert, caused many a shipwreck. Many mariners consider these waters the most treacherous to be found anywhere on the globe, but, because of men with experience, like Captain Neroutsos, the ships arrived safely on time day after day.

In 1904, Cyril became the father of a son, Cyril Houlton, and during this period he was promoted to the rank of lieutenant commander in the Royal Naval Reserve having qualified on HMS *Swiftsure*. He came ashore in 1911 as the marine superintendent and ultimately was appointed general manager of the BCCS. He was destined to play a major role in the future improvement of transportation on the west coast. He concluded that safety was achieved only through professional development, so he prepared and encouraged young officers in their professional skills by making them specialists on their particular runs. One of his responsibilities was to advise the marine designers of the specific requirements that were to be incorporated into all new ships being built on the Clyde for coastal service. There were few assignments on the Pacific Coast that carried the immense responsibility for marine safety as that of overseeing the affairs of this coastal fleet during this early period of few navigational aids for littoral shipping. When the First World War broke out, Cyril immediately reported for naval duty, but was told it was more important that he remain with the British Columbia Coastal Service.

One can only imagine the contributions Cyril Demetrius Neroutsos made to his adopted country, although he has received little credit in Canada's maritime history books. His reserved and unpretentious manner together with his resolute professionalism earned him great respect and admiration amongst mariners and with his peers within the Canadian Pacific Company. Neroutsos Inlet, an inlet on the northern tip of Vancouver Island, is named in his honour.

He was physically strong, and he was tough – on himself, his men and his family. In spite of this, he was highly admired and respected by all who knew him. While determined that his family should live by his code of ethics, he also shared time with them teaching them to swim, canoe and carve wood, and to enjoy the outdoor life together. He would become the one person who would have the greatest impact on the early character development of his firstborn grandchild, Edward or 'Teddy'. His mental toughness was a trait that did not go unobserved by Teddy. Ada Sarah Houlton, his grandmother, also had a great influence on Teddy's development, especially on his character, spiritual education and his appreciation of the arts, for she was a well-educated woman for her generation.

These grandparents also brought him into contact with the world of aviation. Ada's sister Louisa Buchanan's son, Rolf Neill, was a pilot in the Royal Flying Corps during the First World War. The man who had taught Rolf how to fly was Major Mitchell Clarke. Major Clarke also taught flying to Arthur Harris, who would eventually become better known as Sir Arthur 'Bomber' Harris, Marshal of the Royal Air Force. Mitchell Clarke's involvement with Rolf's family went beyond the flying lessons when he married Rolf's sister Eileen.

During the First World War, Second Lieutenant Rolf Neill served with 70 Squadron, RFC, a unit that operated Sopwith 1½ Strutters. Before the war, he had become close friends with his Canadian niece, Winsome Hazel, a friendship that was kept up with frequent correspondence during the conflict. Sadly, on June 3, 1917, Rolf was killed in aerial combat over Flanders Fields, a place forever preserved in the poem by the Canadian army doctor, John McCrae. Needless to say, his death was a severe blow to his family, and Winsome in particular. The 19-year-old aviator received a final resting place in Menen, Belgium.

Around the turn of the century, the Blenkinsops were an established family in the English city of Warwick. They lived in a large house in the centre of the city, a building that still exists to this day. There were 11 children, one of whom was Hubert, who was born in 1890. As a schoolboy, Hubert enjoyed helping out on a farm in nearby Snitterfield in his spare time. He adored horseback riding, and when the First World War broke out, he became a horse riding dispatch rider in the Royal Engineer Signal Service of the British Royal Army.[1]

As a boy Teddy was not only influenced by the exploits of his father Hubert, but also the gallantry of his uncle and namesake, Edward Winnington Blenkinsop. His uncle was a tall, extremely handsome and dashing young infantry officer attached during the First World War from the Royal Warwickshire Regiment to the Royal Welsh Fusiliers when he was killed at Loos-en-Gohelle. One of his men said, 'He was a gallant leader as he was the first officer to reach the barbed wire at the front of the German trenches. He was leading the charge or as they say "going over the top" into the wire. They had 300 yards to go over open country and within 40 yards of the German trenches and realising the wire was not cut, and without hesitation, he gave the order and last words to his men, saying, "Come along boys" and we got through the wire. The Germans were no more than 30 yards away from us. He then fell backward onto the wire mortally wounded.'[2]

Having many family role models definitely had an influence on Teddy Blenkinsop's character. They had a bearing on how he would conduct his life, especially during the perilous events that were soon to follow.

When the First World War neared its end, Hubert was discharged as a sergeant and returned home, not for long, however, for soon after he immigrated to Canada with his other brother Gerald. Both men were attracted to the outdoor life, and they started a cattle ranch in the relatively fertile area near Big Creek in the Chilcotin region in the interior of British Columbia.

They built a log and sod-roofed ranch house on the property and gave it the name 'Bell Ranch' after the branding icon used on their cattle. Both brothers filled their days corralling, nursing and milking the cattle. Big Creek was a remote and sparsely populated place, with only some of the more determined farmers able to make a living there. In late 1918 or early 1919, Hubert became acquainted with a Victoria city girl called Winsome Hazel Neroutsos. Despite the considerable difference in their ages, it was love at first sight. The two of them wrote letters to each other frequently, even though Hubert had to ride his horse for more than 15 kilometres to the nearest post office. After having seen each other only a few times, the couple became engaged in May 1919.

[1]Dispatch riders were used to bring important military messages to the addressee, often frontline unit commanders, as quickly as possible. The horses initially used were replaced by motorcycles later in the First World War.

[2]Copy of a letter from Corporal W. Cashmore to Edward Winnington Blenkinsop's mother. He was with Blenkinsop when Blenkinsop was killed in action at the age of 23. Lieutenant E.W. Blenkinsop is buried in the Chocques Military Cemetery.

Hubert did everything he could to make the ranch a clean and snug home for his future bride. He was hardly able to make both ends meet and knew that city girls like Winsome were used to a higher level of comfort. Her letters show that Winsome loved Hubert very much, but she was only modestly attracted to the outdoor life in an isolated log cabin. In his letter to Winsome of September 28, 1919, Hubert wrote, 'You know by this time that you are marrying a poor man', and 'I have lived in this house for quite a long time without doing anything to it at all. It is good enough for me but I did not consider it would do for you'.

Hubert and Winsome were married in November 1919 in Victoria, and Winsome moved to the ranch in Big Creek. She took her 15-year-old brother Cyril Houlton with her to help on the ranch and to keep her company. Winsome soon adapted to country living and the times at Bell Ranch were happy ones. When she became pregnant, however, it was obvious that she could not stay long at the ranch, and the couple decided it would be best if she spent the last weeks of her pregnancy with her parents at their home on the original Dallas Avenue in Victoria.[1] At least there she would be nearer any medical assistance should complications arise.

On October 8, 1920, Winsome gave birth to a healthy son. The deliriously happy and proud parents chose the names Edward Weyman which they soon shortened to 'Teddy'. On November 16, 1920, the child was baptised at the Anglican Christ Church Cathedral in Victoria. His godparents were Henry Maxwell Blenkinsop and Cyril Houlton Neroutsos on the one hand, and Margaret Shaw on the other. Teddy spent the first years of his life at Bell Ranch. He adored the open air and spent hours on the riverbank, fishing with a thread and bent needle. When his Grandpa Neroutsos visited and saw this, he quickly disappeared, only to reappear with a real fishing rod and some proper bait.

Historically, the Colony of British Columbia and the Crown Colony of Vancouver Island had a predominate English immigrant population whose sympathies, understandably, were generally pro-British, but nevertheless, with the promise of a railway, a unified province called British Columbia entered the Canadian Confederation in 1871. Prior to that period, Canada, as we know it today, had only begun the process of coming together as a result of the Act of Union in 1841. Canadian colonists wished an end to the old colonial system and wanted self government. After the unsuccessful American attempts to take over its northern neighbour in the early nineteenth century, many of the colonists became fed up with some aspects of British rule. This resulted in brief rebellions in anglophone Upper Canada (Ontario) and francophone Lower Canada (Quebec). The Act of

---

[1]The house still exists today, denoted by a plaque, at the corner of the now Battery and Paddon Avenue.

Union united these two regions into the Province of Canada. As time went by, of course, the British did not want to lose Canada completely and decided on confederation as a form of government. This allowed for a central Canadian administration to have some collective powers, but at the same time to devolve other powers to the existing provinces and those territories wishing to join them in the future.

Growing Pains

In 1926, Teddy moved from the ranch at Big Creek and into the city of Victoria. He was turning six and would soon have to attend a school. While Winsome accompanied her son on the move to Victoria, it took Hubert another year to bid farewell to the farmer's existence and trade it for the city life. He initially accepted a job as an agent for Imperial Life Insurance, but later became a real estate agent for Vandervliet, Cabledu & May. The young family moved into the home of Winsome's parents in Victoria at 1076 Joan Crescent.

Teddy spent a considerable amount of time with his grandparents. Grandpa Cyril, affectionately called 'the Skipper' by the family for obvious reasons, was very fond of Teddy, and these feelings were mutual. The Skipper would continue to have a great influence on the development of Teddy's character.

Until the age of 12, Teddy successively attended Craigflower and Monterey elementary schools. He was very intelligent and achieved first-class results. He excelled in sports, in particular swimming, undoubtedly a talent he acquired from his grandfather. From the age of ten, he successfully represented Craigflower in various interschool swimming contests, which were mostly held in the Crystal Garden Pool in Victoria. In October 1931 he won one contest and finished second in two others, all in the category for boys under 12. In 1932 he was selected to represent the local Young Men's Christian Association, now winning almost every race he entered. A Victoria newspaper reported on April 9, 1932: 'Teddy Blenkinsop made a clean sweep of the under 12 "prep" division to capture the laurels in their different classes.'

As a teenager, Teddy received training as a swimmer from Canada's former Olympic coach Archie McKinnon, who regarded Teddy as winner material. In 1936, Teddy became a swimming instructor for the YMCA and the Royal Lifesaving Society.

On July 24, 1933, Monterey Elementary School granted Teddy his high school entrance certificate, entitling him to enter any high school in the Province of British Columbia. Thereupon he moved with his parents into their new home at 2362 Zela Street in the Oak Bay district and was admitted into Oak Bay High School. He had some fine years there, as is remembered by one of his former classmates, John MacDonald: 'Ted was not only a good scholar and a good athlete, but also very popular with his classmates, both boys and girls'[1]

But it was John Uhthoff who quite abruptly became Teddy's best friend. John recalled what happened:

> I first met Ted when we both entered Oak Bay High School in Victoria in 1934. Ted was a forceful sort of individual who decided, apparently quite suddenly, that we were going to be friends. He rode up to me one day as we were leaving school and gave me a bone-jarring lift home on the crossbar of his bicycle. We became firm and constant friends for the four years of high school.
>
> We spent many hours and days together, talking and building model boats and steam engines with the help of his father, Hubert. For a considerable period of time, Ted was forced to wear a rigid body cast because of a severe back problem. This meant that he often had to lie on his bed, and it was at these times that we told each other wild and improbable stories of our doings when we were not together.
>
> He had his share of fights at school, though I don't remember any specific ones, except for one in the neighbourhood where we lived: a boy named Walter Wickson said something to Ted as he and I were passing Walter's house one day and Ted leapt the fence to give Walter a roundhouse beating with his fists. Ted had a habit of playing a curious pantomime with me in which he would take a series of violent swings at my head, just missing me by a few inches. I think that if one of those wild, swinging punches had landed, I would not be writing this letter now. I preferred him when he was a little quieter, which fortunately he was – most of the time.[2]

Teddy developed back problems at the end of 1936. The doctors obliged him to wear a rigid body corset on a regular basis to relieve his spine.

Despite Ted's restless nature he continued to do well at school. It was obvious that both his parents and grandfather had succeeded in keeping some level of discipline in the young boy. His grade nine report card for the school year 1933-1934 showed first-class marks in mathematics and satisfactory ones in languages, and these results continued to improve over the next few years. By Easter 1937, Ted was second of 24 students in grade 12, his top subjects being algebra and geometry.

Ted seemed to have no interest in girls, at least until he met Margaret Jukes. Margaret's sister Yvonne vividly remembers:

> The first time I saw Teddy was while walking to school. He used to pass us on his bicycle – he and John Uhthoff. He had a cast on his leg

---

[1]Letter from J.C.F. MacDonald, August 9, 1989. John MacDonald was a signal officer in the Royal Canadian Artillery. He landed on the Normandy beaches in June 1944 and fought his way through France, Belgium and Holland to Germany. After the war, he worked for 35 years in cancer research and treatment.

[2]Letter from John Uhthoff, January 6, 1990.

> – a broken bone – but with his usual persistence, he was overcoming an obstacle and pedalling hard with one leg only. I was pretty impressed and used to watch for him every day. My sister Margaret used to tease me about having a crush on someone I didn't even know. We moved from that neighbourhood and it was nearly a year before I saw him again. We had a snowfall, unusual for Victoria, and the snow lay on the ground for a few days. My sisters Shan, Margaret, Maureen and brother Arthur and I went out onto the golf course pulling a toboggan. Maureen did not walk very well because of polio. Teddy was there watching us having fun going down the hills, and we asked him if he would like to join us. We did not realise that he had a cast on his back at this time. He was a little shy and reserved; he didn't seem very at ease with girls. He was probably only about 16. We didn't see much of him again till that summer.[1]

The Jukes family normally rented a house during the summers at Finnerty Bay, about ten miles from Victoria. It had 18 acres of woods and a private beach. Mrs Jukes was a generous person and used to let the friends of her five children come up for a week or two, or on the weekends for those who had summer jobs. Because of the body cast, Teddy was not allowed to work in the summer of 1937. Mrs Jukes asked him, at the urging of her daughters, to spend the summer with them. Winsome, unusual for women in those days, had a job and wasn't home very much, so she agreed. Teddy had told his parents that he was visiting with a friend called Arthur Jukes, completely neglecting to mention the girls in the family.

And so it was that Ted spent a great part of the summer of 1937 at Finnerty Bay. He quickly felt at ease with the Jukes sisters and their many friends and had a wonderful time. Having grown up as a single child, he liked the change of being with a big family. And what about Arthur? He had gone off to a militia camp and was not even there. Grandpa Cyril was uneasy about Teddy being with a family he knew nothing about and so arrived one day unannounced to look things over. He was a bit surprised to find his grandson completely surrounded by girls, all the boys being in town at jobs of one sort or another. Nevertheless, his visit began a long friendship between Cyril and his wife Ada and the Jukes family.

Despite the fact that there were sometimes other boys present at the summerhouse – classmates or boys from the neighbourhood such as Noel Grattan, Wally Earl and Joe Adams – Teddy soon developed into the natural leader of the group. Reserved and shy as he had been at first, he quickly turned out to be an incorrigible rogue, full of practical jokes, with an inventive mind for exciting entertainment. One of his remarkable exploits is evoked by Yvonne Jukes:

---

[1]Correspondence and telephone conversations with Yvonne and Margaret Jukes, 1990.

> We had a great big old boat, and one day decided to go 18 miles across to the USA. The boat was too loaded and another boy brought an outboard motor to put on it. We started out and halfway there the seams in the boat began to open up from the vibration of the motor. We were all pretty frightened; the Straits of Juan de Fuca were quite dangerous, so Teddy took charge and took us to an island. He very resourcefully beached the boat, built a fire and collected resin from some trees. He heated this and filled the cracks in the boat. After it hardened we managed to get home.

On another occasion some of the boys went fishing. One of them, who had been eating the Jukes family out of house and home while demonstrating quite appalling manners, wanted to take his catch into town to sell. Teddy was horrified by the idea of not bringing the fish to the family, so he took the fish and hid it. This, according to his friends, was perhaps another characteristic he inherited from Skipper Neroutsos – integrity.

Teddy treated Yvonne, Shan, Margaret and Maureen Jukes like dear sisters and they all greatly adored him. He confided all his dreams and feelings to them, such as his ambition to become a doctor and his closeness to his father Hubert. However, his mother seemed to him a bit reserved, at least until Teddy was older and more interesting.

And that's how the summer of 1937 ended as perhaps the most enjoyable one in the life of Teddy Blenkinsop. The months and years that lay ahead of him, would be far more challenging.

Far from Teddy's summer days at Finnerty Bay, the political scene in Europe became increasingly tense in 1937. Germany's newly elected Reichskänsler, Adolf Hitler, had decided to take Germany out of the League of Nations in October 1933. In March 1936, in spite of the Versailles Treaty, Hitler further created concern by re-militarising as a reaction to a French-Russian treaty. This created a psychological shock and greatly worried other European governments. In 1937, the Spanish Civil War, in which the German Condor Legion supported General Franco's fascist army, reached its climax, while on the other side of the globe the Sino-Japanese War was turning into a massacre with hundreds of thousands of civilian victims.

Independence

After graduating from Oak Bay High School, Teddy and his parents reflected on his future. George Winter, the father-in-law of Winsome's brother, was the resident partner with the prestigious firm of chartered accountants Riddell, Stead, Hodges & Winter. With Teddy's maths talents as trump card, family connections were called upon and the firm decided to give him a position as an apprentice accountant. He moved to Vancouver on August 23, 1937, where he and John Lambeth, an old friend who had also been hired by the firm, occupied a few rooms in a house on Nelson Street.

These were long and demanding days. During the day, both boys worked at the firm or were alternately trained by a tutor who gave them several lectures a day. At night, they studied and did the assignments the tutor had sent home with them. What little time there was left for leisure, the young men used for a walk, a swim, a game of tennis or the odd visit to the movie theatre or to a local dance. They made new friends and quickly found the big city to their liking. Teddy had to support himself, apart from the occasional extras that Grandpa Cyril or Hubert slipped to him. An apprentice's salary was poor and the city life was not inexpensive, so he was hardly able to make ends meet. Still, as a good accountant, he kept the books balanced. In weekly letters to his parents, he described his experiences of the past days, while asking their advice in a variety of matters. His correspondence is so enjoyable yet factual, that it is a genuine pleasure to quote from some of it, like the note he wrote to his parents on September 13, 1937:

> I'm enjoying my work at present and am doing quite well. I'm going to take a bookkeeping course as advised by one of the fellows in the office who has been through the mill. Yesterday Johnnie Lambeth and I hired bicycles and rode all around Stanley Park in the morning. We then went to Third Beach and lay around until about 4:30 in the sun. We then came home for supper and went out to see a numerologist I heard about. He was absolutely the bunk. To us he was a fake right through. We got home at about 11:30 and went to bed.
>
> Tonight I'm staying in to write letters, wash and mend socks (I put on a clean pair each day to try and avoid holes as I walk at least six miles to and from work), and do some studying.
>
> I'm very comfortable now and have a radio which one of the girls here has lent me for a few weeks. Don't worry about me, I'm not lonely and feel well. If I don't like what they give me I raise a shindig and get what I want. Hope all's well and the worries aren't any worse than usual.
>
> Your loving son, Teddy

Now on the verge of his 17th birthday, Teddy was turning into a strong and tall young man. The physical exercises he had been performing so conscientiously for his vertebrae started to pay off and his back did not bother him so much anymore. The workload at the firm increased every day, but the young men were organised and ambitious enough to deal with it, leaving spare moments to take a break and have fun. They were happy and determined – the world lay at their feet. Ted's parents, who had recently moved back into the Skipper's large home at 1076 Joan Crescent, received the following letter on December 19, 1937:

This week will be a busy one. On Wednesday night Johnnie and I are going to a party given by a Mrs and Dr Mayhood for their son and daughter. Johnnie knows them quite well and he took me up to see them. Later they asked me to the party.

I'm almost through my course at Sprott-Shaw and will be ready for the Institute course in February. After a couple of years in that I will be well prepared for my Intermediate exams. I have no doubt as to my ability to pass both them and my finals. I feel sure that by the time I'm 22 I shall be a chartered accountant and earning $150.00 a month. After that I know just where I shall head and what I shall become. But all this is just as I have it planned in my own mind and it will take much to make it a reality. What I have already said is quite enough for the present and I shall make good that boast before I say any more. It will be a hard climb full of obstacles, but I will make it.

I hope this hasn't sounded like the empty boasting of an ambitious but foolish child for it's not meant that way and I hope you will understand. I hope you will say nothing but just sit back and wait, for it's the accomplishment itself that counts, not the word.

But that's enough of that, and as there is no more to say I will say goodnight and goodbye till Friday.

Teddy returned home to Victoria on Friday morning, December 24, to celebrate Christmas with his family. Margaret Jukes and John Uhthoff were there to greet him when he got off the ferry that had taken him across the Georgia Strait to Victoria. In the weeks that followed, Teddy saw a lot of the Jukes sisters. There were parties thrown at the Jukes's residence, while friends John Uhthoff, Phil McMaster and Noel Grattan also organised a party to mark the reunion of the clique.[1]

While Yvonne Jukes had an indubitable crush on Teddy, he himself had fallen in love with her pretty and more outgoing sister Margaret. Still, there wasn't a single spot of envy in the other three sisters who continued to be fond of Ted as if he was their brother. These sisterly feelings had various effects, ranging from taking Ted shopping to fit him for a new suit to sharing their emotions with him or asking his advice in relational matters with boys. From his side, he continued to be the brother who was always full of fun and banter, but who also had a solution for every problem that popped up. One time he strapped Maureen Jukes into a ship's stretcher and tied her onto a car roof, so they could all go off to a party together.

When Ted returned to Vancouver after New Year's Day 1938, he and Margaret kept in touch by letter. By now, his parents were aware of his

---

[1]Both Phil McMaster and Noel Grattan were later killed in an air incident. Flight Lieutenant McMaster (pilot) lost his life on May 26, 1945, when his B-24 Liberator was shot down over Burma, while Flight Sergeant Grattan (air gunner) did not return from a bombing mission in a Vickers Wellington on May 31, 1942.

relationship, and they invited Margaret to their home to celebrate Easter with them. She made a splendid impression, and everybody became extremely fond of Teddy's girl. The summer holidays were again spent at Finnerty Bay. Ted had a summer job as a camp councillor and swimming instructor at a YMCA summer camp for kids, following which he again spent two additional weeks of his vacation with the Jukes family.

After being evicted, for some reason, from their Vancouver lodgings by their landlord in March 1938, Teddy and Johnnie Lambeth moved into rooms on Bute Street, in a house owned by Mr and Mrs Franklin. This middle-aged couple took good care of the boys; Mrs Franklin even did their laundry and some ironing. Still, when they returned to Vancouver after the summer break, Ted and Johnnie yet again had to look for another place to stay. This time they ended up with Mr and Mrs Goodall in Broughton Street. Both young men were still taking lessons in various aspects of accountancy. They worked very hard and this showed in the results they achieved in examination subjects. Ted's marks were hardly ever below 80 per cent. In a hasty letter to his parents of September 21, 1938, he wrote:

> I know that this letter is a little late in coming but there is so little time for anything but work. You may think this an exaggeration but since last Thursday I have put in 20 hours studying. Our class instructor has given us exam papers totalling 11 hours in accounting, with law yet to come. On top of this are two classes a week, extra study, and later on, office night work.
>
> There's nothing much to tell you as I haven't been going out lately. I went to a hit of a party Saturday night and quite enjoyed it. All the rest of the time I have been studying.
>
> The boarding house is fine so far and the food is the best I've had anywhere. I get a glass of milk outside every day, that is, if there's any money to get it with.
>
> That's all for the present. Will write again as soon as possible.
>
> Your loving son, Teddy

In the meantime, a new apprentice had turned up at the accountancy firm. Frank Darling became a close friend of Ted and Johnnie's. He set off on the same training program as his two predecessors, who became his mentors as well as his tour guides in Vancouver. The threesome went to parties together where they met many other interesting people. Teddy met numerous girls and that often resulted in later dates. But even when she was Frank Darling's attractive sister or niece, a pretty local nurse, the daughter of family acquaintances, or any other young lady, none of them really caught his interest, for the love of his life was still Margaret. He started seeing her more often on weekends and their relationship became more serious. Still, it did not keep him from having a good time in Vancouver whenever his work schedule allowed it. On October 3, 1938, he reported to his parents:

> Last Tuesday Frank, the new junior in the office, asked me out to dinner. Afterwards we went to a movie, he took his girlfriend and I his sister. As Helen, his girl, wanted to see one picture and Kay wanted to see another we wended our various ways to different theatres after parking the car. We went to see *Mr Moto* and *Carefree* at the Orpheum and I think we made the better choice. Anyway, we had a lot of fun and more laughs than a barrel of monkeys.
>
> Saturday night I went to a dance with Jane Murdock, a girl I met at the McDiarmids two or three weeks ago. After the dance we went back to some girl's place and had something to eat and danced till about 2.30am. I had a swell time of it. (How do you get lipstick off a collar?)
>
> In spite of the gadding about I seem to have done a lot of work, about 15 hours last week. I will most likely have some to do over the holidays too. I'm enclosing also a letter to Grandfather.

It was obvious that Ted quite fancied the presence of the opposite sex. The girls, for their part, fell for his debonair and polite yet subtle manners, not to mention his exceedingly good looks.

On the other side of the world, on the night of November 9-10, 1938, the notorious Kristallnacht took place in Germany. During these appalling nightly raids, innocent Jewish citizens were routed, murdered and tortured. More than 90 Jews did not survive the night, while 35,000 were arrested and put in concentration camps. Seventy-five thousand Jewish shops were destroyed and plundered and over 100 synagogues arsoned. Jews all over Europe shuddered, political leaders all over the world looked the other way. Earlier in 1938, Germany had annexed Austria and the Czech Sudetenland, which resulted in a general mobilisation of nearly all of Germany's neighbouring countries.

Around the beginning of 1939 the Skipper organised a cocktail party for his grandson. Ted had just turned 18 and was doing exceedingly well in his Vancouver accountancy job, so the Skipper decided to show everyone how proud he was of him. Naturally he invited Margaret and her mother, but he also asked his good friend Pat Russell, his sister and widowed mother. Pat was an officer in the Canadian Navy. The Skipper could never have anticipated how the party would turn Teddy's life upside down. This event was Margaret's introduction to her future husband, Pat Russell. He was older, maybe more sophisticated and quite different from Teddy. In the coming weeks and months, Margaret had a hard time sorting things out, but she and Teddy finally came to a parting of the ways in the summer of 1939. Teddy was hurt and told the other Jukes sisters that he thought Margaret had fallen for the naval uniform and that her infatuation would not last. However, about one year later, in December 1940, after Pat's ship had been sunk, he came home on survivor's leave. He and Margaret were married a week later. Some of Ted's closer relatives always thought Ted never really got over it. Margaret's picture was among his personal effects sent back to Canada in late 1944.

Was it after breaking up with Margaret that Ted seriously started thinking about joining the service? We will never know exactly, but his girl leaving him for a naval officer certainly hurt his feelings. The fact remains that he began to give some thought to a career in the air force in the summer of 1939. From then on, the Jukes sisters only saw Teddy infrequently, except for Maureen, whom he did see from time to time. He had long conversations with her in which he would give her encouragement and they did raise her spirits. She always remembered their last encounter:

> One day Teddy asked me out to a show. This time he seemed very upset. When we came back I asked him to have tea or coffee with me, and he asked for a fire. I told him that the wood needed to be cut but that it was in the basement and I couldn't go down. Ted picked me up and carried me down where I could sit and watch while he chopped. We went back up and lit a fire, made some tea and talked until late at night. That was the last time I saw him.

CHAPTER TWO

The Call of Duty

Near the end of August 1939, Adolf Hitler signed a non-aggression pact with the Soviet Union. Western European countries, like Belgium and the Netherlands, had already lost hope of a peaceful solution of the tensions in Europe and were mobilising their armed forces. On September 1, 1939, the fear of many became reality when German troops brutally invaded Poland, leaving a trail of death and destruction behind them. Two days later, Great Britain and France declared war on Germany. Canada followed with the same militant response on September 10, 1939, while Belgium, the Netherlands and other countries anxiously confirmed their neutrality. Unfortunately, the United States Congress maintained its isolationist stance during the initial phase of the war. President Roosevelt did what he could within the law to help his allies. In March 1941, Congress passed the Lend-Lease Act authorising the shipment of US war materials to nations under Axis attack, primarily Great Britain and the Soviet Union. A loan was arranged with the US after termination of their aid to Britain under this program at war's end. Final payment of this loan was made to the US in 2006. Generally, Britain stood alone in Western Europe, although tens of thousands of European men would escape German tyranny and join the British armed forces to continue the fight from the British Isles.[1] Unfortunately, the United States only entered the war against Japan following the attack on Pearl Harbor on December 8, 1941.

In those days, as the German army overran Poland and their submarines caused disaster wherever Allied shipping was to be found, thousands of volunteers besieged Canada's recruiting offices. Anticipation of the thrill of adventure and the prospect of visiting foreign shores undoubtedly influenced the decisions of many early volunteers, but as news from across the Atlantic grew more sombre, these feelings were gradually replaced with a quiet sense of duty. The Canadian government, via the media, reminded

[1]As an example, 29 Belgian pilots arrived in England in time to fight the Battle of Britain at the side of British, Canadian, Polish, American and Czech pilots. About 620 more Belgians served as aircrew in the Royal Air Force in the war years to follow, several of them eventually rising to command RAF squadrons and even wings.

everyone of the menace the Commonwealth countries now faced and urged each to share the burden. The First Canadian Division was in England for Christmas 1939, and the British Commonwealth Air Training Plan, a cost-shared program to train aircrew and ground crew was signed in December 1939. Canada was selected as the host country for this plan, partly due to its vast size and suitable terrain for airport construction.[1] Good year-round weather and its remoteness from direct hostilities were some of the other considerations.

In his letter of September 6, 1939, Teddy wrote to his parents:

> Regarding the Air Force, I have collected a lot of information and am studying it carefully. I think my application would be acceptable providing I can pass the medical. This would mean that they would put my name on the waiting list and they would call me when they required me. That might not be for some time.
>
> I wonder if you would mind sending my birth certificate over. They require the nationality and birthplace of the applicant's parents, could you give me this – I don't know whether Dad considers himself English or Canadian or whether you consider yourself American. Would you send this as soon as possible as I will need them quickly after I have made up my mind.
>
> Do not be afraid that I will rush into this. I'm waiting for some indication of policy by the government. I shall have to swot up one or two little subjects to help out my application too. I wonder if you would mind asking the Doctor and Mr Eastman if I may use their names as references.
>
> That is all for the present. I am carrying on as usual at work. Mr Winter assured me that my job would be held for me if I joined up, and there is some talk about the intermediate standing being given to volunteers.
>
> I will let you know before I take any final steps so don't worry.

However reassuring he was trying to be in his letters, it was quite obvious that Ted had made his mind up about joining the forces. He had always been fascinated by his father's stories of his exciting experiences as a dispatch rider in the First World War. The story of his Uncle Edward as an infantry officer, the gallant exploits at sea of his grandfather and the daring life in the Royal Flying Corps of his mother's cousin Rolf Neill had enthralled him since childhood.

When Canada declared war on Germany on September 10, 1939, Teddy knew the implications of the policy taken by his government. Shortly afterwards he sent in his application forms and informed his parents of his

---

[1]Canada trained 44 per cent of the 340,000 Commonwealth aircrew graduated between 1939 and 1945.

decision. Meanwhile he continued to study hard, convinced that the air force would not need him immediately, if they ever needed him at all. Although he was still getting top marks in his assignments and accountant exams, aviation was piquing his interest, and so during that October he started watching the aircraft take off and land at Vancouver's Sea Island Airport. At any opportunity he talked to engineers he met about aerodynamics and piston engines. Around this time, Teddy often spent his spare time while in Vancouver in the company of some peers with whom he had attended school in Victoria – Harry Clarke, the brothers John and Hugh MacDonald, Tom McMartin and Dudley Smithies. They spent their Sunday afternoons walking through the city, followed by games of bridge at the home of Irving Dwinell.[1]

On December 23, 1939, the first Canadian troops arrived in France. Many eager Canadian airmen or applicants joined friendly air forces, such as Britain's Royal Air Force.[2] In the period of November 1939 to March 1940, the world witnessed a bitter fight between the Soviet Union and Finland. The Soviets suffered tremendous losses and the Finns retained their sovereignty. The period was also the start of the longest military campaign of the war, the Battle of the Atlantic. Meanwhile, the German government continued constructing concentration camps and filling them with Jews and other 'undesirable aliens' that did not fit Hitler's Aryan dream.

On March 8, 1940, Teddy received a letter from the Department of National Defence, Air Force, telling him:

> The revised terms of entry and service under the British Commonwealth Air Training Plan have made it necessary to reconsider all applications now pending for elementary flying training appointments in the Royal Canadian Air Force. Your application is one of a great many of good standing that have had to be held over because of an excess of offers of service over actual needs to date. You are invited to peruse the attached memorandum carefully with particular reference to the terms of entry and service under the new plan....
>
> Regulations now in force make it necessary for you to submit a new application, provided that you are desirous of offering your services under the revised terms of entry....
>
> While the intake of air personnel is likely to be greatly increased in

[1]Correspondence with Harry Clarke and John MacDonald, 1989. Harry Clarke and Tom McMartin served in the Royal Canadian Air Force during the war, Hugh MacDonald and Dudley Smithies in the Royal Canadian Navy, and John MacDonald in the Canadian Army

[2]During the Second World War, the RCAF expanded almost 200 times its peace time strength, from 1,150 to a peak of 206,350 in 1943. In total, 93,844 RCAF personnel were in direct service with the RAF overseas in both RAF and RCAF formations. 25 per cent of all RAF flying personnel were Canadian.

the near future, it is desired to inform you that due attention will be paid to the priority earned by your original application.

(signed) A T Cowley, Group Captain, for Chief of the Air Staff.

The attached memorandum contained all kinds of conditions applicants had to abide by. There were the limits of age – 18 to 28 years for a pilot and observer, 18 to 32 for a wireless operator or air gunner. Education requirements were junior matriculation or its equivalent, and the applicant had to be 'of pure European descent' and resident in Canada. They had to be prepared to serve anywhere in Canada or overseas. Lastly, applicants were 'required to be of good character, observant, alert, self-reliant, keen on flying, practical and possessing intelligence and personality'.

On April 9, 1940, German armies invaded Norway and Denmark. Belgium and the Netherlands still cherished a hope for a bystander's role in this European calamity, while it was obvious to some that their Prussian neighbour was preparing for an offensive in their direction.

Teddy continued to work and study from his Vancouver digs, and there wasn't much news to report in his letters, except for one thing – he had met an interesting girl and had taken her out a couple of times. Her name was Helen Woodcroft. She, like Teddy, had grown up and lived in Victoria. She later attended the University of British Columbia.

The Skipper and Granny Neroutsos did not particularly like the idea of their only grandchild going off to war. Ted's uncle, Cyril Houlton, who had been a militia officer since 1926 and assigned to the Three Rivers Tank Regiment in September 1939, visited him in Vancouver. He told Teddy in no uncertain terms that there was no point in two from the same family going to war, but Ted had made up his mind.[1] In a letter to his parents, he wrote on May 19, 1940:

Uncle Cyril took me to lunch yesterday and we had quite a long talk. I guess Granny has a pretty good reason to be proud of him. The Winters took us for a drive in the afternoon and we went back there for dinner before Uncle Cyril caught the train. It was nice to see him and it was good of him to take so much trouble to see me.

Johnnie went down to the Air Force and told them he would like to get in. They gave him an X-ray and told him to report for another medical Monday morning. If he passes, he will leave for Toronto the same night.

Have been working pretty steadily both at the office and at home. I have my course all planned out and broken down into sections for study and intend to go at it pretty hard from now on.

---

[1]Uncle Cyril was honourably discharged on December 7, 1944, because of injuries incurred while serving with the Royal Canadian Armoured Corps. He held the rank of lieutenant-colonel and was the commanding officer of the King's Own Calgary Regiment. He was decorated with the Distinguished Service Order in the Italian campaign as a result of his performance in planning and executing the battle to secure the San Leonardo bridgehead.

Ted's letters did not make it easy for his parents to assess what was on his mind in those days. By describing Johnnie Lambeth's experiences, he obviously tried to get them used to the idea that he was going to join the forces, but, on the other hand, he continued to take his studies and accountancy job seriously, as if this was going to be the only important matter in his near future. In spite of all this, he soon filled in his new application to join the air force and was planning to hand it in at the RCAF recruiting centre in Vancouver. After his Uncle Cyril had paid him an ultimate visit on that morning of Monday June 3, 1940, Ted crossed the street to the recruiting centre and enlisted. The staff there could not say anything about his chances of becoming a pilot, only that he would be assigned to aircrew training if he passed the medical. Most of the day he spent dressing and undressing in various offices and being subjected by impersonal doctors to a thorough aircrew medical.

The following day he returned to the enlistment office, lined up with some fellow recruits, was officially sworn into the Royal Canadian Air Force, Aircraftman Second Class Blenkinsop, E.W., R57933, and ordered to report to 1 Manning Pool in Toronto. His document folders were marked P/O, indicating that he would, if all went well, be trained as a pilot or observer. While the individual volunteer could express his preference, the air force would make the binding decision on the basis of performance at the initial training school as to whether he would be washed out altogether or selected for training either as a pilot or observer. That same night Ted bade goodbye to his parents in the Vancouver Railway Station and boarded the train to Toronto.

CHAPTER THREE

Into the Service

The objective of the British Commonwealth Air Training Plan was to train pilots for the Commonwealth Air Forces, and not just for Britain's RAF, but its success as well as the continuing need for aircrew soon led to its expansion. From October 1943 onwards, the plan had 10,906 training aircraft at its disposal. Experienced civilian and military instructor pilots, many having returned from operations, delivered 3,000 well-trained pilots every month into the system. In the end, 131,553 flyers received their badges at the 97 CATP schools.

After a long and uncomfortable train journey, Ted arrived at Toronto's Union Station on Saturday morning, June 8, 1940, from whence his group of volunteers were bussed to 1 Manning Depot at the Canadian National Exhibition grounds overlooking Lake Ontario. These manning depots of the RCAF were basically stations where civilians were transformed into uniformed raw material suitable for further training. Ted was one of over 5,000 volunteers who were bedded together in the Canadian National Exhibition's old cattle and horse show buildings called the 'Horse Palace', an immense room filled with rows and rows of double deck iron bunks.

With the issuing of uniforms and kit came the endless hours of polishing shoes, buttons and brass. The new airmen were continually lined up for a parade of some sort, be it dental, medical or equipment inspections. Inoculations took place in the bunk area of the Horse Palace and for unsophisticated young men it was a rather traumatic experience. They were lined up at their bunks where medical officers attacked both arms with shots against unheard-of diseases. In addition, they were sometimes ordered to drop trousers and drawers for what was called 'short arm inspection', a check for venereal diseases. There were morning wake-up physicals, drills, parades, route marches, and lectures on deportment and behaviour. Officers were to be saluted whenever and wherever, and so was the country's flag. While there were always individuals who would cross the street to avoid having to salute an officer, the country's flag was a symbol respected by everyone. The vast majority of volunteers sincerely believed they were there to serve Canada in her hour of need.

As usual when young men congregate, horseplay took place and in the air force it was common practice. On top of that, the new recruits were the lowest ranking humans at the station, and the non-commissioned officers (NCOs), corporals and sergeants made their presence known and drilled the recruits into recognising their supreme authority. Disrespect was dealt with in many unpleasant ways, such as confinement to barracks, loss of passes and disagreeable jobs, like latrine duty. When on parades, tricks used by the NCOs to get volunteers were many and varied. For example, when men with driver's licences were given the order to step forward, they believed they were going to be drivers, when in fact they were detailed to washing dishes or garbage disposal. Ted and his cohorts quickly learned not to volunteer any information. Many young men who were away from home for the first time had second thoughts about having joined up. They began to wonder how they could have volunteered to get themselves in such a situation. Still, life could be enjoyable too, during this period of adjustment. For those who liked long walks, the route marches were agreeable when the weather cooperated. Soccer and basketball occupied the more athletic types, while reading and study areas were available for those devoted to educating the mind. Concerts and shows in the evening kept busy all who were so inclined. The inevitable discussions at any hour of the day between young men from varied backgrounds and education were both enlightening and often good for a laugh. How Canadians in different parts of the country lived triggered many a chuckle or a laugh. This atmosphere of being in the dumps together and trying to make the best of it developed a sense of perspective and camaraderie amongst the inductees. This was to stand the recruits in good stead – and they would continue to build upon it in the months and years ahead.

Ted did not know any of the other boys in his section at Manning Depot. Johnnie Lambeth had arrived there a few weeks earlier and was about to leave again and move on.[1] Still, Ted sounded quite satisfied in his letter of June 13, 1940:

> Things are going just fine. We were inoculated and vaccinated Monday, dentist yesterday and IQ tests today. They're just pushing us through as fast as possible. The first in at 07:45 a.m. and the dismiss at 04:15 p.m. After that we may leave barracks and stay out till 10:30 p.m.
>
> I polish buttons and shoes three times a day. It's not bad now with one uniform but next week we get our summer issue of light khaki and then there will be two to do and two pairs of boots.
>
> We're going to the Hunt Club next week which is a very snooty place taken over by the air force and used to train aircrew. We'll spend

[1] Johnnie Lambeth would eventually train to become an observer.

4 weeks there and then be assigned to flying schools. It's possible I may get back to Vancouver to the Sea Island base.

Johnnie and I went with Shan Jukes to the Rees' Tuesday night and had a very nice evening. We took Shan to dinner last night and I am taking her out on Saturday night.

Haven't made any particular friends as yet though I've met quite a bunch of fellows since I've been here. It takes me a little time.

I'm really happy now. This is what I like.

Your loving son Teddy.

After three weeks at Manning Depot, those in Teddy's draft that were selected for aircrew went to the Eglington Hunt Club situated on Avenue Road in Toronto on June 24. The Royal Canadian Air Force had appropriated the grounds and buildings of this elite private club to set up the 1 Initial Training School there. The young volunteers, once again, were bunked in horse stables that had been converted to sleeping quarters.

ITS was a ground training centre for would-be aircrew and here matters became much more serious. The pace was hectic, but morale was sky high, for many of the subjects on the curriculum were clearly linked to the flying training that lay hopefully ahead for these young men. Additional to that, the students were now clearly marked as flight cadets, as they were entitled to wear a white flash in the front of their wedge caps. There were several subjects: mathematics, navigation, wireless including Morse code, armaments, law and discipline, sanitation and hygiene, plus four to six hours in the Link Trainer. The Link Trainer was an enclosed, revolving box with instruments, in which they learned the basics of flying. Additional lectures were engines, theory of flight, aircraft recognition, meteorology and war gases and how to deal with them. Drill, parades and physical training filled the remainder of the on-duty hours. Students were awakened at 06:00 a.m., made beds, shaved, washed, showered if there was time, polished shoes, shined buttons, cleaned and dusted their room, had breakfast, and went to parade for the officer's inspection. Classes began at 08:00 a.m. and ended at 05:00 p.m., with one-hour lunch breaks in between. For most students, navigation was the most intensive subject. Whether becoming a pilot or an observer, a working knowledge of aerial navigation was absolutely essential. In their four weeks at the Hunt Club, Ted's class received almost 200 hours of navigation lectures and in the evening problems and plotting for homework. The instructors, many of whom were former schoolteachers, tried to determine the aptitude of the cadets. At the end of the ITS course and on the basis of their assessments, they recommended the best cadets for further training, either as pilots or observers.[1]

Perhaps the toughest test of all at ITS was the M2, the second medical.

[1]Observers were later called navigators.

This was a four-hour ordeal, consisting of careful colour and in-depth vision checks and all kinds of seemingly odd items, such as testing the student's sense of balance. Many students were washed out following their M2, but Ted passed it without difficulty on June 21, 1940. Another important hurdle was the personal interview, where the interviewing officer tried to fathom the student's motives, preferences and character, to subsequently assess him as 'P' or 'O' material. Despite the tempo at ITS, Ted was able to write a letter to his parents on July 8:

> Well, this course is over halfway through now and everything is going well. My average mark rather amazes me – it's 100%! On one of my papers the officer wrote 'a very superior paper' and that is considered a pretty high compliment.
>
> Had my personal interview last week and was told that I would be recommended as a pilot. So all in all everything is going along pretty well.
>
> Had a 36-hour leave this weekend so I went to St. Catharines with Ed Burton who bunks just above me. We had a pretty good time of it too.
>
> There are some nice fellows up here and we all have a pretty good time. We have quite a bit of sports and one thing and another.
>
> Well, I have an exam tomorrow and I must get a good mark so I must study. Remember me to Helen if you see her and say I will write soon. Ditto to John Uhthoff.

When examination time came, some students had to study late every night, even after lights out. For others, like Teddy, fresh out of school, most of the exams were fairly easy. After having completed all exams, Teddy and his friends were issued with two flying suits, one helmet and a pair of goggles. They still did not know their fates but were told that in three or four days the evaluations would be complete and they would get their promotions to leading aircraftman and their postings. Obviously, the tension mounted noticeably. On July 20, the verdict came. Ted and his fellow-students were issued with their new insignia of rank, a propeller badge to sew on their sleeves, and told to fall in to learn their classification and postings. All in all, 485 candidates from the 509 in Teddy's draft had successfully completed the ITS course, and 250 of these were selected for pilot training. Teddy was one of them, and came out 20th of 485, with a final result of 95 per cent. Twenty-four spots were available at the Sea Island Elementary Flying School in Vancouver. They were given to 23 students from British Columbia plus one from Toronto.

Learning to Fly

During the last weeks at the Eglington Hunt Club and then while travelling on the train together to Vancouver, Teddy became close friends with Robert

W. 'Bob' McRae, a young man from Vancouver.[1] They were amongst the 24 selected to start flying training at 8 Elementary Flying Training School. Ted's group was the first class of pilots under the British Commonwealth Air Training Plan to be trained there. 8 EFTS, installed in the 'Aero Club of BC' buildings on Sea Island Airport in Vancouver, opened officially on July 22, 1940.[2] Ted's class arrived the next day.

While 8 EFTS was an RCAF training centre, it had grown out of a private flying school and was operated like one under a station manager. The discipline was not rigid and relations between students, teachers and flying instructors were friendly and informal. The school had about 50 training aircraft at its disposal, the de Havilland 82C Tiger Moth. With a wingspan of 29 feet 4 inches, the Tiger Moth was a very attractive biplane, with a perspex canopy to cover the two tandem seats. Weighing not much more than 1,000lbs, the aircraft had a 145 horsepower Gipsy Major engine, which was extremely reliable. Being a training command aircraft, it was painted the standard and eye-catching bright yellow.

Training started immediately upon their arrival and, with his instructor J. Jacobson, Teddy logged his first 30 minutes in a Tiger Moth on Tuesday, July 23, 1940. He was overwhelmed. The following days he flew two or sometimes three training sorties a day, even on Sundays. And then, before the normal ten hours, his instructor stepped out of the back seat of Tiger Moth 4051 that sunny morning of August 2 and secured the empty safety belts in the back. Ted's heart came up in his throat. To his great relief the 20-minute solo flight went well and he made it back in one piece under the watchful eye of his instructor. After he had taxied back to the apron, Jacobson and some of his classmates walked up to congratulate him. Teddy glowed with pride. A first hurdle towards becoming a pilot had been taken successfully. The days then followed in quick succession. The students attended ground school classes either in the morning or afternoon and flew during the other half of the day. Ted did solo confirmation check flights on August 3 and 4, and more solo flights on most days that followed. He successfully passed his 20-hour test on August 14 and proudly reported to his parents that same day:

> Passed my 20-hour test today. There were several that have to have another check at 30 hours but I was lucky enough to get by without it. So I'll be a pilot for another 30 hours anyway. We start aerobatics pretty soon now, that's going to be a lot of fun.
>
> Well, at last I'm a LAC and not an AC2. Our promotions came

---

[1]Bob McRae was of tremendous help when the author started researching Ted Blenkinsop's life in the mid-eighties. He particularly threw light on Ted's early RCAF years. After the war, he joined Trans Canada Airlines, but retired for medical reasons and became the chairman and majority shareholder of a very large and successful group of mutual funds, the Universal Group. He died in Toronto on July 21, 2004.

[2]The Sea Island Airport is the site of today's Vancouver International Airport.

through just a day or so ago. With flying pay we get about $2.30 a day now.

We may get off on Monday again though it's not definite yet. If so, I'll be home Monday morning again.

As training proceeded, Teddy came to love the little Tiger Moth aircraft more and more. It was a beautiful craft and amazingly rugged. Some of the student pilots bounced them all over the aerodrome like rubber balls, while others lost control and ground looped, sometimes dragging a wing tip. Ted completed no less than 52 training sorties or 30 flying hours in the month of August alone – an incredible average, which was driven by a desperate need for pilots.

There was an acute shortage of pilots in England, where the Royal Air Force was engaged in a ferocious air war now known as the Battle of Britain. In fact, for the RAF, a new and serious phase of this battle commenced on August 8, 1940, when bombing attacks by the Luftwaffe intensified. Fierce air combat developed with high losses to both sides and a month of attrition began in which the British system was strained to the utmost. By husbanding his resources, RAF Fighter Command's Commander-in-Chief, Sir Hugh Dowding, showed a moderate but steady build-up in personnel and surprising increases in aircraft strength and reserves. On August 3, he had 708 fighters available and 1,434 pilots, a marked improvement over the figures of the preceding months. But still nobody seemed to know exactly what the coming months would bring, although it was obvious that Hitler was trying to break Britain's back.

While the flying training at 8 EFTS continued at a rate of one or two sorties a day, seven days a week, the last ten days were also devoted to writing final examinations in ground school and taking flight checks. Thursday, September 5, was the stressful 'ground school exams' day, but at noon Ted and his fellow students were in for a real treat that largely compensated for the tension they had endured during the morning. To honour the first graduating class in British Columbia of Royal Canadian Air Force student pilots under the British Commonwealth Air Training Plan, the Kiwanis Club of Vancouver hosted a special luncheon in Hotel Vancouver's ballroom. In early 1940, there had been a sentiment voiced by the citizens of Vancouver that they were not being given an opportunity to do their part in preparing young men for service in the air at a time when the British Empire was greatly in need of reinforcements. Several high profile Vancouverites demanded that city facilities be used to their fullest capacity. With funds raised at an 'Air Supremacy Drive', training aircraft were purchased, while Kiwanis Club president Les Martin personally obtained authorisation for a school to give elementary flying training. Within a few days he had gathered a staff of instructors and set himself the task of organising and supervising the work of the school. There were 1,000 guests invited to the luncheon, an incredible number, made up of local business leaders, government representatives and high-ranking RCAF officers. A grizzled veteran of air warfare, Group Captain Leigh F. Stevenson, organiser of western Canada's air training schools and Officer Commanding 4 Training Command, congratulated the students on the completion of the first third of their training course. Stevenson, who was an army veteran of the First World War, had joined the Royal Flying Corps in 1918 and later served the RCAF in many capacities. In his opening address, he said:

> When we finish training you, you won't have fear of any Jerry. No Canadian in the last war ever turned tail on a Hun. Canadian airmen are getting twice the amount of training that Germany's best pilots are receiving and are flying superior machines.
>
> Our hardest task is to select pilots, gunners and air observers from the material we get, which is uniformly first rate. Everybody wants to be a pilot, although the gunners and observers are often more important positions.

Group Captain Stevenson concluded by paying tribute to the successes already achieved by the first fighter squadron to see action in the RCAF. In fact, at the time of his speech, two all-Canadian squadrons were involved in the fierce air combat of the Battle of Britain, 1 (F) Squadron, RCAF, and 242 (Canadian) Squadron, RAF, comprised of nearly all Canadians.[1] In total, 87 Canadians flew alongside their British colleagues of the RAF in the Battle of Britain. Twenty of them would be killed in action by the time it was over.

Another guest of honour who was loudly applauded was William McKnight, whose son had been recently awarded a Distinguished Flying Cross for outstanding service with the RAF. Then the Honourable T. D. Pattullo, Premier of British Columbia, presented awards in the form of silver identification disks bearing the crest of the RCAF to all 23 graduates of 8 EFTS. The event was graced with music played by the Seaforth Highlanders' regimental band and vocal numbers by soloists Isabelle McEwen and George Kent. Canadian citizens were proud of their young volunteers and made no effort to hide it. Naturally, Teddy and his friends glowed with pride, not least when they saw the articles and photos covering the event in the next day's issue of the *Vancouver Sun*.

Despite the 'graduation' luncheon offered by the Kiwanis Club, the elementary flying training was not quite finished yet for Ted's class. While his official service records show September 15, 1940, as his graduation date at 8 EFTS, his logbook showed several more elementary flying training sorties beyond that date. Ted's momentous day came on September 18, when the testing officer, Flying Officer Poag, appeared to take the 50-hour flying test. In a letter to his parents he reported the following day:

[1] 1 (F) Squadron would later become known as 401 Squadron, RCAF.

> Passed my exams second highest with an average of 85%, which wasn't too bad. Also took my 50-hour test and came out well. The examining officer told my instructor I was okay and would make a good pilot. It must have been okay because he said he would recommend me for whatever I wanted. I said 'bomber pilot' though it was a tough decision to make. But so many want to be fighter pilots and only a few will be so I thought I might as well apply for the big planes before they stuck me on them. You see I'm good on aerobatics but far better on instruments. Besides these fighter planes are too damned uncomfortable and anyway I black out easily.

Notwithstanding his taste for instrument flying, it remained arduous work. Once the student pilot pulled the linen hood attached to the underside of the coupe top over his head, his world shrank to the blacktopped control stick, the throttle, the rudder pedals and the instrument panel in front of him. There was absolutely no way he could see anything outside the cockpit. Through the ear tube the instructor would then order the student to carry out a series of flying manoeuvres. The Tiger Moth cockpit was not equipped with an artificial horizon, so the student pilot had to find out whether he was climbing or descending by reference to the altimeter and the rate-of-climb indicator, both of which lagged a little before responding. The turn-and-bank indicator, which could also be persuaded to reveal, indirectly, whether the wings were level or not, revealed the turning action of the aircraft. The blend of mechanical and human imperfections resulted at first in the aircraft following a dreadful roller-coaster path through the sky, weaving and skidding from side to side at the same time. For half an hour or more the student pilot had to keep his eyes roving rapidly from one instrument to the other at the same time trying not to overcorrect by concentrating all his attention on rectifying one undesirable gauge. Needless to say, instrument training was very demanding, but after several sessions the student pilot learned to develop a relaxed but steady crosscheck of all instruments, which allowed him to keep steady control of the aircraft without reference to the outside world.

The atmosphere in Ted's class was excellent. The pacing at EFTS was intense, but the student pilots were well aware that they were part of a unique experience and generation. Though originating from various backgrounds and localities, they helped each other where possible, and some strong and long-lasting friendships were forged. Ted's best chums were Bob McRae and John Thorne; the latter was also his bunk-mate. Ted completed his last flight at EFTS on October 8, 1940, his 20th birthday. His logbook now contained 83 flying hours on Tiger Moths, half of which were flown solo. He stood second in his class and again registered his preference for bombers. His request was granted, and on October 11, he and his classmates were on a train to Saskatoon in the province of Saskatchewan. There, 1,200 kilometres from Vancouver and in the middle of the Canadian Prairie, the young men reported for duty at 4 Service Flying Training School. They joined a party of about 15 student pilots who had received their elementary flying training at Windsor, Ontario. Both the fighter and bomber aspirants in the group would take their advanced flying training course at 4 SFTS.

After settling in and filling out the necessary paper work, Ted's class immediately went to work. On October 16, Teddy was introduced to one of the workhorses of the British Commonwealth Air Training Plan, the twin-engine Avro Anson. The Anson was a reliable aircraft, stable and steady for its size with a cruising speed of about 120 mph, and it could stay aloft for a maximum of four-and-a-half to five hours. There were no effective heating arrangements in the aircraft so it was miserable to operate in very cold weather. After a familiarisation flight, his instructor Flying Officer MacLean took Teddy up again in the afternoon for his first flight of the conversion course. He did two more instructional flights with F/O MacLean the next day, and on the morning of October 18, Flight Lieutenant McKnight took him airborne for his solo check flight. After 30 minutes, McKnight had seen enough and ordered Teddy to land the Anson. The Flight Commander of 'B' Flight jumped out of the airplane, leaving Ted to take the Anson up alone. The solo flight went smoothly, and shortly afterwards F/L McKnight and Teddy finished the day with a subsequent conversion ride, seven flights in three days. The pace at 4 SFTS was not going to be any slower than it had been at EFTS, but Ted felt good about that; he liked to set his heart on something and get on with it. The sooner he could get to England and into the fighting, the better. In a long letter written on Sunday, October 20, he recounted to his family:

> Well, this is a God-forsaken spot here – the most dreary looking place I've ever seen. Our quarters aren't so bad, though someone forgot to put a heating system in them, making it pretty cold as you may well imagine.
>
> I'm flying Avro Ansons now. They're used as patrol planes in England but are mainly trainers now. They carry pilot, co-pilot, navigator, wireless operator and gunner, a crew of five in all. They carry bomb-load too. Not bad planes, easy to fly, but rather boring in a way, though at first they keep you so busy you don't know what to do first. I soloed on Friday and I think all of the Vancouver crowd, both on Ansons and Harvards, have soloed. The Harvards are trainers for fighter pilots. I rather wish I were flying them, but later we'll get into something bigger and better.
>
> We had a 48-hour leave this weekend and most of us hardly knew what to do with it. We didn't want to stay at the barracks yet we're at loose ends in town. Oh well, maybe it's a good thing, we'll be able to save a little money.

Ted's class of 42 neophytes was organised in two groups, called 'flights'. Ted and Bob McRae, along with Ed Burton and a few others, found themselves initially in 'B' Flight. Their regular instructor was Flying Officer MacLean. On most instructional flights more than one pupil was taken up, so that everyone could learn from the mistakes made by others. Ed Burton would become Ted's 'twinned' student. The switch from Tiger Moths to Ansons was a big bite for Ted and the others to digest at first. There were many differences to get used to, since the Anson was a twin-engine aircraft and hence heavier and more powerful. It had higher cruising and approach speeds and a greater range. Fitted with flaps and retractable undercarriage, it was a more sophisticated aircraft all around, and the instrument panel reflected the change. Engine instruments now came in pairs, and a directional gyro and artificial horizon added to the other instruments they had grown accustomed to in the Tiger Moths. At SFTS the emphasis in the daylight flying program lay on cross-country navigational flights, instrument flying and reconnaissance missions on which the trainee was expected to make sketch maps of designated towns, outlining road networks and other features that would have particular military significance. The course also contained formation flying, various radio exercises in flight and simulated bombing runs. Night flying was to be given much more prominence than at EFTS and, after the class had gone solo and done a few weeks of day flying, including some periodic tests, they went on several night cross-country flights. The whole flying syllabus had a markedly more advanced stamp to it; it was obvious that a good deal more responsibility and maturity would be expected of the students in the air, where they would log approximately 150 hours, double the elementary quota.

The ground school course was also much heavier at SFTS. Navigation remained the primary subject and was allotted the greatest number of hours. Another significant topic was armament. It included a course of lectures on the various pyrotechnics in use as signalling devices, as well as the manual on the Browning machine gun, which had to be memorised by the students. The class spirit was exemplary. Everybody helped each other where possible, understanding that they would more easily make it as a group rather than as an individual. The ten youngsters of the Vancouver-Victoria area formed a tight inner faction in the class.[1] On October 25, a day on which he had flown three missions, Ted wrote in a letter to his parents:

> We were told today that we will finish our course here on January 12 and that most of us will be instructors. That means we won't get our

[1]Although Teddy grew up in Victoria, he counted himself one of the Vancouver boys as a result of his long period of study and work there. The cities of Vancouver and Victoria are only about 80 kilometres apart.

wings until then. It's almost as tough as being a chartered accountant!

I have about 4 hours solo in these flying greenhouses now and am just beginning to get the hang of them. There really isn't much to it, they're just big, that's all.

Our classes are pretty strenuous here; I've never worked so hard in lectures, especially the navigation. I have to do my own work and show Thorne how as well and that keeps me humping. The Vancouver bunch is doing well here. We had a barrack inspection and our room was the best and is held up as an example. We had a signals test and the first eight were all from Vancouver. I think we're holding our own in the flying end too. We stick together pretty well, and when we want anything done we manage to get it. They're putting in a proper heating system for us and that's a big relief as you may well imagine.

Will write again soon, hope all O.K. Teddy.

When the young fliers received 48-hour passes over the weekend, the Vancouver gang, or at least part of it, usually went into town together, looking for a way to relax and unwind a bit. On one occasion six of them went to tea at the home of a friend of Phil Shannon's. There were quite a few rather nice girls present, and the sextet took some of them to a supper dance and had quite an evening. Teddy and his bunkmate John Thorne also visited the Harrington family from time to time, friends of an acquaintance of Ted's parents. The Harringtons were very kind and assured Ted and John they could come up any time they were in town. It must have felt good to have a place to go to when they were more than 1,200 kilometres from home.

In the meantime, Teddy became very interested in navigation and became a standout in the class. He went on cross-country navigation flights where he often hit the waypoints right on the nose and within seconds of the planned 'time over target'. The flight lieutenant who was the navigational instructor began using Teddy as an assistant whenever Ted had finished his own work. It is very likely that his above average performance in navigation at SFTS to some extent may have influenced his ensuing postings.

While only six months had passed since their training as military pilots commenced, Ted and his cohorts were continuously made to realise that such training was serious business. Five per cent of those who had trained with them at the Eglington Hunt Club and had been selected for pilot training had been killed during their subsequent schooling and over 20 per cent washed out, so they became quite conscious that achieving their ambition was not as easy as a lot of them seemed to think at first.

In mid-November 1940, there was some hope of Ted's finishing his class prior to Christmas, so the work tempo was even increased. Lectures and flying started at 07:00 in the morning, straight through till 05:30 p.m. Half the class had to take lunch from 10:30 to 12:00 a.m. and the other half from 12:00 to 01:30 p.m. There were extra lectures in the evening and all 48-hour passes were cancelled until further notice. It clearly seemed that the school was in a hurry to get them through. Still, it became quite clear that they were not going to be sent overseas. The program seemed to be preparing Ted and his mates to ferry aircraft all around Canada for a while and then to go to an instructor's school. It was a tremendous disappointment for most of the class and some swore they were going to get to England no matter what, but the British Commonwealth Air Training Plan was in dire need of instructors, and it seemed Teddy's class were just the people needed.

Teddy kept in regular touch with his family, and they informed him of Margaret Jukes's upcoming wedding. He did not want to pay much attention to the event and asked his parents to send Margaret a card and gift. In his letters however, it is quite obvious that he still felt let down by her.

Ground courses, Link Trainer sessions and flying tests continued to follow each other in quick succession, and some student-pilots began to show symptoms of stress disorder. In a letter to his parents, Ted recounted:

> Thorne had a funny experience the other day, he lost his temper and dove one of these ashcans of ours up to well over 200 mph and pulled it out too quickly. He bent the fuselage and burst in two windows and damn nearly froze coming home – it's about 40 below zero up topside, so he'd had a chance to cool off in more than one way!

As the work-crammed days flitted by, Teddy spent a lot of time in the air. Towards the end of November, he flew four or five training sorties a day, while spending the rest of the time in the classroom or Link Trainer. Work was never finished before 10:00 p.m., with the next day starting just eight hours later. Ground school exams took place in late November, which started to turn up the pressure a little more. Nevertheless, having worked steadily all along, Teddy was fairly confident about getting good results. On December 18, Teddy went up in the air a record-breaking seven times, doing three day and four night trips. Altogether he logged five hours and 55 minutes that day. Still, somewhere during that same day he found time to write to his parents:

> Haven't written for quite some time but things have been happening so quickly we don't know whether we're coming or going.
>
> We are getting our wings on Friday and are leaving here the same night but where we're going I don't know. We've been flying day and night ever since we finished our ground school exams and I haven't had a chance to get into town for over two weeks.
>
> Thorne cracked up yesterday – he came in without putting his wheels down. Fortunately he wasn't hurt and the plane wasn't

> damaged much. We've been flying so much that everyone gets tired and fed up and don't give a damn what happens.
>
> Had a little fun the other day – there was a low cloud and fog bank 20 feet above the ground when I was on a cross country so of course I had to fly under it. So I got down on a railway track about 15 feet off the ground and bowled along at about 160 mph and did steep turns over every village on the way. It's rather fun to watch the people duck as you come down on the town.
>
> Didn't do so well in ground school this time. The navigation paper was so easy everyone got a good mark, which cut down my lead. However I was first in the twin engine group and fourth out of the whole class with 80%.

The following day came the ultimate challenge at SFTS, the wings test. While the recent flight tests in navigation, formation and instrument were all very important – in fact each was a *conditio sine qua non* – and kept the students honed to a fine edge, the crucial one, marked on the syllabus forebodingly as 'wings test', was the last one to come. Its status as the 'make-or-break flight' had loomed for weeks in the minds of the class. After having flown four more trips, one solo and another one as a passenger, Teddy's name was called to take the test. He went up in Anson 6080 with Flight Lieutenant Gross, Officer Commanding the Anson Squadron, as testing officer. After 45 minutes in the air, during which time Gross put Teddy systematically through the complete repertoire, Teddy landed the Anson and was told by the chief instructor that he had passed the test. F/L Gross marked in his logbook next to 'wings test' the grade 'satisfactory'. Ted now totalled 148 flying hours, and was a qualified pilot of the Royal Canadian Air Force. It had taken him a little over six months. That same evening he sent a telegram to his family in Victoria: 'Wings Parade tomorrow – Leaving Saskatoon tomorrow night – Don't know where to.'

Friday, December 20, 1940, was the day Ted and his friends had worked for so hard over the past six months, the day they had dreamed of so often, the awarding of their pilot's wings. The presentations were made in a simple but impressive service conducted by Group Captain Duncan Bell-Irving, Officer Commanding 4 SFTS and a war ace of the First World War. Representatives of the other armed services, together with about 75 friends of the graduating pilots, attended the function, which was held in one of the large hangars at the training school. After the customary congratulatory speech by the group captain, 38 students received their coveted pilot's licence out of his hands. As the group captain pinned the wings badge on the carefully pressed blue uniform and shook hands with each new pilot, there was a generous round of applause from the enthusiastic spectators. One student, Leading Aircraftman Bernard 'Barney' Boe, received a special distinction as a result of obtaining an average final score of 85 per cent in both theory and flying. Six others obtained a distinguished pass, by averaging between 80 and 85 per cent in theory and flying. These were Leading Aircraftmen Arthur Coles, Phil Kennedy-Allen, Edward Blenkinsop, Geoff Mackie, Mick McGuire and Robert McRae. All seven had graduated from the first training class at 8 EFTS at Sea Island Airport.[1] Teddy had come out first of the twin-engine group and fourth overall. He was very satisfied with the result. The remaining 31 graduates were L.H. Huffman, L.J. Bryant, S.W. Campbell, S.D.R. Lowe, W.E. Yeates, L.A. Unwin, Jim Grant, John Thorne, F.R. Shedd, Maurice Belanger, Ed Burton, G.R. Robinson, Alex Milloy, Ed Fleishman, R.B. Aitken, Geoff Lancaster, Will Strachan, W.S. Clarkson, D.G. Kelsey, W.L. Marr, Nelson Spencer, J.M. Lillie, W.W. Southam, Larry Hickey, C.J. Ladouceur, T.P. Flint, C.F. Harwood, Phil Shannon, J.A. La Roque, L.M. Parsons and J.E. Reade.[2]

After the Wings Parade, came the time to celebrate. A 'Wings party' had been organised, a refined little soirée financed by the graduating class. Ted and his chums had been looking forward to this evening and were determined to have a good time. The guest list started with the social elite, the instructors; it was common practice to invite deserving persons with whom the students had a strong affinity, the line chiefs, the Link Trainer operators and the WAAF's from the parachute section and flight office. Several journalists were present as well, and there was ample coverage of the whole event in the Saturday morning newspapers.

One important question remained unanswered: which of the new pilots would be commissioned as officers? The customary practice was to award commissions to the top third of the class and to promote the remainder to the rank of sergeant pilot. The issue was resolved the next day, when Teddy and about ten others from his class were commissioned as pilot officers; Ted received serial number J3467. In the meantime there was the critical issue of postings to be settled. Ted's class was told that they would not be going home for Christmas but had to stay at 4 SFTS to take a special one-week course following which the posting would be published. Thirty-three of the new graduates were posted to the Central Flying School at Trenton, Ontario, to become flying instructors, while the remaining five were transferred to the recently-opened 1 Air Navigation School at Rivers, Manitoba, to take an advanced navigation course. Ted was amongst the

---

[1]Sadly, Bob McRae would be the only one of the seven to get through the war unscathed. Flight Lieutenant Boe, 441 Squadron RCAF, was killed in action on September 25, 1944, when German fighters shot down his Spitfire Mk IX while he was patrolling over Arnhem. Art Coles was shot down and made a prisoner of war on the Eastern front. Pilot Officer Phil Kennedy-Allen, instructor in 9 SFTS at the time, was killed on April 26, 1941, when his Harvard collided with the one flown by his student. Pilot Officer Geoff Mackie, instructor at the Central Flying School in Trenton, was killed on February 15, 1941, when his Harvard crashed in the Bay of Quinte near the school. Flight Lieutenant Mick McGuire died on August 31, 1944, when his Halifax of 1664 HCU crashed near Caernarvon, Wales, during a cross-country training flight.

[2]Nine survivors of the graduating class gathered in July 1991 to unveil a memorial stone at the Sea Island Airport where they had started their pilot training 51 years earlier.

latter group, and so were Bob McRae, Jim Grant, Maurice Belanger and Ed Burton. They travelled to Rivers on January 4, after having celebrated the New Year in Saskatoon. Rivers, a town about 200 kilometres west of Winnipeg, was reputed to be one of the coldest places in Canada.

Per Ardua Ad Astra

While all pilots received training in navigation during the ground school part of their training, as well as map reading for tactical navigation, only a few were selected for special navigation training. The purpose of sending Ted and his four colleagues to Rivers was undoubtedly to have them specialise further in the art of direction finding, probably with the ultimate objective to produce five new navigation instructors for the BCATP. Whatever it was, Ted and the others did not know; they were hoping that they were posted to the school in anticipation of being sent overseas.

The quintet arrived at Rivers on January 4, 1941, and was right away impressed by the clean and comfortable quarters. Ted and Bob McRae were the two officers in the group of five sent to Rivers and shared quarters in the officers' mess. They had no duties to attend to anymore, as they were assigned batmen to shine their uniform buttons, polish their shoes, keep their room clean and make their beds. This was exactly the type of living Teddy enjoyed, devoting himself totally to his work without having to worry about the little everyday things of life. A further benefit of being an officer was the substantial pay raise. As a pilot officer he now made $6.25 a day, but this did not turn his head. Being practical by nature, he invested straight away in a new uniform and a Victory bond. At the same time he asked his parents to start looking for a house that he might buy.

Bob McRae had been married 'without permission' in September 1940 in Vancouver, and nearly lost his commission when it was revealed on his arrival at Rivers. In the early war days, only singles were permitted to join the air force, on the grounds that singles were 'free of mind'. Some, however, argued that it was a government attempt to avoid paying the numerous widows' pensions it might have to assume because of the war. Even so, Bob and his young bride rented a small house in Rivers, so he seldom used his assigned quarters he shared with Ted, except when they studied together.

Despite the fact that the quarters at Rivers were quite adequate and that his fellow officers seemed to be a friendly bunch, Ted was pretty disappointed. He had hoped to be sent overseas and into the action, and felt that the course at Rivers was costing him valuable time. However, he realised that he had to reconcile himself to the situation, and decided to continue to do his utmost best in whatever the air force had in store for him. Furthermore, Ted and his friends were made to understand that there was a promise of good things to come for a select few who achieved high marks on the course. One of these would be a promotion to the rank of flying officer, while some had the prospect of being held over for an 'astro' navigation course. That was quite something, as there were so few astro qualified pilots in the air force.

1 Air Navigation School had moved from Trenton, Ontario, to Rivers and was opened on November 23, 1940, with the purpose of providing much-needed observers for the bomber, Coastal Command and reconnaissance aircrews of the Commonwealth air forces. The school was commanded by Wing Commander Arthur Miller and was equipped with Avro Anson aircraft that were arriving in quantity from the UK.[1] The instructors were an interesting lot. The chief instructor was Squadron Leader Gillson, an ex-professor of mathematics from Montreal's distinguished McGill University. He was a lantern-jawed type, a brilliant lecturer and conversationalist but not a particularly good organiser. Larry Cooper was another first-rate mathematician from McGill's mathematics faculty and Kenneth Maclure was an actuary trained at McGill. Mowatt Christie was a well-known geology professor from the University of British Columbia. In addition there was an Australian, Andy Guinand, who was top-notch. All in all, they were an impressive group of tutors and each one a specialist in geometry, astronomy and navigation.[2] The 1 ANS at that time had two types of courses for pilots: a long navigation course of six months for senior pilots and a short navigation course of about eight weeks during which pilots trained as navigators, hopefully to the same standard as professional air observers. Teddy entered No. 7 Short Navigation Course that started on January 6, 1941. The first course instructor was Flying Officer Larry Cooper. He was replaced later on by Flight Lieutenant Mowatt Christie. Mowatt recalls:

> I remember No. 7 Short Nav well. Prior to that I had been in charge of No. 6 Short Nav which was not a very satisfactory class and one that had a bad time at Rivers. While on a night exercise, a dense snowstorm came up and two aircraft crashed, killing four of the group. This was only part of the problem as both before and after the accidents the class lacked the keenness one was accustomed to.
>
> No. 7 Short Nav was the exact opposite and a good part of the credit was due to Ted Blenkinsop and another chap called Bob McRae. I remember one sat behind the other in class and there was terrific good-humoured competition between them. Both were very bright and their critical enthusiasm seemed to lift the interest of the whole class.[3]

---

[1]Arthur Miller later rose to the rank of Air Marshal and became commander-in-chief of the Royal Canadian Air Force.

[2]At that time, there was no airborne navigational radar equipment. Navigation was by dead reckoning and map reading supplemented by navigation by the positions of celestial bodies, and to a lesser extent by Radio Direction Finding (RDF).

[3]Letter from Dr Mowatt Christie to the author, November 20, 1990.

Ted and Bob had witnessed the crash recounted by Mowatt Christie. They were studying in their quarters when they heard an aircraft in difficulty and then crash not far from their window. All the occupants died in the fire while Ted and Bob watched emergency services trying to rescue them. It was the first time both of them realised that people who fly airplanes could get hurt if they are not both lucky and careful.

The lectures included using a sextant to obtain star shots to fix a position. The students learned how to find selected stars suitable for navigation and how to take daytime sun shots. The long navigation theory sessions were now and then interrupted by practice direction-finding flights with the Ansons. During these flights, the students had to take sun or moon shots to navigate by or plot a course by using the stars or by 'direction finding'. A Mercator map was used to outline where to go, taking into account predicted wind speed and direction. On the return leg, the students frequently had to direct the aircraft to drop a practice bomb onto a target on a nearby firing range. During these missions, two students were on board, one acting as first navigator, the other one as second navigator, whose task was to corroborate the work done by the first nav. These trips usually lasted three hours, which was just long enough to prevent the young map-readers from freezing to death in their flying classroom. Teddy flew on five such trips in January 1941 and another seven in February. On his first one, on January 17, he was first nav and won the everlasting admiration of Bob McRae, his second, by hitting all three route points in a three-hour flight, a feat none of the others in his class could equal. On January 30, he reported to his family:

> Work is getting pretty heavy here now. We have lectures six hours a day and for the last week I have had to go back and work till 11.00 or 12.00 nearly every night – a little too much of a good thing I think. I've got a busy evening, we're flying first thing in the morning and I have maps to prepare besides doing a lot of trig and various other things that are a little behind.
>
> We're having a dance in the officers' mess tomorrow night, I hope my date turns out alright. They bring in 30 or 40 girls from Brandon for the affairs and it usually turns out pretty well.
>
> I guess I make more money than is good for me at this age and am likely to make even more soon. It should be a good opportunity to salt a little away till the day I can carry out a little ambition of mine. Anyway, don't let it worry you. I won't turn into a confirmed drunkard or anything!

Ted's date that Friday night, January 31, was Frances Martin. She recalled the event clearly:

> In late 1940, shortly after the RCAF Station at Rivers, Manitoba became operational, the Adjutant, Flying Officer Jim Boyd organised

> dances for the officers. He arranged for a number of girls (many were graduate nurses) and their friends to travel by bus from Brandon to the officers' mess at Rivers, returning later in the evening to our homes. As a friend of a relative of Adj Boyd I received invitations to the dances.
>
> Early in 1941, at one of the dances, I met a very tall young officer named Edward Blenkinsop. He wore a ring engraved with his family's crest. Subsequently, my girl friend and I received an invitation from Ted and his friend to attend a dance at the Prince Edward hotel in Brandon. I believe they were celebrating their graduation.
>
> I recall Ted asking what colour my evening gown would be. I replied pink and mauve. Having just emerged from the Great Depression we were lucky if we had an evening gown, usually a graduation dress.
>
> On the evening of the dance, as I entered the place where I boarded, my landlady handed me a florist's box that had just been delivered. Nestled inside lay an exquisite corsage of pale pink flowers tied with a mauve ribbon. We all admired their beauty and perfection and it was with delight that I pinned the flowers to my gown that evening. Almost 50 years have passed, but I will never forget the loveliness or the thrill of receiving my first corsage. It was an exciting beginning to a lovely evening.[1]

The officers' mess provided comfortable distraction to the young officers, even on nights when there were no dances. It was a restricted area where they had dinner, read a newspaper, wrote a letter home or engaged in conversation over a cup of coffee. In the late hours, some of the young officers might even become a little obstreperous after a few drinks, but Teddy always remained a shy, retiring type who minded his own business. He was always a gentleman and unobtrusively lingered in the background. What is more, he did not spend a lot of time hanging around in the mess, as he was usually studying in his room or helping others. Fellow student Bus Imrie later recalled the many hours that Ted painstakingly spent with him, pointing out the names of the stars that were important to recognise in astral navigation. Ted seemed much more proficient in star recognition than the rest of the class.

On March 1, 1941, No. 7 Short Navigation Course was completed. Ted received a certificate signed by Wing Commander Miller, stating that he had passed the course with 90.8 per cent of the total marks and had been assessed as 'exceptional', the only one of the class. He and his four friends were finally allowed to take some leave, and on March 4, Teddy travelled home to spend a fine ten days with his family, whom he had not seen in six months. He spent some of his time off with his friends John Uhthoff and

---

[1]Letter from Frances Martin to the author, September 25, 1990.

Frank Darling, who were impressed by his recent adventures and would themselves soon join the RCAF, but seeing his girlfriend Helen again was the cherry on the cake.[1] She and Teddy soon became 'an item', and it was apparent that Helen Woodcroft was going to be the girl who would erase Margaret's image from Teddy's mind. Helen told Teddy during this visit that, upon graduating from the University of British Columbia, she planned on joining the RCAF and making herself useful to the war effort.

Ted's family drove him back to Vancouver on March 15, from where he took a train back to Rivers. Back at the Air Navigation School, he and Bob McRae embarked on a new course the next day. These lessons were called astro extension navigation, and would last four weeks. Ted passed this course with 87 per cent and was assessed 'above average'. While being proud of his results, he could not but regret the inevitable consequence; the school wanted to retain him at Rivers as a navigation instructor.

And so Ted began the next phase in his air force career. His new function was going to include classroom instruction as well as night flying as check pilot to test the work of other non-flying ground school instructors. Being a tutor did not mean that life was going to be easy for Ted. Things would keep running at a terrific pace, with instructional work, studying and catching up on his own flying skills; by now he had not sat at the controls of an aircraft in three months. On April 14, he took an Anson up for a two-hour practice flight, and the following day he did the same. The days thereafter he took every opportunity to take to the air and brush up his instrument and navigational proficiency.

His first assignment was as an instructor of the No. 11B Air Observers Course, starting around April 20. The air observers, a poorly chosen name later changed to navigator-bombardiers, had been through Manning Depot, Initial Training School, Air Observers School, where they learned the elements of navigation, and bombing and gunnery. The Air Navigation School was the final stage of their training before going into war. Air observers courses lasted four to five weeks, whereupon the graduating navigators left the school and were replaced by a new bunch. With 11B Air Observers Course Ted was working with Flight Lieutenant Kenneth Maclure, who had just proposed a new system for navigation in the high Arctic.[2] As a result, the moment the course was well on track, Chief

---

[1]John Uhthoff earned his pilot's wings on December 3, 1942, and served in England as a fighter pilot. Frank Darling joined the forces in July 1941 and became a navigator in 644 Squadron, RAF, on Halifax bombers. He was severely wounded by flak on October 1, 1944, and was repatriated to Canada. He died in January 1976.

[2]In the Arctic, one is so close to the magnetic pole that the compass is unreliable and, in addition, the lines of longitude converge at high angles so steering by reference to magnetic north is no longer practical. Ken Maclure proposed navigating with reference to the Greenwich Meridian, with rules for checking course by astro and a system for changeover from the normal magnetic routine to the Arctic grid routine. His system, called grid navigation, became the polar standard used throughout the war by the RAF and USAAF. Ken Maclure, a member of Canada's Hall of Fame, died of a heart attack in March 1988 while on holiday in Mexico with his wife.

Instructor Maclure turned out to be very busy with writing reports and the like, so Ted and his fellow instructors Bob McRae and Fred Brand had to do practically everything. They were flying three-hour navigations nearly every night, arriving back at the mess around 05:00 a.m., out of bed again at noon and lecturing all afternoon, and flying again all night. And so it went, with exams and corrections thrown in on top of it all. Besides all that, Ted was doing a fair amount of studying on his own at the request of Squadron Leader Gillson. Ted could not figure out why, but Gillson and Ken Maclure had been after him quite a bit to find out how much he had been doing. It would become clear at a later stage what the two had in store for him. When 11B Air Observers Course was completed, a new bunch of navigator students was already waiting. Ted's next class was No. 13 Air Observers Course, an all-Australian group. He liked instructing them very much and praised their keenness, discipline and good manners.

Whenever he had the time, Ted took a 48-hour leave pass and travelled to Saskatoon, to spend the weekend there with some of his friends from pilot training, Phil Shannon and Barney Boe. He always had a great time with them, although on one occasion they brought him the awful news of classmate Phil Kennedy-Allen's loss in a mid-air collision with his student.

In July 1941, Ted was informed of his next posting. Despite the urgent appeal sent in by Squadron Leader Gillson to keep him at Rivers, the commanding officer in charge of setting up the new 2 Air Navigation School at Pennfield Ridge, New Brunswick, made a special request for Pilot Officer Blenkinsop and was not to be put off. The astro course at Pennfield had to become an exact duplicate of the ones at Rivers, and Ted seemed to be the right man to make that happen.

But before that, Ted was allowed to take a break. He left Rivers on Friday, July 25, to go home for a longed-for ten days of leave. He took the train to Vancouver, where he boarded the afternoon ferry to Victoria. It surely felt good to sleep in his old bed and savour homemade cooking again, after all the months spent in the officers' mess. He thoroughly enjoyed the company of his parents and grandparents, but it was the outings with old friends and the amorous afternoons with Helen that pleased him most. However, good things never last long, and on Monday, August 4, Ted arrived back at Rivers. He found his class back where he left it and resumed ground courses and night flying. He flew three-hour trips on nearly every night following his return, finishing the class on Friday, August 15. The weekend was spent packing, finishing paper work, turning over his various jobs and getting his clearance papers signed. On Monday, August 18, Ted left Rivers for good. Thus he parted with Bob McRae, Jim Grant and the others. Ever since July 1940, Bob McRae and Ted had spent more time with each other than with anyone else. Now they would both take different paths and never see each other again. Bob, who affectionately called Ted 'Blenkie', is undoubtedly the best source of Ted's developing personality in his first year in the service:

> Blenkie was a *very* hard working, *very* patriotic, *very* intelligent young man. He would straighten my uniform cap on my head, in fact he did everything in the proper manner. He was great at drill, I was terrible. He was about five years younger than me and was what we considered 'blue blood'. I was not.
>
> Blenkie was tall, thin, unbelievably good-looking with pink cheeks and jet black waving hair. He walked erectly and was everything the air force wanted in an officer. (I was screwball looking but had more fun.)
>
> He was obsessed with the desire to get into action. We were all volunteers, but I was in no rush to die, but quite willing to get on with it when required. All of us were like lemmings – all wanted to get on ops but had no idea of what it was all about.
>
> I do not remember the exact dates, but in July 1941, I think, Blenkie was sent to Pennfield Ridge in the Maritimes to help set up an astro school there. That was the last I saw of him. So, from July 1940 to July 1941 I had spent part of every day flying, teaching, eating, and working with Blenkie. However, we were seldom alone together for heart to heart discussions. He was no drinker! And a real fitness nut. I was the reverse. We had a mutual respect for each other's flying and teaching capabilities, but he always considered me a bit of a maverick who he had to discipline slightly. We took every opportunity to work on our flying ability, he to win the war when he got on ops, me to do the same but at the same time try to save my neck. I really do believe that he was brave beyond comprehension.
>
> We had several like him on our course. They were all killed. You will note from the listing that all the 'best' pilots got killed.[1]

The Other Ocean

The journey to Pennfield Ridge was long and wearying. Fortunately Ted had time to spend in Toronto, so he paid a visit to Shan Jukes, who was trying to make a living there. He took her out on two or three occasions and the two of them had a good time reminiscing about the pleasant summers spent at Finnerty Bay, but there were also more uncomfortable moments in their conversations, as when Teddy revealed to Shan that he still had deep feelings for Margaret. Shan for her part let it slip that her sister Yvonne was in love with Teddy. This made Teddy quite upset and he

[1]Letter from Bob McRae to the author, April 25, 1988.

never connected with the Jukes sisters again.[1] So he travelled on, arriving at Pennfield Ridge on August 24, 1941.

Pennfield Ridge was a little place in Charlotte County, in the Maritime province of New Brunswick, on the eastern side of Canada and more than 4,000 kilometres from Victoria. It is situated on the Bay of Fundy, about 50 kilometres west of St. John, the biggest city in New Brunswick, with about 50,000 inhabitants. Bounded by the Shore Line Railway, the main highway and the old road, the area possessed outstanding advantages for use by bomber and commercial aircraft: a large flat area unobstructed by high land for miles in all directions, self-draining soil, convenient to highways and railway transportation and with an ample source of electric power. Construction on the airport, located not far from the larger centres of population in Charlotte County, began during the summer of 1940. The air base officially opened for training on July 21, 1941. Wing Commander F.R. Miller, the commanding officer, opened the school in the presence of several hundred men who were ready to start training. The school was described as 'splendidly situated' to provide training under diversified weather conditions, including operation in fog similar to that encountered over sections of Europe.[2]

The Second World War was nearing the end of its second year. Hitler's troops had invaded the Soviet Union on June 22, 1941, and were rapidly advancing east in a new edition of their infamous Blitzkrieg. The battle for Moscow, starting in early October 1941, was a first real test for the Wehrmacht, which was eventually brought to a halt by a combination of tenacious Soviet soldiers and volunteers, muddy roads and the sudden arrival of a bitterly cold winter. In 1941, American efforts at neutrality became increasingly difficult as Axis aggression was escalating around the world. Soon American naval and air bases were being constructed in Britain, supposedly for British use. While western European citizens were suffering severely from the Nazi oppression, the Jews were being terrorised. In September 1941 Hitler issued a decree ordering German Jews to wear a yellow star visible on their clothing. At the same time, the first Jews were being gassed in the Auschwitz extermination camp.

---

[1]Yvonne Jukes enlisted in the RCAF in March 1942 and served in England with 6 Group. After the war she joined the British Military Mission at the Pentagon and was involved with the intelligence service. She later transferred to the Canadian Department of External Affairs where she was assigned various foreign postings. In later years, she was with the Department of Supply and Services in Ottawa. She retired in 1983 and lives in Ottawa. Maureen, not to be outdone though paraplegic, worked during the war in a plant making military radios. She lived in Toronto from 1941 and died there in 1999. Shan Jukes married Whit Bissell, a renowned Hollywood actor and lived in California. She died of cancer in 1959. Their brother, Arthur, joined the Canadian Scottish Regiment and served overseas as a commando. After the war he joined T. Eaton & Co and has retired in Vancouver.

[2]Today the field is used to dry seaweed, which, once dried, is used as fertilizer for plants.

In March 1941, Royal Air Force Bomber Command was diverted from its strategic campaign against German cities, ports and airfields to maritime operations. German successes at sea, predominantly by U-boat operations against the North Atlantic convoys, had torpedoed a great number of Allied ships in recent months. A number considered detrimental to the war effort. In the first quarter of 1941 alone, German naval forces and aircraft had sunk nearly one million tons of Allied shipping carrying supplies bound for Britain and the number was increasing monthly. Four months after being forced to turn its attention from Germany to help with the war at sea, Bomber Command was released and was free to resume its strategic mission. The danger at sea temporarily receded and, because the main strength of both the Wehrmacht and the Luftwaffe was now deep into Russia, the prospects once again appeared to be favourable for an uninterrupted continuation of the bombing offensive against Germany.

The relocation to Pennfield Ridge brought quite a change for Teddy. He had grown up in a city and province near the Pacific Ocean, and now he ended up across the other side of Canada by the Atlantic Ocean. He didn't know a soul in the whole area, but he settled in, flew a familiarisation flight in an Anson on August 31, and reported to his parents on September 1:

> You know by now I'm at Pennfield no doubt. It's rather hard to give an opinion of the place just yet as it isn't quite completed. However it has great possibilities, there's a nice bunch of chaps down here and our mess will be first rate once it's fixed up. I was very fortunate and managed to get myself a single room and will not be bothered by someone coming in and out at odd hours.
>
> I've been out once or twice but everything is over around here now and the only remaining thing to do is go into St. John where I don't know a soul. Don't forget to write and tell me if there's anyone who knows people here.
>
> I was awfully busy when I got here. We're terribly short of instructors and a new Short Nav course came in the day I arrived, so they put me in charge of it. Though I took the course last winter you can appreciate the difficulty of teaching it in five minutes notice without having worked on it for some time. However I got organised and had everything running quite smoothly when they switched me back to Observers and someone else took over. Made me pretty fed up after all that ground work.
>
> I was told today to apply for my 'Specialist Navigation' course and have just finished the letter. If it comes through I get "N" after my name and six months seniority. However there doesn't seem to be much hope down here as we're so short staffed. If I'd stayed in Rivers there might have been some hope.
>
> Quite a tough country for flying down here. We've lost two machines already, both of them the day I got here. One crew bailed

out and were okay but the others were all killed. Not much to say. Love, Ted.

In addition to teaching his first class, No. 24 Air Observers Course, in the classroom, Ted registered a record flying month in September. He flew 19 trips totalling over 60 flying hours, alternating between day and night navigation exercises with his students and the odd adaptation flight. The school was very short of night instructors, so Ted had to put in extra time in the air. Ted was course commander of No. 24 AOC, which meant he was not only responsible for their training, but he also signed off and then presented the students their certificates of qualification.[1] Ted's promotion to flying officer also came through on September 1 in a special letter from headquarters. His fellow instructors soaked him for drinks, of course, but they all were happy for him that he received this elevation in rank. During the following weeks things went along pretty smoothly. Ted passed his 21st birthday on October 8, but he did not celebrate at all and let it go by unnoticed. He must have felt alone on that day, but he always seemed to be capable of suppressing feelings of loneliness by concentrating fully on his assignments. When Chief Instructor Flight Lieutenant Roy Harris, RAF decided to get rid of his number two man because he was ineffective and causing inconvenience to the other instructors, he selected Ted to become his new deputy. Roy Harris and Ted immediately got along very well and became instant friends. Both were workaholics and shared the same ideas about navigation and how to run the courses. They also formed a very efficient team in flight, switching roles as pilot and navigator. Ted silently hoped he could go into war with Roy, and when Roy eventually left Pennfield for a posting back to England, Ted missed him deeply.

Ted did not go out much, but he attended the occasional dance in St. John. On October 31, he even organised an airmen's dance, for which he rounded up 150 young women from St. John, which contributed largely to the evening's enormous success.

In December 1941, Ted's qualification in the world of navigation was further enhanced when he was put in charge of another observers course. He was actually put in over the heads of three more senior instructors, two of them of higher rank. He realised that, before long, a promotion to flight lieutenant might be in the offing, but he hoped to be overseas by then. He continued to fly almost every day when he wasn't grounded by one of his recurring colds. He even considered making plans to take an Anson and fly it to Victoria during the Christmas period. He gave up the idea when calculations showed the total flying time would exceed 40 hours. Besides, it became clear that he could not be spared at Pennfield Ridge over

[1]One of Teddy's students in No. 24 Air Observers Course was former Member of Parliament Donald W. Munro, who showed the author his certificate of qualification signed by Flying Officer E.W. Blenkinsop.

Christmas because of the continuing shortage of instructors there. So he spent another holiday season away from his family. Still, it turned out to be a happy time after all, as it appears from his letter written on January 2, 1942:

> Roy Harris was here for Christmas, his boat was held up so he came over from Halifax. We both stayed with Buggy Turnbull and then went to St. John on Christmas day for dinner and the dance afterward. A good party all around, it was fun to have Roy here for one last go. When I get his address I'll send it to you with money as the extra parcels will be so nice for him. I miss him quite a bit.
>
> Things are looking brighter here now, I've got three assistants and am going to take life easy for a bit. Oh yes, my number 2 stooge is a flight lieutenant, I seem to get all the green men to train. However I get first choice and pick the best of them which is quite a big item.
>
> Been doing a lot of agitating to be moved away from instructing and am going to have a talk with the CO very shortly. After all, I've done my share and should be given a break. I'm doing a flight lieutenant's job now and soon we'll have some who can take over if I leave. If I stay they'll either have to promote me or push me down and neither are likely. Some of the chaps are going overseas now and so it looks as though I should get a whack at it soon anyway.
>
> Not much news for you, things are going along as usual. I imagine there's more excitement in Victoria than here with the new war going. Sounds funny to hear you talking of blackouts and so on. Maybe it'll help the recruiting out there.

One might recall that on Sunday morning December 7, 1941, a Japanese carrier task force's air element bombed Pearl Harbor and the war extended into the Pacific. America, England and the Netherlands declared war on Japan the day following this surprise attack, to which Germany and Italy responded by expressing their unconditional support to the Japanese emperor. On the morning of December 11, Germany, emboldened by the Japanese victories in the Pacific, declared war on the United States. Within hours, the United States Congress responded with a declaration of war against Germany and Italy. Singapore, the Philippines, Indonesia and the Solomon Islands soon fell to the Japanese, and Darwin, the northernmost city in Australia, then came within range and was bombed with regularity. The Allied circle was completed; the lines were drawn. The involvement of the United States in this war now gave the Allies the productive capacity and manpower needed to win this conflict.

In the last week of December 1941, US, British, and Canadian representatives met in Washington DC to build a military alliance for the prosecution of what was now truly a global war. This Arcadia Conference lasted three weeks, until January 14, 1942, and was composed of a series of meetings attended by high-ranking military officials, mostly from the US and Great Britain. These officers functioned as combined chiefs of staff. However, on occasion military officers of the USSR were also present. In addition, most of the conferences met in plenary sessions and were presided over by President Franklin D. Roosevelt and British Prime Minister Winston Churchill. Several tripartite meetings were held where Roosevelt and Churchill met with Marshal Stalin of the Soviet Union. Out of the earlier Lend-Lease Act emerged a sidebar agreement to be employed if the United States should be forced to enter the war against both Japan and Germany. Called ABC-1, it was a plan whereby the US President agreed that, if faced with a war on two fronts, American forces would employ primarily a defensive reaction in the Pacific, while committing the majority of its assets to Europe. Essentially the philosophy was to 'throw everything we've got at Europe to defeat Germany first, then take care of matters in the Pacific'.

Churchill and British military planners tended to take a very literal interpretation of ABC-1, anticipating few American assets would be committed to the Pacific campaign. President Roosevelt, on the other hand, though remaining true to the spirit of the 'Europe first' doctrine of the agreement, could not forget the humiliating blow struck against the American Pacific fleet at Pearl Harbor. Throughout the last weeks of 1941, seldom did he meet with his own generals that he did not reiterate his desire to strike a blow against the Japanese homeland as quickly as possible. Meanwhile, Allied planners turned the majority of their attention towards planning for an invasion of the European continent to strike a deathblow against Berlin.

Following the attack on Pearl Harbor in 1941, the Americans had a fear of being bombed by the Germans, as well as the more realistic threat of U-boat operations in the western Atlantic. Coastal 'blackouts' and 'dim-outs' went into effect along a 15-mile-wide strip of the American eastern seaboard. They required that the lights of all houses and neighbourhoods along the shores be blackened at specified curfews. On the Pacific coast, however, fear of a Japanese invasion was widespread. For many Californians and British Columbians, during the early months of 1942, it was not 'if' but 'when' and 'where'. Men and boys, organised into the ARP (the Air Raid Patrol), carried deer rifles and shotguns, patrolled the bluffs, night and day, and scanned the beaches and the sea for Japanese submarines and landing craft. Other men patrolled the streets at night, checking for any light leaking from blackout curtains.

The Japanese carried out a limited number of attacks on the American mainland. In February 1942, a Japanese submarine shelled an oil field up the beach from Santa Barbara and damaged a pump house. That following June, another one shelled a coastal fort in Oregon, and in September, that submarine's crew assembled and launched a small floatplane that dropped incendiary bombs, starting a few small forest fires. In British Columbia, a Japanese submarine shelled the facilities at Estevan Point on the west coast of Vancouver Island and the Japanese constantly launched balloons that transported incendiaries into the forests of central British Columbia. Still, the only real incursion onto North American soil was when Japan attacked Dutch Harbor at the base of the Aleutian Islands on June 3, 1942. It was partially a diversion to cover the attack on Midway Island and was only of limited military significance. The capture of an Alaskan island forced the United States to establish a northern defence perimeter.

While the winds of war were storming across the world, Teddy's life at Pennfield Ridge remained routine. The days were filled with teaching, flying, writing letters to his family, and of course to Helen, and interspersed with the sporadic dinners or dances in St. John or at the officers' mess. At the end of March 1942, his logbook recorded over 660 flying hours, half of which were flown at night. He had become so used to night flying that he found it much easier than day work. On January 24, 25 and 26 he established a new record for himself, by flying a total of 22 hours during three consecutive nights. He now also had a larger staff to direct, including a flight lieutenant who had been a flight commander at 8 SFTS at Saskatoon. It was therefore not surprising that the school's commanding officer recommended Teddy for a promotion. In mid-March he was informed that there soon would be a possibility to take some leave, so he informed his parents on March 16, 1942:

> You mentioned something about leave in your last letter, Mother. I shall be home for lunch on April 26th and will have a full two weeks there, so prepare to kill the fatted calf.
>
> Was on a good party last Saturday – Eric invited Ian MacPherson and I to a cocktail party on the ship and we went to the dance at the hotel afterward. I finished putting people to bed at about 04.30 hours Sunday!
>
> So the Jukes family is moving to Toronto at last. Wonder what made them decide? And Arthur is engaged by all accounts too. Things are happening pretty quickly now.
>
> How has the rationing affected Dad? Is he under a preferred category? I wrote to Helen and told her she'd better figure on plenty of walking this time as we wouldn't be using the car at all.
>
> Glory halleluiah! I'm exempt from Income Tax this year. The government owes me about $125 to boot!
>
> Well there really isn't much more to say. Sure be glad to get home though, it will be nine months all together and that's a pretty long stretch. Your loving son, Teddy

And then, when Teddy was preparing for his leave while growing increasingly worried about never getting away from instructional duties, he received an unexpected new assignment. He was to be sent to New Zealand to inspect navigational training procedures in conjunction with the Royal New Zealand Air Force (RNZAF) and the RAF Overseas and to implement a new air navigation program there if required. He was instructed to report to Air Force Headquarters in Ottawa, where the purpose of the mission would be further explained to him. So, on April 24, he sent a hasty telegram to his parents: 'Leave cancelled – Posted elsewhere – May be home first – Letter following.'

The following day he left Pennfield Ridge and travelled to Ottawa, where on arrival at HQ it was explained to him that this was primarily a training assignment. The New Zealand air observer trainees were not achieving the same training standards as the British, Australian and Canadian entries, and he and Flight Lieutenant Mowatt Christie were to fly out there and determine the problem and then make recommendations on how it could be resolved. They would travel aboard a US Army Air Force aircraft acting as navigators on the way there and back. It was estimated the whole exercise should be completed in about two months. This, of course, was a challenging assignment and Ted was pretty excited. It was not the posting overseas he had been hoping for, but this was something special and he felt lucky to get this chance. Even the reports of a Pacific war going on with great intensity could not throw him off. Meanwhile, and without Ted's knowledge, Wing Commander Miller added a confidential 'on posting' report to Ted's service records for the RNZAF on April 30. In it was a numerical indication of professional efficiency, where Miller circled a 6 on a scale of 1 to 7. He went on to recommend Ted for accelerated promotion and for a posting to active service, and concluded in the 'Remarks' section: 'This officer has been employed for 14 months as astro-navigation instructor. He has developed into an excellent instructor and very good all around officer. Intelligent, good bearing and appearance and a marked ability to accept responsibility.'

CHAPTER FOUR

Going Down Under

Almost as soon as Ted left the Air Force Headquarters, things began to go wrong. First, he and Mowatt[1] were informed that their assignment probably would last more than the estimated two months, perhaps up to six. Then the Americans decided that they did not want unknown navigators as crew aboard their aircraft. It was decided that Ted and Mowatt should go by sea. Not only that, the first British ship headed that way sailed not from the west coast but from New York, so they left Ottawa for New York on April 29 to catch the ship, the *Port Huon*. With them went three New Zealand sergeant air observers who had just completed their courses in Canada and were to be posted back to an operational unit in their home country.

Mowatt decided to stop off in Montreal to say goodbye to his parents, so Ted and the three New Zealanders completed the last part of the trip without him. Ted checked into the McAlpine Hotel in New York. In a telegram to his parents, he had asked them to wire him the names of any of their friends who might be living in the big city. Immediately upon receipt of the wired message, the Skipper contacted one of his former associates and personal friend with the Canadian Pacific Railway Company, the vice-president for the CPR in Montreal, H J Humphrey. Mr Humphrey right away wired his colleagues at the American Locomotive Company in New York to inform them of Teddy's stay there. As none of Ted's family was there to say goodbye, the Skipper appreciated that someone would contact him so Ted would not feel too alone. The message did not miss its effect as a couple of American Locomotive Company co-workers immediately went out to meet Ted in his hotel. Frank Foley and two of his office associates showed him around the stock exchange and other places of interest, and gave him quite a good time one night. In a cable to Mr Humphrey they reassured him that Ted was being well looked after and in fine spirits. Another one of the Skipper's friends, Colonel

[1]Ted called Mowatt Christie 'Chris'. Air Force nicknames were (and are) often just abbreviations of last names.

Peabody, owner of the Black Ball Ferries out of Seattle, also acted as Ted's host and took him out to dinner several times.

The *Port Huon* was moored well out of town at the explosives dock. She was a ship of the British Port Line, a merchant navy company, about 14,000 tons, with a cruising speed of 14 knots and named after an obscure port in New Guinea. The ship had British officers and crew and by all accounts a very pleasant group. Ted and the others were told later that the *Port Huon* had the largest shipment of arms ever sent to Australia – Tommy Guns and small arms ammunition enough for an army division, and six-inch shells for the US Navy. It was remarked that if the ship was torpedoed, the passengers wouldn't need life jackets but parachutes.

The group of two officers, Mowatt and Ted, and three sergeants, were the only passengers so they were well provided for with two-bed cabins. They messed with the ship's officers who proved an interesting lot. The ship was armed with one cannon that was mounted on the afterdeck. This gun was under the command of a Royal Marine NCO but manned by the merchant seamen. The *Port Huon* sailed from New York on May 3, 1942. It was arranged at the beginning that Ted and his four colleagues would do lookout duty as part of the crew and all would do two hours on and eight hours off on the ship's schedule until they reached the Panama Canal. Once in the Pacific the risk of interception was considered negligible so the lookout program was discontinued. During this period German submarines, operating out of northern Europe, had been sinking merchant ships within sight of the American coast so the *Port Huon* was given a naval escort, a nondescript craft, doubtless a converted commercial vessel.

The *Port Huon* was proceeding down the coast with her escort ahead and seaward following a line of marker buoys when suddenly the vessel bumped up on a submerged sandbar and there she stuck. The ship's officers checked their position with respect to the marker buoys and found that they were in the designated channel. It was suggested that a German U-boat might have hauled the buoys inshore. Fortunately the tide was low when the ship went aground, so a few hours later she backed off the sandbar and carried on down the coast. Still, orders were received to put into the naval base at Norfolk, Virginia, to have the ship's bottom inspected. The inspection showed no appreciable damage but the ship's captain was instructed to wait in Norfolk as the Navy was making up the first American convoy to go down the coast. It was seven or eight days before orders came to sail. There were about 30 ships in the convoy organised in five lines of six ships in each line. The *Port Huon* had the best and safest position as lead ship in the centreline. There were two destroyers in the convoy and aircraft provided air cover together with cable balloons. Radio silence and blackout were imposed. Everyone aboard the *Port Huon* was impressed with the protection. The convoy had a variety of ships, general cargo ships, bulk carriers and many empty tankers sitting high in the water bound for the Gulf of Mexico, Trinidad or Venezuela. The *Port Huon* had been in many Atlantic convoys and was very efficient compared to the rest, for most of whom this was a new experience. Each ship seemed to have a character all its own, varying from efficient to awkward. Some were good at keeping station and passing messages, while others kept falling behind despite the slow speed of the convoy. A few old-fashioned ones did not have Aldis lamps for signalling but could only pass messages by the semaphore flag system, useless in the dark. There was a particularly unwieldy one, the *Angelina*. She did not have an Aldis lamp. One dark night she mistook a flare signal requiring a turn to port and turned starboard cutting across the convoy and nearly colliding with several ships.

The convoy sailed down the coast without serious incident as far as Key West. Here the flotilla, of necessity, broke up as ships were heading in all directions, some to the Gulf of Mexico, a few to the West Indian Islands, and others to Panama or Venezuela. When the convoy broke up and the escort disappeared, the *Port Huon* increased speed and set out on a zigzag course for Panama. After a short run through the Gulf of Mexico it was necessary to go through the Yucatan Channel to reach the Caribbean Sea. At the Yucatan Channel, only 120 miles separate the Yucatan Peninsula of Mexico from Cuba, so it was an obvious place for submarines to intercept traffic. The *Port Huon* went through at full speed at night, zigzagging as usual. On the way through, Ted and the others saw flashes of gunfire to the east and picked up a radioed SOS from the *Angelina*, saying she was being shelled. When the *Port Huon* reached Panama news came through that six ships from the convoy had been sunk, two of which were Mexican. Shortly afterwards Mexico declared war on Germany.

There was plenty of time to write letters, and on May 21 Ted reported to his parents:

> We're at sea somewhere in the Caribbean and it's damned hot, too much for me. The thought of another three weeks of it seems pretty sickening, I'd sooner be at Rivers at 40 below. It's not too bad at night though. I slept on deck last night and it was fine, quite cool and comfortable.
>
> Getting a fair start to a good tan. I must make the most of the sun while it's possible'cause we're going right into mid-winter again.
>
> Been playing a few deck games, bit of bridge and some chess to pass the time, but on the whole have been resting and getting healthy. I was pretty worn out when I left Pennfield.
>
> Getting to know the other passengers a little more now and they all seem to be a good bunch though their bridge is horrible, even by my standards!
>
> Watched some naval vessels going after a sub with depth charges the other day. Quite interesting but we couldn't see very much.
>
> Don't worry if you don't hear from me for some time. If you

continue to write as usual, the mail will go through in a month or so. It will be about three months till you get another letter from me but I will try and write regularly along the way so that you will have a book by the time it reaches you. If possible I will cable arrival but it will be a couple of months before that comes too. So don't fuss or worry, everything is OK. Love to all, Teddy.

Three days after passing through the Yucatan Channel the *Port Huon* reached Panama. After a stop at Cristóbal in the Canal Zone, where Ted posted his letter, the next day the vessel continued through the Panama Canal and then south past the Galapagos Islands, avoiding the normal shipping lanes. Then she set course for Melbourne, Australia, when again no escort was required as the Pacific was so large that the chance of encountering an enemy warship or submarine was negligible. The anti-submarine watches were discontinued, and Ted and his fellows enjoyed the fine weather, reasonably good food and comfortable accommodations on the ship. They had a long way to go and despite the fairly good supply of books and magazines aboard, they had read everything they could get their hands on before the ship reached Melbourne.

On Tuesday, May 26, the *Port Huon* and her passengers 'crossed the Line'. This event was celebrated with the traditional ceremony that converts 'Pollywogs' to 'Shellbacks'. All sailors who had not crossed the equator are considered to be Pollywogs, while Shellbacks were sailors who had previously made the crossing. The night before the vessel reached the equator all of the Pollywogs on board were issued subpoenas by 'Davey Jones' to appear before King Neptune's court the next day. The next day, upon crossing the Line, Ted and his fellow passengers were brought to 'trial' and accused of various crimes by the ship's crew, disguised as an elaborately costumed court of crusty Shellbacks and their leader King Neptune, who accused them of intruding into his domain. More rituals followed, designed to be revolting, humiliating, and hilarious. Finally their 'punishments' ended with a baptism and it was not water with which they were baptised. After enduring the humiliation all the Pollywogs were presented with certificates by the captain confirming their crossing of the equator, and proclaiming them to now be trusty Shellbacks.[1] Ted and Mowatt thoroughly enjoyed the whole event and thought it was a lot of

[1]The ceremony itself, which is thought to have its roots in Viking tradition, is a naval event no sailor ever forgets. With few exceptions, those who have been inducted into the 'mysteries of the deep' by King Neptune and his Royal court, count the experience as a highlight of their naval career. Members of King Neptune's party usually include Davey Jones, Neptune's first assistant, Her Highness Amphitrite, the Royal Scribe, the Royal Doctor, the Royal Dentist, the Royal Baby, the Royal Navigator, the Royal Chaplain, the Royal Judge, attorneys, barbers and other names that suit the party. Officially recognised by service record entries indicating date, time, latitude and longitude, the crossing of the equator involves elaborate preparation by the Shellbacks to ensure the Pollywogs are properly indoctrinated. The ceremony can range from simple to elaborate but most follow the same general outline.

fun and a great way to liven up a long ocean crossing.

While the ship's gun crew took advantage of the time to polish up their sighting techniques by shooting at targets dropped from the ship, Ted and Mowatt enjoyed observing the navigation skills of the ship's officers. They were found as impressive in this as in other things. In clear weather, they obtained accurate fixes in daytime, using the sun plus the moon, planets and brighter stars, even when the planets and stars were not visible to the naked eye. From a large star map and knowledge of their ship's approximate position, they obtained an approximate bearing and elevation of the planet or the star of interest. Their sextants were equipped with a small telescope that permitted them to sight the planet or star if they knew its approximate position. They set the estimated elevation on the sextant and searched on the pre-calculated bearing until the star appeared in the telescope, then measured the elevation accurately, thus obtaining a position line to combine with one from the sun to give a fix.

After ten days or so of good weather, the *Port Huon* headed into the very rough seas associated with the Roaring Forties, below 40° latitude south. The giant waves down under travel from west to east and for this reason most ships in these latitudes go round the world from west to east. In this instance they were going the wrong way into these impressive waves.[1] The ship took quite a pounding and often had to reduce speed to ease the shocks. She passed well south of New Zealand in order to deliver her precious cargo in the shortest time possible to Australia. The *Port Huon* reached Melbourne on June 24. Ted immediately sent a telegram to his parents to inform them that he had arrived safe and sound.

Unknown to Ted and the ship's crew at the time, the historical Battle of Midway had raged in the midst of the Pacific Ocean during their journey. Approximately 8,000 kilometres north of their route, this naval battle, seen by historians as one of the turning points of the war, had reached its climax on June 4, 1942. Japanese Combined Fleet Commander Yamamoto had moved on the tiny US mid-Pacific base at Midway atoll in an effort to draw out and destroy the US Pacific fleet's aircraft carrier striking forces. The US forces had embarrassed the Japanese navy with the mid-April Doolittle raid on Tokyo and in the Battle of the Coral Sea in early May. Yamamoto planned to quickly knock down Midway's defences and establish a Japanese air base there. Yamamoto had expected the US carriers to come out and fight but also figured that the US would arrive too late to save the base at Midway. In addition, he also expected they would be of insufficient strength to avoid being defeated by the tested air power of his superior

---

[1]In the southern hemisphere, south of the trades wind belt, the westerly winds create waves that are particularly strong. In the northern hemisphere, the world is divided into Atlantic and Pacific oceans. In the southern hemisphere, south of 40° latitude, there is no major landmass to interrupt a wave once started. A wave theoretically and probably could actually go right around the world at these latitudes and arrive back where it started.

carrier force. But Yamamoto's intended surprise was thwarted by superior American intelligence, which deduced his scheme well before the battle was joined. This allowed Admiral Chester W. Nimitz, the US Pacific Fleet commander, to establish an ambush by having his carriers ready and waiting for the Japanese. On June 4, 1942, the trap was sprung. The perseverance and sacrifice of US Navy aviators, plus a great deal of luck on the American side, cost Japan four irreplaceable fleet aircraft carriers, while only one of the three US carriers was lost. The base at Midway, though damaged by Japanese air attack, remained operational and later became a vital component in the American trans-Pacific offensive. Prior to this action, Japan possessed general naval superiority over the United States and could usually choose where and when to attack. After Midway, the two opposing fleets were essentially equals, and the United States soon took the offensive.

Ted and Mowatt bid farewell to their good friends on the *Port Huon*, which again was anchored well out of town. Their orders were to report to Sydney as soon as possible to catch a ship to New Zealand, so after a quick look around Melbourne they caught the night train to Sydney. The trip took about 24 hours and they arrived in Sydney the day following an unsuccessful attack in Sydney Harbour by two Japanese mini-submarines, which had apparently penetrated the defensive booms and nets at the harbour entrance by following a ferry into the basin. Ted and Mowatt eventually spent ten days in Sydney and enjoyed their stay although they were required to be ready to leave at any time, which prevented making any plans. They visited Taronga Park Zoo and marvelled at the number of playing fields, tennis courts and the magnificent harbour setting. Finally they left on a troop ship in really crowded conditions and six days later anchored at their destination in Wellington, New Zealand. They had been over two months en route.

Setting the Standards

Ted and Mowatt found the Air Force Headquarters in Wellington and reported to Squadron Leader Hudson, who was in charge of all navigation training for the Royal New Zealand Air Force. He explained their training system and the various problems they were encountering. There were six training stations in New Zealand where navigation was taught, so it was decided that Mowatt and Teddy should separate, each taking three stations and visiting each for about a week to scope their problems, then return to Wellington to report. They agreed to skip manning depots but to pay a visit to initial training schools, elementary flying training schools and service flying training schools. The first one they did together, the Initial Training Wing at Rotorua, was a place situated in the centre of the North Island about 250 kilometres south of Auckland. They arrived there on July 10. The main attraction at Rotorua was the geothermal activity. Here and there about the town, jets of steam and hot water came from beneath the surface and were harnessed to heat the buildings. Ted liked the station, but there wasn't any flying, which was rather a nuisance to him. After observing the training sessions or giving lectures himself, he usually relaxed by playing basketball, and he was introduced to, as he put it in one of his letters, 'the noble game of golf'.

During their time at Rotorua, Ted and Mowatt went to Auckland on four days of leave and had a decent time there. Ted took a girl he had met to a movie a couple of nights and to the local zoo on a Sunday. Much to his regret, however, there were no parties worth mentioning as there was no liquor to be had, only sherry, port and weak beer. He also could not get used to tea, New Zealand's national institution. It seemed that people had it seven times a day, and some got quite huffy if they missed it. Nevertheless he liked the friendly and convivial New Zealanders and often expressed the hope he would be able to see more of their country.

When they had seen enough at Rotorua, Ted and Mowatt went their separate ways and agreed to meet in Wellington from time to time. Ted relocated to 2 EFTS at New Plymouth, a place on the west coast of the North Island with about 20,000 inhabitants, and arrived there on August 6. He immediately felt a liking for the place. It had a wet but much warmer climate, and, above all, it was a flying school. Some of the flying instructors allowed him to take up a Tiger Moth every once in a while, which he thoroughly enjoyed. He did a practice flight on August 10 and two more the next day. They also took him along on a couple of parties and he had a great time.

After finishing up in New Plymouth, Ted travelled to 3 EFTS at Harewood on August 15. This station was located just west of the city of Christchurch on the South Island. Ted had worked there for less than a week when, on August 21, he and a LAC Irwin borrowed one of the school's Tiger Moths and flew a two-and-a-half-hour trip along the South Island's east coast to 1 EFTS at Taieri to visit Mowatt there.[1] It was a happy reunion and the two of them spent some fine days together. While there, Ted was introduced to two new twin-engine aircraft, the Lockheed Hudson general reconnaissance airplane and the Airspeed Oxford advanced trainer. He did a passenger flight in each, on August 22 and 23. On August 24, he and LAC Irwin returned to Harewood in the Tiger Moth.

On September 3, Ted reported for duty at the newly formed 4 General Reconnaissance (GR) Squadron. When Japan attacked Pearl Harbor in December 1941, New Zealand only had three reconnaissance squadrons equipped with a few modern Hudsons and aged Vincents. In the summer of 1942, 4 GR Squadron, now fully equipped with Hudsons, carried out regular reconnaissance duties patrolling the Cook Strait and the

---

[1] 1 EFTS Taieri had been established on the Dunedin Aero Club's aerodrome shortly after war broke out.

approaches to Wellington. This squadron at the same time served as a training unit to reinforce squadron crews in the forward area. After all, enemy submarines were still active in Fijian waters. Ted recounted to his parents:

> Moved again. I'm in a very nice little place called Nelson on the north east coast of the South Island. I'm having a pretty good time of it here. People are very good and the lads on the station look after me pretty darn well, including me in any parties that are going and so on. I've met dozens of people in the past couple of months and seem to be improving somewhat in my ability to remember names and faces. Shall be here for about ten days altogether. I'm still living out of a suitcase and haven't unpacked since leaving Canada. Makes things a bit awkward and is rather hard on my clothes. Have a tough time getting my laundry done and I have to darn my socks as the laundries here don't do it.
>
> Your letters have started to arrive, they're taking between two months and ten weeks to get here, quite a long time.
>
> Went on a terrific party Wednesday night and finally got home at 5.30a.m! A beer party it was at someone's summer cottage. Had a really good time.
>
> Too bad about Noel Grattan being missing, but maybe he'll show up again, so many of them do, you know.
>
> I have taken quite a few photos in this country. Have become quite a tourist as a matter of fact and hardly move without my camera. You will have quite a photo collection by the time I come home.
>
> Won't be long until my attachment is finished though it's possible I may be kept for another year. That will be okay if I get the job I want.

Ted loved every minute of his time at Nelson. He caught every ride he could on the Hudsons, and on September 14 Flight Lieutenant Bradshaw even cleared him to fly solo on one of the squadron's Oxfords. Two days later Ted's time at Nelson was up, and Flight Lieutenant Bradshaw personally flew him to Auckland. There, on September 18, he was picked up by an Oxford and taken to Waipapakauri, the most northerly station in New Zealand and which had been used since 1941 by aircraft making sea reconnaissance over the northern approaches to the country. During 1942 7 GR Squadron had regularly occupied it. The place was a real bush station and quite isolated, and seemed to offer nothing but rain, whirlwinds and mud. Ted did not regret being flown out of there and leaving the place behind on September 25. He transferred to his next inspection assignment, this time 5 GR Squadron based at Gisborne, on the east coast of the North Island. This unit operated obsolescent Vickers Vincents and a flight of Short Singapore flying boats. After a week there he had seen enough to make an assessment, and he was taken on a two-hour flight from Gisborne to Whenuapai in one of the ancient Vincent biplanes. It was quite an experience, as the Vincent had a very large open two-seater cockpit situated behind a radial engine. It was a 1930 vintage aircraft and cruised about 90 miles per hour. There were so many wires between the two wings that it was rumoured a standard rigger's test was to place a canary in a certain spot and if he could get out there was something missing! Whenuapai, located just outside Auckland, was the home base of 1 GR Squadron that was responsible for patrolling the approaches to Auckland and the seas around the North Cape. On October 6, one of the squadron's Hudsons flew Ted out to Levin, where he hitchhiked a ride in an Oxford taking him to Rongotai Airport, in the middle of Wellington city.

In Wellington, Ted reported to the Air Force Headquarters, where he was happily reunited with Mowatt Christie. Chris had also crossed the whole country over the previous couple of months, visiting several other schools and units. Now they would have to write their joint report. It quickly became evident that there were no differences in their assessments and they agreed on the recommendations to be made to the Royal New Zealand Air Force. In short, their suggestions were:

1) The RNZAF should require a higher scholastic standard for their navigator trainees.
2) Changes were needed in curricula at the different schools.
3) All navigation instructors should be given a short course in practical air navigation.

Ted and Mowatt had understood that their assignment was to make an analysis and recommendations, but now Squadron Leader Hudson instructed them to implement the recommendations and in the first instance to organise short courses for the navigation instructors. Ted and Mowatt were provided with Oxford aircraft for exercises and with some sextants and Astro compasses. The courses, held at Rotorua, were successful in updating the participants in new techniques and also – an additional point Ted and Mowatt had perhaps overlooked – the opportunity for navigation instructors to meet face to face to discuss their various problems amongst themselves. When the second course started, Flight Lieutenant Parry from the RNZAF came in to take charge of the course. He was the senior navigation officer for the New Zealand Coastal Command operations. He had a lot of experience island hopping throughout the Pacific, and contributed a great deal to the course. Now it remained to implement the first recommendation, to upgrade the initial training school navigation course. To this end Ted and Mowatt settled down in Rotorua and rewrote the ITS Nav Course outline, the detailed exercises and so on. This was completed by the end of October 1942, and they had made their recommendations and had implemented them as best they could.

It was time to go home. Ted had telegraphed his parents already on October 7 to tell them to stop mailing letters to New Zealand. Before that, he had made arrangements for Helen's birthday, on October 2, by sending his parents Helen's birthday card and a present well before that date. Through the Padre at Rotorua, he had also obtained a genuine Maori necklace of greenstone and gold, to be given to Helen as a present for graduating from the University of British Columbia that past May. However, Ted's return was not definite until the very last moment. Indeed, in his records there is a file undersigned by a RNZAF group captain on October 15, 1942, which reads:

> Flying Officer E.W. Blenkinsop is now due for return to the RCAF after his short period of attachment. He is willing to remain on loan, however, provided he could be posted to a GR Unit. There is a need for one Astro-navigator in each GR Unit in the Pacific area, and he might be considered for posting to the 'Catalina' Squadron now forming. This matter will have to be taken up with the RCAF to ascertain whether they agree and finally for Ministerial approval.

At this time a GR Squadron of Hudsons based near Auckland was flying patrols escorting shipping in and out of the area. As they did not have airborne radar they often had trouble locating the ships they were supposed to escort, especially when there was poor visibility. Sometimes this was due to faulty navigation by the aircraft's crew, or at other times the ship was not at or near its forecasted position. A major argument developed between Air Force Headquarters intelligence and the squadron about failures of interception. Ted and Mowatt were invited by both sides to get involved to help resolve the problem. Mowatt insisted they should not unless so instructed by Squadron Leader Hudson. Although Ted would not have minded to take a closer look at the reconnaissance squadron's problems, Mowatt wanted to return to Canada. His favourite brother, Squadron Leader George Patterson 'Pat' Christie, had been killed in a flying accident over Lac St. Louis near Montreal on July 6 and he was eager to get home.[1]

It is interesting to note the progress of the war at that time. Shortly before Ted arrived in New Zealand the country had been vulnerable to attack as the Japanese had taken Singapore, the Philippines, New Guinea and the Solomon Islands. New Zealand had long before sent her army to

---

[1]Squadron Leader 'Pat' Christie, DFC and Bar had flown Hurricane fighters with Nos. 43 and 242 Squadrons in the Battle of Britain, and Spitfire aircraft with 66 Squadron. His air-to-air victories include six and one shared 'confirmed destroyed', 3 'probables', and two and one shared 'damaged'. One of his victories was a Messerschmitt Bf 109E of JG 51, which crash-landed at Manston. Pat Christie landed alongside and had a nice half-hour conversation with the pilot, Lt Teumer. The Messerschmitt is today being displayed in the RAF Museum at Hendon near London, UK. Pat was chief flying Instructor for RAF Ferry Command at the time of his death. He was 24 years old and is buried in the Field of Honour, Lakeview Cemetery, Pointe Claire, Québec.

the Middle East and Crete where they had sustained serious losses and required constant reinforcement, so the country, to put it mildly, was inadequately garrisoned. About the time of Ted's arrival numerous American troops had also arrived and the country began to breathe more easily. While Ted was in New Zealand, the American marines, after a difficult fight, eventually took Guadalcanal, one of the Solomon Islands. This signalled the beginning of the American offensive in the Pacific and one of the defining moments of the Second World War. Meanwhile, in Europe, the strategic bombing offensive against Germany was in full swing. The United States Army Air Force heavy bombers joined the RAF offensive for the first time on August 17, 1942, bombing marshalling yards near the French city of Rouen.

Home by Christmas

Both Ted and Mowatt had been told, when posted to New Zealand, that it was expected that the assignment would be for about two months. It had now been six months, including travel time, and they were impatient to be off. Finally it was arranged that they should sail from Auckland to the US at the beginning of November. They were going to be joined by a draft of about 150 RNZAF trainees who were bound for Canada and the air training scheme there. Mowatt was the senior officer and was put in charge of the draft. He had arrangements to make, signing for certain equipment and borrowing from the air force in Auckland two cooks and two bakers to cater to the draft on the way across. There were three other officers: Ted was in charge of 'A' Flight, trainee pilots; an RNZAF flight lieutenant accountant was responsible for 'B' Flight, apprentice air observers; and finally a flying officer air gunner was in command of 'C' Flight, the neophyte air gunners. The ship was the *Marie Maersk*, a Danish merchant ship of about 18,000 tons still with its Danish captain and crew who spoke very little English and kept pretty much to themselves. The cabin space was equipped as a hospital ship and carried seriously wounded American marines injured at Guadalcanal. Most of the deck space was taken up with latrines and showers. The air force recruits were allotted the ship's hold, which was divided into spacious high 'rooms' with tiers of bunks six deep up the sides. Fortunately they were few enough so that not more than two bunks were required in the vertical, but on a previous trip, the ship had carried a load of sheep's hides and the hold smelled pretty foul. There was no effective ventilation system and at night it was necessary to cover the hold exits with blankets to maintain the blackout as lights had always to be left on in the cargo space. In this fashion they were to cross the equator.

Everyone was to be aboard on November 1 at 03:00 p.m., to be ready to sail that evening. At noon, Ted and Mowatt received an order to report immediately to the commanding officer of the Auckland area, a group captain. He had just received a signal from Washington posting Ted and

Mowatt, on temporary duty, to the United States Army Air Force as navigation specialists. The group captain said that, as they were due to sail in two hours' time, they could do as they wished; he was willing to hold up the receipt of the cable until they had left. He asked them to make up their minds in ten minutes and let him know. Ted and Mowatt thanked him and went into the corridor to consult with each other. They did not take long to make up their minds. Both preferred to return to Canada to be with their countrymen while still hoping to be assigned to European operations. Besides, they were set to sail and the prospect of a visit home was appealing. For Mowatt the chance to see his family again was precious, while Ted very much looked forward to embracing Helen again after such a long separation. So back they went and gave the group captain their decision to proceed to Canada.

The *Marie Maersk* left the Auckland harbour at the arranged time, destination San Francisco. Aboard were several US marine officers who had been in Guadalcanal and also Commander Green of the Royal Navy who had been on the *Ajax* at the Battle of the River Plate. It was interesting to listen to their experiences. The weather during the trip was fine although very hot in the tropics, so no one really enjoyed the voyage. During the journey, Mowatt put out daily routine orders, which included the naming of duty officers, inspections, times for callisthenics and so forth. Interestingly enough, the recollection of one of the RNZAF trainees on board the *Marie Maersk* was recorded. Colin Pattle, who had been selected for advanced pilot training in Canada, recalled:

> Our initial flying training had been completed in New Zealand and towards the end of October we gathered in Auckland and sailed from there on the *Marie Maersk*. Our course number was 32 and probably contained about 60 young men. Flying Officer Blenkinsop was returning to Canada I presume, and was placed in charge of us. I will tell you what I can conjure up from that long dim past. We, a rather sceptical bunch, thought Ted Blenkinsop a bit stuffy and an unnecessary disciplinarian. This probably arose from the shipboard circumstances which as time went on proved to be pretty awful. Conditions were poor, the ship was dirty and the food disgusting. Many of the meals were inedible. There was a Danish crew and of course they ate well. We were reduced to raiding their stores at night and these activities helped our diet. We had trouble keeping clean and wore anything but uniforms. Flying Officer Blenkinsop tried a daily routine of physical training but under the tropical sun and heat we soon rebelled against that nonsense. It seems to me that the poor fellow succumbed to the conditions and spent the rest of the voyage given over to surviving like the rest of us.[1]

[1]Letter from Colin Pattle to the author, January 18, 1991.

On the morning of Tuesday, November 17, 1942, the *Marie Maersk* entered the port of San Francisco. Mowatt and Ted were happy to turn over the draft to an RNZAF squadron leader from Ottawa. Ted immediately wired his parents to let them know he would arrive at Vancouver railway station on the afternoon of November 19. He asked his parents to bring Helen with them to Vancouver and to stay at the Georgia Hotel at his expense. Then followed the long train journey north, during which both men reminisced about their adventures in New Zealand and looked forward to seeing their loved ones again after such a long time. Arriving in Vancouver, Ted and Mowatt shook hands and wished each other all the best. They agreed to keep in touch and to look each other up after the war, upon which Mowatt carried on to Ottawa and Montreal. Minutes later Ted was reunited with his parents and Helen. Evidently, the reunion was a warm and emotional one – it had been almost 16 months. The biggest surprise however was seeing his mother in an RCAF uniform. Indeed, on September 29, 1942, Winsome had left Victoria to join the Air Force, and had since been stationed at 6 Training Depot in Toronto as an officer cadet. Not only had she felt it her duty to help the war effort but also continuing to live under the same roof with her parents had made her a bit uneasy. And although Hubert very much disliked the idea of her joining up, both the Skipper and Ada were delighted and proud.[1]

Mowatt Christie never saw Ted again. He concluded one of his letters to the author as follows: 'Ted was, of course, highly intelligent, quiet and reserved but not excessively so. I found him very supportive always and cannot remember an angry word passing between us.'[2]

After having spent a lovely two days with his family and Helen in Vancouver, Ted boarded the transcontinental train bound for Ottawa, where he was to report to the Air Force Headquarters. Squadron Leader 'Buggy' Turnbull, who had been one of his instructors at Rivers as well as a friend of the Neroutsos family for a long time, was at the time working at Air Force HQ and offered Ted a room in his sizeable house in Ottawa. At HQ, Ted was told to keep himself at the disposal of the RCAF for a forthcoming posting. He made it noticeably clear to the personnel officers that he had become quite frustrated with instructing and was 'chafing at the bit' to get into operational flying. He then gave a briefing to the air staff about his assignment in New Zealand, while at the same time dealing with other administrative matters. After a few days, Ted was summoned to the personnel branch again, where he was informed that he was to prepare for

[1]Winsome was later promoted to a special services officer and section officer in Western Air Command, Joint Services HQ, Vancouver, and continued to serve there until the end of the war.
[2]We are greatly indebted for the memoirs, written especially for the author, by Mowatt Christie about their exploits in New Zealand. It took Jim Grant and Dick Wynne three years to locate Mowatt, and it goes without saying that if he had not been found, the New Zealand episode of Ted Blenkinsop's life would have remained largely unwritten.

a posting overseas. He was allowed 14 days' 'disembarkation leave', in view of his past and future extended duties away from home. He crossed the country yet again and arrived at Victoria on December 5, 1942, his mind and heart filled with excitement about what lay ahead.

From then on things followed in quick succession. Ted received orders to report to 1 Embarkation Depot in Halifax, Nova Scotia. He went by train there via Ottawa, reaching his final destination on December 18. The RCAF 'Y Depot' in Halifax, was ordinarily the last stop before airmen embarked for overseas. The schedule there was far from arduous, but there were medical tests, including three decompression tests of which one was from 35,000 feet. Ted received some more inoculations, passed tests for night visual acuity and packed all the material he needed to go onto operations. Documents parades were called to have the combatants prepare their will and complete a series of other forms with seemingly innocent queries as to the identity of their next of kin. On the more pleasant side, Ted received news that he was being promoted on December 21, 1942, to the rank of flight lieutenant.

Yvonne Jukes, who had enlisted in the RCAF in March 1942, was stationed in Halifax. She shared an apartment with Margaret and Pat, but Teddy never made the call. It probably would have been an awkward situation to visit both Yvonne and Margaret at the same time.[1] After having spent a few days in Halifax, Ted managed to snatch some of the days owed to him for disembarkation leave and he returned home to Victoria. He was finally going to spend Christmas again amidst his loved ones, the first time since 1939. Winsome and Hubert tried to make it a very special Christmas, realising that their only son was soon to go into harm's way. Winsome and Granny Neroutsos, or Bonnie as she was called, put on a fine Christmas dinner with all the trimmings. There were friends and relatives visiting so the house was quite crowded. Teddy received a lot of gifts and items to use while away.

On December 26, 1942, Ted went back to Halifax to prepare for his posting overseas. He was in high spirits about his future adventure, although leaving Helen had been quite painful, but there was a job to be done, so he tried to focus on what was to come. On his train trip to Halifax, Ted was joined by his old friend Frank Darling, who was also en route to England where he would eventually end up a navigator in a bomber crew. It was a happy reunion and they would have plenty of stories to tell during the long days of waiting for a draft at Halifax and the eventual boat trip to Britain. On arriving at Halifax, Ted was given a hearty greeting by John Uhthoff, who was also preparing to sail to the centre of the Empire.

In late 1942, the war had taken a decisive turn in favour of the Allies.

---

[1]Margaret died in Ottawa in 2002. Her husband, Pat Russell, retired in Ottawa having risen to the rank of rear admiral.

Rommel's Afrika Korps had finally been driven back by Montgomery's famed Desert Rats, and on the night of November 7-8, 1942, the Allies had landed on the beaches in Morocco and Algeria. In January 1943, Churchill and Roosevelt would meet at the Casablanca Conference, where it was decided that a second front in Europe was absolutely essential. Meanwhile, an around-the-clock strategic bombing offensive was to break the resolve of the German people and the vigour of their industry. A dogged Red Army surrounded Hitler's elite troops at Stalingrad on November 22, 1942, which eventually led to a costly German defeat in this frigid Russian city.

On January 31, 1943, the proud Sixth Army, led by the illustrious German Marshal Paulus, surrendered at Stalingrad. Hitler had repeatedly refused Paulus's requests to withdraw, resulting in the demise of tens of thousands of elite German troops under ghastly conditions. The survivors who were able to escape the siege were not only starving, hypothermic and exhausted, but also and perhaps more importantly, utterly demoralised. Lastly, on the Pacific front, American marines had been victorious in a horrendous fight for Guadalcanal. On January 4, 1943, Japanese forces withdrew from Guadalcanal, leaving behind 23,000 casualties.

CHAPTER FIVE

To Father's Land

On January 4, 1943, Ted's troop ship set sail for England. In spite of the marauding German U-boats they arrived safely, after an eight-day voyage. The most inconvenient feature of the journey had been that all travellers, no matter what rank, had to carry all their own baggage from place to place. Trunks, haversacks, web equipment, gas masks and tin hats, everything was hung around the neck or clutched in both hands. After docking at Liverpool, British military officers came aboard to brief the unit commanders on security and so forth. Everything was well organised, with trains waiting to take each group to their particular destination. On January 13, the day after he had disembarked, Ted was dispatched on an eight-hour train trip to Bournemouth, a city on the south coast of England about 80 miles south-west of London, site of 3 Personnel Reception Centre.

Bournemouth was a beautiful city that, in happier times, had been a soothing south coast haven, catering to the middle-aged and elderly citizenry. They crowded there to take pleasure in its mild climate, beautiful beaches and headlands, its lush gardens and parks and grand hotels. The war had transformed the peaceful aspect of the city, and now the beaches were heavily mined, all access to them barred by coils of rust-encrusted barbed wire. The elegant hotels had been taken over by the Air Ministry and were filled with Canadian airmen, most of whom must have struck their hosts as overactive teenagers compared with the dignified clientele of earlier years. Nevertheless, the city's splendour remained apparent despite the huge invasion of boisterous servicemen. Ted and John Uhthoff immediately arranged to room together at one of the hotels that had been commandeered by the military to billet the thousands of Canadian recruits. The officers' mess was located almost on the sea front in the swank Royal Bath Hotel. It was wonderful to be able to have a hot bath and a decent shave and to eat prepared foods again, even though it was at the Royal Bath Hotel that Ted and the others were introduced to the taste of powdered eggs, often masquerading on a slice of scorched toast with a small piece of grease-drenched Spam.[1] Teddy had had a cold during the trip

[1]Spam was a canned meat product made of spiced ham and pork and introduced to the troops during the Second World War.

but got rid of it in very short order after arriving in England. He felt pleased about being in England, and was looking forward to seeing more of his father's native country and finally meeting some of the Blenkinsop family members.

3 PRC was an orientation facility, the first stopping point for all newly arrived Canadian airmen. There they received medical checkups and prepared for more flying training as soon as the advanced flying units were able to make space available for the new draft. The first order of business was to issue the airmen with battle dress and a generous allotment of clothing coupons, which they would need for every article of clothing they bought thereafter. Next they had their photographs taken and were issued with their form 1250 identification cards. A couple of days later they received the latest in flying equipment: warm suits, silk and fleece-lined boots, chamois leather gloves, helmets and goggles. On the financial side, the Canadian airmen were not going to be paid in cash anymore. As an officer, Ted would now have £21 per month deposited to his account in a bank of his choice and the balance of his pay sent home or held to his credit.

In Bournemouth, Teddy ran into quite a number of chaps he knew. There were some of his ex-students, as well as several classmates from pilot training, such as Phil Shannon, Stu Campbell, Jim Grant and Nelson Spencer. As soon as he gained his first leave pass on January 25, Teddy telephoned his Uncle Max 'out of the blue', telling him that he had leave and would like to come over and stay with him. Teddy did say he had previously written to his uncle, but when he later produced the letter from his pocket in evidence, everybody concluded he had forgotten to post it. However, Hubert Blenkinsop had some time before informed his brother Max of Teddy's impending mission overseas, at which point Max, promptly and without hesitation, opened his home to his nephew. Uncle Max and his family lived in Woodland Grange, a beautiful and grand manor house in Royal Leamington Spa, a fashionable Warwickshire town deep in the heart of England, boasting Georgian and Victorian architecture, tree-lined avenues and squares surrounded by glorious gardens. This popular pre-war resort area would become a second home to Ted during his entire service in England.

When Teddy arrived, the whole family were enchanted with him and adored him on first sight. The general consensus was that Ted was a typical Blenkinsop, and he and Uncle Max bonded from the start. Max, the eldest of a family of 11 children, was very like Ted's father Hubert, both in appearance and in manner. This made Ted feel quite at ease in his company and quite at home at Woodland Grange. Ted also met his father's sisters, Lucy and May, who had a little place right next to Uncle Max's office in neighbouring Warwick. He got a bang out of Aunt Lucy, whom he described in his letters as 'a pretty lively sort of person'. Max and his wife

Yetta had eight children. Ann was the eldest at 21 and was nursing in Oxford, Alan had spent a year at sea and was now a 'middie' in the Navy, while Gerald was taking a six months' course at Oxford before joining the Royal Air Force.[1] The younger ones were at schools in various parts of the country. The family had gained plenty of experience entertaining airmen from the Dominion, as they had two or more staying with them during their leave most weeks. They liked a number of them, did not care for a few, but none made the impression that Teddy did.

On the second day of his leave, Teddy had lunch and tea with his aunts Lucy and May, who tried to rake up a good meal for him – not too easy to contrive in those days. Much to his aunts' delight, he did it justice and especially seemed to enjoy a bottle of beer they had managed to persuade the wine merchant to provide from under the counter. After lunch, Aunt Lucy took him, on rather reluctant feet, to view Warwick Castle from the river bridge. Lucy reckoned Hubert would be scandalised if Ted returned to Canada without even a glance at Warwick's showpiece. A government ministry occupied the striking fortress, so Ted was saved a tour of the buildings. After tea, Max took Teddy out and bought him a bicycle. Bicycles, in England in those days, were the only means of transportation except feet, particularly if one was away from the towns or not near a railway. The next day Uncle Max and Aunt Yetta took him on a cycling trip to nearby Stratford-upon-Avon, Shakespeare's hometown. All in all, Ted had a very enjoyable week, and to top it all, he took Ann to a superb dance in Oxford on Friday night, January 29. When his week of leave had ended, he said a temporary goodbye to the whole family, who all hoped he might be stationed near Leamington Spa for a time at any rate.[2]

On Thursday January 28, Aunt May wrote to her brother Hubert, who was affectionately called Toby by the whole family:

> What a shame you can't both be here too. I think even your proud hearts would be satisfied if you knew how much we think of Teddy – he is a darling, so good-looking (but very like you, Toby, all the same) and he has the most delightful manners. He gets on very well with Max who thinks a lot of him, but needless to say teases him all the time – however Teddy only grins and says nothing. He looks well, but too thin to please us – but he says he used to be thinner, so I suppose it's just the very strenuous life. He seems absolutely absorbed in his job, as though it was the only thing in the world at present – but that's rather the way the Air Force takes them.
>
> What strikes me as unusual about Teddy is his mind – he seems to have thought so much, and he talks like a man, not a boy. Of course

[1]Alan ended up serving as a pilot in the Fleet Air Arm and was killed in 1950 while attempting to land on an aircraft carrier. Gerald became a second pilot on Lancasters in early 1945 and was ready to go out to Japan when the war ended.

[2]Correspondence with Ann Gillett (née Blenkinsop), 1988-1989.

by now he has been about quite a lot and has seen a great deal, and no doubt it has given him a wider outlook than is usual in boys of his age. But from the way he speaks, I think that whatever his circumstances had been he would have had a very active intelligence and nothing would be thrown away on him. He has a lovely sense of humour and I should think he would be sweet to live with and not be fussy about trifles.

He came in to lunch on Tuesday. I was alone when he got here and he immediately offered to help me get the table ready, and although he nearly touches our ceiling, he seemed to fit into the kitchen very neatly. Of course, we had no sooner sat down than we all embarked on a violent discussion – Teddy didn't agree with all we said by any manner of means and I noticed that he was very well able to hold his own.

Now here is Teddy, so I'm going to stop. He says he has written, so I hope you will have heard all you want to know – anyway he *is* a dear. Love, May

Back at Bournemouth, Ted and John continued their daily routines at 3 PRC and were both becoming rather restless because of the delay. They paraded twice a day, at 09:00 a.m. and again at 01:30 p.m. There was so little work to be done that frequently they were dismissed immediately after roll call. However, Ted got into a spot of trouble through no fault of his own. On coming back from leave, they were assigned to various classes, and the one Ted joined was shortly afterwards paraded before the commanding officer to be reprimanded for considerable misconduct. The OC wound up his remarks by saying the innocent would be punished with the guilty. In almost three years' service Ted had never missed a parade or received any reproach, so naturally he took a dim view of it and asked for redress of grievance. He got the redress and managed to clear himself but still had to endure the punishment. He wisely let it go at that but it still rankled him. No doubt the exercise was good for him, though.

Many and varied were the facilities generously put at the airmen's disposal by the good citizens of Bournemouth, from archery ranges, cricket pitches to golf courses and sailing facilities. On occasion they marched to a large indoor pool, known as Lynden Hall Hydro, where they spent the afternoon swimming and practising crawling into rubber dinghies thrown onto the surface of the pool. Finally, on February 15, 1943, word came through there was an opening for a contingent of pilots at 3 (Pilot) Advanced Flying Unit at Long Newnton near Tetbury. Teddy was posted there the next day, and bid farewell to John Uhthoff and the others.

Long Newnton, situated in Wiltshire, was one of several temporary airfields constructed by the RAF in the early war years and had two steel mat runways, blister hangars and provisional accommodation. Quarters were good but naturally suffered by comparison with the Bournemouth hotels. The huts were neat and clean, and the Canadian volunteers enjoyed the novelty of being awakened in the morning by WAAF batwomen who brought them steaming hot tea that got them off to a good start.[1]

There were three objectives at the Advanced Flying Unit. One was to improve general flying skills and thus take the additional step toward the standard required for flying on operations. Another was learning to find your way about over the English countryside under weather conditions worse than the Canadians had previously been permitted to fly in. The last objective was to become familiar with the flying characteristics of a heavier aircraft. The aircraft they were to fly on this course was the Airspeed Oxford, an aircraft Ted had been checked out on in New Zealand five months earlier. The twin-engine advanced trainer, described as a reasonably demanding but thoroughly reliable aeroplane, had little secrets left for Ted, so he was already one step ahead of his peers. The AFU course was divided into three separate sections. The first segment, after the ground school, took three weeks and was designed to completely familiarise the new trainees with all the flying features of the Oxford. Once solo, the students would embark upon a series of 200 and 300-mile cross-countries to brush up navigational skills. Interspersed between these trips were frequent sessions of instrument flying, some with an instructor, some with a classmate acting as safety pilot.

On February 18, Ted had his initial flight at 3 (P) AFU with Flight Sergeant Hooper, who became his regular instructor. He performed two more general familiarisation and solo preparation flights, before soloing on the 20th. He had spent a total of two hours and 30 minutes before taking an Oxford up by himself, whereas the other students in his class averaged eight hours prior to doing the same. On that same February 20, Ted made three more flights, and he continued with a lot of flying in the following days. On February 24, 26 and 28 he made three or four flights a day, adding about five hours flying time in each of those days. The cross-country navigations proved quite challenging. These flights forcibly brought home the realisation that what the Canadian volunteers had called map reading at home was child's play. In their native country they had grown accustomed to the uncluttered countryside tidily divided off by the section roads into neat squares lined up with the cardinal points of the compass. Even more importantly, they were in the habit of looking ahead and around in unrestricted visibility, while in England there was often a low overcast or mist that restricted forward visibility. Lastly, map reading was rendered infinitely more difficult by the overwhelming density of the detail on the ground. Railway lines were like webs spun by industrious colonies of spiders, while roads, all of them paved, were hardly ever

[1]WAAF is the abbreviation for Women's Auxiliary Air Force, a female auxiliary of the RAF. They were active in the manning of barrage balloons, in catering, meteorology, radar, transport, telephonic and telegraphic duties.

straight. Fortunately, Teddy had a lot more theoretical and practical navigational experience than anyone else in his class and as a result outshone each and every one of them.

Flying at the AFU continued on Sundays, and there was an obvious reason for the high tempo at the training facility. At the beginning of March 1943, RAF Bomber Command was launching the first of the great aerial offensives for which its indomitable commander, Sir Arthur Harris, had been struggling to organise. Bomber Command had not yet attained its ultimate size that would be achieved a few months later, but even now it could launch a mixed armada of over 500 heavies. Operational statistics show that in early 1943, nearly 3 per cent of Bomber Command's aircraft did not return from nightly raids. It was calculated that, on average, nearly four bomber aircraft were lost every 24 hours. With losses of these dimensions, it was apparent that hundreds of new crews would have to be pumped into the Bomber Command system to fill vacant squadron positions so as to continue the build-up for future operations. It is probable that Harris had Berlin in mind as his ultimate target to force Germany out of the war but Berlin was too difficult a target for Bomber Command to reach at that time, so the logical place to fight Bomber Command's first pitched battle was the Ruhr. The Ruhr, with its sprawling complex of industrial cities, could easily be reached in the shorter nights of spring and summer. However, the flak and searchlight defences around the Ruhr cities were already the most advanced and powerful in Germany.[1] The night fighter units manning the skies on the routes between the coast of Europe and the cluster of industrialised cities were already the most experienced and best equipped in the Luftwaffe. The coming period was going to be a major test for the participants and the levels of death and destruction were about to mount dramatically.

In spite of the pace at the AFU, Teddy found time to write to his parents on February 20, 1943:

> I'm flying again now after such a long spell away from it. I'm rather glad of it to say the least. I can tell you nothing of my whereabouts or of anything connected with my work, so you'll understand why I make no mention of it. Can't even say what sort of weather we're having. Uncle Max teases me about my reticence and I know other people talk a lot but still 'it ain't right'.
>
> I'm with a fine bunch of lads who are training with me, we have a lot of fun in a very quiet way. I'm very busy now, never seem to have enough time to do everything, but I'm supremely happy, everything I've been striving for during the past two years is beginning to work out. It won't be so very long now.

---

[1]Flak is short for *Fliegerabwehrkanone*, which is German for anti-aircraft guns. Flak was a term generally used by aircrews, including the Allied crews.

Had one cold when we first arrived in this country but have been in tip-top shape ever since. Something about the atmosphere makes me eat enormously too, I always seem to be hungry.

John is no longer with me. One of these days one of us will get around to writing to the other and we'll get together again. It was good to be together again after so long a time.

Well, it's late and I'm very sleepy. I will try to write more regularly (the same old ending). Teddy.

Ted's flying skills gradually expanded to accommodate the additional demands imposed by Oxford flying, and he was soon looking for new fields to conquer, confident that he should be able to pass the various tests included in the AFU syllabus. The days passed quickly, and in no time he was in his third week of the first segment of the course and ready for the test he knew must be almost upon him. The test came on March 14, and Ted passed it without difficulty. The initial course at AFU was now finished. Ted had logged 32 training sorties and done a couple more as safety pilot for others in his class, and he now had a little over 700 flying hours under his belt. He was immediately detached to 1531 Beam Approach Squadron at Cranage, another temporary airfield, in Cheshire. There he would complete the second segment of the AFU syllabus.

Meanwhile there were a lot of things happening on the family front. Despite a praiseworthy struggle, Aunt May had not recovered from a bad form of flu she had contracted in mid-February and died in early March. Her passing was a blow to the whole Blenkinsop clan and to many others outside the family. In Canada, Winsome, now a flight lieutenant in the RCAF, was posted to Vancouver, where she would spend the majority of her service. Hubert was left alone in Victoria to look after himself, and he divided his time between his office on 1212 Broad Street and the home of his parents-in-law at 1076 Joan Crescent. His letters show that he never adapted to the idea of having a wife in the service. As if that weren't enough, Teddy received word that his girlfriend Helen had also answered to the call of duty. She officially joined the RCAF in April 1943, thus following in the footsteps of her elder brother, Sub-Lieutenant Derek Woodcroft, on active service in the Royal Canadian Navy, and of Helen's mother, who had served in the Scottish Women's Hospitals in Macedonia during the First World War. After her training in Canada, and much to her delight, Helen was posted overseas and ended up serving on a RCAF bomber station in Britain.

Most of the flying time on the Beam Approach Training, or BAT course, was devoted to practising bad weather approaches and landings using radio beam homing signals. The homing exercises were flown entirely on instrument under the hood, except when the visibility allowed the instructors to leave the hood off. On Monday, March 22, Ted made his final flight of the BAT course. For six days, he had lived with the radio beams, seeking their blended on-course signals from every point of the compass, listening closely to the transmitted Morse codes and translating their cryptic messages into developing mental images of his aircraft's position relative to the aerodrome. For 16 arduous hours, 11 in the air and five in the Link Trainer, he had flown exclusively on instruments, drawing from the ubiquitous monotone of the radio range signals to enable him to find the airfield, position himself on the centreline of its main runway, and descend gently at 100 miles an hour to the concrete strip he sought. He was a qualified beam pilot now, and if the need arose could fall back with confidence on its lifesaving potential.

Ted and the rest of his draft rode to Long Newnton to carry out some extra flights of the curriculum there, before being posted on April 4 to Lulsgate Bottom. There he embarked on the third phase of the AFU program, a two-week concentrated session of night flying that completed his training at 3 AFU. Lulsgate Bottom was situated about ten kilometres south-west of Bristol in Somersetshire. On April 4, Ted went up with Flying Officer Clarke for his first stint of night dual in an Oxford. After 40 minutes, Clarke had seen enough and ordered Teddy to land the aeroplane. After having taxied back, Clarke jumped out and sent Ted off on his first night solo on the 'Ox-box'. The next day, Sergeant Shorney gave him another 25 minutes of night dual before clearing him on an additional hour of solo. The following days were devoted to beacon flying, referred to by the trainees as 'pundit crawling'. These were night navigational exercises consisting of flying to four or five aerodromes in a sequence designed to take about one to two hours. Every aerodrome in the country had a tiny red beacon or 'pundit' mounted on it or near it, which began flashing low-powered Morse code signals at dusk. This enabled pilots, who had a current list of the various codes, to identify the aerodrome. Finding these aerodromes was quite difficult, as the pundits were practically invisible until you were nearly on top of them. In addition, the weather on most nights during this period was marginal for flying, which added significantly to the strain of the pundit crawls and the ability to carry out the landing circuit. Ted counted himself fortunate for the substantially higher amount of night flying hours he had accumulated compared to the others in his group. Obviously, these potential bomber pilots realised that flying at night would become a more than sizeable portion of their operational flying.

On April 15, Ted and the rest of his class completed the AFU program. He had his time certified and his course assessment entered in his logbook. To his great delight, Squadron Leader Swanston, the officer commanding 3 (P) AFU, wrote 'above the average on Oxfords'. In a letter home, Teddy reported in his typical unassuming manner:

> By the way, at AFU I was top of the class in flying marks though we were all ex-instructors and staff pilots. One of the only two classified 'Above Average pilot'. Maybe I'm not as poor as I'd thought, though

> the future alone will tell. Never have rated myself as much of a pilot actually, so I'm quite pleased.

Ted was allowed five days' leave and ordered to report on April 21 to 22 Operational Training Unit (OTU) at Wellesbourne Mountford. Five days of rest wasn't much, but it was no doubt a result of Bomber Command's desperate need for more crews, as the force was getting ready for its main offensive. Sir Arthur Harris had guided Bomber Command through the recent winter with great competence, recognising that the time was not yet ripe for an all-out assault. He had conserved and built up his force, constantly experimenting with new bombing tactics, while at the same time he continued to introduce new technical innovations into the inventory. Now, in March and April 1943, all was ready for a continued and major effort against Germany.

During this period Bomber Command received important reinforcements. At the start of 1942, the RCAF had four bomber squadrons in England of which two were not yet operational. In June 1942, another Canadian squadron had been formed in England. This was only the beginning of a huge expansion for the RCAF bomber force, for during the months of October and November 1942 six more units were formed. This tremendous increase in what was to become Canada's major contribution to the air war preceded the creation of the new all-Canadian 6 (RCAF) Group within Bomber Command, a unique formation which was entirely funded by the Canadian government. The group formally came into existence on January 1, 1943. Seven RAF stations were initially handed over to the group, all in Yorkshire and all previously used by Canadian units. By the start of March 1943, when 405 Squadron was transferred from 4 Group to join the new outfit, 6 Group had nine squadrons on strength. During April 1943, however, the group temporarily lost 420, 424 and 425 squadrons when these units were detached to North Africa to help prepare for the imminent invasion of Sicily and Italy.[1]

Things Get Serious

Wellesbourne Mountford was located eight kilometres east of Stratford-upon-Avon, only a cycling trip away from Uncle Max's house. This was a lucky coincidence, as there were several other OTUs throughout the country, and this one gave Ted the opportunity to spend his entire five-day break at Leamington and subsequent days off which followed. When Ted reported to 22 OTU on Wednesday, April 21, he immediately sensed that this was going to be a different ball game. To start with, he learned that the 'final test' of the training course would be a mission over enemy-held

[1]Of the 48 RCAF squadrons deployed offshore by 1944, 16 were in Bomber Command, 18 were with the Second Tactical Air Force, five with Fighter Command, five with Coastal Command, and another supporting the Eighth Army in Italy. There were also three transport squadrons operating on the Western Front and two in Burma.

France to drop propaganda leaflets. The twin-engine Wellington III aircraft looked very much like what they were, battle-weary operational heavy bombers. These aircraft were still in use by several units in Bomber Command, although their numbers were in steady decline as each new four-engine Halifax and Lancaster arrived on the station. He heard the stories of how fatal accidents were nothing unusual at OTU. The poor condition of the Wellingtons was the contributing factor to the high accident rate. Most of the OTU Wellingtons had come from operational squadrons, and were mostly time-expired before they were assigned to the OTU. The engines were de-rated, since opening the throttles fully could easily result in a blown cylinder.

Ted ran into several familiar faces at 22 OTU. Bill Strachan, who had trained with him at Sea Island, was there, also Bill Thompson, who had been on Short Nav with him, Clive Sinton, who instructed at Rivers, and five ex-pupils from Pennfield Ridge. Ted was quite shocked when an Australian squadron leader wearing the coveted Distinguished Flying Cross stopped him on his first day at Wellesbourne and said, 'You taught me navigation at Rivers, remember?' Teddy looked and sure enough, it was one of his star pupils, now the chief navigation officer, with his underlings now instructing Ted at OTU. Everyone was very decent at OTU and treated the trainees well. Meals were pretty good on the whole and work was absorbing. Teddy was happy as a lark.

Shortly after the arrival of the new draft of apprentices, the instructors and administration officers organised the group into classes and laid out the curriculum. They announced that within a few days the new arrivals would be teamed up in crews of five, each consisting of a pilot, bomb aimer, navigator, wireless operator and air gunner. The procedure was that about 20 of each trade were brought together in one building and left to sort themselves out into crews. If any five could reach agreement and form a crew, the Air Force would oblige and crew them up officially to fly together. All those who had not made their own arrangements would then be crewed up at random by the staff.

This opportunity to crew up on the basis of mutual and personal choices, although genuinely proposed, was largely illusory. Most of the pilots considered it a hopeless task to pick a crewmember on the basis of the scanty information available. They did not have a clue about the air gunner's or navigator's marks in gunnery or navigation school and had to go on a glimpse of him in class or the type of wing on his chest. Of even greater importance, perhaps, the pilots could only guess at the psychological make-up of their potential new crewmembers. Were they up to the hazardous and nerve-racking task of flying a bomber into a hostile environment on a dark and stormy night? Conversely, the other crewmembers were as anxious as the pilots. They were trying to size up the pilots, and the consequences of a poor selection were even more frightening. A second-rate, slow-witted or reckless pilot was likely to get everyone in his crew killed. They knew that if a pilot had been commissioned on graduation he had stood well in his class, but that was often an unreliable guide as the finest pilots in combat had frequently been NCOs. The bottom line remained simple: the motive for anyone wishing to crew up and fly with a particular individual was generally self-preservation. One wanted to have crewmembers who were good at their trades and who could perform them skilfully under the overpowering stress in operational conditions.

Despite the impracticability of attempting to pick other trades, Ted decided that there might be some merit in trying to size up the navigators from the way they performed in the classroom discussions of navigational issues. He was determined not to sit back and take what the Air Force gave him; he wanted to create the crew he was going into battle with himself. Not only that, but he also aspired to move quickly and pick out the best in every trade before other pilots beat him to it. After having observed his classmates carefully for one or two days, Ted made his move. He and a large number of RCAF pilots, navigators, bomb aimers, air gunners and wireless operators, including a few RAF wireless operators who ended up in their group, were put together in a briefing room and told to mingle and get to know each other. Ted approached a navigator named Theodor 'Ted' Howlett and asked him to join his crew. Pilot Officer Howlett had earned a BA and an MA degree at a Nova Scotia university and was a high school teacher in English and maths for eight years. In 1941, when teaching in Yarmouth Academy in Yarmouth, Nova Scotia, he became bored with his job, while also growing increasingly dismayed at the large number of air casualties among his former students. He decided to enlist for pilot training in the RCAF, but he was soon rerouted to navigator training. He graduated as a pilot officer from Air Observers School in September 1942 and promptly sailed from Halifax to Glasgow. He was six foot two inches tall, as was Teddy, but much more heavily built than he. At the age of 26, he would be seen as the 'grandpa' of the crew, but Teddy liked him and considered him a real asset, very quiet but steady as a rock. In a letter written years later, Ted Howlett reminisced about those days:

> I think Blenkie chose me as his navigator at least partly because I had made very good marks on navigation, mathematics and other subjects in the RCAF ground schools in Belleville, Ontario and Ancienne Lorette, Quebec. In the air, I was not, I must confess, as excellent a navigator as I had been in ground school.
>
> Ted was always dignified and restrained in his reactions, and thus he was perhaps not so popular in the officers' mess as some of the other more natural, outgoing men. He had a distinct British accent,

> but that is a customary manner of speech in very-British Victoria, his home city.[1]

It is very likely that Ted made use of the network of former colleagues in the air navigation or air observer branch to ascertain which of the navigators present at Wellesbourne Mountford had stood out in navigation training. He might have done the same for the bomb aimer he was going to pick out, as bomb aimers also passed through observers training. He selected John 'Johnnie' Miskae, a young and keen pilot officer from Winnipeg. He had been two-and-a-half years in the service and was a sergeant fitter at Calgary before joining the flying ranks. He was a 22-year-old, blondish and jovial second or third generation Ukrainian, who had also been top of his class in training. Johnnie Miskae picked up a little hands-on flying as the crew progressed through OTU, and so he became a sort of co-pilot in addition to being the bombardier. He might have been able, in an emergency, to fly back and land the aircraft. Then Ted needed a wireless operator. Dennis 'Ren' Renvoizé recalled what happened:

> After completing a wireless and gunnery course at Penbury in south Wales I was posted to Wellesbourne Mountford with the intention of being 'crewed up'. I was with two of my other English pals when Blenkie came over and asked me if I would like to join his crew. Blenkie was a tall, distinguished and rather handsome man – someone who made you look at him straight away. As at the time I was a sergeant and he was a flight lieutenant, I was quite flattered and naturally said 'Yes please!' This I have never regretted.[2]

Ren Renvoizé was of French descent – being Huguenot originally, but his family had been in England for many generations. When the war broke out, he was thinking of studying to become an architect. Instead, he joined the RAF shortly after his 18th birthday and came out top of his class in wireless school. He was – and still is – a stylish and friendly gentleman of medium height, who had already proved himself as a skilled and experienced wireless operator and very cool in crises. He and Teddy shared many the same ideas about going to war and shared many common values in life, and the two of them would get along very well. Ren was the baby of the crew, at age 21. Lastly, Ted needed an air gunner to man the Browning machine guns in the rear turret of a Wellington. He chose a strong and likeable young fellow from Toronto by the name of John 'Jack' Nash. Jack was easygoing, laughed easily and was always positive in his outlook – not a bad quality for a rear gunner.[3]

---

[1]Letter from Theodor Howlett to the author, November 29, 1988.

[2]Letter from Dennis Renvoizé to the author, August 6, 1990. Ren, his wife Gwen and daughter Penelope have become very close friends with the author and his wife ever since the first contact in 1990.

[3]In 1967, Jack Nash officially had his name changed to Albert John MacDonald.

Right from the start the Blenkinsop Crew, as they were referred to, connected exceptionally well. They knew nothing or almost nothing about one another's past, and, strangely enough, were never curious or interested enough to ask. Everybody minded his own business more or less, and the rapid sequence of events did not leave much time for chitchat. But, they were all keen, all itching to get on with the job and all in harmony. They were very pleased with each other. On April 29, Ted conveyed to his parents that he was really happy and that everything seemed to be coming along the way he had always hoped it would. Little did he realise that his luck would run out in exactly one year hence.

What followed was a number of ground school sessions to assist the newly formed crews to coalesce into combat-ready entities. Lectures covered all subjects and equipment the crew would be using in the Wellingtons Mark III and X, like the innovative 'Gee' system. This was a device which enabled a bomber's navigator to fix his position by consulting a 'Gee Box', which received pulse signals from three widely separated radio stations in England. These showed as blips on the radar screen in front of the navigator that could be plotted on a chart. By computing the difference between receipts of these signals, the navigator could obtain an instant fix. Although being primarily a navigational device, some attempts were made to use it for blind-bombing targets where there was overcast cloud. The foremost benefit of Gee was in enabling crews to reach the general target area when they encountered winds that were not as forecast and might have taken the aircraft badly off course, a major problem that had highly degraded Bomber Command's effectiveness in the early years of the war.

One of the ground exercises at OTU simulated the navigational and other problems a crew could expect to encounter on a bombing raid. It was carried out in a large building that contained a number of twin-level studios, each housing one crew. While the exercise was going on, simulated engine noise necessitated the use of intercom between the different crew positions. A variety of problems surfaced during the raid and were similar to those studied during their classroom plotting exercises. An additional complication was introduced. The large wall clock that paced all the crews' actions operated at one-and-one-half times normal speed. This, according to OTU policy, would compensate for the interminable strain during real operations, which inevitably led to slower reaction times and affected one's normal reasoning. All the OTU's were under tremendous pressure to get crews through the extensive course assignments prescribed and have them ready for posting to the Bomber Command squadrons, or to Heavy Conversion Units if their assigned squadrons were flying four-engine aircraft. Because of the nightly attrition in the heavily engaged line squadrons of the main force, i.e., the regular heavy bomber squadrons, and the insatiable demand caused by the continuous expansion of the force, there was a constant urgency for extra bomber crews.

On Tuesday, May 4, Teddy had a few spare hours and took his bicycle to visit Uncle Max. The next day he again rode the half-hour trip to have tea and supper with Aunt Lucy. He enjoyed the hours away from work, and Max and Lucy did their utmost to feed their nephew well and give him a warm welcome. Flying finally started the following day. Pilot Officer Moore was to be the flying instructor assigned for the first familiarisation flight of Teddy's crew in a Wellington. Before the flight, Ted had taken his crew and pilot's handbook to a remote dispersal area. There they crept through the aircraft for an hour or so in what they called an acclimatisation tour, getting used to the cockpit arrangement and memorising the height of the aircraft from the pilot's seat as it sat on the ground. This was something a pilot had to do on each new aircraft, particularly when moving from a relatively low one, like an Oxford, to a Wellington, which stood over 17 feet high above the ground. The Vickers-Armstrong Wellington III was a big aircraft by the standards Ted and his crew had trained on so far. Fully loaded, the bomber weighed just over 30,000lbs, a 400 per cent increase from the Oxfords they had just mastered. It could haul 4,500lbs of bombs to a target located within a round-trip distance of over 1,500 miles. It was more aircraft than Ted had ever handled before and had the reputation of being a very rugged machine, thanks to its geodetic body construction. With two Bristol Hercules XI engines capable of delivering 1,500 horsepower each, the pilot had four times the power available than he had grown accustomed to at AFU. A much more complicated hydraulic and petrol system and sleeve-valve radial engines required new handling techniques. All neophyte crews could not help but gain a new respect for these well-worn warhorses. Ted meticulously studied all the diagrams and manuals for several days, and he felt ready to take the Wellington into the skies.

Exactly at 09:30 a.m. on the morning of Thursday, May 6, Teddy took off in a Wellington X, with Pilot Officer Moore sitting in the 'second dickey' seat and Johnnie Miskae and Dennis Renvoizé manning their bomb aimer and wireless operator positions. The flight lasted exactly three hours. Teddy went through a seemingly endless routine of circuits, approaches, touch-and-go's and overshoots, while being informed by Moore about the Wellington's particularities. It wasn't until next Tuesday, May 11, that Ted, Johnnie and Ren were on the flying schedule again, this time for a trip in the company of Flight Lieutenant Hudson. After two hours of check circuits and bumps and all kinds of procedures, Hudson found it sufficiently satisfactory to approve Ted's progress and send him on his way for his first solo flight in a Wellington. As soon as Hudson had cleared out of the aircraft, Ted took Johnnie and Ren up for an hour and five minutes of solo flying. Both of his crewmembers jovially congratulated him after his fine performance and called him amiably their skipper. Teddy enjoyed the moment thoroughly.

While Teddy did two more solo trips with Johnnie Miskae and Ren Renvoizé on May 13 and 14, Ted Howlett flew with experienced instructors to practise taking fixes and homing with the Gee system. He also went on a couple of cross-country navigation missions. On the afternoon of May 14, Teddy flew the first flight with his complete crew. Flight Lieutenant Powell accompanied them in the second dickey seat. The mission was a so-called bull's-eye exercise, where the crew had to find a training target on one of the firing ranges and then bomb it with 10.5lb exercise bombs from 10,000 feet. These projectiles produced a flash when they hit the ground, and shot out a billow of snowy white smoke to mark its point of impact. After each exercise, the crew got the miss-distance figures supplied by the observation post in close proximity to the target area. The Blenkinsop crew carried out several of these missions in the days following.

Besides actually dropping practice bombs on the heavily solicited range, the crew also practised simulation bomb runs using a camera that gave the bomb aimer bombsight practice, which was as valuable as the real thing. These high-level bombing missions were a science that called for the utmost in cooperation and understanding between the pilot and bomb aimer for success. Once a bomb was released, it continued forward at the same speed and in the same path relative to the ground as that of the aircraft. While the bomb aimer had to accurately work his bombsight, taking into account the bomb ballistics as well as the airspeed, bombing height, bomb time-of-fall and a set of other variables, his performance was contingent upon the pilot's flying accuracy. Even from the relatively moderate heights the practice bombing missions were being flown, it took the bomb 20 to 30 seconds to fall, so the bomb aimer had to release it while the aircraft was still a mile or more from the 50-foot square target. All the bombsight settings assumed that the aircraft would be kept perfectly straight and level with no variance of airspeed and height. The slightest errors in either of these variables would produce unflatteringly large errors in the desired point of impact. Getting direct hits required nothing less than perfection, and perfection entailed arduous practice and extreme concentration. The pilot and bomb aimer had to blend their skills as two piano players in a composition for four hands. Teddy and Johnnie got the hang of it quite quickly, with all but one of their bombing scores being well inside 100 yards, while most of the other crews doubted they would ever get less than a 100-yard error. On May 17, they set their crew's high-level record with a miss-distance of 42 yards, while on a low-level bombing run the day prior their bomb load had hit the ground 16 yards from the practice target.

From then on, Ted's crew flew almost every day, sometimes two missions a day, and steadily continued to make progress. The last portion of their OTU training put heavy emphasis on long-range night cross-country navigations, some of which incorporated special exercises against searchlight and night fighter defences. In addition, the crews flew 'combat load' sorties in aircraft that were loaded to the maximum permissible takeoff gross weight. These missions served the objective of making the crews familiar with high-weight manoeuvring and the slower response and reduced performance of the aircraft at these weights. Instructors joined them when new procedures were introduced, such as formation or low-altitude flying. Some of these missions included air firing on a drogue target, allowing a keen Jack Nash to show his gunnery talents. On May 20, Ted's crew completed their first night training mission with Flight Lieutenant Hudson. The next day Flight Lieutenant Powell gave them their night solo test and allowed them to go by themselves after two hours of night circuits and bumps. Two more local night trips followed on May 22 and 23. Teddy's crew was then dispatched on their first night bull's-eye mission. On May 25, Flight Lieutenant Hudson witnessed their bombs falling only 36 yards short of target, and released them for a solo trip.

Missions on May 30 and 31 marked their first experience with the use of infrared beams for night simulation bombing. A device was mounted on the practice target that transmitted an infrared beam toward the sky at the appropriate angle and along the predetermined line of the bombing run. In this way, if the bomb aimer had the pilot tracking correctly on his run and had the target centred in his sight when he pressed the button and activated his camera, the invisible IR beam would leave a trace on the exposed film. When the film was developed in the photographic section at the base, the results were recorded and could be assessed. Obviously more practice bombing was always prescribed, but Teddy's crew now seldom turned in bombing scores outside 50 yards. They now had about 60 hours on Wellingtons and were just about ready for combat.

Royal Air Force Bomber Command was still compelled to devote a large percentage of its effort to bombing targets in Germany while still assisting with the war at sea with mine-laying and attacking ports, railway yards and airfields in occupied countries. But science was now more than ever coming to the aid of Bomber and Coastal Commands. Alongside other inventions, new and more powerful depth charges were introduced to attack the U-boats that were creating havoc amongst Allied shipping in the Atlantic. Admiral Karl Dönitz, the supreme commander of the German Kriegsmarine, finally on May 24, 1943, ceased further U-boat operations in the Atlantic, following their heavy losses experienced the previous month.

The new H2S navigation and bombing aid had begun to be used operationally in January 1943. Entirely self-contained in the aircraft, it produced a radar map of the terrain beneath the aircraft, showing clearly features such as coastlines, rivers, lakes and towns, even through dense cloud.[1] Almost simultaneously, Gee was superseded by a far more accurate and less easily jammed radar navigation aid known as Oboe, which proved to be an ideal navigation aid for the versatile Mosquitos that had recently joined the newly formed 'Pathfinder' force.[2] For some time Bomber Command had been using raid leaders in attempts to improve target marking. Most squadrons contained a proportion of crews who, by survival and experience or above-average skill, showed a consistent ability to find and bomb their targets. The obvious suggestion was made that these crews should be gathered together permanently into a target finding force. This concept of an elite element was strongly opposed by Bomber Command Commander-in-Chief Sir Arthur Harris along with most of his group commanders. Their objection eventually led to a revised concept that gathered together six 'ordinary' squadrons to be stationed in close proximity to each other to exchange ideas so as to develop new target-finding tactics. Harris still resisted, but Air Chief Marshal Sir Charles Portal, Chief of the Air Staff, ordered Harris to abandon his opposition and stand up this new force.

All was finally ready on August 11, 1942, and the first raid for the pathfinders took place one week later. The new force, consisting of only four ordinary squadrons, immediately faced many problems. Initially the pathfinders never received the much-wanted pick of the best crews from the groups that were responsible to supply replacements. The force was operating four different types of aircraft – Halifaxes, Lancasters, Stirlings and Wellingtons – and had no special bombs for marking targets, but the pathfinders gradually evolved and soon were able to justify their existence.

Among the better-known exploits of the Allied air forces in mid-1943 are certainly the daring and brilliant attacks by 617 Squadron on the Möhne, Eder and Sorpe dams. Although costing eight of the 19 participating Lancaster crews, breaking these 'unconquerable' concrete structures with the astonishing 'bouncing bomb' created a significant morale boost for both the Allied forces and the British public. Less well known are operations like those mounted by Bomber Command in support of Operation Torch, the invasion of North Africa in the autumn of 1942. When Torch had achieved its objective, Eisenhower prepared for the first stage of the Allied liberation of Europe, the landings in Sicily and Italy.

---

[1]H2S was a self-contained scanning radar. It consisted of three parts, a generator driven by the starboard outer engine, a rotating radar scanner mounted in a pod under the aircraft, and a cathode ray tube, in front of the observer. The scanner rotated once per second, and reflected from buildings, etc., directly below and forward of the aircraft. No reflection was received over water, but the coastline could be identified, as could reflections from towns and villages along the route. From these, a bearing and distance could be calculated and used in determining course, wind velocity and ground speed. H2S was a ground-mapping radar 'avant la lettre'.

[2]Oboe was a combination of radar pulse signals from two UK-based stations. By knowing the distance to a selected target and with one station tracking the bomber, the intersection of the two signals (or arcs) became the bombing release point.

The brutal extremes of Nazism continued to yield thousands of innocent victims. At the Wannsee Conference held on January 20, 1942, German leadership had discussed the issue of the large number of inmates in Germany's concentration camps. As a result, it was decided to make the extermination of the Jews a systematically organised operation, and give it the horrifying name Endlösung or Final Solution. Extermination camps that had the capacity to annihilate large numbers of people were prepared, including Belzec (15,000 a day), Sobibor (20,000), Treblinka (25,000) and Majdanek (25,000). Between July 22 and October 3, 1942, 310,322 Jews had been deported from the Warsaw Ghetto to these extermination camps. Conditions in the Warsaw Ghetto were so bad that between 1940 and 1942 an estimated 100,000 Jews had died of starvation and disease alone. As news of the mass killings at these death camps leaked back to the ghetto, despair gave way to a determination to resist. It was then that the Zydowska Organizacja Bojowa or the Jewish Fighters Organisation, mostly young Polish Jews in their teens and early twenties, was formed and moved to take control of the ghetto. In January 1943, SS leader Heinrich Himmler was tired of Polish resistance and gave instructions for Warsaw to be 'Jew free' by Hitler's birthday on April 20. On April 19, 1943, the Waffen SS entered the Warsaw Ghetto. Although they only had two machine-guns, fifteen rifles, 500 pistols, a number of grenades and petrol bombs, the 1,500 desperate resistance fighters opened fire on the Germans. The Germans took heavy casualties and retreated, only to return shortly afterwards to set fire to all the buildings in the ghetto. Thousands of Jews were murdered, arrested or buried alive under the rubble of the buildings. Still they didn't give up and, using guerrilla tactics, the ghetto fighters continued the battle from cellars and attics. On May 8, the Germans began using poison gas on the insurgents in the last fortified bunker. The gas killed everyone except roughly a hundred men and women who survived by escaping into the underground sewers. The Warsaw revolt came to an end on May 16, 1943. About 7,000 Jews were killed in the fighting. Over 55,000 were transported to the death camp in Treblinka. After the defeat of the uprising, the Germans razed the ghetto to the ground. When the Germans left Warsaw in January 1945 there were only 20 Jews left in the city. The Warsaw Ghetto Uprising was probably the largest single resistance operation organised and executed by a partisan body during the Second World War.

First 'Op'

At the time, the atrocities committed by the Nazis were little known to Allied soldiers. Ted and his crew, like most lower-ranking officers and men in the Allied forces, were kept informed of the war's progression only by means of the news reports at the local movie theatre, newspapers and maybe a military intelligence report. Their sense of duty was fed by a determination to help stop a war that was started by an insane dictator who was threatening the free world, especially the British Empire and Commonwealth.

On June 4, 1943, when Ted and his crew showed up expecting to be sent on another high-level bombing exercise, they were in for a little surprise. Ted's name was on the Ops Board and had him and his crew flying Wellington 'S-for-Susy' that night on a 'nickel' raid, the code name for a leaflet-dropping mission. Thereupon Ted's crew gave 'S-for-Susy' the most rigorous air test they had given any aircraft up to that point, even test-firing their guns with meticulous care as a final step. Shortly after returning to Wellesbourne, they were told that the mission was scrubbed due to forecasted poor weather over the target area. Next day, the merry fivesome reported again for duty, and right away noted their skipper's name on the schedule for the night mission. Briefing was at 04:30 p.m., prior to which time they learned that four other crews were flying the operation with them. Inside the secured briefing room they sat for a few minutes, then rose as the station commander entered, escorted by the flight commander, the intelligence officer and all the section leaders. For the first time the 25 young airmen experienced the tension of sitting before the covered wall map, watching anxiously as the curtains parted to reveal the red route tapes, and listening to the intelligence officer as he signified with his pointer and began his customary but ever dramatic 'Gentlemen, the target for tonight is....'. Teddy's crew's target was Vichy, a town lying some 200 miles south of Paris. It struck them that for their first combat undertaking the target was a long way into enemy-held territory. The other crews had objectives in the same general area. The trip would take just over six hours all told and, with the light load they were taking to France, they would be able to carry one hour of reserve fuel. The intelligence officer explained how carefully the route had been chosen so as to keep the five crews clear of major flak installations and the known areas of night fighter activity. Despite his laudable efforts to bolster confidence, the tension was clearly visible on all faces in the audience. As the briefing went on, Ted looked in fascination at the tape and pins that traced the route, particularly the red trail leading from the sea into hostile territory. Undoubtedly some of his colleagues were wondering how frightening it would be to be fired upon and have shells explode near them in the darkness. Others were probably mulling over their chances if a Ju 88 or Me 110 night fighter got them in their sights, knowing that the answer was not very encouraging.

When the briefing was over the crews had a couple of hours to wait before they went to the mess for their first traditional pre-ops meal. This treat – and it really fell in that category – consisted of a fried egg and toast supper, a real fried egg! Squadron aircrews also got milk to drink every day, plus a fried egg snack after each operation, so being admitted to the ops fraternity that night did not do the morale of Teddy's crew any harm.

Because of the lateness of June sunsets, take-off was delayed correspondingly, and the five crews waited what seemed an endless period in or near the crew room. Finally, after having smoked too many cigarettes and having rehearsed the mission details a number of times, the crew bus came to pick them up. Everybody now seemed in a world of his own as the bus drove out to the hardstands. Teddy and his chums climbed into 'S-for-Susy', got their gear stowed, strapped themselves in, and waited for Ted to start the engines. Cylinder head temperatures and magnetos were checked, while Ted Howlett and Ren Renvoizé tested their equipment and Jack Nash readied his rear turret machine guns. Around 10:30 p.m. the Wellingtons started to move one by one, and began rolling toward the active runway. Ted taxied up to the takeoff point, and at exactly 10:45 p.m. Wellington 'S-for-Susy' received the signal for takeoff and took to the skies. Exactly three years and one day after Teddy had joined the armed forces, he now had embarked on his first combat mission.

Navigator Ted Howlett remembered well what happened on their number one op:

> When we reached about 20,000 feet over France, the oxygen-feed became faulty and my 'Gee' radar box began to give a fuzzy, meaningless picture. Also, the rear gunner Jack was convinced that a German night-fighter was following us, and, as a result, Ted began a series of evasive actions that continued for quite a long time.
>
> Well, the night-fighter – if there was one – never fired at us and we eventually dropped our 'load' somewhere near the target area. But my attempts at navigation had been almost fruitless. I had to rely heavily on the flight plan. In the end, we did reach England, but a friendly flashing beacon near London indicated that we were about 40 miles off track! Result: I felt very 'low' for a couple of days.[1]

Wireless Operator Ren Renvoizé concluded:

> We were flying over France on a very moonlit night, when a German night-fighter flew alongside. We thought that it was our end, but it turned out that he was unarmed apparently. I think that we were all pretty scared at the time.
>
> On this trip, we were supposed to cut the strings on the bundles of leaflets and throw them through a certain hatch. But I think it was Jack who opened the wrong one and as fast as we threw them out, the leaflets came back in again. The aircraft soon resembled a newspaper office. All we wanted was to get rid of them – which we eventually did – and hope and trust that some of Marshal Pétain's countrymen read them!

[1]Letter from Ted Howlett to the author, November 29, 1988.

The Blenkinsop crew landed at Wellesbourne at 04:45 a.m., closely followed by the four other Wellingtons. Ted and his chums were tired but satisfied; they had finally entered the battle and proudly noted their first op in their logbooks. After intelligence had questioned them for a few minutes on the features of the trip, they headed to the mess for their post-ops breakfast.

To Africa

On June 10, 1943, Ted got his times certified by the chief instructor and his flight commander. He had received a total of 20 hours and 40 minutes dual on the Wellington III and X and had flown as captain an additional 61 hours and ten minutes, making a total of just short of 82 hours. In total he now had 828 flying hours. When he picked up his logbook he found in it the assessment 'above average as pilot and navigator'. Much to his delight, most of his crewmembers had been given the same appraisal. Shortly after, Ted and his crew received the news of their next posting. They were soon to be transferred to North Africa as a replacement crew, to take part in operations there with the newly formed 331 Wing, RCAF. Initially, they were ordered to report to 311 Ferry Training Unit, but not before a well-deserved 11 days of leave. As could be expected, Teddy spent this interlude at Uncle Max's and had a marvellous time. He took maximum benefit of this time off at Woodland Grange before going into war for as long as it would take.

Ted and his crew reported back at 22 OTU on June 26, and Warrant Officer Pullar took them up on a short check flight the same night. The crew was immediately back on track, and two days later they left Wellesbourne Mountford for an airfield just 15 miles south of there, Moreton-in-Marsh. On this temporary airfield, which was the home of 311 FTU, they were going to train in the art of ferry flying, since for the first time in their career, they would soon have to fly an aircraft across different countries and over water. Their FTU training consisted mainly of three long cross-country flights in a new Wellington X, with serial number HE266. On July 5 they completed the first one, a trip of almost nine hours, followed by a second flight of 'only' six hours and 20 minutes the following day. While during these flights the Blenkinsop crew concentrated their mind on recalling their individual skills and crew responsibilities, the lengthy cross-countries were predominantly serving as a consumption test. The Wellington was known for its complicated fuel system, especially the nacelle tanks which contained a specified quantity of reserve or emergency fuel. New pilots were told to make sure to have an earnest chat with one of the ground crew fitters before taking up an unfamiliar serial number if there was any likelihood of requiring the use of these nacelle tanks. Wellington HE266 was just out of the factory, so Teddy wanted to make sure the fuel system was operating the way he expected.

On the morning of July 8, Teddy and his crew performed a last air test with Wellington HE266, before preparing for their journey to Africa. The day before, Teddy had packed up his gear and sent his excess baggage to Uncle Max. In an accompanying letter he expressed his wish that Max's family would make good use of the soap flakes, hot chocolate mixture and Bovril. He hoped that Gerald might like the sweaters and woollen socks he had used for flying training, while he trusted that Alan could make good use of a very heavy sweater while on sea duty. Lastly, he thanked Uncle Max for his being able to treat Woodland Grange as home, and he uttered his hopes to see the family again soon.

After the air test was finished, the aircraft was loaded with all the baggage plus some spare parts. The crew was briefed on the navigation track to be flown and what they could expect along the route. They were told that they might run into fighters around the Bay of Biscay and were instructed to fly close to the cloud base so they could take cover in the clouds if fighters were encountered. At exactly 04:30 p.m. on Thursday, July 8, 1943, Teddy and his crew took off from Moreton-in-Marsh in Wellington HE266, and set course for Portreath in Cornwall. This was to be their last stop before leaving England. There they changed their air force uniforms to army battle dress – ready for the desert – and were issued their .38 calibre revolvers.

On the morning of July 10, they departed from Portreath with destination Ras el Ma in French Morocco, a flight of more than eight hours, bypassing neutral Spain and Portugal. Shortly after taking off, Teddy shifted to the overload petrol tank. This created an airlock, which caused the engines to sputter and run erratically. Teddy immediately lowered the nose of the aircraft to gain airspeed and the Wellington began to slowly descend towards the Scilly Isles. Needless to say, this caused much anxiety among the other crewmembers. Fortunately, a quick re-engagement of the main fuel tank ended the crisis so the crew continued their journey.

28 Squadron of the South African Air Force occupied Ras el Ma, a desert airfield situated some ten kilometres west of the historic city of Fez. During the approach to the airfield, the green Blenkinsop crew almost had an abrupt ending. Ren Renvoizé related:

> One story against myself at that time cost me a few native drinks! On the approach to Ras el Ma I had put out the trailing aerial – to assist in picking up radio signals. With the excitement of landing in a strange country, I forgot to wind it back in. I forgot the length of it – at least 100 feet or so with lead weights on the end to make it hang down below the plane. As we were landing, Flying Control screamed out: 'Wind in that bl--- aerial!' It had just missed the power cables by a few feet. I understand a week earlier another aircraft did the same and all were electrocuted.

When Teddy finally landed, there was a very high wind blowing out of a heavy sandstorm in the area, so he and his comrades had to sit for a long time in their aircraft in unbearable heat. When they were finally able to leave the aircraft and take out their gear for their overnight stop, they were accommodated in tents. During the evening, Jack Nash and Ren fancied a stroll around the camp. As they were returning to their tent in the dusk, they were challenged and nearly shot by a very fierce Ghurkha guard who did not speak English. Not wanting to argue with an armed Ghurkha, Jack and Ren beat a retreat and made it back to their tent in one piece. Thus ended an eventful first African day for the Blenkinsop crew. Teddy secretly hoped that things would go a little more smoothly in the days and weeks to follow. The next morning, the Allied invasion of Sicily was the news of the day, which lifted everyone out of bed early that morning.

In January 1943, the Allies held a conference codenamed Symbol in the Anfa Hotel in the French Moroccan city of Casablanca. Churchill, Roosevelt and the Joint Chiefs of Staff attended, along with France's General De Gaulle, America's General Eisenhower and Britain's Field Marshal Alexander. The aim of the conference was to decide future strategy, with an attack against the Germans in France high on the agenda. Eisenhower had already proposed a landing in France, planning an operation that depended on massing US troops on British shores. Britain was not in favour of this plan, believing that the priority should be to grind down German military strength before meeting the Germans head on. In the absence of Russian representation, the Americans and British had decided on the policy that Germany, Italy and Japan should surrender unconditionally. They also agreed on an invasion of Sicily and Italy, the first stage of the liberation of Europe, only after Operation Torch had achieved its object and Africa was secure. It was also decided that a combined British and American strategic bomber offensive against Germany would be conducted out of Britain. Furthermore, both Churchill and Roosevelt agreed to give aid to the Soviet Union.

Operation Husky, the Allied assault on Sicily, was conceived in a very methodical manner. First the enemy's communications were attacked, then the nine days preceding the actual landings, the enemy's airfields were targeted. The next big job was to protect the invasion fleet of 2,000 vessels as it assembled at sea. Finally, on July 10, 1943, as the ships neared the landing beaches, 1,200 men of the First Airborne Division were towed over the island in Hadrian and Horsa gliders, while paratroops of the US 82nd Division jumped further west. Although this first Allied airborne operation was not a conspicuous success, the airside of Operation Husky went smoothly. The opposition was ineffective, and while strategic bombers hammered supply lines in Italy, the tactical air force gave the armies all the close air support they could wish for. The invasion of Sicily was the logical conclusion of the North African campaign, since capturing the island meant removing it as a base for Axis shipping and aircraft, while also regaining control of most of the Mediterranean. The Allies achieved a second goal by forcing German leadership to pull land and air forces away from the eastern front in order to defend its southern terrain, thereby easing the pressure on the Soviets. Lastly, the assault on Sicily put pressure on the Italian regime, with the hope of eventually knocking Italy out of the war. This action also acted as a precursor to the invasion of Italy, although not agreed to by the Allies at the time of the invasion. The Americans resisted a commitment to any action that might conceivably delay the invasion of France. However, the situation would soon become somewhat confused following the dismissal of Mussolini on July 25, 1943, and Italy's decision to change sides. Whichever side they were on, it made little difference. The German air and land forces intended to contest every inch of the ground that brought the Allied armies closer to the German frontier.

CHAPTER SIX

Into the Ops Zone

On July 13, 1943, the Blenkinsop crew completed the last leg of the ferry flight to their new operational unit in Africa. They left Ras el Ma at 09:00 a.m. and flew further east to the airfield Pavillier, some 50 kilometres south-west of the city of Kairouan in Tunisia. The airfield was fairly close to the mountains that form the western part of that country. They reached their destination at 02:15 p.m. This trip counted as their second op. Pavillier was the home station of 424 Squadron, RCAF.

The Tunisian campaign of early 1943 was the final stage of the fighting that had raged back and forth along the North African coast since the first Italian drive into Egypt in 1940. Originally controlled by the French Vichy government, Tunisia had been occupied by German forces following the surrender of the Vichy forces in French Morocco and Algeria in November 1942. The combined American and British First Army advancing into Tunisia from Algeria hoped to move quickly through Tunisia to meet up with the British and Commonwealth Eighth Army advancing across Libya after the victory at El Alamein, thereby crushing the Axis forces between these two armies. However, this action was slowed by the rapid reinforcement into Tunisia with German troops from Sicily and a series of skilfully executed defensive operations. Gradually, however, after much hard fighting, the First Army advancing from the west met the Eighth Army advancing from the south and together they pushed the Axis forces into a pocket around Tunis. Cut off from supplies of rations, ammunition and fuel by an Allied naval blockade, the fate of the Axis forces around Tunis was inevitable. The last pocket of resistance surrendered on May 13, 1943. More than 50,000 Axis soldiers were killed and 291,000 taken prisoner during the campaign, while 600 intact aircraft were left behind on Tunisian airfields. These airfields were now available for operational use by the Allies to bomb targets in Italy.[1]

Early in April 1943, the Air Ministry requested that three bomber

[1]H. Bernard, *Totale Oorlog en Revolutionare Oorlog*, vol. III (Brussels: Belgian Royal Military School, 1976) 31.

squadrons from 6 Group be moved into North Africa. Canada selected Nos. 420 'Snowy Owl', 424 'Tiger' and 425 'Alouette' squadrons, forming what was to be known as 331 Wing, which was then assigned to take part in the Sicilian campaign. Canadian Group Captain Clarence R. Dunlap was selected to command the proposed 331 Night Bomber Wing. This formation was subordinated to 205 Group of the British-American North African Strategic Air Force, commanded by the illustrious Major General 'Jimmy' Doolittle.[1] All personnel received shots for tropical diseases and their aircraft, Wellingtons Mark X, were especially protected to deal with dust, sand and the heat. The ground staff sailed to North Africa in late May, while the three squadrons left Portreath between June 2 and 4 with destination Telergma, Tunisia. On their way there, and despite taking a wide route over the Atlantic, they were attacked, losing two crews from 420 Squadron and one from 425. Meanwhile, Group Captain Dunlap had reconnoitred sites to situate the airfields needed for the wing. On May 31, he was granted authority to utilise the two airfields on the plains near Kairouan rather than those already designated by higher command in the mountainous regions of Tunisia. In later years, Air Marshal Dunlap would recall those days:

> There were four Wellington Wings surrounding Kairouan, three of them RAF and one RCAF. 331 Wing was the last to arrive on the scene. Hence, we had slim pickings as regards to location. Nothing survived by way of shrub or bush. The only shade was beneath the wing of the aircraft. In that shade the temperature on occasion rose to more than 50° Celsius.[2]

Runways, taxiways, dispersals and camp sites were immediately laid out by Group Captain Dunlap and his staff at Zina and Pavillier, and on June 7 the preparation of the new airfields was completed by the local detachment of the US Army Corps of Engineers. Building these facilities was not easy because of the 55° heat and the unexpected summer rainstorm.

On June 17, 1943, instructions were received from higher authority to the effect that dispersal and other operating criteria would make it impossible to co-locate the three squadrons at Zina. As a consequence, it was decided to move 424 Squadron to Pavillier, which had been prepared as a satellite airfield for Zina. Two days later, 420 and 425 squadrons left Telergma and deployed to their assigned airfield at Zina – also referred to as 'Pavillier East', while 424 flew into Pavillier on June 23. On June 25, 331 Wing was declared operational.

The Canadians soon became aware of the physical and meteorological

---

[1]The North African Strategic Air Force was part of the North-West African Air Force, headed by Lieutenant-General Carl Spaatz. The NWAAF was part of the Mediterranean Air Force, commanded by Air Chief Marshal Tedder.

[2]Letter from Air Marshal C.R. Dunlap to the author, November 12, 1987.

nature of their new environment. There was eternal sand and heat, and there were, periodically, torrential rains that transformed the airfield into what looked more like a swamp minus the bulrushes. There were the sand-laden winds that the locals called the sirocco. These winds blew out of the desert, they seared the eyes, dust-draped everything in sight and finally dried everything up, making it possible for this miserable cycle to start all over again. The Canadians had traded the mud, wind and rain of England for the mud, wind and rain of Tunisia, with extreme heat thrown into the bargain. And while it was blisteringly hot during the day, the nights were very cold by comparison. Disease was prevalent and, over the course of the campaign, the men of 331 Wing would have to deal with dysentery and diarrhoea. Another menace was the countless mosquitoes, carriers of the life-threatening malaria disease. As a preventive measure, everyone had to take a quinine tablet each day. This proved to be no extravagance, when a corpse of a dead mule was hoisted up from the bottom of the water well. Little did they know the water trucks had been using the well for the past several weeks.

Just when the Canadians were getting reasonably adjusted to their new situation, they were called upon to attack their first theatre target. Their immediate concern was the softening up of Sicily in preparation for the invasion. 420 and 425 squadrons joined the other forces of 205 Group for an attack on the port-town of Sciacca – a predetermined landing point – on June 26, while 424 Squadron bombed San Giovanni on June 27. Misfortune hit the first raid of 331 Wing, with two aircraft dropping their bombs before take-off; fortunately neither exploded. German night fighters and Italian anti-aircraft fire resulted in the first African campaign losses for the wing, which led to a casualty rate for 331 Wing in June 1943 of 5.3 per cent. Despite these losses, 331 Wing Wellington bombers carried out successful attacks on harbours, airfields and railways in Sicily and Sardinia during early July 1943. On July 9 and 10, they supported Allied forces making amphibious landings and patrolled the coastline using their jamming devices, effectively hiding the invasion force from the enemy.

Little did Ted know that his Uncle Cyril's armoured regiment had embarked in LSTs from England on July 1, 1943, Canada's Dominion Day. He was the commanding officer of the King's Own Calgary Regiment attached to the First Canadian Division. His regiment was planned to conduct amphibious landings onto the beaches of Sicily about July 9.

These events were all taking place around the time that Ted Blenkinsop and his crew arrived at Pavillier as replacements. Much to the disbelief of 424 Squadron's adjutant, and like all replacement crews before, the Blenkinsop crew had arrived without water bottles, very little bedding, but with greatcoats! Their Wellington HE266 was reassigned upon arrival, never to be seen again. Ted and his friends attributed any welcoming indifference to the fact that there was a war going on at this station. They were temporarily posted to 424 Squadron on July 15. However, 424 apparently didn't really want them, and on July 20 after Teddy's strenuous insistence, they were officially transferred to 425 Squadron at nearby Zina airfield. On arrival there by truck, they immediately felt welcome.[1]

425 Squadron, a French language unit, had the noteworthy characteristic of being mostly French Canadians, especially the ground crew. By establishing this squadron, the Canadian government aimed to lift the language barrier that kept many Quebecois and Francophones from other parts of Canada from enlisting in the RCAF, where generally English was the accepted operational language. For its motto, the phrase, 'Je te plumerai,' was appropriately picked out of the popular French-Canadian song 'Alouette, gentille Alouette'. 425 was formed at Dishforth in June 1942 under the command of Wing Commander Joe M.W. St-Pierre. The unit started flying in August and became operational the following October. On January 1, 1943, the squadron became part of a new formation under the jurisdiction of the newly formed 6 Group of the RCAF. When Teddy's crew arrived, the squadron already had three weeks of operations in the Mediterranean theatre under its belt. After having hit targets on the isles of Sicily and Sardinia in preparation for the Allied invasion of Sicily, the 'Alouettes' began to deliver a series of good kicks on the shin and toe of Italy. They went after docks, rail yards and airfields in the Naples area, and ports bordering the Strait of Messina. Several crews had been lost during these raids, so the Blenkinsop crew arrived in the nick of time.

Sun, Sand and Sickness

Teddy and his crew were very proud of their squadron. They felt accepted and wanted, and the squadron seemed like a well-knit and conscientious group. As soon as they arrived and had been presented to their respective flight commanders, they were put through the rest of the mundane routine involved in getting them squared away at a new station. The squadron intelligence officer briefed them on the military situation and the results of the preceding days, while the squadron admin officer, Flight Lieutenant Edmond Danis, took care of administrative tasks and getting them billeted. The crew's living quarters on this Tunisian desert airport was a small tent, barely large enough to hold three rather flimsy cots for the three officers. There was just enough space on the ground for mattresses for the two sergeants, Ren and Jack. Officers had folding wooden washstands with canvas bags, but airmen and NCOs washed and shaved out of their tin helmets or out of left-behind German petrol cans. This undemocratic

[1]According to 424 Squadron's Operations Record Book, Ted flew a mission as second pilot with Flying Officer Brown's crew on the night of July 19, 1943, to bomb Capodichino airport near Naples. However, he did not record this mission in his otherwise meticulously kept flying logbook, so we assume that he didn't take part in it after all.

situation greatly embarrassed Teddy. Another source of discomfort to him was that Ren received RAF pay of about Canadian $1.50 per day, whereas Johnnie, as a flying officer, made $8.50 and Teddy, as a flight lieutenant, earned $10. In addition, the Canadian officers received a small 'hardship' allowance. Luckily, money did not occupy their minds. Their principal preoccupation was remaining sane in spite of the extreme heat and the millions of flies, and completing a tour of operations of about 30 bombing missions so that they could get back to England... or Canada.

The whole wing was under canvas. A large tent or marquee was used for briefing and de-briefing. Two large marquees together served as the station hospital. Three trailers housing power generators were supplying electricity for the administrative and operational sections of the camp. On returning from operations, crews had to be debriefed by the intelligence officer. The strain was eased because of the consumption of rum-spiked tea or coffee and Benson & Hedges cigarettes in small red tins. Teddy was a reasonably heavy smoker like most of the other aircrew at that time.

Outside of duty hours, there wasn't much to occupy the men except storytelling about home and sunbathing for the foolhardy. In the scores of tents spread out over the plain, the crews scheduled for night ops were resting during the day. A few had phonographs and sometimes the mellow voice of Dinah Shore or another contemporary star wafted across from one tent to another. Other amusements included the odd softball game or attending the frequent movies that were shown outdoors at night. For armourers and ground crews an afternoon siesta was a necessity. The scorching midday sun heated aircraft fabric, metal parts and bombs until they became too hot to handle. There were 1,200 men in the wing and only one woman, a nurse. In reality, though, women did not occupy the minds nearly as much as food did, good food, which the men rarely had. The one occasional treat they enjoyed was steak. It was on the menu perhaps once every ten days. After a while, crews knew in advance when they were going to have steak, for 'Padre' Maurice Laplante always appeared at the airport that day. Besides the intermittent steak, the food was usually tinned stews, known as 'bully beef', hard-tack biscuits and tea, over and over again. Of course, there was the desert butter that would not melt in the sun – and therefore would not dissolve in one's mouth either. The food was cooked in clay open ovens and drops of water were added to the burning oil to give the desired heat, very makeshift, but very effective. There were some long, unpainted wooden tables for airmen's meals, and seats were provided by using heavy cylindrical cardboard cartons in which bomb tailpieces had been received. Jack Nash recalls conditions in the mess tent: 'We mostly stood up to eat our meals and used 45-gallon drums as table. We had to kick the scorpions away and also had to be on the lookout for snakes. The flies in the mess tent were so thick that you had to keep brushing them off the slice of bread you were trying to eat.'[1]

Water was a problem; it came in service bowsers and it was strictly rationed. All men were allowed only a pint or so per day for drinking and shaving. Ren Renvoizé can remember one occasion when the crew had sufficient water to have a cold shower. The water was put in a large square tin with holes punched in the base and it was then filled and suspended on a pole. Then one of them pulled the rope attached and down came the water. Lavatories were just holes in the ground with an improvised wooden seating construction over them. It often was a common meeting place. Ren Renvoizé continues:

> There was a lounge tent with a trestle table that served as an All Ranks Bar, I cannot remember any chairs. It was very seldom open, as there was usually nothing to drink. But, on one occasion, the barman – a member of the ground crew whose name was Andy – went missing for a few days and finally returned with some native cherry brandy, which we drank in earthen cups. I had six of these and can still feel my throat and head throbbing with the thought of it![2]

Everyone in Teddy's crew, at one time or another had a bout of diarrhoea during the stay in Tunisia. No one in the crew caught the more serious illness, dysentery, although some members of the unit did. Some seemed to cope with the conditions better than others, but Johnnie Miskae suffered at times from quite severe headaches.

Into Battle with the 'Alouettes'

After lunch on the day of his arrival, July 20, while his crewmembers were occupied with various tasks encountered with a posting such as interviews with their respective section leaders, things were a little different for Teddy. He was informed that he was flying that night, briefing at 04:00 p.m. He was told to report to the squadron adjutant, Flight Lieutenant Réal St-Amour, who would take him in to meet the squadron commander. Wing Commander Joe St-Pierre DFC, a slim, dark moustached Quebecois, welcomed Teddy to the squadron. He informed him in a friendly, but businesslike manner, that a lot was expected from him. It is not at all far-fetched to assume that Group Captain Dunlap, who was a close friend of Teddy's mother and his Uncle Cyril, had informed Joe St-Pierre of Teddy's performance to date. Then the adjutant took Teddy over to meet the pilot with whom he was to fly that night. Flight Lieutenant Blakeney, though in the RCAF, was an American hailing from Texas, and was one of the more senior pilots on the station. He introduced Teddy to his crew, Flying Officer

---

[1]Letter from Jack Nash to the author, March 2, 1990.

[2]As remembered by Ren Renvoizé in a letter to the author, dated August 6, 1990.

Gabriel Taschereau, Sergeant Phinnay, Pilot Officer Hutton and Flight Sergeant Goyette. On the first mission flown in theatre by the 'Alouettes', Blakeney's Wellington had been attacked by a Junkers Ju 88, whose presence was realised only when they were fired upon. His gunner, Flight Sergeant Goyette, although startled at first, hit the firing buttons and sent the German prowler down blazing into the Mediterranean. Claimed as destroyed, the Ju 88 was 425 Squadron's first aerial victim. Teddy was going to fly with Blakeney as a second pilot or second dickey. Each new squadron member of a crew was, in most cases, initiated in this manner to gain needed experience, but just as importantly it was a means of getting the feel of operations from the beginning and a way of being introduced to squadron and battle theatre procedures.

Events now followed each other in quick succession. Teddy felt excited, but calm. Here he was, just arrived in a completely new part of the world, and about to take part in his first real combat mission. The day had actually arrived for which he had worked so hard over the past three years, and he was determined not to fail. His mind was occupied with many questions. How was it going to be to fly in this theatre? Was he going to leave a good impression? Was he going to be a competent captain and manage his crew appropriately? But soon confidence prevailed over his nerves and his mind seemed at ease. He knew he was a good pilot, and he was going to do his utmost to excel and get his crew through this unscathed.

In the early afternoon, the main centre of activity was in the operations tent in the heart of the camp. Wing Commander Joe St-Pierre entered the tent with his flight commanders, Squadron Leader Baxter Richer and Squadron Leader Jean-Claude Hébert. Squadron navigation chiefs were meanwhile conferring in another tent with the senior navigation officer about the routes to and from the target. The target for the night of July 20 was Naples. The conference discussed tactical and navigational problems, the best avenue into the target and the smoothest way out, how to elude known anti-aircraft gun concentrations, etc. When it ended, everything was ready for the briefing of the crews. Briefing was usually held outdoors, and so it was this time. A nervous, noisy crowd was suddenly silenced and stood to attention as Group Captain Dunlap and both squadron commanders arrived and made their way to the front. After the target for the night was revealed, the intelligence officer and squadron commander gave their briefings and illustrated their instructions with maps pinned to a huge board outside the operations tent. Meteorology in turn passed on the latest weather information. One after another the leaders of the various sections spoke to the crews. Maintenance addressed the pilots regarding bomb and fuel loads, optimum engine performance and expected consumption. The signals leader then informed the wireless operators of the radio frequencies for that night, the authentication codes and their change times.

Take-off was after sunset. Flight Lieutenant Blakeney's Wellington took into the Tunisian skies at exactly 11:03 p.m. Blakeney's crew was called the 'Illuminators'. His Wellington HE261 was being loaded with 36 flares, no bombs. The importance of their task that night was described by the then Group Captain Dunlap:

> Target illuminators – a sort of pathfinder job – was an assignment reserved for the best crews. This was quite a responsibility, requiring precise flying and navigation. All the aircraft on the mission, not only those of 331 Wing but also those of the other three wings, relied on the 'illuminators' to go in first, identify the target, and then turn night into day by releasing large quantities of reconnaissance flares. 331 Wing and its crews were renowned for their aptitude for this task and very frequently were selected over the other wings to deal with the more difficult missions.[1]

Identifying the target was one of the problems the crews were facing in the Mediterranean theatre. Finding it was another one. Navigation over the Mediterranean was right back to basics, as there were no electronic aids like Gee or H2S to use. Astro navigation was the main means and with few clouds it was easier to use the sextant than it had been in Europe. Navigators plotted their positions by means of star shots, visual pinpoints, flak positions, and quite often by the glow of mounts Vesuvius and Etna.

The mission went well, with little flak or searchlights in the target area, which came as a surprise to Flight Lieutenant Blakeney and his crew. They landed back at base at 05:10 a.m. Teddy experienced a sensation of relief and contentment; his first mission over Italy was now a fact. He followed the crew in for interrogation, took a cup of coffee and a cigarette, and went down to find his trunk and tent. There, his crewmates were already awake, stirred by the droning of Wellingtons in the landing circuit. They immediately fired a number of questions at Teddy. 'How was it, Blenkie?', 'Seen any flak or fighters?', 'When will we be allowed to go?'

Teddy's crew only had to sit back for another two days, as on July 22 all of the Blenkinsop crew were on the mission schedule. All of them were down to fly with an experienced crew: Teddy would go with Sergeant Hawkins and his men, Flying Officer Stafford, and sergeants Bunting, Moreau and Platana. The target was marshalling yards near the Italian city of Salerno. Wellington HZ468 was loaded with a single 4,000lb bomb, a so-called 'cookie'. It was dropped from 7,000 feet and Teddy and the others saw it burst on the rail installations. After the attack, a number of leaflet bundles were released over the city, containing propaganda messages for the Italian people. On return to Zina airfield, the Hawkins crew reported 'a successful mission' to the intel officer.

---

[1]Letter from Air Marshal C.R. Dunlap to the author, November 6, 1987.

In anticipation of his crew achieving the required preparatory missions under their belt, Teddy went on another second dickey trip on July 26. This time he had the privilege of flying with the veteran crew of Pilot Officer Courtney Spooner. Captain Spooner, Jim Leigh, Scotty MacKay, Ferdie Le Dressay and Stew Blackert had been one of the original crews that formed 425 Squadron at Dishforth in September 1942. After completing 21 raids from Dishforth, they were now scheduled to carry out their 12th operational mission from Africa. One week later, on completion of their 35th op, they would be sent home. Spooner's 'personal' Wellington HE931, named 'Blues in the Night', was equipped with 18 250lb bombs. These were released on the airfield at Monte Corvino near Salerno. No defences were reported and the crew landed back safely at Zina after a six-hour trip.[1]

The 331 Wing's African mission was originally to last just two or three months, or as long as it took to secure Sicily, opening up again the Mediterranean shipping lanes, after which they were to return to England and 6 Group. With the fall of Benito Mussolini on July 25, 1943, however, the Allies saw additional opportunities as a result of a weakened Axis partner. The mission was extended to September in order to support an invasion of the Italian mainland. The Sicilian city of Palermo capitulated on July 22, and by the middle of August, German and Italian forces retreated to mainland Italy. Mussolini's successor, Marshal Badoglio, having officially pledged to continue the fight, would in the meantime enter into secret negotiations with the Allies. The Tunisia-based Wellington Wings continued to attack railway yards and airfields around Naples, then turned to attack Salerno in order to prevent a German counter-offensive.

On Their Own

Wednesday, July 28, was the day. Although it would officially be his sixth operational mission since the nickel raid at 22 OTU, this time Teddy was going to take his own crew into combat and drop bombs – not leaflets – on an enemy target. He was raring to go and wanted everything to be perfect. The crew planned the mission in utmost detail, and ran over checks and procedures throughout the whole day. Their objective was the Capodichino airport near Naples. They were assigned Wellington HE900, which was to be loaded with 16 incendiary bombs and seven 500-pounders. In addition, they would have to drop several packs of leaflets, all carrying a declaration by General Eisenhower to the Italian people.

At a quarter past midnight, Teddy advanced the throttles and shepherded the heavily laden bomber into the cold Tunisian sky. All five

[1]After having returned to England, most men of Courtney Spooner's crew were posted for instructional duties. Unfortunately, Flying Officer Spooner, instructor at 84 Operational Training Unit, was killed on January 21, 1944, when his Wellington crashed near Kettering, Northamptonshire. He was 21 years old.

men felt a certain amount of apprehension but concentrated on the task ahead. Not a lot happened during the three-hour flight up to the target area, but once over the aerodrome of Capodichino all hell broke loose. Navigator Ted Howlett remembered:

> On our first trip as a crew, our illuminating and bombing of Capodichino Airport near Naples caused fierce flak from the Germans below. This was one of the occasions on which Ted flew a straight and level course over the target for a seemingly interminable period of time. Finally, Johnnie Miskae shouted: 'Let's get the hell out of here!' And we did, but not before suffering more than 20 flak-holes.

Ren Renvoizé added: 'Some of the raids that we took part in were very naughty. Particularly our first one to Naples Airport sticks out in my memory. We were coned in searchlights several times for what seemed ages.'

Teddy had scared the hell out of his crewmembers by flying as steady a course as possible, three times, over Naples until he was satisfied with the target run-in. He wanted to drop the bombs dead on target no matter what. Over the past three years, he had listened to stories of other bomber crews who had surrendered to the tremendous terror they experienced over a heavily defended target area and delivered their bombs prematurely. It became clear that some of the crew, in particular Johnnie Miskae, weren't too pleased with Teddy's headstrong steadfastness and seemingly fearless qualities. After the raid, Johnnie noted the following forthright comment in his flying logbook: 'Operations as ordered – Naples Airfield, Italy. Stooged over target for 20 minutes to identify target. Lots of flak and searchlights, very accurate. Twenty flak holes in kite.'

It is impossible to imagine the fear felt by the thousands of bomber crews in the Second World War if one has never engaged in aerial combat against a deadly serious adversary. Night after night they risked their lives, sitting in a slow, barely manoeuvrable and poorly armed aircraft, in complete darkness. Suddenly they were coned by three or four searchlight beams, immediately followed by the terrifying fireworks associated with precisely aimed armour-piercing shells, which tore holes into the aircraft the size of a milk bottle. All this time they were attempting to dodge the searching beams of light. Every night, a high percentage of the airmen never returned from a mission. Those who did return, most of them only between the ages of 19 and 22, realised it could be their turn next time. Still, they carried on, trying not to make too many friends and making the best out of every new day.

Despite this bit of friction on their first operation, Teddy was quite satisfied with the outcome of the mission. The ordnance was dropped on the target and he had brought the crew home safely. He must have realised that his cool-headedness over the heavily defended target had made some of his crewmembers a bit twitchy, but he didn't make too much of it. A few days later, he somewhat merrily reported to his parents:

> No doubt it will be a bit of a surprise to you to find me in Africa. We've been down here nearly a month now and have seen quite a bit of the country. We've done several trips, none of them very exciting though. Only one was a bit shaky, and we had about 15 holes in the aircraft when we returned. It's fun dodging the lights and flak, you feel so detached from it all. The thing that bothers one most is the searchlights surprisingly enough. You don't worry nearly as much about flak, mainly because it isn't quite so apparent I imagine.

While still a newcomer in the squadron, Teddy's reputation started to filter out. The then Flying Officer T. J. Stephens, navigator in 425 Squadron, recounts:

> I remember that Ted Blenkinsop had quite a reputation at that time, he was already a flight lieutenant. The general story was that he had joined the RCAF very early in the war and in very short order became a pilot and an officer, and an instructor. After a short time he was sent to New Zealand to help that country set up their air training scheme. After some time, he was then sent back to Canada, but he did not wish to stay there and wanted to get overseas into operations. Ted Blenkinsop was well-liked, and was known as an extremely competent pilot and very dedicated. He had a very clear conviction of what he wanted to do.[1]

As a result, it did not come too much as a surprise that Teddy was given the position of deputy flight commander in early August 1943. After all, he had held the rank of flight lieutenant for quite some time now, and his operational results had proven that he was up to handling more responsibility now in the squadron.

The month of August 1943 brought a lot of action for Teddy and his crew. Twelve aircraft of 425 Squadron took part in an attack on Randazzo, Sicily, on the first of the month, but due to thick haze obscuring the target, Teddy and some of the other crews bombed the secondary objective Milazzo. On their return, the trip was described as disappointing by all the aircraft captains. The next day Teddy's crew was not on the operations schedule, and on the third the squadron was stood down for the day. A swimming party was arranged for the afternoon and in the evening a softball game was held against 424 Squadron, who lost by a score of six to four. On August 5, ten aircraft of the 'Alouettes' were detailed for bombing operations over Capo Peloro not far from the Sicilian city of Messina.

---

[1]Letter from T.J. Stephens to the author, March 30, 1990.

Again there was haze over the target, and bombing results could not be observed. All crews reported a fair amount of light and heavy flak from Messina, but only one 'Alouette' aircraft was slightly damaged. Teddy, just like the other captains, considered the effort not very successful. While returning from Naples on August 6, 425 Squadron sustained its final loss of the Tunisian period. Approaching to land at Cap Bon on the outermost north-east tip of Tunisia, Sergeant Wood's Wellington dove into the sea for reasons unknown. The body of the rear gunner washed ashore next day, but the remainder of the crew were believed trapped inside the bomber and could not be salvaged due to heavy sea.

By August 1943, the situation for the defenders of Sicily was no longer tenable. The Nazis were being chased across and off the island. For them the port of Messina became a miniature Dunkirk in reverse. Thirteen times in 14 nights 425 Squadron combed the evacuation beaches or the sandy strip on the mainland directly across the narrow Strait of Messina. Attempting to hinder as much as possible the shuttle of German troops and supplies to the Italian toe, the bomber crews aimed at barges and ships in harbour and open water, stockpiles of war materials spread over the shoreline and Capo Peloro, roads and railways in the Messina area, and likely looking targets in the city itself. They toted incendiaries along with high explosives, intending to burn and blow up the enemy's fuel and transport along the beaches.

Teddy and his crew returned to Capo Peloro on August 8 and 10. On both occasions little opposition was noted and, particularly on August 8, Teddy reported accurate bombing and a 'successful show'. On August 11, the crews of 331 Wing paid another visit to the beaches between Messina and Capo Peloro. Teddy's four crewmembers were stood down, but he was not. Wing Commander Joe St-Pierre had added Teddy's name to his crew list for a very special assignment that night. While Squadron Leader Richer was detailed for a nickel raid on Florence, Joe St-Pierre ordered his ground crew to load up his Wellington LN436 with 250,000 leaflets that were to be dropped over the northern Italian city of Modena. The rear gunner on the mission, Sergeant Henri Marceau reminisced:

> I will never forget that trip, my own 37th and last one, for the fact that we had no bomb load, but a great quantity of tracts to convince the Italian people to end the war, etc... as if the civilians could do something about it. The dropping of the tracts was a real 'snafu' – instead of dropping bundles from the bomb bay; each small package was ripped open by our Wireless Operator Les Wainwright and Ted Blenkinsop, and stuffed down the flare chute. The pieces of paper were like a cloud behind the aircraft, and it broke our fragile antenna for IFF transmission, that is Identification Friend or Foe.
>
> When we returned to base, using Astro shots to navigate, the USAAF observer on board, Lieutenant Clapp, was amazed of our real

> navigation. He told us that all he knew was dead reckoning or radio signals and some map reading.
>
> When we neared Cap Bon, some cannon fire was aimed at us, but fortunately, as our IFF system was out of order, the fire was anticipated and we bypassed it.[1]

This flight, in terms of elapsed time, was probably the longest Wellington trip ever undertaken by a crew of 425 Squadron. Wing Commander St-Pierre and crew were airborne for eight hours and 40 minutes. Teddy was taken along as second pilot and was given control of the aircraft for the return flight from the target. Only a few days later, Joe St-Pierre was decorated with the American Distinguished Flying Cross. Lieutenant-General Carl Spaatz, Commander of the North-West African Air Forces, personally made the presentation.

On August 13, Teddy and his crew were one of a number of aircraft that attacked the beaches between Villa San Giovanni and Palmi, on the Italian mainland just across the Strait of Messina. Besides delivering bombs, they also dropped 16 packs of special German language leaflets on the Messina area. It was a good trip with satisfactory results. On August 15, five aircraft of 425 Squadron were also among a force of 331 Wing Wellingtons to bomb railway yards near Viterbo, a town some 60 kilometres north of Rome. The Blenkinsop crew took off at 08:00 p.m. in Wellington LN436. Ted Howlett had to navigate completely by Astro, as most of the route to the target was flown over water. When over the objective, Johnnie Miskae's repeated attempts to release the 4,000lb bomb were unsuccessful, and the 'cookie' remained hung up until five minutes after leaving the target area. After their return, Teddy was not too pleased with the outcome caused by the faulty bomb release mechanism, especially since the flight had lasted a full seven hours. Ten aircraft of 425 Squadron were sent against enemy positions on the beaches between Briatrice and Capo Suvero on August 17, but high command had a special assignment for Teddy's crew and a few other ones. They were to attack railway targets in the Pizzo and Lamezia area. The mission went very well, and Teddy's Wellington HE900 released the string of six 500-pounders and six 250-pounders putting them right on the target. After the mission, two crews claimed to have direct hits, the Blenkinsop crew being one of them. Shortly afterward, Group Captain Dunlap congratulated both crews. Around that time, Teddy found a moment for another letter home:

> The heat isn't so bad here, it's been quite cool during the last few days, but the flies are an absolute pest and you never manage to keep them away. We're all under canvas of course and are more or less roughing it. Food is quite good but of course it all comes from cans. The cooks do a damn fine job under the circumstances.

[1]Letter from Henri Marceau to the author, May 31, 1988.

As you may know this squadron is a French-Canadian one and has a pretty fine record too. They're a good bunch and very congenial. I'm a deputy flight commander at present and that's about as far as I shall go for some time I expect.

The crew is in fine shape at present, though we've all been sick once or twice in a mild sort of way, a mild form of dysentery being the general complaint.

We were at a rest camp on the coast recently and had a fine time loafing on the beach and swimming all day in the 'Med'. It's so much cooler and we were able to get thoroughly clean for a change.

Hope everything is okay at home and that you are still happy in the Air Force, Mother.

The capture of the city of Messina on August 16 meant the end of the Allied campaign in Sicily. Axis losses amounted to 164,000 troops, including 132,000 prisoners, of which 32,100 were German. On the other hand, 20,000 Allied soldiers were killed, wounded or missing. On August 18, a letter despatched from HQ North-West African Strategic Air Force over signature of General Doolittle, commended 331 Wing on its outstanding contribution to the success of the Allied operations in Sicily. 331 Wing's bombing missions during the latter half of August and most of September supported a pattern one might expect prior to an invasion. Marshalling yards, key road, rail junctions and airfields from Taranto in the south to Pisa in the north were all in their sights. These targets, all so vital to the regrouping enemy in matters of supply and troop movements and defence, were attacked from the air with great success.[1]

In the evening of August 21, Teddy and his friends were one of 12 crews detailed to bomb marshalling yards near Battipaglia. He took the recently arrived Sergeant Jones along as second pilot. The target was visually identified by the aid of the flares dropped by the illuminators, and the bomb load came down right into the rail yards. On return, Teddy reported 'a good trip' with very concentrated and successful bombing. Only two aircraft of 425 Squadron were scheduled for operations on August 25, and Teddy's name was assigned. Both missions were nickel raids, and Teddy's crew were detailed to drop 200,000 leaflets over the city of Rome. Wellington HE330 took off at 00:55 a.m. in the direction of the Italian capital. Ren Renvoizé remembered clearly: 'I remember on the 25th of August 1943 (my 21st birthday) we had to release leaflets on the city of Rome and its outskirts – with strict instructions not to drop anything near the Vatican. A well-remembered birthday, but without any cake.'

The flight took almost seven hours. It was Teddy's 16th op, and the first one he flew as a captain without his complete crew. Teddy's bomb aimer,

---

[1]The great contribution made by bombing raids to the successful outcome of the invasion of Italy prompted the Allies to adopt similar softening-up methods in preparation for D-Day.

Johnnie Miskae did not take part in this mission and was replaced by Flight Lieutenant Donald Wilson. In fact, Johnnie never flew with Teddy again. The reason for this appears to be medical, although there is a slight suspicion that there were other problems. In Teddy's letters one can read that Johnnie had to stop flying due to serious ear problems, while Ted Howlett indicated that Johnnie suffered at times from headaches. At the same time, Ted Howlett pointed out that Johnnie was sometimes cynical and insecure and that he occasionally grumbled to Jack, Ren and Ted that their skipper sometimes stayed too long over the enemy target and flew too straight and level for their own safety. Teddy was a perfectionist and made high demands of himself and his crew. When errors were made by anyone in the crew, he did not beat about the bush but came right to the point. He believed the purpose of learning from one's mistakes and then addressing them, made the team stronger. Still, sometime during the first half of August, Teddy's flight commander, Jean-Claude Hébert, called Teddy to his office. Squadron Leader Hébert had somehow conceived the idea that Teddy did not have confidence in his bomb-aimer, and uttered: 'Look son, are you a pilot, a navigator or a bomb aimer? Your crew is getting a bit edgy. You should express more faith in them.'[1]

Ren Renvoizé added his views on this. 'I do understand Hébert's point about Blenkie being over-demanding. Personally, it didn't worry me, but I think Johnnie Miskae and possibly Ted Howlett got a little "edgy" at times. But on the whole, we all respected each other's prowess in their own jobs.'[2]

Still, Johnnie Miskae usually achieved excellent bomb-aiming results, which regularly prompted felicitations by his superiors. There are no indications that Teddy assessed him on a regular basis. On the contrary, Ted Howlett declared:

> In spite of my own two or three silly navigation errors on bombing operations, Ted never really complained. After all, he himself was a first rate navigator. He was always a patient man, apparently concluding that I and the other crewmembers were trying to be as efficient as he. Through all the frightening experiences Blenkie maintained an exemplary calm. Although he was almost the youngest of us, he was the steadfast, calming 'father' of the crew. This is, of course, partly understandable. After all, the pilot can see or sense what is happening inside and outside the plane. The miserable navigator and wireless operator tremble – or try to keep busy – in their windowless cubbyholes.

Flying Officer Johnnie Miskae was finally transferred to a personnel depot in Algiers on September 20, 1943. He and Teddy would never see each other again.[3]

---

[1]Quote from Wing Commander Jean-Claude Hébert to Colonel Louis Geoffrion, March 1990.
[2]Letter from Ren Renvoizé, September 5, 1990.
[3]John Miskae passed away on February 13, 1988, after a courageous fight against cancer.

Initially, Teddy always took whoever was available as a bomb aimer, but soon Flight Lieutenant Donald C. Wilson became his regular crewmember in that capacity. Donald Wilson, who before the war lived with his parents on Strath Avenue in Toronto, had graduated from initial training school together with Teddy nearly three years before. Each had taken a different route after ITS, Donald eventually becoming a very talented navigator and bomb aimer. After 32 operational trips over German-held Europe with 51 Squadron, with several hair-raising missions, Donald applied for a posting to 425 Squadron as a 'bombing leader'.[1] He took only a 48-hour pass before he was on his way again for his second tour of operations.

Donald ultimately flew ten operations with Teddy's crew. He was an exceptional talent, and Teddy felt very fortunate to have him in the crew. Many years later, Donald reminisced:

> How I got into Ted's crew, I really do not recall. Perhaps I flew that first flight as a substitute for an indisposed Flying Officer Miskae. However, it had been my wont as squadron bombing leader to fly as a 'quasi-second dickey', to observe on a mission's effectiveness, to inspire confidence in 'green' or troubled crews, to observe on a particular crew member who reputedly was having difficulties in performing his function. Other times, on missions of particular strategic importance, I was nominated to join a crew for that particular mission. Finally, I simply was inspired to fly with Ted's crew to, in RAF parlance, 'get some in' with the least risk of mishap. By process of logical deduction and reference to my logbook, the most probable reasons for that first flight were either to replace an indisposed bomb aimer or to 'get some in'.
>
> Further, I cannot substantiate the premise that Johnnie Miskae and Ted may have been incompatible. Yet I must agree with Claude Hébert that Ted could be 'sometimes too demanding of his crew – too exacting'.
>
> I conjure up a picture of Ted as a very serious determined, intelligent, proficient young man, a bundle of energy, somewhat shy, and idealistic but very confident in his own abilities. My assessment of his skills was that, through his rather long tenure as both a trainee and an instructor, he had become extremely proficient as both a pilot and navigator and probably extremely knowledgeable of the intricacies of gunnery, wireless, and bomb aiming. Whereas each of the other crewmembers entered combat highly skilled in his own trade but with limited knowledge of the other trades, Ted was, theoretically, master of all.
>
> In particular, compared to many other more operationally experienced pilots, Ted knew his aircraft well, knew how to manage

[1]Chief bomb aimer of the squadron.

> his engine handling to coax out optimum performance and to exercise efficient cruise control through every phase of a flight profile. To my mind he was a navigator's dream. He could flight plan and follow that plan to maintain course, speed and altitude in accordance with the navigator's plan or alterations as required. He maintained a steady platform for the taking of 'Astro shots' to assist the navigator in establishing his position. He always maintained a stable platform for the bombing run from start to release point. For him, as for me, the North African experience was an ideal opportunity to put to practice all the theories of flight and navigation without undue hostile interference. I suspect the other crewmembers similarly enjoyed the opportunities to exercise their skills under almost perfect conditions.
>
> I believe that had I known Ted longer we would have grown to be friends sharing a common bond in our aspirations – to always do the job to the best of one's ability.[1]

On August 28, Donald's second mission with Teddy's crew was an attack on Taranto. Three days later came the moment Teddy had been secretly waiting for: his crew was appointed as illuminator on the night mission schedule. As mentioned earlier, illuminators were select crews that preceded the arrival of the main attacking force. Their assignment was to identify and illuminate the target by accurate placement of flares over the area. Only expert crews were selected for this task, as the whole bombing force relied on their precise piloting and navigational competence. On his first illuminator mission, the skilled Sergeant MacLeod joined Teddy's crew to occupy the vacant bomb aimer position. He released the 36 flares from 8,000 feet over Salerno, and the crew reported 'a good trip' to the intelligence officer.

425 Squadron was stood down for one day on September 2. There was a swimming party that afternoon at Sousse, and then in the evening a motion picture was to be shown, *The Life of Louis Pasteur*. Nevertheless, the bombing tempo was maintained throughout September. Practically all of 425 Squadron's raids had been carried out for the direct or indirect support of the Allied ground forces that had stormed the Italian mainland on September 3. On this day, Teddy was once more given the task of illuminator for a raid on the Capodichino airport, and again Sergeant MacLeod dropped the flares right on the target. Teddy's 20th operational mission took place on September 6, when Battipaglia was successfully attacked. He reported after the raid: 'Very successful raid – Bombs exploded in marshalling yards.'

More than eight weeks after arriving in North Africa, Teddy's superiors decided it was time for a break. On September 7, Teddy and Ted Howlett were given 48-hour passes and sent to a French resort hotel at Monastir.

[1]Letter from Wing Commander Donald C. Wilson, DFC, to the author, July 24, 1990.

They made the trip in a small lorry, through the flat, barren and heat-cracked Tunisian desert, speckled here and there with derelict tanks, motorcycles and army vehicles. Immediately upon their arrival at their Monastir residence, they wished they could stay a week. The seaside hotel not only featured real furniture, soft beds and good meals, but the staff seemed very partial to Canadians, so Teddy and Ted were well looked-after by the hotel employees. While at Monastir, Teddy and Ted received the news of the Italian capitulation, which was celebrated with their first-ever swim in the nude, along with thousands of British soldiers and a number of women – clothed – and horses!

The break was over all too soon, and on September 9, Teddy and Ted reported back for duty. The wing was now heavily involved in tactical operations on key junctions around Salerno, the intent being to help the Allies maintain their toehold on the strategic strip of beach they recently had acquired. Pilot Officer Lehman joined the Blenkinsop crew for another illuminator assignment on September 10, this time the city of Formia being the objective. Then, on September 11, 331 Wing's planners had something special in store for Teddy. Group Captain 'Larry' Dunlap, OC 331 Wing, had asked Wing Commander St-Pierre to assign Teddy to the task of transporting him and several of his staff officers to a conference at North-West African Air Force Headquarters. There they would discuss the move of 331 Wing to a new base. Dunlap had made this particular transport request in order to get an opportunity to become better acquainted with Teddy and at the same time to observe his flying capabilities. So away they went and in a little over half an hour Wellington HZ809 was in the landing circuit near Tunis. To be under the watchful eye of the group captain, who incidentally was right alongside him in the co-pilot's seat, and to be landing at a completely strange airfield, must have been somewhat nerve-racking for Ted. At any rate, the approach speed was a bit high, so the aircraft touched down but only to bounce a considerable height and then again, before it finally settled on the ground. Embarrassing though it was, a red-faced Teddy managed to smile and say, 'I really can do better than that.' And so he did on the return flight at day's end when the party returned to base. In fact, he 'greased it on' like a real professional.[1]

Meanwhile, it seemed the war in the Mediterranean was now entering a decisive stage. On September 3, the British Eighth Army had crossed the Straits of Messina in an amphibious invasion of southern Italy. The First Canadian and Fifth British divisions gained a foothold in Italy with the first successful amphibious invasion on continental Europe so far in the war.

The Fifth US Army conducted an amphibious assault at Salerno, 30 miles south of Naples, on September 9. On that same day, Marshal Pietro Badoglio and his cabinet formally accepted the Allies' terms of surrender,

---

[1]Letter from Air Marshal Dunlap to the author, October 27, 1987.

publicly announced as an unconditional surrender, as drawn up by the American, British, and Soviet governments. Allied hopes were high. The Italians separated into two camps: pro-Allied and pro-German factions. Allied planners thought the Italian campaign would be over in a matter of weeks. This campaign turned out to be one of the most difficult of the entire war, largely because of the terrain and the high quality of the German troops who were led by very experienced commanders.

On September 11, upon learning that the Badoglio government had surrendered to the Allies, German forces seized control of the major Italian cities in central and northern Italy including Rome, Milan, Trieste, Genoa, Bologna, Verona, and Cremona. They were determined to mount a vigorous defence against the Allied offensive. The following day, most of the Italian fleet escaped from Italian ports and surrendered to Allied forces in response to Marshal Pietro Badoglio's acceptance of the Allied terms, while German paratroopers conducted a daring raid to rescue Benito Mussolini from Italian imprisonment. Restored to power, Premier Benito Mussolini announced on September 15 the establishment of a Republican Fascist Party and the Socialist Republic of Italy in the northern part of the country that was still under German control.

On September 12, Teddy took part in a night mission to attack a road intersection near Castel Nuovo. For this trip, he carried Flight Lieutenant Les Wainwright as a replacement wireless operator. Les was the regular wireless operator on Wing Commander St-Pierre's crew and he was the squadron's 'wireless leader'. Flying Officer Hutton filled the bomb aimer vacancy, and became the last ad hoc bombardier to fly with Teddy. For the next missions of the Blenkinsop crew, Don Wilson became the regular bomb aimer. Starting on September 14, the crew completed three missions on three consecutive nights, the last one as an illuminator. In spite of not having flown with the crew for a couple of weeks, Don blended in right away. By now the missions of Teddy's crew were habitually annotated with such logbook entries as 'successful' or 'direct hit', while their target photographs were often endorsed with the word 'excellent' over the signature of Group Captain Dunlap. On September 18, Teddy was again assigned as one of the illuminator crews, for a raid on targets near Viterbo. Three more missions, on September 21, 23 and 24, directed towards the enemy ships in the harbour at Bastia, the San Giusto airfield at Pisa, and the Leghorn shipping docks respectively, ended the month of September 1943.

The first rains arrived over Tunisia about September 5. The facility at Zina was in an old lake bed, which slowly began to look more like a lake than an airfield. After a period of uncertainty as to whether 331 Wing would move to a new base or return to the UK, the decision was taken on September 26 to move to Hani East. This base was located only a few miles east of Kairouan, so the move was completed within a few days. 425

Squadron kept operating at full pace, even while engaged in the move that had begun on September 29. While the stay at Hani East would be short-lived for the men of 331 Wing, it turned out to be quite memorable. Bob Hope and Ethel Merman arrived at the airfield one afternoon, and gave their stage show out in the open air. Hundreds, if not thousands, of soldiers and airmen – Canadian, American and British – thoroughly enjoyed their performance.

German resistance in Salerno finally came to an end on September 18, allowing the Allied forces to move north and capture Naples on October 1. By now the Allies had built a force of 189,000 men and 30,000 vehicles. Blown bridges and blocked roads had hampered the initial assault, but the Allies moved quickly and gained 300 miles in only 17 days. The Port of Naples was repaired, so much-needed supplies could now be received by sea. The taking of the airfield at Foggia now provided the Allies with the ability to provide air superiority over the entire battle area. When the Allies crossed the Volturno River on October 14, they achieved complete control over the southern Italian theatre. Just prior to this, the Badoglio government had declared war against Germany but the Germans were not planning to withdraw. Quite the contrary; they were preparing a series of defensive fortifications in very mountainous country, known as the Gustav Line. Studded with pillboxes, the Gustav Line stretched on a north-south line, hinged at the top by the town of Cassino. Ted's Uncle Cyril received the Distinguished Service Order for planning and then directing the attack to secure the San Leonardo bridgehead at the Sangro diversion in the Battle of the Moro River.

In the end, Italy would represent frustration and death for thousands of Allied soldiers in a bitter and stagnant campaign reminiscent of the First World War. It was a year before Allied troops entered Rome, but the invasion of the French Normandy coast overshadowed the Italian victory. This campaign in its later stages was often described as the forgotten front, but it must be noted that these hard fought battles in Italy, against a highly professional German army, were the crucible in which General Eisenhower gained the experience he needed to command a multinational force and thus was ultimately central to the Allied successes in Western Europe.

Out of Africa

The month of October started with some good news. Teddy was appointed to the rank of 'acting' squadron leader, effective October 3. In addition, he was promoted to flight commander of 'A' Flight. In less than 11 weeks a 'green' replacement pilot had progressed to become one of the squadron's senior leaders.[1]

[1]Throughout the war pilots demonstrating leadership or operational skills of a high order were frequently granted acting ranks, which sometimes had to be dropped when their particular assignment ended.

On October 4, Teddy completed his 30th operational mission, an attack on an objective near Formia. It was against the airfield at Grosseto that the 'Alouettes', on October 5, 1943, carried out their last offensive action in the Mediterranean. Less than 48 hours later, word was received from HQ 205 Group that 331 Wing was to cease operations and prepare for return to Britain. The 'Alouettes', during the Tunisian period, had completed 88 operations in 101 days. 311 Wing returned to England with high praise from their commanders. They had flown 2,127 sorties and dropped 3,746 tons of bombs and ten million propaganda leaflets during their temporary duty in the Mediterranean theatre. Only 18 of 331 Wing's aircraft were lost in action.

All the aircraft from 331 Wing were delivered to the Wellington squadrons of 205 Group that were to remain for the time being in Africa. The establishment of airfields in Italy in late 1943 enabled these units to continue the battle and turn the tide in the Mediterranean theatre in the Allies' favour. Teddy's last flights over northern Africa were made on October 12 and 13, when he flew his faithful crew to Blida airfield, near Algiers, and returned to Hani East on his own the next day. After several months of intense operations, the crews were exhausted. Ted Howlett had contracted 'sand fly fever' shortly after arriving at Hani East. When flown to Blida by Teddy, he spent the next few days there in a military hospital. After one night suffering a 40° fever, he recovered in time for the return voyage to England. He had not been alone in the infirmary. Upon arriving in Blida, Don Wilson also entered hospital suffering from exhaustion, delirium and infectious jaundice. He stayed there for at least a week, after which he demanded discharge to ensure he returned by sea to the UK with his squadron, rather than being left alone in Algiers.

By truck to Tunis, train to Algiers, and the SS *Samaria* to Liverpool, 425 Squadron returned to England, disembarking on November 6. Air Vice-Marshal Brookes welcomed the squadron personnel on their arrival back in Liverpool, and the RCAF Band added to the occasion. The three squadrons were once more under the administrative and operational jurisdiction of 6 RCAF Group of Bomber Command. Orders were received to report to their new stations – Dishforth for 425 Squadron, Dalton for 420 and Skipton-on-Swale for 424. Wing Commander Joe St-Pierre, who had led 425 Squadron for more than 15 months, was posted on October 1 and succeeded by Wing Commander Baxter Richer.

CHAPTER SEVEN

Four-Engine Bombers

425 Squadron's arrival at their new station Dishforth was followed by a week of resettlement activity and then 16 days of disembarkation leave. Naturally, Teddy could not wait to see his relatives at Leamington Spa and Warwick again. It was a joyful reunion as there was so much to recount on both sides. Also, at long last there was time to write home and update his parents and grandparents on his African adventures. For, despite the efforts made by Teddy to write letters in the desert heat, it appeared that none of his scribbling reached the home front. Shortly after his return to England, Teddy wrote two letters:

> I have been stationed in North Africa with the Canadian Wellington squadrons since last July and in that time I have done 30 trips. They tell us here in England that we made quite a name for ourselves, be that as it may, we worked pretty darned hard under rather trying circumstances.
>
> I lost a bomb aimer and did most of my trips with a chap called Don Wilson, who was at the Hunt Club with me. He's a second tour man and was a pretty valuable addition to our crew. We were very successful, especially towards the end, and we came through without any worries whatsoever.
>
> The heat and flies were bad out there and we were never free of them. We were rarely clean either. I kept good health though until just before we left to return to England. I went down with a touch of sand-fly fever, then a mild form of dysentery, which was common all through our stay out there, followed by jaundice and finally by a heavy cold from which I am just recovering now. I lost a lot of weight but I'm eating like a horse now and will be in fine fettle once I shake this damn cold. Aunt Yetta is in the process of fattening me up and is succeeding quite well I think. Uncle Max has given me the run of his workshops and I'm busily engaged in building a model sailboat – this sounds familiar, doesn't it? Alan and Ann have both been home for a day or so, but I missed Gerald. He's in the RAF now of course, but it has not been decided whether he's to be a pilot or a navigator as yet.

> I've had altogether 5,000 cigarettes since I left Canada. The Canadian Legion sent me 600 cigarettes and one parcel of food, which I very much appreciated. I would appreciate anything you can send in the way of foodstuffs, tinned fruit and fish, a couple of shirts and some heavy black socks for winter wear. Also razor blades, shaving soap, toothpaste, and a jar of 'Arid' deodorant. I would also like a tin of Ovaltine and some more vitamin pills if you don't mind.
>
> Note the new address, and I think if you send parcels through BC House in London they are more certain to arrive – particularly cigarettes.
>
> I hope everything is going well with you both. Perhaps, Mother, you will be able to get leave for Christmas and New Year. Give my love to Granny and Grandfather. Don't worry about me, I'm in good spirit and pretty fit again now. It's such a comfort to be able to come to Uncle Max, it's just like being home and all the family are so good to me. Love to all, Teddy.

All good things come to an end, and on November 28 Teddy reported back to his squadron. He had spent a restful but joyful two weeks at Uncle Max's, putting back on the weight he had lost in Africa – he gained 16lbs in two weeks. After arriving back at Dishforth, he immediately applied for a second tour of operations. He expected that volunteering for the pathfinders would ensure getting his second tour.

All 425 Squadron personnel were kept busy in their different sections, setting up squadron operations at Dishforth, when the new postings came through on December 6. No less than 59 men said their goodbyes to 425 and proceeded to various training units to do their instructional tours. Ted Howlett, Jack Nash and Ren Renvoizé were amongst the ones departing, Ted being posted to 24 OTU, Jack to 18 OTU, and Ren to 19 OTU. Teddy would never see either one again, despite his efforts to persuade them to go on a second tour with him. Ted Howlett recalled:

> In late 1943, Teddy contacted me to ask if I would like to go with him on a second tour – this time, hopefully, in a pathfinder squadron. I somewhat reluctantly declined – partly because I thought he should get a navigator who was nearer to him in age, ambition (in the RCAF) and skill. My chief interest was in returning to civilian life. My wife Patricia was a British Wren and we first met in London after my return from North Africa. We married in 1945 and have lived happily ever after in Yarmouth, Nova Scotia, Toronto and Hamilton, Ontario. I went back to high school teaching until I retired in 1978.

In his search for a new crew, Teddy also approached his faithful rear gunner Jack Nash. Jack remembered their conversation clearly:

> We were in Dishforth waiting to see where they were going to post us

as instructors. I was posted to Bridgnorth in the north of England as a gunnery instructor. While I was awaiting my posting orders, Blenkie called me to the officers' mess. He asked me if I would like to do a second tour with him as soon as possible. He said rather than go home to Canada for a month's leave we could complete our second tour and then could return to Canada for good.

At this time I refused because I was married with two small children, and I wanted the month's leave in Canada to see them, before taking on my second tour.

Fate is the hunter, and it's a terrible thing.[1]

Teddy never managed to solicit Ren Renvoizé. Ren related what happened:

When after sailing back to the UK in the SS *Samaria*, I lost touch with all the crew. I was then sent to Scotland as an instructor. There I received my commission and in October 1944, I volunteered for a second tour of operations and joined 35 Squadron Pathfinders at Graveley, also in Lancasters – which is rather a coincidence as Blenkie was also in pathfinders and in Lancs. My first operation there was a daylight raid on Essen – four days after I was married!

We all liked Blenkie and I cannot remember any form of disagreement or criticism in all the time we were together – either on the ground or in the air, which must be pretty unusual.[2]

Several weeks later, Teddy sought out Don Wilson for his leadership and bomb-aiming expertise. Don's recollections possibly throw a different light on how some of his other crewmembers really felt about a second tour with Teddy.

I had numerically completed my second tour before I joined Teddy. Still, he asked me to crew with him on his second tour with the Pathfinder Force. In my half-joking/half-serious response which I paraphrase as best as I can remember lies my sole reservation about Ted, i.e., 'There is no way I intend to risk my carcass over the Ruhr Valley with a "keen type" who has yet to learn how to "get weaving" when the tail gunner screams that a Messerschmitt is on his tail, while the bomb aimer yells that the aircraft is coned by search lights and the

[1]After returning to England, Jack was posted to Middleton St. George in Yorkshire, where he joined 419 'Moose' Squadron. He completed a second tour over Germany without too much difficulty, and was awarded the DFC.

[2]When the war in Europe ended, Ren was sent to the Far East for a third tour of operations. However, just prior to going abroad, he was posted to Transport Command instead, where he flew Stirlings to Africa, India and Pakistan, bringing home British servicemen who had been Japanese prisoners of war. He finally left the RAF (VR) in 1946 as a flight lieutenant. He then ran a factory and offices as a general manager and director. He retired in 1984 and lives a happy life in his charming Welsh cottage with his wife Gwen. Ren's brother served as an armoured car commander in the Recce Regiment of the Royal Army, and was killed in the Reichswald Forest just before Ren's marriage. He is buried in Nijmegen.

flak is too close for comfort.' With these words I may have expressed not only my apprehensions but those perhaps of his entire crew, rejoining him on a pathfinder squadron.[1]

All these refusals disappointed Teddy. Don Wilson is still convinced that, in Africa, Teddy was covertly assembling an experienced and skilled crew which he planned to bring with him to the Pathfinder Force or at least start with on a second tour over Europe. However exacting or demanding he sometimes could be, he used the North African campaign as a training or proving ground for the more rigorous assignment to come, the Western European theatre of operations. It is Don's point of view that Ted was evaluating his crew's ability to perform under the most stressful and dangerous conditions that they might ever encounter. In spite of all that, Teddy now had to go and look for a completely new crew. Fortunately, there was time available, as he first had to have a conversion course to the four-engine heavy aircraft used to fly over Europe.

On December 9, 1943, Teddy, Don Wilson and several others from 425 Squadron's decimated ranks, were temporarily detached to 1666 Conversion Unit at Wombleton. It was here the conversion course on the four-engine Halifax III aircraft was given. It started with a week of ground school.

Before regaining the status of operational readiness, the squadron had to complete the long process of familiarisation and do considerable training with their new 'battle-wagons' using the new or modified equipment that they had on board. Also, since their soon-to-be-acquired bombers carried crews of seven or eight instead of the usual five, their strength had to be increased significantly. Teddy and the others returned to 425 Squadron on December 17, which in the meantime had moved to another station, Tholthorpe, the unit's final overseas base. Upon their arrival, the section leaders and flight commanders began to organise their various departments before the arrival of their replacement crews. Meanwhile the new Halifax aircraft began to arrive, and the ground crews started doing the required aircraft modifications.

On December 24, Teddy was granted a 48-hour pass for Christmas. He naturally headed straight for Leamington Spa to spend his leave in the snug surroundings of Uncle Max's home. He felt content and confident. A difficult African campaign had gone well, and he was now really looking forward to trying his hand with the renowned pathfinders. To complete his happiness, he received the news that Helen had been posted overseas and

[1]Don never applied for another tour of operations. He was posted on instructional duties but arranged for an early discharge and pursued his pre-war intent to study engineering at the University of Toronto. He returned to the RCAF as an aeronautical engineer and spent 22 years in research and development. He participated in the development of virtually every fighter aircraft for the RCAF, maintaining his flying status. Later, he served as a director for research and analysis for the federal Department of Supply and Services until he retired in 1984.

might well end up on a bomber command station not far from where he was stationed. He had not seen her in two years.

In the first week of January 1944, Teddy managed to get three trips in a dual-control Halifax under his belt, the first two as a co-pilot, the third one as first pilot. After that, he and his friends from the 'Alouettes' attended various ground school courses in preparation for flying the Halifax in operations. Teddy's instructional qualities were again called upon, when in mid-January he was summoned to give lectures on engine control and hydraulics to pilots, flight engineers and bomb aimers. On January 29, he logged his first Halifax flight as an aircraft captain, carrying a six-man crew on a local flight. Shortly before, he met Helen in England. He reported on January 27, 1944, to his family:

> So glad to hear Mother made it home for Christmas, it must have been nice for you both.
>
> Helen and I spent a couple of days together in York. It was pretty nice to see her again but the time was all too short. She's stationed not very far from me, about three hours by train, so maybe we'll see each other fairly often.
>
> There's not much hope of me getting home this year, so Mother may as well take her leave whenever it's convenient. As a matter of fact, I'm trying to get back on operations right away and have told them I will go back to flight lieutenant to get on if necessary. One short tour after so much instructing is hardly a fair deal and they won't give me a navigation course. Seems to me it's about time I got something other than instructional duties. Haven't much to tell you so I'll say cheerio and love to all, Teddy.

Leading Aircraftwoman Helen Woodcroft was stationed at a training base but was soon posted to an operational bomber unit as an education section assistant. Enthusiastically she wrote to Teddy's mother on February 3, 1944:

> I went to York where I met Ted. He told me such exciting tales of Africa that I felt rather like Desdemona at the feet of Othello! He has put on some weight, which is good, and although his eyes still look tired I think he is very fit and quite happy. He delighted my heart by giving me some Canadian cigs, I ran out ages ago, and a scolding for not asking for them – which I received with mixed feelings!
>
> He told me a bit about his Uncle Max and family – they sound perfectly delightful and he loves staying there. Hope I shall meet them sometime.
>
> Wherever he goes he seems to meet people he knows – we were having a drink one night and the waitress brought two more, a 'gift for Squadron Leader Blenkinsop', but we couldn't find out who it was from because they apparently left immediately afterwards. I thought

that was rather nice, don't you?

Did I tell you that Wally Earle came over on the same ship? He took me pub-crawling because I wanted to go, and added to the enjoyment of the evening by apologising about every pub he took me to – I'm sure he thought I wasn't the type for pubs at all! He secretly amused me much.

Take care of yourself my dear, and give my love to your husband and lots for you, Helen.

Helen's obvious cheerfulness had a very good reason. During their meeting in York, Teddy asked her what she would think of marriage. Naturally she was elated by his suggestion, and the couple decided to send a telegram to their parents to inform them of their intent. No date was set, as Teddy first wanted to complete his second tour of operations before concentrating his mind on matters of postwar family life. Besides, he believed that it was unfair to marry a girl when you didn't know what the future held.

On February 7 and 8, Teddy completed two more local flights in the Halifax, doing circuits and landings, and practising engine out flying procedures. Weather prevented flying on several days in February, when the grounded crews received lectures on various subjects, such as minelaying, air-sea rescue, the latest night fighter tactics and aircraft reconnaissance. On February 11, 425 Squadron suffered its first Halifax loss, when Flight Sergeant Aubin's crew perished in a crash near Birmingham. Also, on the same day, Wing Commander Baxter Richer was admitted to a hospital in York. This had an immediate effect on Teddy – as the 'A' flight commander of the 'Alouettes', he assumed temporary command of 425 Squadron. This was quite a milestone in Teddy's career, and he felt really pleased. Then, on February 18, he formally announced to higher headquarters that 'his' 425 Squadron was ready to resume bombing operations over Germany, if only at partial strength. Accordingly, ten crews were briefed the next evening to assist in the bombing of Leipzig, a leading manufacture and repair centre for the Junkers organisation.

Teddy never took part in squadron operations with their new equipment. On February 21, he took off with a seven-man crew to perform his first night trip in a Halifax, a cross-country and 'Bull's Eye' exercise which lasted six-and-a-half hours. Although completely ready for operations, he would never fly a Halifax aircraft again, as shortly news of his posting came through. With effect from February 28, 1944, Squadron Leader E.W. Blenkinsop relinquished temporary command of 425 Squadron and was posted to 405 (PFF) Squadron, RCAF.

Pathfinders

A lot had happened in the air war over Europe while Teddy was in Africa. Bomber Command had enjoyed mixed fortunes during the Battle of the Ruhr, which was conducted during the early summer of 1943. It had been a period of force build-up and of experimentation in new strategic bombing tactics. Well before the Battle of the Ruhr was over, Bomber Command had decided upon the next step. In late July and early August 1943, Hamburg, Europe's largest port and the second largest city in Germany, received a series of heavy raids in the space of ten nights. An important tactical reason for the choice of Hamburg lay in the target's position on a prominent river and close to a coastline, features that would be eminently recognisable on the H2S radar screens. This equipment, which was installed by now in most pathfinder aircraft and many main force bombers, contributed greatly to increased accuracy in navigation and bombing. Good progress had also been made both in the development and installation of radio and radar countermeasures equipment in the heavy bombers of the RAF, and one major tactical innovation was used in the Battle of Hamburg, a device which enabled the bombers to pass through the German defences and to reach Hamburg in greater safety and numbers. This was called Window, strips of coarse black paper with thin aluminium foil stuck to one side. The length of the strips was directly related to the wavelength of the main German ground radar, which controlled the night fighter interceptions and flak guns, the Giant Würzburg. When a package of Window was dropped from an aircraft, it immediately blossomed out, and the dense cluster of tinfoil strips reflected an echo on the Würzburg that was virtually impossible to distinguish from the echo returned by a real aircraft. It had been proven in trials that if sufficient strips were released in the air, both the German ground radar as well as their airborne radar used by the night fighter crews for bomber interception would be swamped by false returns rendering their equipment virtually useless.[1]

The Germans also continued to improve their defences, for it was clear that the Allies, even if they were not yet ready to set foot on mainland Europe, were bent on destroying German cities and towns both by day and by night. While the Luftwaffe possessed no strategic bombing force capable of destroying the British aircraft industry, it could inflict heavy losses on the Allied bomber formations. These losses, if sustained, conceivably could have halted the Allied bombing offensive altogether.

A number of new devices and tactics were introduced into RAF Bomber Command during the fall of 1943, such as a new blind-bombing apparatus called G-H and the diversionary raid tactic. With the growing mobility and proficiency of the German night fighter force, it was becoming necessary to conceal the actual target from the Germans for as long as possible. For this reason, Bomber Command started flying diversionary raids, sometimes called 'spoofs'. By deploying a small force of ordinary bombers routed on an alternate track, the German air defence controllers could be delayed in

---

[1]Air war experts estimated that, in the ten nights of operations against Hamburg, Window saved over 100 Bomber Command aircraft that would otherwise have been lost.

their application of force. Occasionally the main force was divided into two major raids so as to split the defences. This, of course, invited the inevitable risk that the defences might not split, and simply concentrate on one force of bombers. By and large, however, Sir Arthur Harris preferred to concentrate his heavy bombers in single raids and rely on the techniques at his disposal to blunt the enemy defences.

On August 17, 1943, a precision raid was carried out against the German research establishment at Peenemünde, where the top secret V-2 rockets were being built and tested. During this raid, and for the first time, a so-called master bomber of the Pathfinder Force was controlling a full scale Bomber Command operation. The duty of the master bomber or 'master of ceremonies' was to arrive on target first, in a Mosquito or Lancaster, accompanied with his deputy in a separate aircraft. He directed the attack by VHF voice communications, giving a running commentary of bombing instructions. At the conclusion of the raid he reported to headquarters via a short coded message concerning the condition of the target, in order to give the HQ planners extra time to organise a return trip if necessary.

When Teddy arrived in 405 Pathfinder Squadron, Bomber Command was in the midst of its greatest test of the war. An all-out assault on Berlin had begun on the night of November 18-19, 1943, and it would last a full four-and-a-half months. Bomber Command's front-line strength was now higher than at any previous period, with more than 700 four-engine aircraft available. The command was made up of approximately 60 squadrons from six bomber groups. Embedded in the force was 8 (Pathfinder Force) Group, whose aircraft marked targets for Nos. 1, 3, 4, 5 and 6 Groups, which together formed the main force. 6 Group was administered and mostly manned by the Royal Canadian Air Force. Normally, every Bomber Command squadron contained amongst its crews, citizens from throughout the British Empire. The most efficient of the four-engine bombers was the Lancaster, although many of the heavy squadrons were still equipped with the Halifax. The Halifax was a solid aircraft but had poor high altitude performance and carried considerably less payload than the Lancaster. Morale was high due to the recent successes over the Ruhr and at Hamburg. The accelerated training and aircraft replacement programs were now producing a copious flow of reinforcements.

The major question mark concerning Bomber Command's proficiency, as it entered the Battle of Berlin, was its technical ability to find the precise target location when undertaking extended range operations deep within Germany. In 1939, Bomber Command had been forced to fly at night because its aircraft could not be adequately defended against the German day fighter force. As the war progressed, the German night fighter force's successes further obliged the bomber force to restrict operations to dark moonless nights. Bomber Command's perpetual problem was to find its

Top left: Hubert and Gerald Blenkinsop's cattle ranch near Big Creek in the remote and sparsely populated Chilcotin region in the interior of British Columbia. They named it 'Bell Ranch' after the branding icon used on their cattle. (*Provincial Archives of BC*)

Top right: Hubert Blenkinsop gave up the rancher's life in 1927, trading it for a white-collar job in Victoria as an insurance and real estate agent. (*Blenkinsop Family*)

Bottom left: Family photograph taken at 1076 Joan Crescent, Victoria in 1929. Left to right: Teddy's mother Winsome, Teddy, his grandmother Ada Sarah, and his aunt Edythe Winter-Neroutsos. (*Blenkinsop Family*)

Bottom right: Teddy as a ten-year-old boy doing what he loved most – playing outdoors, in this case with a hand-crafted miniature boat at the family cottage at Mill Bay, BC. (*Blenkinsop Family*)

Top left: Teddy enjoying a holiday at Finnerty Bay in 1937. (*Blenkinsop Family*)

Top right: Margaret Jukes, Winsome and The Skipper in late 1938. (*Blenkinsop Family*)

Middle left: Teddy and Margaret Jukes very much in love at Finnerty Bay in the summer of 1938. (*Blenkinsop Family*)

Middle right: Sunday, October 15, 1939. Teddy and a group of friends who usually walked together on Sunday afternoons before returning home for tea, followed by a hand of bridge. Left to right: Teddy Blenkinsop, Hugh MacDonald, Harry Clarke and John MacDonald. (*Harry Clarke*)

Bottom: Elementary flying training at 8 EFTS at Sea Island Airport in Vancouver. Ed Fleishman, Ed Burton, Jim Grant and Teddy Blenkinsop return from a training flight on a bright day in August 1940. In the background the dependable De Havilland Tiger Moth 82C basic trainer aircraft are seen. (*CAF PL1532*)

Top left: Part of the 38 students that received their pilot's wings at 4 SFTS at Saskatoon on December 20, 1940. Front row left to right: S.D.R. Lowe, F.R. Shedd, Bob McRae, Geoff Mackie, Arthur Coles, Mick McGuire. Second row: Maurice Belanger, L.F. Hickey, Bernard Boe, Bill Marr, A.F.R. Southam, S.W.L. Campbell. Back row: Ed Fleishman, Ed Burton, Teddy Blenkinsop, John Thorne, Phil Shannon and Phil Kennedy-Allen. (*Provincial Archives of BC*)

Top right: A proud newly-commissioned Pilot Officer Edward W. Blenkinsop, posing in front of one of the Avro Ansons of 4 SFTS. (*Provincial Archives of BC*)

Bottom: Teddy was among five graduates from 4 SFTS to be transferred to the recently opened No. 1 Air Navigation School at Rivers, Manitoba, to take an advanced navigation course. Rivers was reputed to be one of the coldest places in Canada. Maurice Belanger, Ed Burton and Jim Grant are standing in the back row first, second and third from the left. Mowatt Christie is sitting fifth from the left in the front row, while Teddy Blenkinsop sits fourth from right, with Bob McRae on his left side. (*Bob McRae*)

Top: When Teddy arrived in England in January 1943, Hubert's brother Max promptly opened his home to his nephew. Uncle Max and his family lived in Woodland Grange, a beautiful manor house in Royal Leamington Spa, a fashionable town deep in the heart of England. This popular pre-war resort area became a second home to Teddy while in England. (*Ann Gillett-Blenkinsop*)

Middle: Uncle Max and his family at Woodland Grange in 1943. Max and Yetta had eight children. Left to right back row: Mary, Alan, Yetta, Max and Ann. Front row: Ruth, Guy, Jane and Dick. Gerald was not present when the photo was taken. Ann was the eldest at 21 and was nursing in Oxford, Alan was serving in the Navy, while Gerald was about to join the Royal Air Force. Alan later served as a pilot in the Fleet Air Arm and was killed in 1950 while attempting to land on an aircraft carrier. Gerald became a second pilot on Lancasters in early 1945. (*Ann Gillett-Blenkinsop*)

Bottom: In late April 1943, Teddy 'crewed up' with these four gentlemen at 22 OTU, Wellesbourne Mountford, to form an operational Wellington bomber crew. Standing from left to right are: Sergeant 'Ren' Renvoizé (wireless operator), Sergeant Jack Nash (rear gunner), Flight Lieutenant Teddy Blenkinsop (pilot), Pilot Officer Ted Howlett (navigator) and Pilot Officer Johnnie Miskae (bomb aimer). (*Lee Miskae*)

Top: On July 10, 1943, Teddy and his crew left England for North Africa, where they joined 425 Squadron RCAF. During the next three months, they would take part in bombing operations by 331 Wing over Italy, flown from bases in Tunisia. Here, a 331 Wing Wellington X is seen flying over North Africa in 1943. (*RAF Museum P4667*)

Middle: The living quarters for aircrew on the Tunisian desert airfield consisted of a small tent for each crew, which was barely large enough to hold rather flimsy cots for the officers and mattresses on the ground for the sergeants. This tent belonged to the crew of Pilot Officer Courtney Spooner. Scotty MacKay is shown in typical desert attire. (*Scotty MacKay*)

Bottom: One of the few photos showing Teddy Blenkinsop in Africa. He and other squadron officers are obviously having a good time. Left to right: F/L Les Wainwright, S/L Baxter Richer, W/C Joe St-Pierre, F/L Teddy Blenkinsop, F/L Tex Blakeney and S/L Claude Hébert. Kneeling: F/O Freddie Belanger and F/L Jerry Bell. (*Don Wilson*)

Top: Wellington HE931 'Blues in the Night', assigned to Pilot Officer Spooner's crew, is being 'bombed up'. The cockpit section and tyres are being protected against the sun. (*Ted Howlett*)

Middle: An official RCAF photograph of Teddy Blenkinsop and Don Wilson, taken in early 1944 at 425 Squadron in England, while the pair glance through Don's photo album. (*PL22598 via Provincial Archives of BC*)

Bottom left: Teddy's girlfriend Helen joined the RCAF in April 1943, following in the footsteps of her elder brother Derek Woodcroft, who was on active service with the Royal Canadian Navy. After her training in Canada, she was posted overseas and ended up serving on a RCAF bomber station in Britain. (*Blenkinsop Family*)

Bottom centre: Pilot Officer Robert 'Bob' Booth, who had just completed his first operational tour over Europe, took the position of flight engineer in Teddy's new crew in 405 (Pathfinder) Squadron RCAF. (*Harry Booth*)

Bottom right: Flight Lieutenant David Ramsay DFC became the H2S set operator and (visual) bomb aimer in Teddy's pathfinder crew. The talented David had completed a tour as a bombing leader with 420 Squadron over North Africa. After returning to England in early November 1943, he declined to be posted as instructor for a well-earned rest after having completed nearly 40 operational missions. Instead, he requested a posting to 405 Squadron. (*Peter Ramsay*)

Top left: After graduating from university in 1940, Larry Allen received a Bachelor of Arts degree in journalism. He enlisted in the RCAF in January 1942, and became Teddy Blenkinsop's navigator on 405 Squadron. He had previously completed an operational tour as the exceptionally talented navigation leader of 420 Squadron in North Africa. (*June Handley*)

Top centre: Flight Sergeant James 'Sonny' Bradley was the wireless operator in Teddy Blenkinsop's pathfinder crew. Originating from Gloucestershire, England, he was the only non-Canadian of the crew. (*Michael Parker*)

Top right: The Blenkinsop crew, being tasked as deputy master bomber, resulted in David Ramsay's switching to the extra visual bomb aimer crew position, which meant the need for a new H2S set operator. This vacancy was filled by Flight Lieutenant George Smith, who had just completed a first tour of operations. (*Herman Smith*)

Middle: Warrant Officer Nicholas Hugh Clifford was the last one to join the Blenkinsop crew, filling the post of rear gunner. At the age of 35, Hugh Clifford was unusually old for operational aircrew duty. He was posthumously commissioned pilot officer. (*Robert C. Dickson*)

Bottom: Warrant Officer Leslie A. Foster manned the mid-upper turret in Ted Blenkinsop's 405 Squadron Lancaster. Leslie strongly disliked war, but still applied for a second tour of operations after finishing a hazardous first one. He did this in order to return home sooner to his wife and two little daughters, having then completed his commitment. Leslie Foster was posthumously commissioned pilot officer. (*Leslie W. Foster*)

Top: Lancaster LQ-X of 405 Squadron. The Blenkinsop crew flew this aircraft on a training sortie on March 14, 1944. (*National Archives of Canada PA113730*)

Middle left: Lancasters of 405 PFF Squadron en route to a target at dusk. (*Chaz Bowyer*)

Middle right: Lancaster JB286 LQ-O. Teddy and his crew flew this aircraft on operations to Tergnier on April 18, 1944. (*405 MP Squadron*)

Bottom: The Bomber Command operation to Montzen on April 27-28, 1944 was supposed to be a 'milk run'. The vast railway yards would be easily detected and the route to the target was relatively short, but heavy night fighter opposition caused havoc among the bomber force. Still, considerable damage was inflicted on the railway facilities. (*NSCWOII*)

Top: Under-tail view of a Bomber Command Lancaster. This was a favourite position from which German night fighter pilots chose to attack RAF heavy bombers in 1943-44, approaching from astern and below where their own aircraft would be least visible. At the last moment the enemy fighter would pull up to fire its nose-mounted guns at the bomber's fuselage or wing fuel tanks. (*RAF Museum P106110*)

Bottom left: Despite a very efficient Luftwaffe night fighter force, German anti-aircraft guns constituted an even bigger threat to Allied aircraft. The flak batteries were aided by powerful searchlight installations, feared and hated by the bomber crews more than anything else. A pilot trapped in a large cone had little chance of escaping the anti-aircraft guns. (*Wilfried Roels' Collection*)

Bottom right: German night fighter crews of NJG 1 are passing the time while on night alert at St. Trond airfield in Belgium. Left to right: Leutnant Fries, Hauptmann von Bonin, Feldwebel Staffa, Oberfeldwebel Meinel and Oberfeldwebel Johrden. Eckart von Bonin ended the war with 39 air-to-air victories. (*Author's Collection*)

Top: Evocative aquarelle showing the shooting down of the Blenkinsop Lancaster. (*Original painting by Wilfried Roels*)

Bottom: Original raid plot made by RAF intelligence officers after the Montzen raid. Last known positions of all aircraft that did not return are indicated. Note the position of the Blenkinsop Lancaster, denoted by '405/S'. The cause of the loss is indicated by 'Fi (Prob)', which stands for 'Probably enemy fighter'. (*PRO AIR 14/3222*)

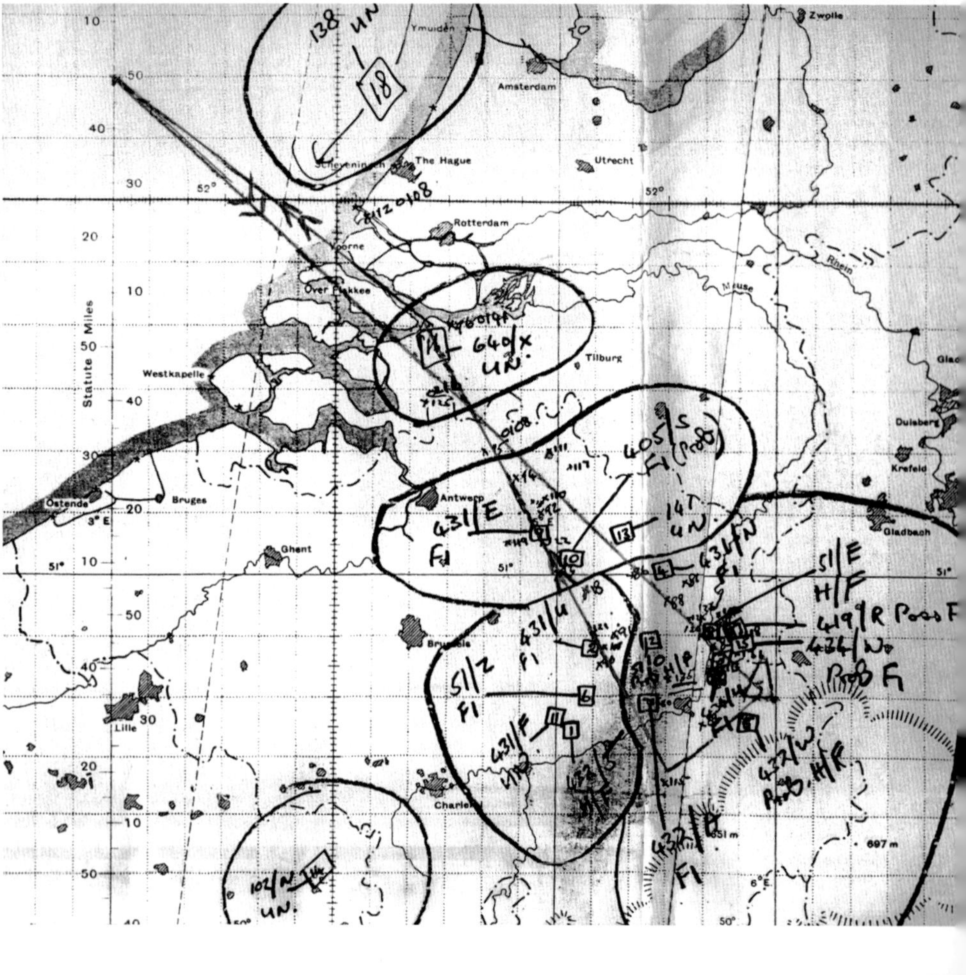

Top left: A leader of the fascist VNV is awarding loyalty decorations to some NSKK troops at the instruction centre of the NSKK, set up at the ancient Citadel of Diest. (*NSCWOII*)

Top right: One of two purpose-made photographs carried by Teddy in his escape kit. As a standard procedure, Resistance organisations always provided evaders with false identity papers, using the snapshots carried by aircrews. Teddy never received such papers, and the photos remained hidden at the Pypen farm until after the war. (*Paula Pypen*)

Bottom left: Oberleutnant Johannes Hager, the 24-year-old Staffelkapitän of 6./NJG 1, was the German top-scorer during the night of April 27-28, 1944. After claiming two Halifaxes over Belgium, he logged his third victory two kilometres south-east of the city of Diest in Belgium, the exact position where Teddy Blenkinsop's Lancaster came down. (*Wim Govaerts*)

Bottom centre: Teddy Blenkinsop and Hilaire Gemoets on May 1, 1944, three days after the crash. 20-year-old Hilaire was a dedicated resistance fighter. His folks sheltered Teddy during the first days and nights after escaping from his downed Lancaster. (*Lea Gemoets*)

Bottom right: Frans and Maria Van Dyck, the couple that hid Teddy in their home at Assent for about two weeks. (*Maria Van Dyck-Simons*)

Top: On July 6, 1944, Teddy was placed by resistance leaders in the home of the Pypen family in Meensel-Kiezegem. Here Mother Pypen poses with her daughters in May 1947. Left to right: Augusta, Octa, 'Mama', Paula and Mia. (*Pypen Family via Provincial Archives of BC*)

Bottom left: Prosper Natens, member of the NKB Resistance movement, who ultimately regarded himself as the overall leader of the Meensel-Kiezegem Resistance. (*SOMA*)

Bottom centre: Natens' right-hand man, 21-year-old Adolf Hendrickx. Irresponsible decisions by both Natens and Hendrickx, driven by their desire for post-war recognition, ultimately ended in the arrest of Teddy Blenkinsop. (*SOMA*)

Bottom right: Maurice Merckx, one of the three Merckx sons who brutalized their fellow citizens. (*BRT*)

Zelle Nr.

Kasse Nr.

Blenkinsop — Name

Edward — Vorname

8.10.20 — Geb. Tag

Wohnort — Dienstgrad —

Wohnung — Truppenteil —

INHALT:

Anerkannt:

Den 12.8.44.

Unterschrift

Empfangen:

Den

Unterschrift

Top left: During the SS raid of August 11, 1944, several hundred villagers were brought together within these walls of the Meensel Community Girls' School. (*Author's Collection*)

Top right: Entrance of the dreaded St. Gilles prison in 1944. The prison is still in use today. (*Author's Collection*)

Middle: German document listing Teddy's personal effects and signed by him on August 12, 1944, one day after his arrest. His signature includes his rank of squadron leader. (*Provincial Archives of BC*)

Bottom: Notorious Flemish SS leader Robert Verbelen, who ruthlessly headed the command cell that made the arrests at Meensel-Kiezegem during the raid on August 11, 1944. (*Frans Craeninckx*)

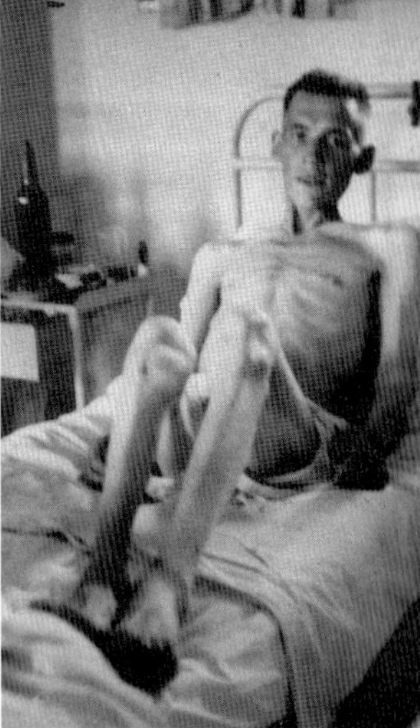

Top left: Dreadful living conditions in the Neuengamme concentration camp. The drinking water was heavily polluted. (*Neuengamme Photo Archives*)

Top right: July 1, 1945. Jozef Claes in hospital after his return from Germany. He was one of only eight men to return to Meensel-Kiezegem alive. (*Frans Craeninckx*)

Middle: The death register at Neuengamme indicates approximately 40,000 prisoners perished at this camp by April 10, 1945. (*Archief Stichting Vriendenkring Neuengamme*)

Bottom left: Document from the Belgian authorities stating Teddy's date of death and his recovered personal effects. (*Provincial Archives of BC*)

Bottom right: Charles and Odile Jonckers in the early 1990s. Charles was an active member of the Group 'G' Resistance movement and was the first Belgian resistance worker to make contact with Teddy. His young wife, Odile, had a sister who was a courier for the Underground. (*Author's Collection*)

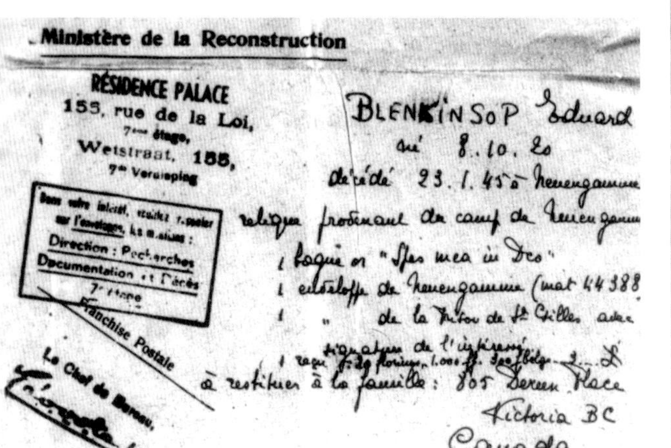

Ministère de la Reconstruction

RÉSIDENCE PALACE
155, rue de la Loi,
7me étage,
Wetstraat, 155,
7e Verdieping

Dans votre intérêt, veuillez rappeler sur l'enveloppe, les mentions :
Direction : Recherches
Documentation et Décès
7e étage

Franchise Postale

Le Chef de Bureau,

BLENKINSOP Edward
né 8.10.20
décédé 23.1.45 à Neuengamme
reliques provenant du camp de Neuengamme
1 bague "Spes mea in Deo"
1 eitelsloffe de Neuengamme (mat 44388
1 " de la Prison de St Gilles avec signature de l'infirmier
1 reçu [illegible]
à restituer à la famille : 805 Dereen Place
Victoria BC
Canada

Top: The last resting place of the Blenkinsop crew, as it appears today. Left to right: F/L George J. Smith, F/L David Ramsay DFC, F/L Lawrence Allen DFC BA, P/O Robert A. Booth, P/O Nicholas H. Clifford, P/O Leslie A. Foster, F/S James S. Bradley. Clifford and Foster posthumously received the rank of pilot officer, effective date April 26, 1944. (*Author's Collection*)

Middle: Two brave ladies who tried their hardest to get Teddy back to England safely; Paula Pypen and Jeanne Beddegenoodts at the annual remembrance ceremony in Meensel-Kiezegem in August 1989. The author's grandfather, Albert Stas, is seen at the extreme right. (*Author's Collection*)

Bottom: Concentration camp survivors of Meensel-Kiezegem at the annual remembrance ceremony in 1989. (*Author's Collection*)

Top: Remembrance photo of the Meensel-Kiezegem victims. Teddy Blenkinsop is included top left. Only the eight men in the bottom row returned alive. (*Albert Stas*)

Bottom: The memorial headstone for Teddy Blenkinsop in the remembrance cemetery in Meensel-Kiezegem. Unfortunately, both the date of his birth and death are incorrect. A hero's symbol of flowers of remembrance is placed at the front of each headstone on All Saint's Day each year and on the day that Meensel-Kiezegem pays tribute at a ceremony each August. (*Author's Collection*)

targets in that darkened sky condition. This condition led to the creation of the Pathfinder Force (PFF), which some believed should have been called a target-finding force, in August 1942.

The idea of a special precision force to lead the main bomber streams had not appeared as a bolt out of the blue. In 1941, Group Captain Sydney Bufton, Director of Bomber Operations at the Air Ministry, had suggested that six squadrons should be grouped in close proximity to each other, and their aircrews enriched with 40 of the Command's most highly experienced crews. But, Bomber Command's chief, Sir Arthur Harris, immediately condemned such a scheme as more likely to foster elitism and hence dampen morale. Further up the hierarchy, the pendulum of opinion swung back again, and Harris received orders from Churchill, through the Chief of Air Staff, to create this separate force. It was to be commanded by Group Captain Donald Bennett, a young Australian officer, who had made a name for himself before the war in the RAAF and also in Imperial Airways. Because of his brilliant navigational skills, he was asked to form Ferry Command earlier in the war. He achieved great success in delivering Hudson and Liberator aircraft across the ocean from Canada and the US to Britain. Precise navigation was to be the cornerstone of the pathfinders' success, so it was logical that an experienced pilot-navigator should lead it.

By early 1944, the pathfinders had already made quite a name for themselves. Becoming a member of this organisation was not an ordinary event. 405 Squadron's previous leader, Group Captain Johnny Fauquier, had been particularly known for declining more potential pathfinder crews than any other commanding officer, much to the annoyance of the AOC of 6 Group.

Identifying potential crews to join the PFF, and encouraging crews to accept a posting in 8 Group, was not an easy task in the early days of establishing this elite unit. However, in March 1943, Group Captain Thomas G. 'Hamish' Mahaddie had been promoted to 8 Group training inspector and was solely responsible for the selection and training of all future pathfinders. The reason for assigning Hamish to this task was to arrest and reverse the flow of indifferent crews arriving at the pathfinder squadrons. Hamish began to study the bomb plot charts issued by Bomber Command after each sortie, and the crews who consistently returned with their targeted photos were carefully noted. Then he went to visit their station, and enquired about these 'star' crews and why they had not volunteered for PFF. Some claimed that they had volunteered to no avail, and so now, when identified, were immediately posted within a few days to the Pathfinder Training Unit at Warboys.

Teddy had the necessary credentials to apply for a posting to pathfinders. He had proven himself as an outstanding pilot and navigator and had achieved excellent results during the illuminator missions flown out of North Africa. An aircrew posting to the PFF was conditional on two things. First, the mandate of PFF was that an entire crew had to volunteer. Secondly, one had to accept a tour of duty of 45 sorties, half as long again as a standard bomber tour. A crew could then take some rest before being called for a second tour of 20 additional operations. But, if a first-tour crew so wished, they could continue directly on after 45 operations to the magic number of 60. This counted as a double tour and relieved them of the obligation to return for a further tour. By this means the force gained the maximum potential input from these highly experienced crews; as they possessed 'the right stuff' needed for blind and visual marking of difficult targets in all weather conditions. It is important to note, however, that the average survival rate for a PFF crew beginning its 45-op tour in early 1944 was about 40 per cent, so this meant that out of every ten pathfinder crews, only four would survive long enough to reach the projected 45 operational missions. One year earlier, this figure had been as low as 20 per cent![1] The compensation for this hazardous tour extension was the likelihood of achieving a higher rank than normally found in the main force. Of course, there was an increase in pay, but a much more compelling motive was the exclusivity, honour and glamour of being a pathfinder. Pathfinder crews who completed five operational trips were permitted, as a temporary award, to wear the pathfinder badge – a gilt eagle – on the flap of the upper right hand pocket of their dress uniform. It was not permitted on the battle dress, which was worn while flying, because if PFF crews were captured by the enemy, they would certainly undergo more severe and intense interrogation.

In April 1943, two additional Lancaster squadrons augmented the existing PFF. One of these was 405 Squadron RCAF, based at Gransden Lodge.

[1]T.G. Mahaddie, *Hamish, The Memoirs of Group Captain Mahaddie, DSO, DFC* (London: Ian Allan, 1989) 85.

CHAPTER EIGHT

405 'Vancouver' Squadron

405 'Vancouver' Squadron, the first bomber squadron of the RCAF overseas, was formed at Driffield, Yorkshire, on April 2, 1941, and equipped with Wellington II aircraft. The unit carried out its first operation on the night of June 12, 1941. Until the end of the war in Europe it was actively employed on offensive operations over land and sea, participating in most of Bomber Command's heaviest and most telling assaults on targets in Germany, the occupied countries and northern Italy. On April 19, 1943, upon joining the elite of Bomber Command, the PFF, the unit moved to Gransden Lodge, Bedfordshire, just in time to celebrate its second anniversary. A typical wartime station, well dispersed and unusually set away from roads and amidst fields, Gransden had the customary three runways. There were a couple of hangars along with 36 hardstands. It was a smaller station than many, with accommodation for about 80 officers, nearly 200 NCOs and over 800 airmen.

From this time forward, the 'Vancouver' Squadron continued to add to its laurels by steadily increasing its efficiency rating, as a result of outstanding squadron leadership combined with a remarkably low loss rate in view of their bombing successes. In August 1943, the unit's illustrious leader, Wing Commander John E. Fauquier, received a Distinguished Service Order for his sterling leadership in raids against Peenemünde and Berlin. One month later the growing importance of the squadron was recognised when Fauquier was made a group captain. In October 1943, the squadron's last battle-worn Halifaxes were time-expired and the crews converted onto Lancasters. They flew these aircraft for the duration of the war.

In January 1944, the squadron bade Group Captain Fauquier farewell, who, having completed two tours, was elevated to a more responsible assignment. Wing Commander Reginald Lane took command of the squadron for the next eight months. It was a period of tremendous activity. The squadron carried out an unusually high number of bombing raids throughout its time in Britain, more than any other Canadian squadron. Operations in the month of January 1944 alone resulted in the loss of ten 405 Squadron crews, while many aircrew had been injured – it was the second worst month of the entire war during this period – so February had commenced with a heavy training program for replacements after January's heavy losses. Teddy Blenkinsop, an experienced aircraft captain, was one of several substitutes who arrived at the right moment. On February 28, the day of his posting, he reported to his parents:

> At last I've achieved my ambition and am starting my second tour of operations on pathfinders, of whom you've no doubt heard. Reg Lane from Victoria is Commanding Officer of the squadron, he used to be at the 'Y' when I was there, you may remember him, Dad. I've picked up a very good crew, two of them being the navigation and bombing leaders of one of the squadrons. We have all the makings of a perfect team if I can hold my end up. I think we will do about 25 or 30 trips and should be finished by August. Anyway, I don't want you to worry about me 'cause it's all in a days work and it's something I set my heart on a long time ago.
>
> Haven't seen Helen since our first meeting, but I hope we will manage to get leave together sometime in March. It never occurred to us that our telegram would cause so much surprise. I wouldn't get married without giving you some sort of warning anyway.

After his Wellington crewmembers' decisions to decline his request they crew up for a second tour of operations, Teddy had been on the lookout for new candidates to join his team. In Tunisia, and later at Dishforth and Tholthorpe, he had become better acquainted with several individuals of his own 425 Squadron, in addition to several others from 420 Squadron who shared the airfield at Zina with the 'Alouettes'. Two of them had stood out on operations in Africa and later, when back at Dishforth, had applied for second tours: Flight Lieutenant Lawrence 'Larry' Allen, who had been the navigation leader in 420 Squadron, and Flight Lieutenant David Ramsay, DFC, the respected bombing leader of that same outfit. When Teddy asked them to join him for a second tour, this time with pathfinders, they both immediately accepted. The three of them quickly developed a good and happy understanding as the nucleus of what was to become a top-rated pathfinder crew. Together, they would find the others needed to complete their team. There were seven men in a standard PFF Lancaster crew, consisting of a pilot, navigator, bomb aimer – who was actually the H2S-set operator, wireless operator, flight engineer, mid-upper gunner and rear gunner. The set operator was usually also a qualified navigator.

A Dream Team

Larry Allen was born on June 27, 1917, in Edmonton, Alberta, of Jewish parents who had immigrated from Lithuania and Poland to Canada around 1915. He grew up as an only child on Rankin Boulevard in Windsor, Ontario, where he attended Prince of Wales Elementary School and Sandwich Collegiate Institute. He graduated with matriculation and commercial course credits and was accepted into the University of Michigan at Ann Arbor. Larry was very articulate and had given memorable Shakespearean performances at the Sandwich Collegiate drama club. Other hobbies included golf, photography, amateur radio, badminton and tennis, flying, hunting and fishing. His biggest interest, however, was journalism. He had an arrangement with the Sports Editor of *The Windsor Star* to cover several sporting events, including the University of Michigan football games for which he received by-lines. He was a natural at putting words to paper. On graduating from university in 1940, he received a Bachelor of Arts degree in journalism. He wanted to get into the newspaper business or ultimately radio reporting. In the meantime, he managed the Temple Theatre in Windsor, one of his father Max's several family-owned movie theatres of the Premier Operating Corporation. In his spare time, he loved playing golf at a course adjacent to a lake where his parents had a summer home. He was an excellent player and spent as much time as possible there with his cousin Julius Goldman. Being Jewish, Larry was very mindful of the pictures, published in *Life* magazine, of the terrible atrocities the Jewish people were suffering in the German prisons and detention camps. He went to a recruitment office in Windsor in November 1941, where he was interviewed and placed on a special reserve list. When the Japanese attacked Pearl Harbor in December 1941, he could wait no longer. He told his teenage sweetheart, June Handley, that this was *his* war, and officially enlisted in the RCAF on January 6, 1942. He expressed his wish to enlist for flying duties.

To complete the portrayal of Larry Allen, June Handley-Peters added the following:

> Larry had good facial features – with thick, wavy, dark brown auburn hair, laughing blue eyes, an engaging smile and a very pleasant personality. He had many friends and was an idealist. He was a 'man of substance', he 'pursued excellence'.
>
> Larry and I became engaged the summer of 1941, and were planning to marry after he got home from the service – not thinking too much of the ordeals of a mixed marriage, always figuring it would somehow work out. His mother and father were disappointed of course, but they were civil to me. My family accepted and respected Larry, we were all very comfortable together.[1]

Larry would have liked to become a pilot; he loved flying and had a good taste of it after receiving lessons at the Windsor Flying Club. But, on enrolment, he volunteered to become an observer. He needed glasses for

[1]Letter from June Handley-Peters to the author, May 7, 1992. June's brother Jack served in the Essex Scottish Regiment, and was taken prisoner during the Dieppe raids in August 1942. He spent the rest of the war at Stalag 8B.

reading and close work and in addition suspected that he would not meet the air force's stature requirements for pilots. He was not a tall man, but his RCAF Medical Board assessment read 'Intelligent, physically fit, sincere, alert, keen and a pleasing personality'. Larry entered 5 Initial Training School at Belleville, Ontario, in April 1942. He obtained excellent results there, and the assessment of his superiors read: 'Excellent observer material – cool and clear thinking'. He then proceeded to 1 Air Observers School at Malton, Ontario, where he was assessed above average and was awarded his Air Navigator's badge on October 9, 1942, and commissioned to Pilot Officer Lawrence Allen, J-14769. He was then sent overseas, and arrived in England on November 4, 1942. He joined 22 OTU at Wellesbourne Mountford, where Teddy also received his training five months later. There, the navigation officer considered Larry to be 'a very efficient navigator. Is very confident and will do well operationally. Above the average'. He was 'crewed up' and subsequently posted to 420 Squadron, and went along to North Africa with his unit and the rest of 331 Wing, operating out of Zina airfield. There, he completed 35 operational missions. In Tunisia, he had been promoted to flight lieutenant, and assigned to the task of squadron navigation leader. On being posted to 405 Squadron on February 27, 1944, his commanding officer, Wing Commander Danny McIntosh wrote in his confidential posting report: 'An outstanding squadron navigation leader who has trained his aircrew with skill and enthusiasm. His personal operation ability has been exceptional. Strongly recommended.' It was obvious that Teddy's new navigator was an ace.

David Ramsay was the third son of Scottish parents. He was born on December 30, 1920, in Dysart, Saskatchewan, where his parents were farming. In 1922, during the 'difficult period' for the farmers on the prairies, the Ramsay family moved to Port Alberni, British Columbia, where David attended Alberni Elementary School and the Alberni District High School, graduating with high standing in 1939. During his boyhood, David was active in athletics. Learning to swim and dive at the age of five, he continued his interest in aquatics and was a successful competitor in the Sproat Lake Regatta events and in other local swimming meets. Basketball was perhaps his favourite sport, but baseball, lacrosse, track and field, softball and tennis all claimed his interest at various times. He coached several junior basketball and softball teams, and in 1941 he successfully managed and coached the Alberni Junior Girls Basketball Team for the British Columbia Provincial Championships. This success attracted wide attention in the district and David became well known and popular with the businessmen and young people within the Port Alberni area. After graduating, he was offered a position in the Port Alberni branch of the Bank of Montreal, which he accepted in July 1939. His dedication to his work there earned early recognition, and in 1940 he was given teller's duties.

One of his brothers immediately went on active service at the outbreak of hostilities in 1939. This increased David's interest in the armed forces with the result that he joined the RCAF in Vancouver on August 28, 1941. He was an outstanding student during his training period and graduated in April 1942 as an observer at 2 Air Observers School at Edmonton, Alberta. He was then posted to 1 Air Navigation School at Rivers, Manitoba, where he completed the last 'long course' conducted by the RCAF in Canada in August 1942, qualifying as a navigator, air gunner and bomb aimer. He was commissioned to Pilot Officer David Ramsay, J-12973.

By this time his brother was with the Canadian Scottish Regiment in England, and David therefore immediately applied for posting to join his brother overseas. He arrived in England in early September 1942, and was almost immediately posted as a replacement bomb aimer to 420 Squadron, RCAF, flying Wellington IIIs at Skipton-on-Swale in Yorkshire. On October 13, 1942, David participated in his first op against the enemy, a memorable run to Kiel. This dangerous mission was accentuated by a mid-air collision with a German night fighter on the return journey over the North Sea. Their Wellington limped back to base although without a rudder, a tribute to the flying ability of the crew. David's operational period with the 'Snowy Owl' Squadron was served under the experienced captaincy of Squadron Leader Danny McIntosh, DFC and officer commanding 420 Squadron.

In late May 1943, David and the others of 420 Squadron were ordered to North Africa, where David, by now a flight lieutenant, was soon appointed to squadron bombing leader. For the excellence of his leadership in subsequent operations, David was awarded the Distinguished Flying Cross. The citation for his DFC was published in the *London Gazette* on November 30, 1943, and read: 'This officer has been bombing leader in his squadron for a period of seven months and during that time has taken part in a large number of operations against German and Italian targets. Flight Lieutenant Ramsay has, by his enthusiasm and leadership, set a splendid example of accurate bombing to all crews and has himself on several occasions made a second or third bombing run.'

After returning to England in early November 1943, David was asked to report to an OTU as instructor for a well-earned rest after having completed nearly 40 operational missions. However, a visit in late 1943 to his army brother convinced David that the invasion of north-west Europe was forthcoming and there was a need for experienced aircrew for the softening-up of the invasion area. In fact, at this time he inferred that he would go into the invasion with the army if he could not continue flying operations against the enemy. Eventually, however, David succeeded in gaining a posting to 405 Squadron.[1]

[1]With thanks to Brigadier-General Peter F. Ramsay, ED, CD, David's brother, who served in the Canadian army from 1939 to 1946, finishing the war with the rank of major.

While at 420 Squadron, Larry and David had become acquainted with James Bradley, a British wireless operator. James Sydney Bradley was born on May 4, 1922. James, affectionately called 'Sonny' by his parents and four sisters, spent his childhood in the Wye Valley and the Royal Forest of Dean in Gloucestershire, England.[1] His hobbies were fishing, cycling, nature study and playing the piano. After finishing school at Churchdown, he trained as an acetylene welder at the Llantony Welding Works in Gloucester City and went on to work in an aircraft factory. He joined the Land Defence Volunteers in 1940 but decided to enter the RAF Volunteer Reserve in June 1941. James completed his initial training at 7 Initial Training Wing at Newquay in Cornwall, whereupon he was selected to become a wireless operator. Flight Sergeant Bradley was crewed up at OTU and eventually joined 420 Squadron, which he followed to North Africa in June 1943. Upon their return to the UK, James and his crew started training on the four-engined Halifax bomber at 1659 Heavy Conversion Unit. On January 18, 1944, however, their Halifax suffered engine failure and crashed near their home station Topcliffe, mortally wounding bomb aimer Joseph Sharpe and rear gunner Leslie Petry. Pilot Fred Baker was repatriated to Canada for hospitalisation, leaving James and navigator Ted Harkin behind in England. After having recovered from the initial shock, James took heart and applied for a posting to start a second tour. It is very likely that either Larry Allen or David Ramsay introduced him to Teddy referring to him as their new wireless operator.

Robert 'Bob' Booth, who previously had also completed a first tour, took the position of flight engineer in Teddy's new crew. Robert Alexander 'Bob' Booth was born in Carberry, Manitoba, on September 24, 1918. At a very early age, he moved with his parents to Winnipeg, Manitoba's capital city. There he was educated and later employed with the Canadian Pacific Railway, where he worked as a mechanic on cars and motorcycles. Before enlisting in the RCAF on November 15, 1940, he had served for one month as a private with the Winnipeg Light Infantry at Portage La Prairie. He was initially rejected for aircrew because of a suspected heart murmur. After completing his initial training in October 1941, he was posted overseas. He then served in 404 Squadron, RCAF, as a technical sergeant, until he was able to re-muster to aircrew and become a flight engineer on March 1, 1943. Shortly afterwards he was posted to 419 Squadron, RCAF at Middleton-St-George, where he completed 22 operation missions on Halifaxes. He took part in Bomber Command's most daring raids of that period, including Hamburg, Peenemünde and Berlin. On December 16, 1943, Bob was commissioned to pilot officer, serial number C-19795.

[1]During the war, two of James's sisters, Anne and Marjory, served in the Queen Anne's Imperial Medical Nursing Service Reserve.

Shortly afterwards, he was posted to 434 Squadron, RCAF, based at Croft. There, he took part in one operation, a memorable attack by 823 bombers on Leipzig on February 19, 1944, from which 79 bombers did not return.[1] It is uncertain when and why exactly he was posted to 405 Squadron shortly thereafter, but it is assumed he applied to fill one of the flight engineer vacancies there. Teddy likely asked him to become his flight engineer during their pre-operational training.[2]

Now two more important spots had to be filled in Teddy's team, perhaps the most important ones. He needed two sharp-eyed air gunners that would defend his aircraft and crew in the likely event of attack from an enemy night fighter. He found them in Leslie Foster and Hugh Clifford.

Leslie Arthur Foster was born at Medicine Hat, Alberta, on June 25, 1917. Together with his two brothers and three sisters, he grew up in that city and went to school at Connaught School and Alexander High School. His other interests included swimming, baseball, physical training and photography. In the mid-30s, his father Winfred passed away, leaving Leslie and his two brothers to support the family. His brother Allan was employed at the Boeing Aircraft Company's assembly plant at Vancouver's Sea Island airport and his other brother Wynn became a schoolteacher. After finishing high school, Leslie chipped in as a shoe salesman and as a loader. In 1938, Florence Kreller married the handsome and athletic Leslie. She bore him a daughter, Wynnona, in January 1940.

Leslie's brother Wynn gave up school teaching in 1939, and enlisted in the RCAF.[3] Despite his young family, the call for duty was irresistible, and Leslie followed his brother's example shortly, signing up on August 14, 1940. At 1 Manning Pool in Toronto, he was selected to join the Service Police. In August 1942, Leslie re-mustered to aircrew, and following training at 4 Initial Training School at Edmonton and 3 Bombing and Gunnery School at MacDonald, Manitoba, where he came second in his class. Sergeant Leslie Foster was sent overseas on January 25, 1943. Only six weeks before, his daughter Leslie Carol was born. He spent a fine two weeks of leave with his wife and two babies. His heart sank when he had to kiss them goodbye at the train station on his way to the duty ahead.

In England, Leslie missed his family deeply, and in letters to Allan he implored his brother several times to take care of Florence and the kids if anything should happen to him. Leaving his family behind put him on an emotional roller-coaster ride like many of his fellow-volunteers in the Allied air forces. Filled with homesickness, he thought about quitting, but somehow something wouldn't let him and seemed to keep drawing him on.

---

[1]This was the highest loss of the war in a single operation to that date.

[2]With thanks to G. Harry Booth, Bob's brother, who successfully completed a Bomber Command tour of 33 missions over Europe.

[3]Wynn Foster served in the RAF Coastal Command. In December 1942, while on a transfer flight from England to Cairo, Egypt, his Wellington aircraft went missing with its entire crew. Wynn left behind his wife Helen and daughter Donna-Rae.

In March 1943, he took an advanced gunnery course, by which time he expected to be posted to a bomber squadron. He confessed to Allan, 'This is just a suicide job and married men should never go into it, so stay where you are.' In April 1943, Leslie was posted to 77 Squadron, RAF, flying Halifax bombers out of Elvington in Yorkshire. As a rear gunner, he joined the crew of Sergeant Richardson, which was composed of five Englishmen and one other Canadian gunner. He still wasn't very happy, and confided to his brother that he 'wouldn't mind England if Florence was here, as seeing beauty without your loved one is like a thorn in your heart'. However, in spite of these thoughts, he immediately gained confidence in his crew, which led to his conviction that he would get through okay. On May 13, 1943, Leslie and his crew flew their first op to Bochum in the Ruhr Valley. More operational missions followed in quick order, and Les reported to his brother:

> I know every flak gun in Belgium, Holland and Germany. Jerry is no fool or coward either; you often see him flying right through the Flak and it is his wits against ours. We have had the upward luck (and by luck I mean just that) so far and I hope it keeps on. I will be home by Christmas if my luck continues to hold. When I get back, a nice safe job in the post office will suit me fine.

Leslie continued to take part in all the important raids of the summer of 1943, including Hamburg, Peenemünde and Berlin. He confided to his brother that he was going to drop into air force headquarters right after his tour was finished and put on a big 'moan' to go back home to his family. On September 6, 1943, Leslie completed his 24th and last mission with 77 Squadron, an attack on the city of Munich. His crew was subsequently split up and sent to different stations as instructors. Leslie ended up in 1664 Conversion Unit at Croft, as a gunnery instructor. He still very much longed to go home to his girls, by now one and three years old, but he reconciled himself to the situation, knowing that he would be in England for only another six months or so. By now a flight sergeant, Leslie was quite fed up with instructing, but was resigned to the fact that at least it was a safe job. He reported to his brother Allan:

> Sometimes I wish I could go on operations again but I always come to my senses again before I do anything. Out of 40 gunners that were on my course over half are gone now, but I guess I was born lucky wasn't I? I sure miss Flo and the kids but just have to put up with it, I suppose, and we will make up for it when we get back home together. I will be due to go home in March, but there's a roster and it will take much longer. We get a month's holiday and are allowed a month's leave for travelling so should have lots of time at home. That is the one thing that keeps me going.

Leslie also admitted to his brother that he hated flying. He told him that he was 'sick and tired of seeing aeroplanes' and that the limited amount of flying at the conversion unit 'suited him fine'. Still, much to his brother's surprise, he soon volunteered for another tour of operations. The reason for this was the same as for many other servicemen applying for a second tour. He did not see much sense in going home for a month or so, getting to know the family and settling down, and then having to break away again and go back overseas. Indeed, aircrew going home for leave after a first tour of operations were expected to report back in any case after their breather for a second tour of duty. By requesting a second tour right away, he expected to be home by August, and this time for good. He asked his brother not to say anything to Florence and their mother, as he knew they would worry too much. So, Leslie applied for a posting to an operational bomber squadron, and ended up in 405 Squadron, RCAF, where Teddy selected him to man the top turret of his Lancaster, as 'mid-upper gunner'.[1]

Nicholas Hugh Clifford was born in North Bay, Ontario, on January 10, 1909. He was named after his father Nicholas Albert Clifford, so the family soon called him Hugh to avoid a mix-up. Together with his parents, two brothers and two sisters, Hugh moved to the city of Hamilton at the age of six, attending Hamilton public schools and Hamilton Technical College there. After graduating, he worked for eight-and-a-half years in the sheet metal and roofing business, spending some of this time in the United States with a roofing firm. After that, his father employed him in a dry cleaning business and with J. Irving Roofing before he joined the RCAF on October 16, 1939. After enlisting, Hugh served a number of years in ground duties at 3 SFTS in Calgary, until applying for aircrew duty in November 1942. Hugh entered 3 Bombing and Gunnery School at MacDonald, Manitoba, on December 6, 1942, where he became acquainted with Leslie Foster. He was awarded his air gunner's badge on March 13, 1943. Sergeant Clifford was sent overseas in early April 1943, and posted to 432 Squadron, RCAF. In this unit, he completed about 30 operations as a rear gunner on Wellingtons, operating from Skipton-on-Swale, and on Lancaster IIs, flying from East Moor. He did not feel much like putting in the required spell as an instructor after that, so he right away applied for a second tour of operations. He was transferred from 432 to 405 Squadron on March 9, 1944, ten days before being promoted to warrant officer. In 405, Teddy immediately welcomed him into his crew, where he would man the position of rear gunner. At the age of 35, Hugh Clifford was unusually old for operational aircrew duty, and he unquestionably became the 'grandpa' of the Blenkinsop crew.[2]

---

[1]With many thanks to Leslie W. Foster, son of Allan Foster and named after his uncle Leslie Arthur Foster. Florence Foster only found out that Leslie had gone on another operational tour after he was reported missing.

[2]With thanks to Hugh Clifford's nephew, Robert C. Dickson.

Warboys

On arrival at 405 Squadron, Teddy and the rest of his crew – minus Hugh Clifford who had not been posted yet, were attached to the Pathfinder Force Navigation Training Unit, in short NTU (PFF), at RAF Warboys. At this station, main force crews were initiated into the challenging art of target finding and marking. The airfield was a very large establishment and housed a number of other units. The station had about 100 aircraft, mostly heavies, and a number of Mosquito type aircraft used in pathfinder training on the Oboe equipment.

But before they started to fly, the newly arrived crews received a number of ground school lectures on various subjects related to their new assignment. At NTU, the aircraft used were Lancasters, so the station also served as a conversion unit. They studied the aircraft systems on the Lancaster, different navigation techniques, the peculiarities of the new aircraft and the various payloads it could lift. Pathfinder aircraft did not just carry a load of bombs to the target but were equipped as well with illumination material. The initial pathfinder operations had been hampered by a lack of an effective 'marker bomb'. In early 1943, a purpose-built marker, called the target indicator (TI) had been produced for pathfinder use, most of the work being done by the pre-war firework industry. It was basically a 250lb bomb casing filled with 60 pyrotechnic 'candles' and fitted with a barometric fuse. This fuse exploded the canister and ignited the candles at a predetermined altitude, which then bloomed into a magnificent splurge of colour and cascaded slowly to the ground. Red, green, and yellow were the standard PFF colour variations. Once on the ground, the TI stayed burning for about three minutes. The TI proved to be reliable, vivid, distinctive and not easily copied by the Germans. In fact, the RAF sometimes changed the sequence of the marker colours so as to fool the Germans, who sometimes made dummy red fires to confuse the bomber crews. Around the TI, the pathfinders developed marking techniques that were used until the end of the war.

The crews were also trained in jumping with a parachute, should it become necessary. This jumping technique was simulated in one of the hangars using a rope-and-pulley method. One end of the rope was anchored to the roof truss in the hangar ceiling, the other end extended down an incline to the floor. The airman, sitting in a sling supported by a pulley on the rope, rolled down the length of the rope and, at the sudden stop near floor level, had to land on his feet, then roll into a pile of hay bales.

The Lancaster was a bomber pilot's aircraft of choice, and was equipped with all the latest navigational equipment. On March 5, 1944, Flight Lieutenant Everett took Teddy and his crew airborne for the first time in a Lancaster III. Teddy acted as second pilot. They were involved in a mock pathfinder operation, where they were introduced to the different PFF concept of operations. The next day this routine was repeated, this time with Flight Lieutenant Coldham at the controls. On March 7, Flight Lieutenant Weber continued the preparation of the novice crew, which upon finishing had now ten hours of specific pathfinder training under their belt. Navigator Larry Allen and bomb aimer David Ramsay had exhibited their natural skills to the NTU instructors, who concluded that, together with their pilot and other crewmembers, they were exceptionally apt for PFF work.

On March 8 and 9, Teddy completed his training at Warboys, with three more Lancaster flights to further train in circuits, three-engined landings and night landings. The Lancaster had completely different takeoff and landing characteristics from the Halifax, so these instructional flights were spent doing the 'circuits and bumps' routine. He soloed the Lancaster on March 8, taking it around the Warboys circuits for a mere 15 minutes. Now he was prepared, and on March 10, he and his crew checked out from Warboys, and returned to 405 Squadron at Gransden Lodge.

Into Battle, Again

After a crew had left Warboys and returned to its PFF squadron, the idea was to put the crew quickly on an operation. Teddy and his crew realised that soon they were going to be in for it. They were assigned to the squadron's 'C' Flight, which was the training flight and headed by one of the most experienced men in 405 Squadron, Squadron Leader Gordon Bennett, DFC. Back at Gransden, Hugh Clifford joined Teddy's crew, and was welcomed by everyone. Despite his age, he seemed an unflappable and self-assured airman, quite the type Teddy wanted.

The Blenkinsop crew arrived in 405 Squadron at a critical time for Bomber Command. In February and March 1944, the force's casualty rate would reach the most appalling numbers of the entire war. In fact, during the month of March 1944, the chance of a Bomber Command crew surviving the entire tour that month was only 13 per cent. This period was the zenith of the German night fighter fortunes, after their full recovery from the technological deprivation experienced in the summer of 1943. Since the start of the Berlin raids in November 1943 and until mid-March 1944, almost 900 Bomber Command aircraft had been lost over enemy territory. There had been a horrifying six-week period between December 16, 1943, and the end of January 1944, when 87 pathfinder crews became casualties in missing or crashed aircraft. Furthermore, aircrew morale was undoubtedly put to its severest test during the Battle of Berlin. Surprisingly, there was not a widespread drop in crew confidence, though there was a deterioration of efficiency as a result of limited flying during periods of poor weather, longer routes resulting in fuel displacing bomb tonnage, and the reliance on inexperienced crews as a result of the casualty rate. There were no freshman raids for the main force boys; a new crew could arrive at a squadron from a training unit and a hazardous task to Berlin in midwinter might be their first ops flight. The last major RAF raid on Berlin was flown on the night of March 24-25, 1944. Some of the raids had caused serious damage in Berlin, but the overwhelming success sought by 'Bomber' Harris proved to be elusive. Berlin was not reduced to ruins at the end of the battle and the Germans would be nowhere near surrender by April 1944 as Harris had foretold.

Just like Larry and David, Teddy was well aware of the fact that operating a heavy bomber over occupied Europe would be quite different from the missions they had flown from Tunisia in 1943. The Lancaster was twice as large and heavier than the Wellington, with a crew of seven, and not five. The skies over Europe were renowned for the presence of the Luftwaffe's 'top gun' fighter crews, and intelligence reports on Germany's leading night fighter aces were common topic among the Allied aircrew. And then there was the anti-aircraft artillery – flak. Italian anti-aircraft fire, both in point of accuracy and intensity, was nowhere near on par with the German proficiency. Another difference was that the Mediterranean operations did not require the deep penetration into enemy airspace, although they did involve relatively long transits over water. On the other hand, in the European theatre of operations, crews had navigational aids like Gee or H2S at their disposal to guide them, in addition to a skilled pathfinder force there to mark the target's aiming-point. The pathfinders were the main force's guide, not only as route-markers on the long hazardous trip to the target but also over the target itself, where, with their better navigational techniques and technology, they had the task of pinpointing the areas where the bombs should be released.

The pathfinders were critical to the success of the bombing raids, which were planned to the minute on an exacting timetable. They had to reach the target despite all the difficulties of navigation – changing weather conditions, unforecast winds, German night fighters and flak defences – and then arrive on target within a tolerance of only one minute. They had to drop their target indicators on exactly the right spot even though the whole scene might be enveloped in dense cloud or adverse winds which could shift the flares miles off target. When they failed, which on occasion they did, the resulting confusion had a disastrous chain reaction on the entire main force.

The PFF used two navigators in each aircraft, the observer or set operator and the plotter. On completion of their training course at NTU, after discussions amongst themselves and with their instructors, it was decided who would function better as the set operator and who would be the plotter. In the Lancaster, both men operated in a completely blacked-out compartment. The only illumination was from a small lamp the plotter used to see his charts and his Dalton computer. Additional light was provided by the glow from the set operator's Gee-set and the light from his

H2S cathode ray tube which lit the plan position indicator. Despite the use of two navigators in pathfinder aircraft, there was no time for chitchat during a mission. Larry and David sat side by side on a narrow bench at a compact table with barely enough room for their charts and logs. Under the Lancaster's nav table were various pieces of equipment, which seemed to consist of nothing but protruding electrical connections that effectively prevented straightening one's legs and assured knee damage if tried. The aircraft of both the main force and PFF, with certain exceptions, always observed a complete blackout and radio silence during night operations. In the nav compartment, it was always completely dark. Both navigators had no visual indication of whether they were flying in daylight or darkness. Except for takeoff and landing, and possibly over the target if time permitted, they saw less of the war than anyone else. Both Larry Allen and David Ramsay met the criteria for flexibility for each could do either one of the two navigator tasks. In view of their experience, however, they had no difficulty in deciding that Larry would become the plotter or 'nav one', and David would be the set operator or 'nav two'.

Except on special flights, PFF did not use a forward gunner or a bomb aimer as such. The flight engineer was given training to enable him to operate the bombsight with additional information provided by the set operator. Depending on the raid, the flight engineer would drop the bombs visually, with information from the set operator and plotter for setting the bombsight. During this time the pilot would be given the course to fly over the target while he was to hold the plane perfectly straight and level during the last five miles to the release point. When it was a blind bombing raid, the operator set the release switches, timed and released the bombs and flares from his position, based on his reading of the H2S scan.

While March 11 was spent getting settled in after arriving at Gransden, the day following Teddy was scheduled on the training board. He flew a beam approach training sortie in an Airspeed Oxford, with Flight Lieutenant Gardner as his instructor. On March 14, Teddy took his entire crew airborne twice. The first mission was a day cross-country in Lancaster III 'H-for-Harry', while the second one was a two-and-a-half-hour night trip in 'X-for-X-Ray'. After landing, he was informed to be ready for the next day, as his flight commander intended to send him up – as a second dickey – for his first operation in the squadron.

On March 15, Teddy was scheduled to fly with Flight Lieutenant McDonald and his crew. He tagged along with his tutor during the entire day, keen to absorb as much as possible about the task ahead. The mission on which Ted acted as the co-pilot was to be a major raid with 863 bomber aircraft involved, 16 from 405 Squadron. The target was Stuttgart, and after a six-and-a-half hour mission, the crew returned safely to Gransden. Bombing had been very scattered due to cloud cover, and the raid was assessed as poor. Thirty-six aircraft did not return from the raid due to enemy air defence. One of 405 Squadron's crews, captained by Flight Lieutenant Fyfe, was listed as MIA or missing in action. But Teddy was deemed mission qualified, so 405 Squadron could draw on one additional crew for the next operational duty schedules.

However, before going on operations as a crew, the Blenkinsop team had to complete some more training. Day cross-countries were flown on March 17 and 18, before the crew was sent on a week's leave. On March 19, Teddy wrote to his parents:

> Well, at last I'm operational again and very glad of it. The new squadron is fine and there are a nice crowd here. I've been very lucky with my crew, they're a good bunch and very keen, we should have no trouble at all.
>
> Had a letter from Helen yesterday, giving me hell for not writing to you, I think it's a conspiracy but it must be effective. By the way, I'm having cigarette trouble again, the February shipment has not arrived. Things were going very well until about three weeks ago, but it may be due to my move. Will let you know if they come or not.
>
> Have my operational ribbon and Canadian Volunteer Medal now, also my operational wing, and will begin to look a bit like an American private by the time this tour is over. Still, if they hand these things out I suppose we must wear them.
>
> I'm going off for a week's leave tomorrow, rather imagine I'll spend some of it in London and some with Uncle Max. It's nice to go up there and loaf about for a bit.

After having spent some days in London, Teddy travelled to his relatives in Leamington Spa. He stayed with Uncle Max until March 28, when he returned to his station. Upon his return, Aunt Lucy wrote an interesting letter to her brother Hubert, interesting, for it sheds some light on Teddy's character, vigour and love for his country, while it also uncovers some of the thoughts of a young man stretched by the unremitting strain of war:

> Teddy turned up a week ago at Max's for 8 days leave and has now gone back. He came over to us for the day, and we thought him looking better than usual and very cheerful. I don't know whether he usually has a high colour, but he certainly had this time and we even thought he had put on a bit of weight. He is very satisfied with his present surroundings and says they are excellently fed and have good quarters.
>
> He went up to London for a few days – probably to meet Helen, I should think, but he was not very communicative, and we never press him to tell us anything – not that it would be any use if we did.
>
> We get a bit worried about the opinion of poor old England that he is one day going to take home with him, and only hope that it isn't shared by all his fellow Canadians. He thinks and says that there is

> nothing Canada can learn from this poor old country, and that it has everything to learn from Canada, and we gather that he does his best to teach all the Englishmen with whom he comes in contact, a process to which they don't take very kindly. Of course we realise that a lot of it is youth with its certainty that it is right, and also that there is considerable substance in some of his criticism, but one can't expect his contemporaries to be equally tolerant, and they would resent his feeling of complete superiority to the whole body of Englishmen doing the same work as he is doing, and might forget what we never can: all he has given and is giving for this country. Don't please say anything to him about this; his self-confidence is essential for his work. Don't imagine that we don't love the boy – we do; and we admire him for being so young and keen and even for his intolerance; but we don't want Canada to think, when he and his fellows return, that we have failed to appreciate them, and, indeed, all that Canada has done for us in every way; but I hope you will see why there may be individual cases of resentment, each side thinking the other feels itself superior. However, the main thing is that he is well and happy and, at present, in the midst of Canadians.

On the day he returned to the squadron, Ted and his crew were scheduled to perform a fighter affiliation training sortie. During this exercise, a Hawker Hurricane, acting as the 'enemy', performed a series of pursuit attacks on Teddy's Lancaster. During these attacks, Teddy had to perform the so-called 'corkscrew'. This manoeuvre was designed to give Teddy practice in evasive action when attacked and the air gunners time to simulate accurate return fire. The manoeuvre should begin when the first fighter attacking was at 600 yards and should be continued throughout the engagement. It usually was the mid-upper gunner, having the best all-around view in his top turret, who gave the command 'Corkscrew port/starboard – Go!' Then followed a series of steep diving and climbing turns, leaving the crewmembers one moment frantically holding on to something to counter weightlessness, while afterwards being slammed into their seats under the gravitational or 'G' forces. All the time Teddy was announcing over the intercom what he was doing so the gunners could apply the appropriate sighting rules and allowances. Although a fine aircraft, it was still hard to imagine that a big Lancaster could be thrown about in such a manner. This evasion was tiring for the pilot and had to be stopped the moment it was clear that no further attacks were developing. Some crewmembers were not too badly affected by these violent manoeuvres but it left some feeling rather unwell. However, the more aggressively the manoeuvres were executed, while maintaining sufficient airspeed obviously, the greater the chance of shaking off a German night fighter. German night fighter leaders taught their crews to stay with the corkscrewing bomber and to wait until it was changing direction at the top of his climb, when its wings would be level and they would have an easier 'non-deflection' shot. If they did not manage to hit the bomber at this time, they were told to break away and search for an easier target, for the violent corkscrews carried out by some Lancaster pilots were truly amazing.

Two days later, on March 30, the Blenkinsop crew appeared for the first time on the Pathfinder Force operations order. Their first pathfinder mission as a crew would become a memorable one.

The Nürnberg debacle

On Thursday, March 30, just as on any other ops day, briefing was in the afternoon with takeoff three to four hours later. All crewmembers attended the briefing, where the commanding officer and all the section heads, plus the met officer and intelligence officer had their say about the trip. The target for that night was Nürnberg, deep into southern Germany. Topics discussed included the target, the inbound route, the estimated time of arrival (ETA), and the exit route to be taken returning to home base. Aircraft were assigned, with the classification of the crews and the raid, and their bomb and flare loads, fuel uplift and alternate airports noted for any returning damaged aircraft. Each crew working from their own table completed the required calculations, and the navigator stayed back to complete the flight plan.

Nürnberg was an ancient imperial city in the south-east part of Germany. Although not regarded as of major industrial importance, there were numerous small factories and, in addition, the city was a fairly important centre for rail and water communications. Having failed in the destruction of Berlin, it was believed by some that the city was selected for a single heavy attack because it was the symbolic birthplace of Nazism. Nothing less than 15 Halifax squadrons and 34 Lancaster squadrons, including seven PFF, were placed on the raid's order of battle. However, any route to Nürnberg would have to pass close to a number of heavily defended areas and be subjected to attacks by fighters from nearby assembly points. As it turned out, the route chosen was complicated, involving a huge dogleg consisting of a long straight flight due east into central Germany before turning south for the final run in to the bombing IP. Such an indirect routing served to confuse the enemy as to the real target. There was always the hope that, during the course of the penetration, the enemy fighter controller would commit his fighters into the wrong airspace. In addition, there was an advantage in having abrupt corners to the routing so that any late aircraft could catch up by cutting the corners. But the selected course passed between two areas of heavy flak defences: the Ruhr to the north and Frankfurt to the south.

To add to the difficulty, the anticipated weather on the way and at the target area caused growing apprehension among the operations staff. The forecast disclosed that weather for the raid night was marginal at best. This particular night was to have been a moon stand-down night for the main force, but the raid was planned on the basis of an earlier weather forecast. This report asserted that there would be a high overcast cloud obscuring the bombers from the moonlight on their inbound route to the target. Furthermore, the target area weather was forecast to be clear for ground-marked bombing. However, a Mosquito aircraft that had carried out a weather reconnaissance around midday reported that the protective high cloud was unlikely to materialise and there could possibly be a low stratus cloud obscuring the target. Still, command headquarters elected to proceed with the raid.

On any deep penetration raid, it was customary to anticipate visual ground marking by the pathfinders, codenamed Newhaven marking. This allowed that, in the event the main force stream became somewhat loosened, a clear view of the ground aiming point would enable the main force bombers to converge on the target as they started their final approach. As a precaution, a small number of sky markers were also carried in the event that sky marking was found to be necessary. If weather conditions over the target were such that the target would be obscured by cloud, blind sky marking was used. The sky markers – small short-burning red, yellow or green flares – were fitted with parachutes to give each flare a very slow descent rate. The PFF primary blind marker crews placed these sky markers in a position above the target and on the run-in to it, so that each aircraft used the flare as the aiming point. The bombs overshot the aerial markers onto the target. It was a challenging procedure as it was very difficult to obtain an accurate target marking due to the cloud conditions, and at the same time, the wind could easily carry the parachutes off line. These blind sky markers, like the attack for which they were used, were code named Wanganui.

The unfavourable weather forecast, delivered in the afternoon by the Mosquito reconnaissance aircraft, had not gone unnoticed by the bomber squadrons. It was generally assumed that the raid would be cancelled at some point. After the briefing, all 781 Lancaster and Halifax crews that were planned for the mission enjoyed their ops meal, where drinking too much tea had to be avoided for obvious reasons. Not all of the more than 5,000 young airmen having their meal that night had the same hearty appetite. More than 100 crews had yet to complete their sixth operation, while 18 were flying their first, but Teddy's veterans were keen and ready to go. After leaving the mess hall, the crew suited up in flying gear and made sure they had all the equipment and maps they needed during the flight. Their personal possessions – money, passports, wedding rings and other items that could give away their background or family ties – were handed to the intelligence officer and put in a sealed envelope until their return. After that a truck took them to the hard stand where Lancaster III JA976 'S-for-Sugar' was parked. This Lancaster would become the regular aircraft used by the Blenkinsop crew while assigned to 405 Squadron. After a final ground check the crew climbed on board, checked the oxygen system and other vital equipment and waited for the ground marshaller to inform them that the mission was on. Besides crew, equipment and a full load of fuel, 'S-for-Sugar' carried five 2,000-lb heavy capacity bombs that night. It struck Teddy how relaxed his crew appeared. Everyone attended to his duties in a composed but concentrated manner. It was obvious that he had picked a top team. Then the green flare appeared and the raid was on; it had not been cancelled.

The basic objective of a planned heavy bomber operation was to obtain a stream of aircraft, all on the same course, with sufficient separation to minimise the risk of collision, which would achieve a sudden compact, yet continuous flow over the target. To accomplish this, the timing of the operation had to start at takeoff. Each squadron taking part was allocated a certain time slot to be over target, and each aircraft was given a time-on-target. Working backwards from this time-on-target the navigators could calculate a takeoff time and an ETA for each turning point on the route.

405 Squadron despatched 14 Lancasters to Nürnberg that night. Takeoff would be at one-minute intervals. At 10:10 p.m., Teddy began his final checks: escape hatches secure, cross-feed valve off, flaps 25 down, pressure in the hydraulic jacks okay. Then he eased off the brake, feeding power to the four Merlins and the Lancaster rolled slowly out of the dispersal bay. At 10:22 p.m., Teddy swung 'S-for-Sugar' onto the runway, set the brakes and inched all the throttles forward to 800 rpm so as to prevent the plugs from fouling up. Another green flare from control and with the brakes still on, he nodded to Bob who then opened the throttles on both inner engines. Brakes off. Teddy now advanced all throttles to full power, the aircraft accelerated forward propelled by four powerful Merlin engines that roared to life under full power. Slowly the heavily laden bomber accelerated. Until the tail came up at about 60 miles per hour, Teddy was able to control the heading by juggling the power fed to the two outboard engines. Tail up now. 'Confirm full power,' Teddy shouted. 'Full power,' Bob repeated the order, firmly ensuring the throttles were against the gate. At the same time he locked the throttles with just the right amount of tension so as they would not retard, yet Teddy would be able to take control in case of an engine failure. With Bob dealing with the throttles, Teddy was now free to use both hands on the control column for lift-off. Teddy, now controlling heading by application of rudder, held the nose down while the speed increased. At 105 miles per hour, he steadily applied a backpressure to the control column so as to initiate aircraft rotation, 'S-for-Sugar' made a slight bounce, then lumbered skyward at 10:25 p.m. Still struggling to attain that positive rate of climb, Teddy called for undercarriage up. There was a whine of hydraulics and a muffled thump as the big wheels tucked nicely into the inboard engine nacelles. He held her in a steady climb at 160 miles

per hour. At around 1,000 feet he raised the 25° of flap selected for takeoff and turned towards the outbound track. 'James, go back and give us a reading from the master,' Teddy called. There was a moment's delay, and then the voice of James Bradley, the wireless operator, came back, reading off the course from the master unit of the DR compass. Teddy and Larry checked their repeaters for compass error.

The bombers of 42 main force and seven pathfinder squadrons were from airfields all over Britain. They flew, in radio silence and in total darkness, across the North Sea to form up the bomber stream off the Suffolk coast. Each navigator had calculated his own flight plan to ensure that, in theory at least, his aircraft would arrive at a pre-determined position in the massive stream. The majority of the pathfinders took their place at the head of the force. This aircraft stream of something like 30 minutes duration gave some measure of mutual protection. Enemy radar blindness could be assumed because of the Window to be released by all aircraft at the appropriate time. At a line considered to be at the fringe of the detection limit of German radar, the skippers set full climb throttle boost to attain the operational height of 16,000 to 20,000 feet, a climb which took up to 40 minutes to complete. Once at altitude, the cruising indicated airspeed of 185 miles per hour was set and the pilot turned inbound at the first turning point. Certain pathfinder crews in the advance wave were designated to report on weather conditions and winds found over the course. These winds were then broadcast to the main force navigators.

Surrounded by dozens of aircraft at night and without lights, was the time when the air gunners earned their keep. The danger of encountering a twin-engine enemy fighter was the same as a collision with a friendly aircraft. This was especially true at turning points where bombers could be swinging in and out of the stream from many directions. Flak was an ever-present danger in spite of the precautions taken to route the stream away from known flak posts.

Despite diversionary mine-laying operations over the Frisians, spoof raids on Aachen, Cologne and Kassel, and the massive use of countermeasures such as Window, German fighter controllers were not fooled that night. They assembled their fighters over two radio beacons astride the bomber route to Nürnberg. It seemed as if they knew the bombers were coming, and from which direction. As usual, the enemy radio listening service had picked up increased wireless traffic in the afternoon, when many of the bombers were flying air tests in preparation for the night's operation. In anticipation of a heavy raid, flak and fighter units throughout Germany had been put on full alert. The advance pathfinders themselves, ironically, provided confirmation that the raid had taken off and was assembling. Some of the crews switched on their H2S sets soon after take-off, unaware that the Germans could now detect the set's transmissions over a long distance. It is fairly certain that the very powerful German Wassermann radar, located on the Belgian coast near Ostend, was watching the bomber stream as it approached.

The German radar operators apparently quickly figured out which aircraft were the actual diversionary force and then focused all their attention on the multiple radar contacts over Belgium. Accordingly, the first night fighters were ordered to take off from their airfields in France and Belgium, and directed to two assembly areas east of Belgium. The bomber stream, which had crossed the Belgian coast near Ostend, turned due east near the Belgian city of Charleroi, and began their long dogleg. At this point, some navigators discovered the winds from the west were stronger than forecast, and the aircraft were being blown off track. Already the first 'found' winds had been broadcast, but these proved both inaccurate and varied by a wide margin. Furthermore, with Gee now effectively jammed by the Germans, and H2S fairly useless over the featureless terrain, only the experienced navigators could obtain star shots and keep a reasonable track. Teddy, himself a talented navigator, realised how fortunate he was to have Larry and David on board.

The first fighters appeared just before the bombers reached the Belgian-German border east of Liège and ferocious attacks ensued in the bright moonlight for the next hour. Several of the Luftwaffe Messerschmitt Bf 110 and Junkers Ju 88 night fighters likely benefited from their newly installed technological innovations: the SN-2 on-board radar which could not be jammed by Window, and the upward-firing cannon codenamed Schräge Musik.[1] Les Foster and Hugh Clifford witnessed Lancasters or Halifax aircraft, one after the other, falling from the sky. By the time the main force was halfway along the inbound route to Nürnberg, the bombers were dispersed across a front of more than 40 miles. The majority flew hopelessly north of track, and some of the Lancasters were streaming condensation trails high in the moonlit sky. Almost 100 enemy night fighters were now within the bomber stream, following the bomber's track revealed by their condensation trails. An astounding number of 82 bombers were lost on the inbound route to the target and many of those losses concentrated near their target. Fortunately, all of 405 Squadron's 14 Lancasters were far enough ahead of the main force and escaped the ferocity of the German night prowlers.

Apparently the pathfinders accurately marked the turning point where the bomber stream was to turn south and inbound the target, but due to the scattering of the main force, relatively few crews identified the turning point and altered course only by dead reckoning. The plan was to be that, at precisely 01:05 a.m., 24 PFF Lancasters, including five of 405 Squadron, would arrive in the area. These blind marker-illuminators, using H2S,

[1]These 20 or 30mm cannons, mounted amidships, enabled German night fighters to attack heavy bombers from directly beneath, completely out of sight of the bomber's air gunners.

would drop green TIs and strings of parachute flares in an effort to show up the target area. Almost simultaneously, 62 Lancasters, called supporters, were to bomb blind using H2S, saturating the area with high capacity bombs and at the same time filling the sky with Window. An attack as described above, where blind radar ground marking was employed, was codenamed Paramatta.[1] Two minutes later, six Lancasters, termed visual markers, employing highly experienced bomb aimers working visually, were to release mixed green-and-red TIs on the aiming point, attempting for more precise Newhaven marking. Then, at 01:10 a.m. or 'zero hour', the first of the main force stream were to drop their bombs on the green-and-red TIs. At three-minute intervals during the course of the raid, the PFF blind backers-up would arrive and place their TIs or incendiary bombs to enhance the existing marking. Such was the plan. In perfect conditions it should have turned night into day, and the German city into a blazing inferno.

In reality, everything that could go wrong did go wrong. Only eight minutes flying time from the target, the first pathfinder crews came upon the edge of a solid deck of cloud obscuring Nürnberg completely. A few crews adapted to the new situation and employed their back-up supply of Wanganui sky-markers. Amazingly, no master bomber had been assigned to orchestrate this major raid, so no instructions were given to the main force to be on the lookout for the sky-markers. A strong cross-wind which developed on the final approach to the target caused many of the pathfinders to mark too far to the east, while it also blew the few sky-markers even further eastwards. On top of all that, the poorly forecasted winds had caused approximately 110 aircraft to stray to the north and ultimately to bomb the city of Schweinfurt, some 80 kilometres to the north-west of Nürnberg. Most of their bombs fell outside Schweinfurt, however, and little damage was done. Countless other misfortunes – including such problems as unserviceable H2Ss, battle damage and continuing interference by German night fighters and flak – led to the majority of the main force arriving over a vast blanket of overcast cloud. Two diffused areas of sky-markers could just be discerned. Most crews had to decide which of these gleams of light coincided with their ETA, and released their bombs accordingly. It was later estimated that only 500 bombers dropped their ordinance and those over a vast area around Nürnberg. There was absolutely no concentration and insignificant damage was done to their targets; only 69 citizens of Nürnberg and its suburbs were killed.

After the bombing run in, the aircraft continued on the same heading to the next turning point, which was only a short distance past the target area. The track home was also zigzagged in order to avoid, as much as possible,

---

[1]Paramatta and Wanganui are small towns in Australia and New Zealand respectively, and reflect the origin of the chief Pathfinder, Air Vice-Marshal D.C. Bennett.

the heavily defended areas. All semblance of a bomber stream had long vanished, as more than 600 bombers struggled back across northern France towards the English Channel. Fighter action was much reduced on the return flight, as most of the German fighters were out of fuel. Ninety-five bombers were lost in total that night, a staggering 12 per cent of the force dispatched. It was the biggest Bomber Command loss of the war. The Nürnberg raid was a complete fiasco.

Not surprisingly, the whole operation came under investigation by Bomber Command HQ, to determine the exact cause of the problem. A repetition of such appalling losses had to be prevented in the future. Some navigation leaders were very explicit in blaming the massive presence of enemy fighters inside the bomber stream on what they considered a suicidal routing so close to known German fighter assembly points. However, the raid against Nürnberg would be the last of its kind. Never again would the Luftwaffe enjoy such success as that of March 30-31, 1944. Besides, with D-Day looming, the Nürnberg raid brought the curtain down, at least temporarily, on Bomber Command's strategic offensive against the Third Reich.

The Blenkinsop crew had been detailed as one of 405 Squadron's four supporters that took part in the Nürnberg raid. The supporters were usually the newest crews. Their role was to support the early marker crews and help achieve saturation of the ground defences. Their first duty was to arrive at the target on time.

Teddy touched down on the runway of Gransden Lodge at exactly 05:23 a.m., and was the last of 405 Squadron's Lancasters to safely return to base. Their maiden trip with the pathfinders had been a nerve-racking and harrowing experience, and the entire crew realised they had been fortunate to return unscathed, as did the other 13 participating crews of 405. The squadron's flight commander of 'A' Flight, Squadron Leader Trilsbach, and his expert crew, perhaps had the narrowest escape of all in 405. Their Lancaster 'A-for-Amigo' was hit twice by heavy flak after leaving the target area. The starboard outer engine subsequently failed and shrapnel riddled the fuselage, but the veteran captain skilfully brought back his stricken aircraft to Gransden Lodge.

The Blenkinsop crew had done well and, while exhausted, was content with the result. Their mission report sounded serene and self-assured: 'Overcast cloud from 10 to 12,000 feet in target area. Load released at 01:13 hours from 20,000 feet. Bombed on windward side of 5 flares, which had been burning 4 to 5 minutes. Landed base.'

During interrogation by the squadron's intel officer, the padre offered them a tot of navy rum, also known as 'Nelson's Blood'. This was to relieve stress and help the crews sleep, which was usually impossible as several officers or crewmembers shared a single Nissen hut where not all the roommates had been on that particular raid. Anyhow, before going to bed, the weary crews looked forward to their 'bonus', one egg with two rashers of bacon.

Forty-nine bomber squadrons participated in the raid. The German night fighters downed 78 heavy bombers that night, and 11 aircraft were lost to flak. Two other aircraft collided over the Continent, while several others were damaged or crashed upon returning to England. The toll in personnel was even more overwhelming, with 535 airmen killed, 25 wounded and 155 taken prisoner. Only nine squadrons reported no missing aircraft. By way of comparison, more men were lost on this one raid to Nürnberg than were lost in the entire Battle of Britain that lasted several months. In the raid against Nürnberg, Bomber Command learned the folly of committing its main strength against a defence that was still not only robust, but flexible, ingenious and, above all, resolute.

Looking at disasters like Nürnberg, it is difficult to imagine how Allied commanders could sustain such losses and still go time and again on these dangerous operations. How was it possible to maintain morale in the heavy bomber squadrons? Operational flying proved to be an exacting test of nerve and self-control, and the strain had a pronounced cumulative effect. The effects of even a dozen operational sorties were discernible on the faces of some crews. Some crewmembers were so tense that they lost their voices or had to leave the briefing room to go and throw up outside. Others had nightmares reliving an operation under fire and would wake up in terror.The outward signs were not so readily apparent in most of the aircrew, but with few exceptions, they were there nevertheless in one form or another. There were the indirect manifestations of pressure as well. Most crews were superstitious, some in the extreme. There were many who always did things in a certain set order, and with certain embellishments, while getting ready for a mission. In every barracks block airmen went through elaborate pre-flight rituals and remained convinced that if they varied the ritual by one single act their safety was in jeopardy. Few aircraft took off without at least one member of the crew carrying a rabbit's foot or some other lucky charm or talisman. Anyone wishing to visualise how intense the strain could become, how suppressed fear could swell and chew away within, should read the excellent book by former Canadian bomber pilot, Murray Peden.

> Imagine yourself in a building of enormous size, pitch black inside. You are ordered to walk very slowly from one side to the other, then back. This walk in the dark will take you perhaps five or six hours. You know that in various nooks and crannies along your route killers armed with machine guns are lurking. They will quickly become aware that you have started your journey, and will be trying to find you the whole time you are in the course of it. There is another rather important psychological factor: the continuous roar emanating from nearby machinery. It precludes the possibility of your getting any

> audible warning of danger's approach. You are thus aware that if the trouble you are expecting does come, it will burst upon you with the startling surprise one can experience standing in the shower and having someone abruptly jerk open the door of the steamy cubicle and shout over the noise. If the killers stalking you on your walk should happen to detect you, they will leap at you out of the darkness firing flaming tracers from their machine guns. Compared with the armament they are carrying, you are virtually defenceless. Moreover, you must carry a pail of gasoline and a shopping bag full of dynamite in one hand. If someone rushes at you and begins firing, about all you can do is fire a small calibre pistol in his direction and try to elude him in the dark. But these killers can run twice as fast as you, and if one stalks and catches you, the odds are that he will wound and then incinerate you, or blow you into eternity. You are acutely aware of these possibilities for every second of the five or six hours you walk in the darkness, braced always, consciously or subconsciously, for a murderous burst of fire, and reminded of the stakes of the game periodically by the sight of guns flashing in the dark and great volcanic eruptions of flaming gasoline. You repeat this experience many times – if you live.[1]

Teddy and his crew were now firmly entrenched members of the pathfinders. They had proved their value in that catastrophic raid on Nürnberg, and now were ready to take on more assignments. Nürnberg had been Teddy's 32nd bomber operation.

The Road to D-Day

Most of Bomber Command's efforts in recent years had been to weaken the general German capacity to resist an invasion of Europe. As the date of the Normandy landings – Operation Overlord – approached, Bomber Command's resources were to be turned, in a far more precise manner, towards the hinterland of the invasion coast. In the west, the Germans had a complete army, including many of his best divisions, some equipped with massive armour. These divisions, moving on interior lines of communication, could reach any part of the Atlantic coast within a day or two, and thereafter an excellent railway system would continuously supply them. The Allies, on the other hand, would take many days to bring any equivalent army across the Channel and put it ashore. That army's supplies would all have to arrive by sea transport and would almost certainly have to be put ashore with most inadequate docking facilities, for it was clearly improbable that the Allies would capture any port intact, and if not, it would be impossible to land anything like the quantity of supplies that the Germans could bring up by rail. If by chance the German army failed to

---

[1]Murray Peden, *A Thousand Shall Fall* (Toronto: Stoddart, 1988), 425-26.

neutralise the Allies as they straggled ashore, then there would be the problem of holding and breaking out of the beachhead, surrounded as it would be by an iron ring of Panzer divisions.

This assessment of the situation was exact in all particulars except one: it overlooked the existence of a heavy bomber force. It might have been expected the German leadership would make this mistake. The Allied bombers had so far confined themselves solely to strategic bombing and had never yet been successfully deployed in a tactical role. Very occasionally, Bomber Command had attacked small targets like Peenemünde, but by far the greater part of its efforts had been directed against large industrial cities. Furthermore, previous experience had shown that the RAF's inadequately armed heavy bombers could not operate by day in the face of any serious opposition, and could not hit small targets by night except when the opposition was negligible and weather conditions exceptionally good. Despite reservations about this new role, mainly over the ability of heavy bombers to surgically hit the many small targets allocated without collateral killing too many friendly civilians, late March 1944 marked the opening of a new phase in Bomber Command's war.

Henceforward the heavy bombers were to be switched to targets closer to home. From time to time the Command revisited German cities and industry, if only to ensure that the Germans retained their home-based night fighter force in place, rather than moving it westward. The main targets were rail centres in France and Belgium, with a view to isolating the German forces in Normandy and deny them any form of rail-born reinforcement. The challenge was to paralyse the entire railway system of north-west Europe, from the Rhine to Normandy. This area had been secretly selected for the invasion. Seventy-nine railway centres were targeted, each of which included adjoining repair shops and depots containing the necessary material needed to repair the damaged marshalling yards.[1] The plan was to select aiming points in such a way that an effective concentration of bombing would destroy or severely damage the repair centres. If railway yards and rolling stock were damaged as well, as it inevitably would be, this would be all to the good. The enemy would then have an abundance of repair work while being deprived of the means to do so.

There were also raids on Luftwaffe fighter airfields on the Continent, military bases, ammunition depots and armament factories in France and Belgium. Then there was the Atlantic Wall, a ring of strong fortifications along great stretches of the north European coastline, including very long-range radar-sighted gun batteries that could sink any warships whose guns were out of range to retaliate, so, just prior the invasion, radio and radar

[1] 37 of these targets were attacked by RAF Bomber Command, while the remaining 42 were allotted to the US 8 and 15 Air Forces and various Allied medium bomber and fighter-bomber units.

stations and these coastal gun batteries had to be destroyed. Meanwhile, one aspect of the plan, of which the bomber crews were unaware, involved deception operations to persuade the Germans that the main landing would be in the Pas-de-Calais area, some 100 kilometres further up the coast from Normandy. For every bomb dropped on the railway system leading to Normandy, almost as many bombs were dropped further north. This deception plan was initiated months earlier by means of spurious army radio traffic and false information revealed through double agents to the Germans. Lastly, cities in Germany were attacked, but only during the most favourable of conditions, to avoid a disaster on a scale of Nürnberg.

Before taking part in this new phase in operations, Teddy and his crew performed two daylight cross-country training flights on April 3 and 4, 1944. The crew received no rest at a bomber station, and a pattern was established for them on days when they were not scheduled for operations. If they were not burdened with ground duties, they would be conducting air tests, practising standard beam approaches and Gee homing, circuit work, fighter affiliation exercises or bombing practice at the local range. After such daylight training flights, Teddy spent a quiet evening in the officers' mess, and on April 3 found time to write to his parents:

> Came back from leave the other day. I spent three days in London and saw a couple of shows and three movies. I went with Larry Allen my navigator, who seems to know London inside out. He took me to some very nice little restaurants in Soho where we had some first class meals. Spent the rest of the time with Uncle Max and Aunt Yetta and filled in a bit of time sawing wood! Gerald and Ann were both home, the former doesn't seem to know what's going to happen to him but it doesn't appear likely he will go to Canada.
>
> I've done two operations on my second tour, Stuttgart and Nürnburg. They don't seem as hard as I had expected. My crew is a very good one and I think we're going to be able to do a first class job. I hope to do at least 30 more trips and possibly another 15 or more after that if they'll allow me. After all, this is what I joined up for in the first place so I may as well get a good whack in while I can.
>
> Have been feeling very well lately and seem to have a pretty good appetite. Should be putting on weight. Oh, I have plenty of vitamin tablets now, and shan't need any more now that summer is coming along. The cakes are wonderful and two parcels of Dad's cookies sent some time ago were awfully good and arrived in first class condition.
>
> Your letters are arriving very regularly Dad, though Mother's are a bit scarce. Glad to hear Mother was home for a while and that you both took a bit of a holiday.

After a couple of additional cross-country training missions on April 7 and 8, Teddy and his crew were posted again in the battle order for the night of

April 9-10. The target was a goods station in the French city of Lille, close to the Belgian border. Only 239 aircraft were despatched for the mission, including 40 Lancasters, seven from 405 Squadron. Teddy's crew was one of the supporters in the pathfinder formation, and 'S-for-Sugar' was scheduled to deliver 13,000lb of bombs on the rail station. It was a very short and uneventful mission, flown in broad moonlight. After a mere two hours and 40 minutes the Blenkinsop crew safely returned to base. Only one Lancaster was lost on the raid, and from Bomber Command's viewpoint, the raid was a success. Many bombs hit their target and caused much damage to buildings and tracks. The majority of the 3,000 goods wagons in the yards were destroyed. Unfortunately, many of the bombs fell outside the railway yards resulting in the deaths of more than 450 French civilians, while 5,000 houses were destroyed. The days following the raid, inhabitants of Lille and its suburbs became very resentful towards the British, as this intense bombing left many feeling they were living their last moments. This was without a doubt the saddest aspect of the raids in France and Belgium. However dedicated the crews and however accurate the bombing, reports such as these would continue to demonstrate that many civilians from occupied countries, who had already endured many years of German oppression, would die by Allied bombs and never live to see the liberation of their homeland. In certain Allied command circles there was unremitting opposition towards the pre-invasion bombing campaign, based on fears it would turn the French and Belgian population against the Allies.

The first attacks on the railway centres were made using old tactics. Pathfinder Mosquitos and Lancasters flying at great height, as in previous attacks on German cities, laid out position markers, but the main force crews were expressly forbidden to bomb if they could not clearly see the markers, a very necessary precaution in order to avoid civilian casualties to the maximum extent possible. Still, the required accuracy was not attained, and before long a master bomber was dispatched in every raid. It was his business to check the position of the markers and to direct the main force to bomb only the most accurately placed markers. On top of that, the master bomber was also to mark the target himself after identifying it visually. Fortunately, most of the railway centres in France and Belgium were defended by only a few anti-aircraft guns, allowing the heavy bombers to attack from a lower than normal altitude. This of course made for increased bombing accuracy with the bomb craters often overlapping each other in the target area. At the same time, Bomber Command's frontline strength continued to increase, and in 1944 three or four targets could be attacked simultaneously.

On April 10 at Gransden Lodge, 405 Squadron was stood down for a Victory Loan drive. On April 11, Teddy's crew was amongst ten from 405 Squadron scheduled for a night op. The target was the German city of

Aachen, and 341 Lancasters were tasked to do the job. Again assigned as supporter, 'S-for-Sugar' carried a full bomb load to the city, and returned to base unharmed after a three-hour-and-20 minute round trip. The crew had seen the odd night fighter, but they kept their distance. Due to the shorter than normal distance to the targets – Aachen is situated very close to the Belgian border – the missions to Lille and Aachen were counted as one operational mission towards the number of missions needed for a tour.

On April 12, the squadron was again stood down, this time for a party and dance that was held to support the Victory Loan campaign. The RCAF Overseas Headquarters' band supplied the music. The following day, Teddy took his crew on a four-hour training flight involving some simulated bombing attacks. The crew was then left alone and they lay about the mess for the subsequent four days, but on April 18 their next mission was announced. That night, four different railway marshalling yards in France were attacked in separate raids: Rouen, Juvisy, Noisy-le-Sec and Tergnier. The Blenkinsop crew was one of 24 Lancasters that accompanied 139 Halifaxes and eight Mosquitos to Tergnier. They took off shortly before 10:00 p.m. for what was to be a three-hour round trip. Teddy did not act as supporter this time but as a visual backer-up. Their task was to estimate the mean point of impact of all the primary marker crews and then drop their TIs visually on this point. Besides the TIs, Teddy's Lancaster also carried eight 1,000lb bombs. Pathfinder aircraft always carried their allocated quantity of TIs and completed their load with bombs, so on completion of their marker drop they continued on past the target, then turned and carefully re-entered the stream to release their bomb load over the target. The raid destroyed 50 railway lines, but six Halifaxes did not return due to night fighter and flak opposition. For the first time since the start of their tour with 405 Squadron, Teddy and his crew had a close encounter with a very proficient air defence system. Upon leaving the target area, Hugh Clifford suddenly alerted the crew that an enemy night fighter was closing in on them. His words had scarcely been uttered when the Luftwaffe intruder opened fire. The dull rattle of Les and Hugh's Browning machine guns was heard through the intercom, while Teddy instinctively started a violent corkscrew manoeuvre. David, Larry, James and Bob were thrown off their respective positions, grabbing hold of anything they could to withstand the alternating increased G-forces and weightlessness. After a period of controlled fear that seemed to last for ages, Hugh called that the fighter seemed to have disappeared. Such was the intercom discipline that there was no more comment about the fighter until they reached home base at Gransden Lodge, although every one realised that it had been a very close call.

As PFF crews grew more efficient, they became eligible for a promotion to more demanding marking duties. The next step after supporters was usually the role of backers-up. As the crew gained experience – i.e., survived – they became visual markers or blind marker-illuminators, progressing to primary visual markers or primary blind markers. At the highest level of the hierarchy were those of exceptional flying and leadership abilities, the deputy master bomber and master bomber. These were mostly second-tour crews. Needless to say, exceptional proficiency standards had to be achieved before any crew could qualify for these demanding assignments.[1]

The Blenkinsop crew's star was rapidly ascending, and for their next operation, on April 20, squadron senior leadership had a choice assignment for them. They were selected as one of only two visual marker crews in a force of 14 pathfinders, all from 405 Squadron, that were going to lead a raid on the railway yards at Lens. Wing Commander Reg Lane was the master bomber for this attack, while main force was made up of 154 Halifaxes. Seven PFF Mosquitos would open the raid using a low-level marking technique.

Visual markers actually were at the top of the pathfinder crew assignment hierarchy. They were the most experienced crews and had to identify and then mark the aiming point visually. No matter how much flying time a PFF crew had logged, they might never achieve the position of visual marker if its bomb aimer did not possess exceptional talents for night vision and concentration. David Ramsay qualified both as an H2S-radar blind marker and as a visual marker, and his skill and application quickly propelled him into the top tier of bomb aimers in 405 Squadron.

The Blenkinsop crew took off in 'S-for-Sugar' at 09:53 p.m. The raid to Lens went very well. The railway yards were bombed, with particular damage to the locomotive sheds and repair workshops. Teddy flew five consecutive runs over the target until he was satisfied with the identification of the aiming point. However, none of the PFF Lancasters had to use their target indicators, and Teddy ended up releasing his bomb load dead on the TIs that had been accurately placed by the Mosquitos. He landed back at Gransden at precisely 01:00 a.m., and was happy to learn that all 405 Squadron aircraft had made it back unharmed. Once again, Teddy's crew had done an excellent job, and he received compliments from both Wing Commander Lane and Squadron Leader Bennett, who had been the other visual marker on the raid. Tergnier and Lens counted for one op, so Teddy now had a total of 34 operations, and more than 1,100 flying hours.

Before the briefing for the Lens mission on April 20, Teddy found time to drop a line to his parents. Sounding upbeat and assertive as ever, little did he realise that it would be the last letter he would ever write to his

---

[1]Squadron Leader H.W. 'Jimmy' Trilsbach generously supplied nearly all of the technical details about pathfinder tactics and techniques in several letters to the author during the period 1988-1991. He was a former OC 'A' Flight of 405 Squadron. Jimmy completed 55 pathfinder ops – six as a master bomber – and he and his crew were one of the most experienced pathfinder crews in the history of 405 Squadron. Following a long illness, Jimmy passed away on February 3, 1991.

family in Victoria:

> Dear Family,
> Well, it seems some time since I last wrote but there's really very little news for you. We've bought a car for the crew and manage to get about the local countryside and into town once or twice a week, it makes a very nice change. We've been going out fairly regularly lately and I daresay you can assume I've been on all the big raids since the end of last month. The crew is shaping up wonderfully and I'm really very proud of them, good workers and very cool. We were in a bit of trouble the other night as a matter of fact, and they behaved wonderfully, speaking calmly and quietly as though we were at a garden party, yet everyone of us was pretty damned scared. It's funny, you know, when you're in a cold sweat and your tummy is slowly squeezing itself to death how you can speak and behave as though everything is quite normal, though I expect you've gone through that a great many times, Dad. Anyway, nothing happened to us much to our surprise and we're a much better crew in a way than we were before – we have perfect confidence in each other. Oh, I have a bit of news for you, it seems I've been awarded the DFC, God only knows why. Anyway, it's nice to know they think I've done a fairly good job.
>
> Well, guess that's about all for now. Going on leave with Helen in a couple of weeks and am looking forward to it. Don't worry about me, everything is going wonderfully. Teddy.

As it happened, somewhere in late March the four officers of the crew, Teddy, Larry Allen, David Ramsay and Bob Booth, had bought a second-hand Ford with 10 horsepower. The car was registered and insured in Larry's name. Larry, affectionately called 'Sea-level Allen' by his buddies due to his small build, was the evident choice for holding administrative responsibilities. He was meticulous, intelligent, and above all, well organised. Teddy, David and Bob had permission to drive the car and shared ownership with Larry. Obviously, all seven men of the crew greatly benefited from this means of self-sufficient transportation.

The citation for Teddy's DFC read: 'This officer has completed many successful operations against the enemy in which he has displayed high skill, fortitude and devotion to duty.' The award was effective on April 11, 1944, and had been awarded to him because of his stand-out performance while serving with 425 Squadron in North Africa. The news of Teddy's award had not gone unnoticed by his family in England. On April 21, Aunt Lucy wrote a letter to her brother Hubert:

> My Dear Toby,
> I enclose a page of today's *Times*, with the notice of Teddy's award of the Distinguished Flying Cross. It is grand news, and we are so glad and proud. If absolute concentration on the job and keenness and

> complete disregard of danger have anything to do with these awards, he has earned his over and over again.
>
> He wrote to Yetta two days ago to say he would be getting leave early next month and would like to spend part of it with Helen at Woodland Grange; that is about all the news we have had of him lately, except that he is busy and happy – he can't be busy enough to satisfy himself and would like to be on the job without a break. I really believe he feels like that, and resents any idea of leisure, which he interprets as slackness. But, you know, the powers that be must have assessed the nervous strain on these youngsters pretty accurately, and decided just what intervals off work are necessary to keep them in good trim both physically and mentally.

Bomber Command was more successful in attacking the small, sensitive targets in France and Belgium than anyone could ever have ever imagined. The use of a master bomber became a standard feature on these raids, where astray bombing had to be avoided. The net result of the various new marking techniques and the use of a master bomber, was that the efficiency of night bombing in April 1944 rose to the point where 200 or 300 Halifaxes and Lancasters could do the pulverising damage to the vital area of a target that a force of close to 1,000 had been required to do earlier in the war. The bomber crews were dedicated and delighted to be associated with the invasion of Europe. Furthermore, they were happy to be attacking military objectives rather than targets within German built-up areas.

Still, shortly after the Lens raid, the high command decided to turn its attention to the German homeland again. A minor attack on the city of Cologne had been the forerunner on the night of April 21, 1944, but an old-style all-out raid was staged on the city of Düsseldorf on the night of April 22. Teddy's name was one of the seven chalked up on 405 Squadron's operations roster, and this time he was again allotted the task of visual backer-up. The raid involved nearly 600 bomber aircraft, including several pathfinder squadrons. The strike caused widespread destruction of large industrial premises, but a serious situation developed when German night fighters penetrated the bomber stream, resulting in 16 Halifaxes and 13 Lancasters being shot down. All but one 405 Squadron aircraft returned safely home that night; Pilot Officer Saltzberry and his crew were missing after a parallel raid to railway yards at Lâon. The master bomber on that mission, Wing Commander Cousens of 635 Squadron, was also shot down.

The Blenkinsop crew had one night's rest and then flew on ops again on April 24. They were detailed to assist in a raid on the German city of Karlsruhe in southern Germany. Once again their assignment was the one of visual backer-up, amid a total of 637 bomber aircraft, the majority being Lancasters. The raid was not a big success. They experienced icing, freezing rain and St. Elmo's fire on the way to the target. Clouds and strong winds blew the marking pathfinder's aircraft far off track, resulting in only the northern part of the city being damaged. Furthermore, aircraft that failed to find the main target hit several German cities to the north of Karlsruhe. To add to the failure, 19 'heavies' were lost on this mission. Teddy put 'S-for-Sugar' safely down at Gransden after a five-hour-and-20 minute foray. This was his 36th mission.

Deputy Master Bomber

With the invasion of Europe now less than six weeks away, the softening-up campaign of the French-Belgian transport system was intensified. On the night of April 26, 1944, over 900 bomber aircraft attacked three different targets: the important German industrial cities of Essen and Schweinfurt and the major French railway centre of Villeneuve-St.-Georges near Paris. Teddy and his crew were part of six 405 Squadron aircraft detailed for the latter attack, that is to say, they were assigned as a key player for the mission. While Squadron Leader Gordon Bennett was again tasked as master bomber, the role of deputy master bomber was entrusted to Ted Blenkinsop. This was an exciting time for the crew. In less than a month and after a mere seven operational pathfinder sorties, they had risen to one of the two top jobs in Bomber Command. The progression and completion of the raid was going to be largely in their hands. 405 Squadron's commanding officer, the then Wing Commander Reginald Lane, remembers the occasion well: 'Edward Blenkinsop had had a fair amount of experience and this was very quickly evident in the way in which he and his crew operated. They progressed rapidly to the point, I made him a deputy master bomber and had him in mind to take over the squadron from me. I was very impressed.'[1]

And so the skill and proficiency of the Blenkinsop crew was being recognised. The job of deputy master bomber required much courage, clear judgement and flexibility to make adjustments. Only the most experienced crews and consequently the most senior were picked for this specialised task. When bombing under the direction of a master bomber, release altitudes were much lower; consequently the associated risks were greater. Master bomber crews quite often became casualties, as they remained flying over the target area throughout the entire raid, sometimes for over 40 minutes. Hence the raison d'être of a deputy master bomber: he was to take over and direct the raid in case the master of ceremonies was shot down.

The relatively new H2S equipment had its shortcomings, both technically and operationally. Even when a set was working well, it took skill to interpret the images on the screen. A tremendous amount of concentration was required to keep moving from one identified feature to the next. Away from coastlines, the task was almost impossible without very close coordination between plotter and set operator, and these two

[1]Letter from Lieutenant-General Reginald Lane to the author, August 6, 1987.

members of Teddy's crew worked exceptionally well together. Larry and David were golden, and their successful cooperation and unmistakable individual talents were certainly a major factor in the selection of the Blenkinsop crew to be assigned as a deputy master bomber.

However, a deputy master bomber crew on each trip carried an extra crewmember, an experienced bomb aimer. This visual bomb aimer took position in the nose of the aircraft, from where he supported the pilot and navigator with visual identification of landmarks or aiming points. In addition, he was an extra pair of eyes to help the aircraft captain in assessing the progress of the raid, and the positioning or regrouping of the TIs as required. The Blenkinsop crew had just the man for this job, Flight Lieutenant David Ramsay, DFC. But his switch to visual bomb aimer meant that the crew was in need of a new set operator. He was found in the person of Flight Lieutenant George Smith, who had recently finished a first tour in a main force bomber squadron before being posted to 405 Squadron.

George John Smith was born on June 22, 1918, at Verwood, Saskatchewan. His parents Paul and Ann, both of Russian descent, had immigrated to Canada in 1906. There they set up a farm and raised a family in a hardworking and Christian home. Farm life in central Canada was tough and all had their chores to do, but George spent a happy childhood with his five brothers and one sister. The Smith farm was a lively place, where lots of local young people would come out to swim and play ball. Mother Smith always had plenty to eat and drink for everyone, including homemade ice cream. After his schooling years, George spent two years on his father's farm before taking a job as a country telephone lineman. A year later he became a truck driver. After work, he enjoyed playing in the local music band.

On July 8, 1941, George enlisted in the Canadian air force and volunteered for pilot training. He passed the medical exams and was accepted, ending up at 5 Elementary Flying School at High River, Alberta, in January 1942. He moved on to 12 Service Flying Training School at Brandon, Manitoba, in May 1942, but ceased training after two months. He was reinstated as a bomb aimer, training at 7 Bombing and Gunnery School at Paulson, Manitoba, and then proceeded to 5 Air Observer School in Winnipeg. On December 4, 1942, he proudly received his air bomber badge and officer's commission, serial number J-21564.

Shortly before sailing overseas in early January 1943, George married Audrey, a girl from the small neighbouring town called Willows. Audrey fell in love with George's kind, lovable, generous and thoughtful personality. After spending the required months in a personnel reception centre and operational training unit, George was transferred to 432 Squadron RCAF, stationed at Skipton-on-Swale in Yorkshire. However, upon arriving there in September 1943, he developed an acute appendicitis and peritonitis and became dangerously ill. He was hospitalised for six days, but he recovered and was again declared fit for flying duties. He immediately rejoined his unit, which recently had moved to East Moor. He joined the crew of Pilot Officer Bill Meaden, with whom he completed 30 operations over occupied Europe. The crew had a narrow escape on the night of January 27, 1944, when a German Messerschmitt Bf 110 attacked their Lancaster II.[1] Upon completion of their tour, the crew was given a rest doing instructional duties. George, however, volunteered for an immediate second tour, hoping to go home for good to his Audrey after the tour. His exceptional skill as an air bomber and H2S set operator secured him a posting to pathfinders, and he ended up with 405 (PFF) Squadron in March 1944. There he met up with several of his old 432 Squadron buddies, including Hugh Clifford. Teddy Blenkinsop and his crewmates welcomed him as their new set operator and he joined the team able and ready to do the job of deputy master bomber.

The raid to Villeneuve-St.-Georges progressed nicely. There were no clouds and visibility was good in the target area. This allowed pretty accurate Newhaven marking and bombing from a relatively low altitude of 6,000 feet. Cooperation between the master bomber, Squadron Leader Bennett, and his deputy, Teddy Blenkinsop, went extremely well. On one of the runs over the target, Teddy dropped illuminator flares for Bennett, as his own bombsight had gone unserviceable. This flawlessly coordinated effort allowed Bennett to accurately pinpoint the aiming point. Immediately after this, Teddy started circling the target, and radioed to the main force where to bomb in relation to the target indicators. The returning crews claimed that the southern end of the railway yards was successfully bombed. Only one Halifax failed to return.

The performance of the Blenkinsop crew won great approval from their superiors. In fact, upon their return to the squadron ops room at about 03:00 a.m., Teddy was asked to prepare for a new mission the following night. Instead of getting the customary 24 hours off ops duty, the crew would have to be ready for briefing again in about 12 hours. Teddy sent his men to the mess for their well-deserved treat of operational crews, a fried egg for breakfast, and a bottle of beer. He asked everyone to 'hit the sack' as soon as possible thereafter. Although the flight had lasted only a little over four hours, master bomber duties were proving to be an exhausting and demanding business.

---

[1]Pilot Officer William H. Meaden was awarded the Distinguished Flying Cross in June 1944. The citation read: 'This officer has shown an unconquerable spirit of determination to achieve his objective. The majority of his many operational sorties have been over heavily defended areas, including five against Berlin, and his coolness and his unusual initiative have won him the respect of his crew and the whole squadron. For his exceptional qualities of leadership, for his coolness in face of danger, for his spirit of determination and devotion to duty, this officer is strongly recommended for the award of the Distinguished Flying Cross.' Bill Meaden died in Toronto on May 3, 2000.

CHAPTER NINE

Disaster over Montzen

Upon showing up in time for lunch on April 27, 1944, the Blenkinsop crew received some heartening news. Larry Allen had been awarded the Distinguished Flying Cross, bringing the total of DFCs for the crew to three. Larry's work as a navigation leader in 420 Squadron had not gone unnoticed, and he felt quite pleased with the news. The others in the crew shared his pleasure and got a lift from Larry's decoration. Morale in the Blenkinsop crew had now just about reached its zenith. Teddy mused at how this exceptional crew had come together to emerge as though from some mystique of chance. The crew's combined prestige had risen abruptly in the squadron and everyone was rather pleased with the job done during the past four weeks. All eight of them genuinely believed that they would make it through unscathed. Although the average survival expectancy for an RAF heavy bomber crew still did not exceed 50 per cent, 405 Squadron had lost only one aircraft during the 96 operational sorties flown hitherto in the month of April 1944. Inspired by the knowledge that an invasion of Europe was imminent, the general atmosphere in the squadron was one of quiet enthusiasm. Still, levelheaded as they were, Teddy and his crewmates realised that it was not over yet. Daily intelligence reports clearly showed that the Luftwaffe was still a formidable threat.

After lunch, the crew hitched a ride to the flight line to check out their aircraft. Seated in the cockpit of 'S-for-Sugar', Teddy listened attentively as the rest of the crew reported in on their various safety checks. He had already run up each of the four powerful engines to see if they were producing the necessary boost and the required 3,000 rpm. He acknowledged his approval as the aircraft was checked out from 'stem to gudgeon': three turrets operating, radio loud and clear, oxygen feeding properly, DR compass and P.4 compass synchronised, bombsight functioning; bomb doors and flaps, trimming tabs, special navigational instruments – all okay. Satisfied, he shut down the four powerful Merlins and consulted his watch – plenty of time for a nap before briefing. Takeoff time was around midnight.

Bomber Command's main targets for this night were important Panzer engine and gearbox factories near the relatively small city of Friedrichshafen in southern Germany. This attacking force consisted of 322 Lancasters and a single Mosquito. The timing of two other attacks, both against railway yards, was coordinated to keep the expected Luftwaffe prowlers west of the German frontier and as far away as possible from Friedrichshafen. In these raids, 144 aircraft were bombing an important marshalling yard on the Antwerp-Aachen rail line at the Belgian border town of Montzen near Aachen. In addition, 223 aircraft were tasked to attack a railway centre at Aulnoye in Northern France. To confuse the German defences even more, a fourth stream of 159 OTU aircraft carried out a diversionary sweep over the North Sea towards Jutland, the homeward turn of which began with a short dogleg towards the Ems Estuary. To draw the night fighters away from the bomber streams, extensive intruder and bomber support operations were also scheduled. Twenty-five Mosquito night fighters of 100 (Bomber Support) Group fulfilled the task of hunting for German night fighters near the bombers' routing, using a device called Serrate. This equipment could pick up the radar emissions of the Luftwaffe fighters.[1]

When Teddy and his crew, still a bit tired from the previous night, attended the late afternoon mission briefing, they were quite pleased to see that they were one of only eight pathfinder crews planned for the secondary Montzen raid. Six other crews of the squadron had to lead the main bomber force to Friedrichshafen, along a drawn out route taking them all over France and deep into the Reich. The trip to Montzen was calculated to take a little over three-and–a-half hours, taking into account the extra time spent over the target during the master bomber orbits. This time Wing Commander Lane was taking on the job of master bomber, relying on Teddy as his deputy. Both these crews would also act as visual markers. The remainder of the 405 Squadron crews assigned to Montzen had the task of illuminators. The vast railway yards would be easily detected and the route to the target was relatively short; this was going to be a 'milk run' or, as crews would often say, 'a piece of cake'.[2] However, the met man on one hand and the intelligence officer on the other offered two causes of concern. It was going to be a clear and moonlit night, which made the flight to Friedrichshafen potentially very dangerous. The recent Nürnberg catastrophe had taken place in similar conditions less than a month earlier but Friedrichshafen was further south and on the limit of German night fighters' effective range. On the other hand, Montzen and

[1]Two 239 Squadron Mosquito crews had confirmed claims on German night fighters. Flying Officer Pepper and Flying Officer Follis claimed one Me 110 and one Ju 88 destroyed, while Flight Lieutenant Reeves and Warrant Officer O'Leary claimed one Me 110 destroyed. One 141 Squadron Mosquito did not return. Its experienced crew, Squadron Leader Vic Lovell, DFC, and Bob Lilley, DFC, was missing in action.

[2]This expression originated in the late 1930s in the RAF and was used amongst pilots to describe an easy mission.

Aulnoye were much closer to the Luftwaffe night fighter lairs in Belgium and Holland. It was not to be discounted that one of these raids would be detected and attacked in the moonlight by a formidable and concentrated German night fighter force. Still, this did not throw the Blenkinsop crew off stride. Lighthearted, they departed their various briefings and went to the mess to eat dinner and kill the remaining time before the mission was on.

The hard-fought battle between Bomber Command and the German night fighter defences was now nearing its climax. The effectiveness of the German night fighter defence had increased steadily during the 12 preceding months. Their tactics had evolved to the point where the highly competent German pilots were ordered to pursue the raiders to the limit of their fuel endurance. They engaged the enemy bombers on contact and only broke off offensive action when their fuel had almost run out. Any losses, due to their fighter aircraft running out of fuel, were a risk their pilots and commanders were prepared to take. This was their equivalent of the Battle of Britain. They fought to defend their homes and loved ones with the same reckless intensity born out of desperation that their British counterparts had displayed in 1940. They did not suffer from want of practice, and all too many of them had become past masters of their deadly art. Moreover, the Germans began to extend the network of beacons, which already covered most of Germany and served as an assembly point for night fighters into France and Belgium. The night fighters themselves were also brought up in large numbers to bases in this forward area until there was a large enough force that could be locally controlled for operations close to their bases. Before long Bomber Command's casualty rate began to rise. Still, whatever happened, they had to go on raiding targets in the same comparatively small area, now with little chance of confusing the night fighters by widely dispersed attacks. Meanwhile, the introduction of the SN-2 Naxos night fighter radar set, which was able to see through the 'smokescreen' of Window, provided the Luftwaffe with an additional advantage in the spring of 1944. For the moment the only effective countermeasure that could be devised was to make the attacks extremely short. A number of separate forces, each usually consisting of a single bomber group, were sent to attack different targets simultaneously.[1]

The two main radar devices in the German defensive network were their long-range detectors, the Freyas, with a range of about 150 kilometres, and the much more sensitive and accurate Giant Würzburgs. The latter had an effective range of about 15 kilometres and fed accurate information on

---

[1]Up to the end of June 1944, Bomber Command carried out 13,349 sorties against the railways of north-west Europe, dropping 52,347 tons of bombs, with a casualty rate of 2.6 per cent. This 2.6 per cent is the average for four months of operations. Casualties were low at first, but steadily increased as the enemy began to appreciate what the Allies were up to and what it would mean to him.

numbers of approaching aircraft, course and altitude, to the German ground controllers and the flak and searchlight defences. The coastline Freya early warning radars enabled the German defences to be alerted as soon as the first of the RAF bombers began circling for height over bases in England. Thus, long before the main force reached the enemy coast, the defenders were making their initial dispositions and preparing to strike the bomber streams with all the force they could muster. The night fighters were guided to the vicinity of the early arrivals, after which it became just a matter of opportunity in selecting their prey – a bomber aircraft. The need for all bombers to be on target within about a 10-12 minute period was simply to saturate the German ground defences. Being too early or too late was not a good idea.

The first aircraft to leave Gransden Lodge that Thursday evening of April 27 were the six leaders of the Friedrichshafen force. They took off at around 10:30 p.m. A crewmember of one of these six Lancasters later noted in his diary:

> Took off at 10:30 and away six of us went in a fairly bright moon. Didn't see a thing 'till around Strasbourg when the fighters came up and took quite a slice out of our numbers. At one time there we saw six kites go down in about three minutes. There was tracer flying all around but we got past without an interception, although Taffy thought that a Ju 88 was after us for a while. H2S was working well and as blind marker illuminator we had no trouble getting there at Zero minus 5. Bombed three seconds early from 18,000 feet.
>
> The target looked vicious running in. The place was thick with searchlights weaving all over the sky waiting to all close on some poor kite (which felt like us). But we got through without a scratch and after turning sharply to starboard we got a good view of the target. We could easily see the whole town exposed by the lights of our flares and the place was fairly getting a licking under the direction of the Master of Ceremonies. The town was hit hard but the nearby forests were well away too.
>
> Not much flak over the target but plenty of fighters. Easy trip home.[1]

Indeed, probably even before the main Bomber Command raid against Friedrichshafen crossed the French coast, the German radar controllers reacted to this threat by sending up an estimated 100 twin-engined night fighters. After making landfall on the French coast at Le Havre, the Lancasters were divided between two routes, splitting south of Paris. Meanwhile, the Luftwaffe fighters that had been assembled over north-east France were fed into the inbound target bomber stream in the area of

---

[1]Diary extract of an unknown airman, obtained from Captain Rolland Cright, 405 Squadron historian, in September 1994.

Strasbourg. Aided by the prevailing moonlight, they shot down 14 Lancasters, the first one at 01:19 a.m. 7 Squadron's Wing Commander W.G. Lockhart, DSO, DFC and Bar, and his crew were all killed in the crash at Reichenbach. Several night fighter pilots obtained multiple victories. At 02:20 a.m., the bomber stream withdrew from the Friedrichshafen target, many bombers flying into Swiss airspace. Only a few combats occurred on the homeward leg over northern France, and a total of 18 Lancasters did not return. Fortunately, these high losses had not disrupted the entire operation, and the bombers that reached the target dropped their loads in an outstandingly successful attack based on good pathfinder marking. Several factories were badly damaged and the gearbox plant was completely destroyed.

While the first German night fighters were unleashed to intercept the Friedrichshafen raiders, the Montzen force was taxiing out. At precisely 11:49 p.m., Wing Commander Reg Lane was the first to take off, followed by his seven accompanying squadron crews, those of Squadron Leaders Trilsbach and McDonald, Captain (USAAF) Copenhaver, Pilot Officers Long and O'Connor, and Flying Officer Stronach. Teddy's 'S-for-Sugar' closed the line, lifting off the runway at 00:01 a.m. Other Canadian squadrons – 419, 431, 432 and 434 – dispatched for the raid took off at various other airfields in Yorkshire, while 51, 78 and 640 Squadrons also participated. In total, 120 Halifaxes, 16 Lancasters and eight Mosquitos were setting course inbound the North Sea. The planned route took them from Southwold on the English coast to a point over the North Sea due east of that town. From there, the bomber stream would set course inbound Montzen, a long straight leg of approximately 150 nautical miles (278 km).

However, unknown to the assembling Montzen task force, German night fighter controllers were vigorously on the alert. They now found themselves confronted with four separate bomber streams that were heading for the Reich. The North Sea diversion of 159 OTU aircraft was, quite correctly, assessed as a minelaying operation of minor importance. This led to a concentrated response towards the Montzen and Aulnoye attackers. While one night fighter unit was sent towards the minelaying operation to investigate, two others, Nachtjagdgeschwader 1 and 2, were sent to an assembly area east of Nijmegen. Once the threat of the North Sea diversion was over, they were released for an interception of the Montzen force, which crossed the Dutch coast south of Overflakkee. The night fighters took some time to catch up with the bombers, though, and the spearhead of the Montzen force reached the target without being intercepted.

Wing Commander Lane and his second-in-command, Teddy Blenkinsop, turned up over the huge Montzen marshalling yards at hour zero; 01:24 a.m. The diligent pathfinder Mosquitos had already started red spot fires in the target area one minute earlier, which facilitated recognition. Wing

Commander Lane orbited the target and started to control the raid, while the six illuminator crews dropped their loads of hooded flares from 12,000 feet that illuminated the entire area. Now the marshalling yards were easily visual. Then, in a closely coordinated effort and from a comparatively low altitude of 4,500 feet, Reg Lane and Teddy Blenkinsop began to drop green TIs, backing these up during subsequent runs with white-and-yellow ones. David Ramsay was in the bomb aimer's position in the nose of Teddy's Lancaster. His main function was to assess the accuracy of the TIs and report to Teddy. In addition to the TIs, both leader crews were able to drop their bomb load of three 1,000lb bombs on the target. Meanwhile they were coaching each other and instructing the main force on which colour of TIs to bomb. Lane's broadcast comments, given in his distinctively Canadian accent, contained reinforced directions to the main force crews sprinkled with words of motivation and general encouragements. A few light and heavy flak guns were active in the target area, but there were no searchlights.

However, while the initial stage of the Montzen raid was going on, German night fighters slowly caught up with later waves. While some of the night fighters, which had been held up by the OTU diversion, never reached Montzen in time, others began causing havoc amongst the vulnerable, target-fixated bombers. The first Halifax was shot down at 01:30 a.m., just prior reaching the target. Others followed in the ensuing minutes.

Wing Commander Lane continued to devote most of his efforts to ensure that the main force pressed right on into the target and did not release their bombs prematurely. It was not easy, as main force crews harassed by night fighters were generally not inclined to listen. They just wanted to get out of the target area as quickly as possible. Still, apart from the average number of overshooting and undershooting bomb releases, the attack went very well. Huge fires started burning in the centre of the railway site and the locomotive workshops were severely hit. Nineteen locomotives and 143 wagons were blasted to pieces, and all railroad tracks were damaged or destroyed. With the exception of two signal houses, all buildings on the site were destroyed.[1]

The attack on Montzen ended at 01:44 a.m. Ten of the raiders were downed in the immediate vicinity of the target or shortly after starting their return leg. For the next hour however, the German night fighters would aggressively resist the withdrawal of the Montzen force over the Low Countries, claiming another five victims.[2]

---

[1]Information obtained from the operations record book of 405 Squadron (AIR 27/1789) and from official records held at the Administration Communale de Montzen-Plombières, Belgium. Sadly, 64 Belgian civilians were killed, ten missing and 150 wounded. 410 were left homeless. Up to 4,000 (forced) labourers were put to work to repair the vital marshalling yards, which were back in service on May 11, 1944.

[2]In the end, 15 bombers were lost on the Montzen raid, constituting an appalling 10.6 per cent of the deployed force.

Towards the end of the attack, Wing Commander Lane called Teddy by radio and told him to return home as the raid was nearly over. Teddy eased his Lancaster onto a heading that would take them back across Belgium to the North Sea. Reg Lane stayed over the target a little longer, to make sure that all the main force aircraft had dropped their bombs. He finally left the target area at 01:45 a.m. and found himself far to the rear of the returning bomber gaggle.

Teddy and his crew were quite pleased with their effort over the marshalling yards, but there was no time for contentment as bomber aircraft were going down all over the place. In his logbook, Larry Allen tried to keep track of reports shouted by his crewmates. Aircraft to aircraft firing was seen at one position, while an exploding Halifax was seen at another. David Ramsay was sitting in the nose turret and keeping his eyes continuously scanning, ready to grab the two machine guns if need be. Meanwhile, Hugh Clifford and Les Foster had their hands ready on the butts of their Brownings. And then, less than 25 minutes after leaving the target area, all hell broke loose. As Hugh Clifford shouted a warning, the air around 'S-for-Sugar' was instantly filled with white flaming shells that flashed past with horrifying speed, and the aircraft shuddered heavily with the pounding of a hail of close range cannon fire. Through the back of his seat, Teddy felt a series of staccato blows that jarred him like the strokes of a wild trip hammer. He instinctively thrust the control column forward while twisting the ailerons to initiate a dive into a violent corkscrew, but in the second it took to commence that manoeuvre, 'S-for-Sugar' absorbed heavy punishment from the torrent of shells the Messerschmitt's cannons were able to deliver into its target. A moment later, combustible materials aboard the stricken aircraft ignited, and Lancaster 'S-for-Sugar' became an airborne inferno. The whole attack had lasted only ten seconds.

Wing Commander Lane, flying about ten kilometres behind Teddy, was one of the nearest onlookers of the tragedy. At exactly 02:05 a.m., he suddenly witnessed Teddy's Lancaster explode in the moonlit sky, a horrifying sight he would clearly remember for the rest of his days:

> Soon after leaving the target, the Halifax ahead of me was shot down by a night fighter. Very rapidly other aircraft were shot down as the German night fighters got into the bomber stream with great effectiveness. As each bomber was shot down, I dropped in altitude as I decided I would rather take my chances with the light anti-aircraft defences than the night fighters. About the eighth airplane to be shot down was attacked by a fighter and then it exploded. With the explosion, the red pyrotechnic target markers also blew up, and I knew immediately that it was Teddy Blenkinsop's aircraft, as we were the only two bombers carrying those specific colours. Needless to say, I was shocked as, not only did we lose a very capable bomber captain,

> but also I was beginning to think of Teddy taking over 405 Squadron from me.
>
> On my return, I reported that Teddy had been shot down, and judging from the size of the explosion, that there was absolutely no chance of any survivors.[1]

Reg Lane tried to concentrate on what he had to do. He struggled to shelve his grief and attend to the survival of his own crew but had difficulty remaining detached. The loss of Teddy and his crew was harder to deal with than others because of their mutual hometown roots and his admiration for Teddy. After their return to their various home stations, the grounded airmen awaited their friends' return. They counted the landings and waited in vain for more. Fifteen bombers never showed up, a heavy price for what was supposed to be an easy mission.

At Gransden Lodge, Wing Commander Lane reported to the intelligence officer what he had seen. His rear gunner, Flight Lieutenant Jim Scannell, confirmed the account of his skipper. Their intel report was factual and impartial: '5057N 0507E – 0205 hrs – 10,000 ft – Saw what first thought to be scarecrow fall from 10,000 ft. But two successive explosions followed, as of petrol tanks and 2 TI Reds cascaded at about 3,000 ft. Believed to be 405/S which would have been at this position and is known to have two Red TIs aboard.'[2]

The following day, surviving aircrews tried their best to ignore the empty chairs in the mess hall. All realised the empty spaces would soon be filled with new recruits. Reg Lane found himself faced with the daunting task of writing telegrams and letters to the relatives of the eight Blenkinsop crewmembers, bringing them the dreaded news about their sons. Officially, the crew had not been heard of since over the target area at Montzen. Although there was no doubt in Lane's mind that no one could have survived the violent explosion, he had to follow regulations and report the crew as 'missing in action'. Much to his surprise after the war, he had assumed wrongly. On April 28, Uncle Max was the first to hear about Teddy's misfortune, when he received the following telegram: 'Regret to inform you that your nephew S/L E W Blenkinsop DFC is missing as result of air operations 27/28 April Stop No information should be given to the press – OC 405 RCAF Squadron.'

Max immediately informed his brother of the dreadful news. Hubert also received a telegram from the RCAF casualties officer on May 1, and a few days later a letter arrived written by Wing Commander Lane on April 29. Then a letter followed by the RCAF casualty officer on May 3, 1944. This letter stated that enquiries had been made through the International

---

[1]Letter from Lieutenant-General Lane to the author, May 21, 1989.

[2]Public Records Office AIR 14/3222, London, UK. A 'scarecrow' was an alleged (but non-existent) German pyrotechnic device simulating the destruction of a bomber in the air.

Red Cross Society and all other appropriate sources. The letter also stipulated that Teddy's name was not going to appear on the official casualty list for five weeks and that his parents could release to the press that he was missing, without including the date, place or his unit.

Needless to say, Helen was also devastated when she heard the dreadful news about her fiancé, but she showed her mental strength and personality in a letter to Teddy's parents written on May 3. The letter is a fine illustration of what thousands of nearest and dearest went through after receiving a 'missing' notice:

> I got a letter yesterday from Ted's aunt, giving me the news. It was a very kind, cheerful letter and helped a lot. After the first shock and agony, I found that I was, and am, quite positive that Ted will turn up again sooner or later. I don't know why I have this feeling, whether I am being foolish or not, but the feeling has taken complete and utter possession of me and I can think of nothing else. Trying to reason it out, he is so efficient in everything he does, and that, plus the confidence his crews have in him, I am sure will bring him through this.
>
> I know how you both are feeling and I wish I could be with you and try to help, and give you some of my confidence if I can.
>
> This is a hellish difficult letter to write – can't write any more.
>
> All my love and hope to you both, Helen.

A Formidable Opponent

Before the war, the commander-in-chief of the German air force, Reichsmarshall Hermann Göring, had boasted that no foreign bomber could attack the Fatherland. When Bomber Command began its long and unrelenting night attacks, he soon realised that flak and searchlights alone would not stop the raiders, and he ordered the establishing of a night fighter force. The Germans applied themselves to this task with their usual vigour, and so began the long air battle in which scientists on both sides played an ever-increasing role as they designed device and counterdevice, to help or hinder offence or defence.

Although night fighting had been undertaken in embryonic form way back during the First World War, the German night fighter force, the Nachtjagd, had to virtually start from scratch when British bombers began to attack German targets in 1940. A chain of radar stations, named 'Kammhuber Line' after Generalleutnant Josef Kammhuber, was established across the Reich from Norway to the border of Switzerland. Nearby night fighter wings, Nachtjagdgeschwadern (NJG), were alerted to the presence of the incoming enemy and ground controllers guided the fighters towards an intercept. These fighter wings were equipped for the most part with heavily armed Messerschmitt Bf 110 and Junkers Ju 88 aircraft. Later these aircraft would be fitted with the Lichtenstein nose-mounted radar.

Despite initial problems, in late 1941 Kammhuber had provided such a proficient night fighter force that bomber losses rose to about five per cent. The learning curve in Bomber Command was steep; one of the lessons learned was that one must saturate the German defences by getting the maximum number of bombers through the target area as quickly as possible. This tactic, plus the numerous electronic and technological inventions discussed earlier, combined with the incredible courage of the young men crewing these bombers, gave Bomber Command the required stamina to continue its offensive. But during the winter of 1943-1944 the German night fighter force was so powerful and dangerous that, on 16 major raids against Berlin, bomber losses averaged more than five per cent. Despite all RAF countermeasures to fool the defences, the loosely controlled night fighters not only succeeded in getting into the bomber stream but also sometimes flew across the North Sea to meet the oncoming bombers. Although air gunners performed brilliantly and scored the odd success, they fought an uneven battle. The small-calibre defensive armament in the bombers was no match against the heavy weaponry employed by the Luftwaffe. This lack of effective weaponry, together with the offensive punch of a very sophisticated German air defence system, left the Allied bomber crews very much on their own once over Continental Europe. German night fighter units, flak batteries, communications, radars, monitoring and observation posts and command and control centres were constantly upgraded and interconnected into the various fighter divisions scattered throughout the various regions. The job of the night fighter controller was to fit all the pieces of information together. The controller then broadcast his running commentary from powerful transmitters that were difficult to jam. The German night fighters, whose effectiveness was greatly improved from early years, now displayed a remarkable flexibility that was typical of how the Luftwaffe adapted. The system now enabled fighter units from northern Denmark to be scrambled and then to intercept over southern Germany, before landing at a nearby airfield to refuel and rearm for a second mission.

By early 1944, several expert night fighter units operated from airfields all over Western Europe. The best-known stations, also acknowledged by RAF intelligence officers and bomber crews, were Leeuwarden, Venlo and Twenthe in Holland, St. Trond and Florennes in Belgium, and St. Dizier and Juvincourt in France. These bases housed some of Germany's top-scoring night fighter aces, a number of them highly decorated by the Führer himself. The basic Luftwaffe unit was the Staffel, which was normally made up of nine to 16 aircraft. Three or four Staffeln combined together formed a Gruppe. The officer commanding such a unit was the Gruppenkommandeur. Three, four and occasionally five Gruppen formed a Geschwader or Wing, headed by a Geschwaderkommodore.

On the night of April 27, 1944, around 200 Luftwaffe night fighters were deployed against the OTU diversion and the Montzen raid, few of which managed to make contact with the bombers. However, the Montzen raiders had the misfortune that several aces of Nachtjagdgeschwader 1 (NJG 1), who had gathered for a meeting at St. Trond the previous day, were scrambled against the attack. The airfield of St. Trond, home station of the leading IVth Gruppe of NJG 1 (IV./NJG 1), lay directly beneath the return path of the Montzen bombers. All crews of this unit were equipped with the latest SN-2-equipped Messerschmitt Bf 110G night fighters. Twenty-two-year-old Oberleutnant Heinz Schnaufer, the recently appointed Kommandeur of IV./NJG 1, took off from St. Trond at 01:07 a.m.[1] He was the first to catch one of the Montzen raiders, a 434 Squadron Halifax, which he sent down in flames with one burst of gunfire at 01:30 a.m. At the end of the war, Schnaufer's official tally stood at 121 victories obtained in just 164 combat missions. His victory total includes 114 RAF four-engine bombers, arguably accounting for more RAF casualties than any other Luftwaffe ace.[2]

Oberleutnant Hermann Greiner, Staffelkapitän of the 11th Staffel of NJG 1 (11./NJG 1), scored two victories during the Montzen raid. He recounted:

> I can still vividly remember my sortie on this night, not because I would be able to consult my flying log book and notes (these were destroyed in a fire during a British night raid on St. Dizier airfield), but because the circumstances of both my own sortie and the RAF raid fell outside the normal scope.
>
> My crew and I were off duty on the evening of April 27. Therefore, I was not at the Nachtjagd Operations Room, but was enjoying myself with my comrades and German girlfriends in the mess of IV Gruppe at St. Trond. Nevertheless, I had instructed the Operations Officer to inform me by telephone if and when any RAF incursions were reported, against which the crews on alert of IV Gruppe would be scrambled. As it happened, I was woken up just after midnight, because incoming bombers had been reported in the area of Brussels, St. Trond and Liège, and I became airborne at around 01:00 a.m. on April 28. As usual, I climbed to operational height, in this case whilst flying in large curves as I did not know the situation in the air and was only informed on general British incursions in the area. I did not observe any of the usual combat activity, such as flak fire, air combats,

---

[1]Letter from Schnaufer's radio operator Fritz Rumpelhardt to the author, January 23, 1989.

[2]Schnaufer was the top night fighter ace of all time and one of the most highly decorated German soldiers. He was taken prisoner by the British in May 1945 but released later that year and returned home to take over the family wine business, his father having died in 1940. His end came when, during a wine-purchasing visit to France, his open sports car collided with a lorry on the main road south from Bordeaux. Schnaufer died in hospital two days later, on July 15, 1950.

aircraft going down and exploding on the ground, light bombs or marker bombs or munitions exploding. It really appeared as if nothing was wrong and I already suspected false alarm or overstated reports, when, all of a sudden, I saw an aircraft crossing my path about 100 metres above me. I was able to get a good visual on the aircraft, without the use of our on-board radar. I had no difficulty getting into a shooting position – some ten to 15 metres directly below the enemy aircraft – because the Lancaster was not weaving, was flying on a steady course, and the rear gunner did not react to my presence.

My 'attack tactic' was always the same; from my position directly below the aircraft, I pulled up the nose of my machine slightly and then, almost invariably, fired one burst into the fuel tanks between the two left-hand engines. (I had a compulsive hesitation to fire into the fuselage of the enemy bomber, and did not do this a single time during any of my 51 victories). Because one does not consciously dive down together with the burning enemy aircraft, but retains one's flying height, only little details could be observed after this point. In this case, I can still remember that I saw tracer ammunition exploding inside the bomber after the fire in the aircraft had increased, but I was unable to observe any members of the bomber crew baling out. If one still had the time, one did register the point of impact of the adversary for the combat report, as many a fire (experienced by myself!) was extinguished after a while.

Only a little later, I caught a Halifax in the same manner, but this time, at least, I knew the approximate heading and height of the bombers.[1]

The attack tactic described by Hermann Greiner, known by the night fighter pilots as the 'von unten hinten' (from below and aft) attack, was a common routine to surprise a night bomber. After having picked up the enemy aircraft on the on-board radar, the night fighter approached it from behind until within visual range. Then, the night fighter descended about 1,500 feet while still closing in on its quarry, thereby aiming to stay out of the cone of fire of the bomber's rear gunner. When the night fighter was in a position where the bomber was inside the lethal range of its cannons, the pilot pulled the nose up sharply, and aimed its nose-mounted cannons at the bomber's fuselage or wing fuel tanks. The rear gunner and the bomb bay were particularly vulnerable to the devastating firepower of the night fighter, and more often than not RAF bombers exploded before the crew realised what had hit them. This manoeuvre was effective but difficult to perform. There was a significant risk of collision and, if the bomb load exploded, it could take down the night fighter too.

---

[1]A portion from the very interesting letters from Georg Hermann Greiner to the author in 1989-1994 (translated by the author).

Oberleutnant Henseler, Staffelkapitän of the Venlo-based 1./NJG 1 and flying a Heinkel He 219, also achieved two confirmed victories during the Montzen raid. Oberleutnant Johannes Hager, the 24-year-old Staffelkapitän of 6./NJG 1, was the night's top-scorer. He and his crew took off from St. Dizier at 00:57 a.m. Flying a Messerschmitt Bf 110G-4 probably equipped with upward-firing cannons, he claimed two Halifaxes and a Lancaster over Belgium. These were numbers 20, 21 and 22 of his confirmed victories. He logged his third victory two kilometres south-east of the city of Diest in Belgium, the exact position where Lancaster JA976 'S-for-Sugar' of 405 Squadron came down.

The new upward-firing cannons, code-named Schräge Musik, offered a better alternative than the attack method described by Greiner above. This allowed the night fighter to approach and attack British bombers in straight and level flight from below, where they would be outside the bomber crew's field of view. Consequently, the gunners were unable to alert the pilot of a night fighter attack, and so the pilot was not able to initiate his evasive corkscrew manoeuvre. Hence, an attack by a Schräge Musik-equipped fighter was typically a complete surprise to the bomber crew, who would only realise that a fighter was close when they were under attack. Some pilots, like Hermann Greiner, one of the more chivalrous Luftwaffe fighters, chose to aim at the wing fuel tanks instead of the fuselage, thereby giving the bomber crew a chance to escape. It is very likely that 'S-for-Sugar' received hits in one or more of the wing fuel tanks, but also in the bomb bay, leading to the ultimate explosion of the unused red target indicators.

It is to be expected that Hager used the Schräge Musik cannons to shoot down his victims that night of April 27. He had used these same weapons five nights earlier to shoot down another four-engine bomber.[1] Some of the experienced night fighter crews were not particularly keen on the new armament and continued to attack in the old-fashioned way 'from below and aft'. But most of the top-scorers in NJG 1, including Johannes Hager, had used the new weapon during night attacks on bombers in the weeks and months before April 27, 1944. By mid-1944, one third of all Luftwaffe night fighters were equipped with this new weapon.[2]

Intriguingly enough, at 02:09 a.m., Major Hans-Joachim Jabs, respected Kommodore of NJG 1, also claimed a Lancaster two kilometres south-east of Diest, but his claim was later turned down, as it is marked as

---

[1]Abschussmeldung 313, dated May 6, 1944. Combat report by Johannes Hager and his radio operator Hubert von Bergen including a claim on a four-engine bomber, using 40 rounds of 20mm MG FF Schräge Musik cannons. He flew Messerschmitt Bf 110G-4 (G9+HP) that night, and it is very likely that he used the same aircraft on April 27-28, 1944. Johannes Hager died in September 1993.

[2]The Messerschmitt Bf 110G-4 variant was equipped with two 30mm cannons and two 20mm cannons in the nose, all four delivering armour-piercing incendiary shells at a very high firing rate. Some Messerschmitt Bf 110G carried two 20mm Schräge Musik cannons.

'unconfirmed' in Luftwaffe victory listings. In the end, upon their return to base, NJG 1 crews claimed 14 confirmed victories, while one NJG 2 and two NJG 4 crews each claimed one certain triumph. This brought the total Luftwaffe tally for the Montzen raid to 17, set against the total of 15 heavies that failed to return from Montzen.[1]

And so it happened that Teddy and his crew fell victim to one of the several battle-hardened German night fighter crews that formed the nucleus of what was probably the most successful night fighter unit to ever exist: Nachtjagdgeschwader 1. Flight Commander Johannes Hager finished the war with 48 confirmed victories, listing him as number 24 in the table of most successful German night fighter aces. Major Hans-Joachim Jabs, wing commander of NJG 1, was a veteran of the Battle of France and the Battle of Britain in 1940. Despite the vulnerability of the heavy Messerschmitt Bf 110 against the more nimble RAF aircraft and the heavy losses incurred, Jabs claimed eight Spitfires and four Hurricanes destroyed. In 1941 the majority of the Bf 110 units were withdrawn from daylight fighting, and Jabs was transferred to night fighting and Reich defence. Interestingly, on April 29, 1944, just one day after his claim of a Lancaster during the Montzen raid, his Messerschmitt Bf 110G night fighter was caught by a flight of Spitfires from 132 Squadron, RAF, led by 15-kill ace Wing Commander Geoffrey Page, during a daylight sortie. In a desperate dogfight Jabs managed to down two Spitfires before deliberately force landing and scrambling for cover before his aircraft was destroyed by strafing.

A Flying Deathtrap

Johannes Hager claimed his third and final victory that cold April night two kilometres south-east of Diest. His situational awareness could not have been better, as his point of reference was the exact position where Lancaster 'S-for-Sugar' came down. There, at the small parish of Webbekom, borough of the provincial city of Diest, in the Flemish north of Belgium, numerous inhabitants were watching with horror as 'S-for-Sugar' descended during its last seconds of flight.

After the short and aggressive fighter attack, Teddy's Lancaster was doomed. Pushing the control column forward into a defensive descent, Teddy tried desperately to keep the disintegrating bomber under control so as to give his crew a chance to bail out, but the uncontrollable fire in the left-hand inboard engine was eating its way through the wing structure, and the fuselage was engulfed in flames as well. At some point the red TIs

[1]Analysing the Luftwaffe night fighter claims, and comparing these to the individual Bomber Command losses in the night of April 27-28, 1944, proved one of the most challenging parts of the research for this book. Additional insight and valuable details were generously provided by three eminent researchers of Luftwaffe night fighter operations; Wim Govaerts, Theo Boiten and Marcel Hogenhuis. We are most grateful to them.

detonated and the resulting explosion was discernible from a great distance. Several inhabitants of Webbekom, alerted by the reciprocal gunfire and high-pitched noise from the Lancaster's Merlin engines, watched in awe as the blazing bomber passed over their homes at a very low altitude. The night fighter's torrential cannon fire had more than likely wounded one or more crewmembers and might have put the gun turrets, radio and hydraulic systems out of action. The dilapidated Lancaster flew on in a north-easterly direction for several kilometres, losing debris along its earthward path. One can only speculate why Teddy did not immediately give the order to bail out of the aircraft. Perhaps the intercom system had failed or chaos aboard the bomber prevented the crew from receiving any communication from their skipper. The most likely reason, however, may have been the fact that one or more crewmembers were unable to bail out, because of wounds or because of unserviceable or scorched parachutes. The parachute packs for most of the crewmembers were stowed adjacent to where each crewmember sat or operated. In case of an emergency, they would normally grab their parachute and clip it on to their harness, which they always wore, then bail out of the aircraft.

The question remains, why was it that none of the able-bodied crew bailed out of the aircraft sooner? Perhaps Teddy tried to make a crash-landing, hoping to give the injured crewmembers a chance of survival. When he realised this would be impossible due to a lack of visibility or aircraft controllability, it was too late. A more plausible explanation could have been the general situation inside the bomber. There simply was not enough time between the attack and the final demise of the Lancaster to scramble to one of the escape hatches and jump to safety. Thorough analysis of all available sources and witness reports show that there were, at best, only a couple of minutes between Hager's attack, and the crash at Webbekom. These minutes must have been horrendous for the crew, as they were trying to get to their parachutes in a blazing and violently descending aircraft, while not wanting to abandon comrades who might have been trapped in their turrets or incapacitated by injuries.

The faltering Lancaster continued along its north-easterly track in the direction of Webbekom, when one crewmember plummeted out of the aircraft and hit the ground in a field just north of the Papenbroekstraat.[1] When locals discovered his body later that morning, it was obvious that this unfortunate flier had not used his parachute as he was partly submerged in the soft ploughed land. Intriguingly, he was found with bandages around his head and body, as if he had received urgent medical care in the aircraft. About 1.5 kilometres further along the Lancaster's ill-fated path, another crewmember exited the aircraft. It would seem that, at this time, the crew had been given the order to bail out, or else individual

[1] 'Straat' is the Dutch word for 'street'.

crewmembers decided to take their fate in their own hands. Although the Lancaster was now flying too low for a conventional parachute drop, this escapee miraculously survived although badly injured. He most likely pulled open the front escape hatch in the bomb aimer compartment's floor, noticing with alarm how close the trees below seemed, and pulled his D-ring to allow himself to be dragged out as the slipstream caught the silk folds. A few seconds later he impacted the ground nearby 'the Grotto', a chapel alongside a dirt road called the Tiensebaan. Mrs Seys-Cauberghs, who lived nearby at the time, emotionally recalled the fate of this crewmember:

> A boy was lying near the Grotto, and he was heard crying until 5 a.m. In the morning, just before dawn, Germans or members of the NSKK were heard 'being active' over there. When we later visited the bodies lying in state, we were told which of the boys was found near the Grotto. It was a very young-looking lad, with wavy hair. He had an obvious shot wound in the neck. The blood had run underneath the facial skin towards his chin. I was shocked.[1]

In a pathfinder aircraft, it was the task of the one occupying the nose compartment to open the front escape hatch and jump out first. This would have been David Ramsay. Moments later, two more crewmembers jumped. One of them was George Smith and the other one might have been Larry Allen or James Bradley. Both men were alive, though injured, following their brief parachute descent. George Smith was quickly found by NSKK members and taken to a German hospital in Diest.[2] The other jumper possibly attempted to evade capture but was quickly discovered by the dispersing NSKK. He did not survive and what happened to him is unknown. It seems possible that he could have been murdered in cold blood.

The bomber then passed slightly south of the village centre of Webbekom, at an altitude not higher than 300 feet. The aircraft then made a sharp spiralling 270° turn to the left, possibly due to structural failure of the left wing as a result of the all-consuming fire. At this juncture the fuel tanks, still containing aviation fuel, ignited in a violent and tumultuous explosion. Immediately, the aircraft fell apart and the remains plummeted earthward.

What happened to each crewmember of 'S-for-Sugar' will always remain something of a mystery, but it is certain that Teddy Blenkinsop was blown out of his cockpit by the explosion of the Lancaster. Likely, his sheer professionalism and tremendous sense of duty stopped him from leaving

---

[1]Interview with Julia Seys-Cauberghs, November 10, 1992 (translated by the author). When shown photos of the crewmembers, Mrs Seys-Cauberghs was positive that this man was David Ramsay.

[2]NSKK: Nationalsozialistisches Kraftfahrerkorps or National Socialist Motor Corps, a paramilitary organisation of the Nazi party.

the aircraft until convinced that the last of his crew were out. He stayed at the flight controls, perhaps with his steadfast engineer Bob Booth beside him, until that ultimate moment. At the minute the Lancaster blew up, the nose and cockpit section separated from the main structure and Teddy was blown clear. He came to, lying on the ground some 300 metres from the location where the majority of the wreckage fell. Teddy later told Resistance leader Hilaire Gemoets that he had been knocked out by the explosion. When he regained consciousness, he found himself on the ground with his parachute open. A Lancaster pilot always wore his parachute and in fact sat on it as it formed part of his seat, rather like a cushion. This saved Teddy's life. He suffered from shock and had a very painful right shoulder, but he was still in this world.

The debris of Lancaster B.III JA976 fell over an area of about 300 square metres. Two engines and a wheel of the main landing gear as well as numerous other parts landed on the Parelsberg, raised grassland just west of Webbekom. The fuselage of the bomber miraculously came to rest between the Webbekom town hall and the farmhouse of Louis Happers. These buildings were no more than 50 metres apart but remained completely undamaged. According to the locals, it was as if the aircraft fuselage had been carefully laid down between both buildings by hand. The remainder of the aircraft came down in the farmyard of the Weckx family, some 150 metres from the town hall. The Weckx parents had awakened their five children when the bomber passed south of the village, and one of the sons, Marcel, aged ten, remembered well what followed:

> The bomber came over a few minutes after a group of about 100 aircraft. The explosion happened at very low altitude, and the wreckage parts were lying all over our farmyard, as if they had been scattered there by hand. The NSKK Blackshirts arrived almost immediately, as if they were in the immediate vicinity. They entered our house and yard, obviously looking for survivors of the crew. At dawn a few hours later, we saw a wing lying just behind our barn. A bit further we spotted some kind of glass cabin and a machine gun. A dead airman was found just beside that cabin, he had a bandage around his arm. He was a well-built man, and he wore a white polo neck pullover. He did not wear a parachute, or maybe he did but it was still unopened.[1]

Some 30 metres from the airman found near the gun turret, another body was discovered. This man did not wear a parachute and had probably died in the crash. Webbekom inhabitants found a third lifeless crewmember in the immediate vicinity of the wreckage, still attached to his deployed

[1]Interview with Marcel Weckx, February 19, 2007 (translated by the author). This story is confirmed by several testimonies of other Webbekom people. When shown crew photographs, Mrs Seys-Cauberghs immediately identified this victim as Les Foster.

parachute. He was lying on the flank of the Parelsberg. The rumour went round that this man was shot just above the ground as he descended with his parachute. He had a noticeable gunshot wound in the back and had obviously lost much blood. According to several bystanders, gunshots were heard just prior to and after the crash. It might have been exploding machine gun bullets of the Lancaster, but some locals insisted that jumping crewmembers were being fired at from the ground. Several others, however, took the view that a number of the crew were shot just *after* landing while still wearing their parachutes. One resident, a known collaborator, was given a serious beating by some local patriots shortly after the war on account of having fired his rifle at one of the helpless airmen. Still, while no evidence was ever found about such crimes, official documents revealed another shocking offence.

George Smith might have lived to tell the tale of the final flight of the Blenkinsop crew. Unfortunately, he did not survive. When certain statements about his fate reached 1 War Crimes Investigation Unit, RCAF in October 1945, investigating officers were dispatched to Webbekom in May 1946. Their findings were appalling:

> A Canadian bomber crashed in a field near Webbecom, Belgium, on 28 Apr '44. Of eight members of the crew, six were killed, the seventh escaped and the eighth, George John Smith, was badly injured and taken to a German hospital in Diest where he was locked in a room, denied medical attention, food and drink for three days, by which time he died.
>
> It is established that Smith was bleeding from the nose, mouth and ears and was unconscious during the entire time.
>
> On the afternoon 1 May 44, the bodies of Smith and the other six members of his crew were buried in the local cemetery. An autopsy performed on all the bodies indicated that the airmen had suffered extensive fractures but that Smith bore no fracture of the skull.
>
> On the day preceding Smith's death, the German Town Major named Berger ordered the preparation of seven coffins and when reminded by the civilians that there were only six dead airmen, was heard to say: 'There is a seventh flier here in Diest at the hospital; he is not yet dead but he will be tomorrow morning and he will be buried in Webbecom with the others who are already dead.'
>
> The German doctor in charge of the hospital, named Mahr, is known to have given strict orders that Smith be not touched in any way and that the door to his room be at all times locked.
>
> The Director of Medical Services, CMHQ, under date of 1 Mar 46, on reviewing the facts of this case presented to him, concludes by saying, 'It is my opinion that even though surgical interference might not have been considered indicated by Dr Mahr, gross negligence was shown by him in the general handling of this case. There has been

obvious neglect of reasonable medical care.'[1]

Berger was the Gruppenführer of the instruction centre of the NSKK, set up at the ancient Citadel of Diest. The NSKK was originally formed as a motorised corps of the Sturmabteilung (SA). In the mid-1930s, its primary aim was to educate its members in motoring skills, while also serving as a roadside assistance group. With the outbreak of the Second World War, the NSKK became a target of the Wehrmacht for recruitment and most NSKK members ended up in the regular military, serving mostly in transport units. Several NSKK recruitment centres were founded in Belgium and France. From May 1941 on, thousands of Dutch and Belgian volunteers arrived at the Citadel of Diest, most of them originating from collaborator organisations such as the Zwarte Brigade (Black Brigade) of the Vlaamse Nationale Beweging (Flemish Nationalist Movement), the Nationale Socialistische Beweging (National Socialist Movement) and the Rexist Party. Initially, the NSKK organisation at Diest aimed at providing the German Army and Luftwaffe with transport personnel. Beginning in 1942, the volunteers received a complete military training, and armed NSKK regiments were sent out from Diest to various front zones. Diest was arguably one of the most important garrison towns of the NSKK throughout the war.

The sympathy shown by a large number of citizens of Diest and Webbekom was in sharp contrast with the atrocities as described above. Theodore Claes and a few other locals were made to collect the bodies of the airmen in the morning of April 28. They were gently assembled on the lawn of the Weckx farmyard. On the afternoon of April 29, Miss Aline Macken, an ambulance driver of the Belgian Red Cross section of Diest, observed that the bodies had not yet been coffined. She immediately warned her chairwomen, Miss Marie Alenus, and together both young women drove to the German Command Post at the city hall of Diest. They pointed out the unsanitary situation to Berger and urged him to take appropriate action. The vindictive NSKK leader was not impressed and waited until the next day to give orders to two local carpenters, Renders and Jonckers, for the manufacture of seven coffins, not six as the latter first suggested. The Red Cross ladies carefully dressed the bodies of the six fliers, whereupon they were laid in state in the parish hall next to the church.[2] A large group of locals soon arrived to lay flowers on the coffins and to bless the fallen airmen with a sign of the cross and holy water, but

[1]Extract from a report of 1 War Crimes Investigation Unit, dated May 28, 1946. National Archives of Canada. Wanted Reports were subsequently filed against Doctor Mahr and his hospital assistants Doornik, Van Roey, Kuehlieg and Tetzmann. A charge against Doctor Mahr was filed with the United Nations War Crimes Commission, but it is unknown whether he was ever convicted.

[2]Letter from Miss Alenus to the director-general of the Belgian Red Cross, May 2, 1944 (translated by the author).

before long Louis Merckx, a local collaborator, arrived. He brutally chased away the villagers, kicking aside the flowers and pouring the holy water over the coffins. He probably regretted his act the next morning, May 1, when fervent Resistance members, Maurice Geyskens and Frans Commers, evened the score by shooting out several windows in the Merckx family home. An agent of the Belgian underground intelligence network 'Service Marc' reported the events to London:

> Friday 28 April 1944 at 2h10, a four-engined aircraft was shot down in flames on the territory of Webbekom, 2 km S.E. of Diest. Six Canadian aviators were dead, one wounded, one escaped.
>
> The inhabitants reported the indecent behaviour of certain local collaborators (e.g., Louis Merckx of Webbekom) and of the NSKK garrison of Diest (e.g., the NSKK officer Berger) on the occasion of the many sympathy manifestations of the majority of the population. Personal observations of VN/AM/223 D.[1]

On May 1, 1944, George Smith died in the German hospital in Diest. He was rushed to Webbekom where, with appropriate military honours, he and his six comrades were buried at the parish churchyard at 03:00 p.m. NSKK soldiers or members of a local German Wehrmacht workshop fired a salute to the fallen airmen.

Despite the involvement of the Belgian Red Cross and the underground intelligence report sent to London, it took until July 5, 1944, before the families of Teddy's seven crewmembers received the bad news. On that date, the Canadian Red Cross, through German information, stated in a telegram that all seven were classified 'missing, believed killed'. The relatives were in touch with one another, and the fact that Teddy's parents had not received such a telegram supported their hopes for all their boys' safety. There had been instances when such reports had been false and the lads had eventually turned up safely.

Less than two years after the burial at Webbekom the graves were reopened and a Canadian War Crimes Investigation Unit performed an examination on all seven bodies. Young Albert Steennot, who had been employed as a translator by the postwar British Town Major, Major Cross, was there:

> In January or February 1946, I was ordered to join an army doctor E. Skutezky, Canadian of Polish descent, to my hometown Diest. After having interrogated several inhabitants about what happened to a Canadian crew of a Lancaster bomber, we went to the local cemetery at Webbekom. There, in the presence of the army doctor, the town secretary and myself, a couple of workers dug up the bodies of the seven crewmembers. It was an unpleasant experience. The doctor

[1]Service Marc, Sheet 98, Courier D4, dated May 15, 1944 (translated by the author).

examined the bodies, and held back two of them for transport to Brussels, where he would conduct a full autopsy on them. Later that night, the doctor telephoned the Town Major, to tell him that both airmen had received a neck shot. This is the absolute truth.[1]

There is a possible explanation for the brutal behaviour demonstrated against the airmen by the NSKK troops at Diest. A government order urged the German population to retaliate against Allied airmen who parachuted from disabled aircraft. On August 10, 1943, SS-leader Heinrich Himmler issued a decree to the security police (SIPO) stating that it was not the task of the police to interfere in clashes between Germans and Anglo-American 'terrorist flyers' that had bailed out. Any so-called Terror Flieger could be accused of indiscriminately and illegally attacking innocent German civilians. The Reich thus claimed that these airmen were to be deprived of any protection customarily accorded to prisoners of war.[2]

Before dawn on April 28, the NSKK and a small number of German soldiers searched through the area surrounding the crash site, leading to the discovery of Teddy's parachute. They now realised that one member of the crew was on the run and they were bent on finding him. Berger ordered a search of the whole area and reminded the residents of Diest and Webbekom that helping a fallen airman was a capital offence that was punishable by death.

Over the years the people of the village of Webbekom considered these seven airmen to also be their warriors who, along with countless others, had helped free Belgium from Nazi oppression. Fresh flowers are still frequently placed at their churchyard grave, and each year on the last Sunday of April, the sacrifice of the crew is remembered by a Sunday mass. On Sunday, May 3, 1964, the Webbekom town council, in the presence of many dignitaries from Belgium, Canada and the United Kingdom, arranged for a special tribute by way of a solemn and moving ceremony in remembrance of these fallen airmen… their heroes.

---

[1]Interview with Mr Albert Steennot, November 9, 1992 (translated by the author).

[2]The Sicherheitspolizei (SIPO) was a term used in Nazi Germany to describe the combined forces of the Gestapo and Sicherheitsdienst (SD) between 1934 and 1939. In 1939, the Sicherheitspolizei as a functioning office ceased to exist. The term survived in common usage, however, and was most often used by local security force commanders who adopted the title Inspektor des Sicherheitspolizei und SD. Such personnel typically had command over all SD and Gestapo units in their area of responsibility and performed duties such as those of a modern day chief of police. The Gestapo was the largest, having a membership of about 40,000 to 50,000 in 1943-1945. It was the political police force of the Reich. The SD was the smallest, having a membership of about 3,000 in 1943-1945. It was the intelligence service of the SS. Since the Gestapo was the primary executive agency of the SIPO and SD, and by far the largest, in most cases the Gestapo rather than the SD carried out the actual 'executive action'. In occupied territories members of the Gestapo frequently wore SS uniforms.

CHAPTER TEN

On The Run

When Teddy came to his senses, he did not fully realise what had happened to him. His body ached everywhere and he figured somehow he had been ejected from his aircraft. Though still in shock, he was conscious of the fact he was alone in a strange country swarming with enemy soldiers who were probably already looking for him. In the distance he could hear what sounded like a thousand dogs barking in a frenzied manner and for a moment he fought back a wave of panic at the idea that the Germans were tracking him with bloodhounds. He assumed that there was a chance other crewmen had also survived, but there was no time to look around, nor would it be wise to call out any names in the dark, so, he struggled to his feet and released his parachute harness. His whole body was still smarting. He noticed that he had lost his flying boots, which were probably peeled from his feet by the shock of the deploying parachute. In only his socks, he ran into the darkness away from the burning aircraft. Almost immediately he spotted a couple of people standing near some houses adjoining the local café, The Tin Pot. They were gesturing to him. They were Alfons Veelaers and his wife, both of whom had very strong feelings against the Germans because of the oppression they had visited on their country. Teddy cautiously approached them. Luckily, they were patriots. Aided by a translation by a French woman who happened to live nearby, he was able to explain to them he was thirsty and in need of footwear. He was hurriedly given a drink of water, some old farmer's clothes, and a pair of wooden clogs. As soon as he was dressed, Clementine Gijbels led him to a small wooded area about 500 metres away and by gestures, Teddy realised he was to hide there. He remained in the woods for a short while but quickly decided to move on while it was still dark. Luck was still with him, since the NSKK Blackshirts, hearing the rumours of a fugitive airman sighting, scoured the woods shortly after Teddy's departure.

During bailout escape and evasion briefings, Allied aircrew were told to bury their parachute and immediately vacate the area and stay out of sight. The crash would inevitably attract the enemy, who would immediately start a search for any survivors. Discovery of the parachute by the enemy would increase the intensity of the search around that area. It was essential to get away from the crash scene immediately by using hedges, ditches and woods as cover, while avoiding crossing roads, and then to find a secure hiding place well away from the scene. There the airman was to remain hidden until the initial search died down. So Teddy, bothered by a very painful right shoulder, followed all those instructions. He found his bearings by aid of his celestial knowledge and proceeded in a southerly direction, probably following the dirt road now called Droomblokstraat or the sunken path Blakenbergstraat. After staggering on a few kilometres and observing the dawn was upon him, he had to find a suitable hideout. He found a haystack and crawled under its cover. There, exhausted after the night's tragic events and from the intense and throbbing pain of his injured shoulder, he dozed off.

The air force escape and evasion doctrine also advised that a downed airman should travel by night and hide by day. Escapees were instructed, if landing in southern Germany, to move south-west in order to try to reach Gibraltar via France and Spain. No guidance was, for obvious reasons, given about the French, Belgian, Dutch or Danish resistance or their whereabouts. If downed over northern or eastern Germany, it was left to the crew's own initiative whether to aim for Switzerland or stow away to Sweden.

To sustain oneself, each crewmember received a Halex escape kit before going on a mission. This small container, usually carried in a knee pocket of the battle dress trousers, contained a hacksaw blade, a rubber water bottle, Halazone water purifying tablets, some fishing line and hooks, needle and thread, chewing gum, shaving tools and matches. For sustenance, malted milk tablets and concentrated blocks of chocolate were in the kit, as well as Benzedrine tablets (amphetamines) to act as a stimulant to increase alertness and suppress hunger. Every aircrew member flying over Western Europe was issued a purse containing French, Belgian, Dutch and sometimes Spanish currency. A silk escape map of the area was hidden somewhere in his clothing. A compass, in the form of a button, was sewn into the battle dress. The magnetized needle pointer of the compass, pivoted on a small fulcrum, was of vital importance as a primary aid of escape. Small passport photos of the holder dressed in shabby civilian clothes were carried by each crewmember. They would be useful when the Resistance decided to produce a fake identity card for the evader. The carrying of identity cards by the local population was made mandatory by the German forces, and all cards carried a photograph of the individual. British Intelligence instructed the RAF that all aircrew were to carry photographs on all operations over enemy territory. Interrogation of successful evaders revealed the type and size of photograph required, including details about the background and the required clothing and certain aspects of the subject. Aircrew were told to carry at least two photographs and ensure that they were kept separately.

An airman was instructed to approach only individuals who were alone. Having made contact with a civilian who was willing to help, an evader could usually look forward to some kind of lodging, food, false identity papers, civilian clothing and transport – sometimes by bicycle or car and, on long journeys, by train. Local resistance groups provided much of the practical assistance.

After a few hours, his shivering body and empty stomach awakened Teddy. The past night had taken its toll on his body, and he realised he had to get some proper food and, above all, medical help for his shoulder. He took stock of his situation and saw two alternatives – find the nearest German and surrender or try to escape. He did not relish the prospect of a German prison camp. He had his escape kit and a fair amount of local currency.

While pondering his options, suddenly two children appeared in front of him. They had been playing in the field and stumbled onto the stranger. After smiling at Teddy for a short while, they ran off. Teddy did not want to risk exposing himself in broad daylight, so he decided to stay where he was. Before long, a farmer by the name of Frans Toetenel arrived at the scene. His children had found Teddy. Teddy addressed him in French: 'Je suis aviateur Canadien – RAF', at which point Frans gestured to Teddy that he had to stay put while he went to get some food. The sympathetic farmer then returned with bread, cheese and milk, which Teddy gratefully gobbled up. Before leaving again, Frans indicated to Teddy that he should stay near the haystack. Then he left.

At nightfall, Frans set out for the home of Jonckers, a carpenter whose family lived at the Papenbroekstraat nr. 7. The three sons, Charles, René and Joseph, were active members of the Group 'G' Resistance movement, and Frans solicited their help. Charles Jonckers later remembered well what happened:

> Frans Toetenel was the owner of a piece of farmland on the Mierenberg at Assent, where his children had found an airman hiding in one of the haystacks. In the evening of April 28, Frans arrived at our home and told us about this, and that he had given food to the Allied flyer. I told him that it was a dangerous situation to have the airman there and that the NSKK and Germans were searching the area looking for the one missing airman. Next I told him that I would come and fetch the airman between midnight and 01:00 a.m., but that I should not be seen by anyone. At night, Hilaire Gemoets, our leader, and I went to the farmland. While Hilaire kept watch on the path leading to the farmland, I cautiously approached the haystack and made my presence known by doing 'psst, psst'. The flyer came out – he was quivering from head to toe. Hilaire and I had to support him in turn while walking to the home of Hilaire's parents. He was much

> weakened and obviously in a lot of pain. When we arrived at the house of the Gemoets family, a remote farm near some woods in the village of Struik near Assent, the flyer seemed relieved. In the light, we noticed that the tips of his hair had turned grey. In our first attempts to communicate with him, in a mixture of French and English, we learned that he was a Canadian and his name was Teddy. He made it clear to us that he had saved himself with his parachute, but didn't know how. He said he probably had been blown out of his aircraft when it exploded, and that he feared that no-one else of his crew survived. He pointed to his painful right shoulder, and we decided that he needed professional help. While Mrs Gemoets helped Teddy wash and gave him a good meal, we sent someone to get Dr Musiek from Diest. He was very patriotic and had a connection with the resistance. He arrived early the next morning, and attended to Teddy's shoulder. It turned out that he had a dislocated shoulder, and a badly bruised collar bone.[1]

Although only 20 years old, Hilaire Gemoets was respected and accepted by other Resistance workers, and soon became a leader of the local cell of the Group 'G'. Hilaire, by rejecting a call up to work for the German war effort, was really a fugitive himself. In 1944, he was high on the wanted list of the Germans for yet another reason. He had organised or at least participated in many sabotage actions in 1943 and 1944. These included armed robberies of town halls to steal ration stamps or destroy forced labourer registers, derailments of trains between Tienen, Diest and Aarschot, and the transport and hiding of arms and explosives. His most daring feat was his armed attack on a prisoners' transport escorted by Gestapo agents in August 1944. Although wounded himself by returning gunfire, he killed all the Gestapo agents and released the prisoners from the lorry. A real daredevil, Hilaire was an example to many in the local Group 'G'. Unbeknownst to one another, his father Charles and sister Lea were also working for the Resistance, the latter as a courier.[2]

Observed by Charles Gemoets, his wife and six children, Teddy spread his escape map on the table. With Hilaire and Charles's help, he established his location. He was in the heart of Belgium, about 50 kilometres east of Brussels. The Gemoets folks gave Teddy a new wardrobe, consisting of old working clothes belonging to the farmer and his son Hilaire.

Teddy knew from his RAF preparatory evasion lectures that an evading aviator had to make every effort to conceal his true identity, in both appearance and behaviour. He needed to adopt the clothing style and

---

[1]Interviews with Charles Jonckers June 10 and September 20, 1989 (translated by the author). Confirmed by Anne and Lea Gemoets, sisters of Hilaire, in January 1991.

[2]Just prior the liberation, on September 3, 1944, Hilaire was caught by retreating Germans during a gun fight in Webbekom. He was executed on the spot. Today, a memorial stone commemorates this tragic event.

mannerisms of the local inhabitants. The daily shaves, neat haircuts, wearing of a wristwatch or walking in a soldierly manner had to be discarded.

The Gemoets family kept Teddy hidden in their home for that day and following night. Then, on the morning of April 30, they brought him to a wooded area behind their property where they had built an ingenious hideout partially dug into the ground. There, about five Russian refugees were holing up out of sight of any German patrols. They had recently escaped from a German POW Camp at Zwartberg in the Belgian coalfields.

Charles Jonckers' young wife, Odile, had a sister who was a courier for the resistance. Shortly after Teddy's arrival, she travelled to Brussels to collect a questionnaire that had to be filled out by any downed airman. This was a standard procedure established by Resistance groups, to check that a supposed Allied airman was genuine, before putting him into an escape line. While Teddy was hiding with the Russians, Paul Wauters, a local teacher visited with him. Paul spoke some English and French, so he could converse with Teddy. Paul explained that Teddy would have to wait in hiding until they received word from Brussels they could accept him and place him into an escape network. Teddy again recalled the lectures given during his training. It was essential to be patient, do as he was told and await guidance from his helpers. He asked Paul if there was a possibility to radio London informing them that he was alive, hoping that the news would reach Helen or his family. Without making any promises, Paul told Teddy he would see what could be done.

Teddy realised he had been lucky. His sore shoulder was taken care of, and he was being fed and helped by people who, although suffering deprivations themselves, obviously had experience in resistance matters. He was in the hands of the organised Resistance, and began feeling positive about making it back to England.

The German intelligence had known for some time of the Resistance movement. Their actions and the potential threat to the German war effort gave them great concern. Much to the frustration of the German hierarchy, it soon became evident the extent to which the population were involved in hiding Allied airmen and then aiding in their escape. Pamphlets were posted everywhere, alerting citizens that supporting Allied escapees would be punished with execution if caught. Still, they never succeeded in stopping the Resistance activities.

Nevertheless, the German threat was real. Ferdinand Alen, an innocent miller who lived near the field where Teddy was found by the Toetenel children, was arrested shortly after Teddy had been moved from there. Ferdinand had nothing to do with the affair, but an unscrupulous woman collaborator let slip that there was a pilot hiding near Ferdinand Alen. The 57-year-old Ferdinand was lifted from his bed by the Gestapo at 09:30 p.m. on May 9, 1944, and taken to the infamous St. Gilles prison in Brussels.

There, he was harshly interrogated, but he obviously failed to disclose any information about the fugitive airman. As a result, he was then put on a train to the infamous Buchenwald concentration camp on May 20. On June 8, 1944, Ferdinand was transported to the Dora Mittelbau camp, the secret German underground factories that were producing the V-1 and V-2 rockets. There, like thousands of others, he slaved to death in the most atrocious circumstances. He passed away on July 13, 1944, according to the German death certificate due to 'heart and blood circulation failure'.[1]

Despite Teddy being tucked away in the woods at Assent, Hilaire made the assessment that the situation was unsafe. He realised that the Germans were still searching for the missing airman in and around Webbekom, and it was common practice to move an evader at the slightest indication of danger, so he arranged for Teddy to be relocated.

[1]Archives of the Federal Service for War Victims, Brussels – Dossiers DDO of Ferdinand Alen (SVG-d148829). The file contains a formal statement by the Jonckers brothers about the careless woman who betrayed Ferdinand.

CHAPTER ELEVEN

The Belgian Resistance

The Germans' early successes in Europe were a setback for Britain. Not only had large quantities of Allied equipment and munitions been left on the Continent but, more importantly, thousands of soldiers were stranded there as well. Many became prisoners of war, but thousands evaded capture. It has been estimated that between the fall of Dunkirk in June 1940 and the end of the war in 1945, 35,000 British, Commonwealth and latterly American soldiers and airmen found their way to Allied lines. Twenty-three thousand were men who had escaped captivity; over 9,000 – mostly downed airmen – evaded capture and returned to friendly territory. The creation of escape routes for Allied servicemen, while only one aspect of the secret war waged by an occupied people, was probably the first manifestation of a resistance after the Nazi-controlled Wehrmacht swept across Western Europe.

In the gloom that settled over the Continent following Dunkirk, scores of British soldiers and Allied airmen were assisted by willing but often inept Resistance groups of citizens from these occupied countries. In rare occasions, these groups received direct or indirect support from British intelligence, but far more importantly, they received unstinting assistance from the local citizenry from all walks of life. A first category of motivated helpers consisted of Belgian veterans of the First World War and other ex-servicemen who had been released by the Germans after the Belgian capitulation or had escaped incarceration. Then there were the confirmed anti-fascists, intellectuals such as doctors and lawyers, but also labourers and unskilled workers. A third group contained farmers and labourers who strongly opposed German forced labour and tried to avoid it for a life in the Underground. Last but not least, many keen helpers were found among the impoverished population, who loathed a neighbour who might collaborate with the enemy out of sheer self-interest. All these helpers gave up their food, their clothing, their time and, only too often, their lives to help air force escapers, or 'evaders' as they were known, to rejoin their units. These helpers wore no uniforms, few of them received any awards and, in a Nazi-dominated Europe, their future was anything but secure.

Many young airmen, cocky and confident in their professional ability and courage, learned the meaning of humility in the presence of these people.

The first Resistance organisations were created fairly soon after the Belgian capitulation of late May 1940. Despite illustrious sounding names – the Black Hand, the Black Legion, the White Phalanx, Victory and Freedom, and so forth – many of them only played a minor or local role. What is more, there were probably too many of them situated in the confines of a limiting Belgian geography. This fact alone increased the chance of compromising their operation.

The Belgian Underground movement in the initial stages spent a great deal of its time gathering intelligence and passing it on to the British and to a lesser extent the Soviets. The information was transmitted by means of clandestine radio transmitters. Numerous independent 'intelligence and action services' spontaneously came into being. It always started with someone who wanted to react against the German oppression. Ordinary people who loved their country rose above themselves to defend it. Many made naïve beginners' errors, which they paid for with their lives. German detectives posing as resistance agents were easily able to arrest careless network members. However, the Resistance workers learned fast, and after the first arrests the remaining networks reorganised and reconsidered their methods and procedures. Those movements that overcame their teething troubles grew into impressive organisations and provided a significant contribution to the course of the war.

These intelligence and action services involved organisations and individuals that provided unvarying assistance to the various Allied intelligence agencies. The factions that gathered intelligence were in touch with the British Special Intelligence Service, while the propaganda organisations worked in cooperation with the Political Warfare Executive. The Special Operations Executive (SOE) for their part tried to coordinate the activities of the action and sabotage networks. Working in utter anonymity and known in England only by their code names, most members of these Underground organisations, unlike their counterparts of the armed Resistance, remained unidentified until after the war. These groups were small, as they only required a limited number of well-placed volunteers. There were only 12 large networks and 18 smaller ones. In addition, these specialist intelligence networks provided liaison and operational information for the armed Resistance or sabotage groups. By early 1944, Resistance movements were printing over 300 different clandestine newspapers that were circulated all over Belgium. In 1943, they managed to publish 100,000 fake copies of *Le Soir*, a newspaper controlled by the Germans. These were sold as authentic newspapers at stands throughout the country.

To illustrate the contribution of the Belgian intelligence and action services, British records from 1942 show that 80 per cent of the intelligence gathered by all Resistance movements in all occupied countries in that year came from Belgium.[1] In particular, the reports sent detailing the location of German radar sites were vital to the Allied bombing campaign, especially prior to the invasion. Tens of thousands of intelligence reports by Belgian agents reached the Special Intelligence Service, 25,000 of which were of acknowledged military value. However, there was a downside to the communication function performed by these intelligence gatherers. The transmitters who sent this vital data to Britain also coordinated armed intervention against the Germans, such as the destruction of bridges or the blowing up of rail lines. Several members of the intelligence and action services were caught as a result – and paid the ultimate price.

The term 'armed resistance' referred to organisations whose primary mission was to provide clandestine paramilitary assistance to the Allied liberation armies. Initially, these formations had very few firearms at their disposal. Furthermore, during the odd clash between untrained and under-armed Resistance fighters and German troops, their losses were heavy. While waiting for the Allied invasion, the armed Resistance groups made themselves useful by hiding and supporting Jews, downed airmen or other runaways, or by organising all sorts of acts of sabotage. Others started their own intelligence service or printed clandestine periodicals.

Aside from the intelligence services, there were several prominent armed resistance networks in Belgium. By 1941, three constituted organisations had been formed from former soldiers of the defeated Belgian military, the Belgian Legion, the White Phalanx and the Reconstructed Belgian Army. These groups ultimately united under the name Belgian Legion (Légion Belge–Belgisch Legioen). This organisation operated throughout the country and was recognised in July 1943 as the military branch of the exiled Belgian government in London. To avoid confusion with the returning Belgian army in exile, they adopted the name the Secret Army (Armée Secrète–Geheim Leger) on June 1, 1944. The first task was to raise 50,000 people who would be under the command of the Allies when required after D-Day. The Secret Army was supplied with firearms and other equipment during night drops from RAF aircraft.[2]

The next most important Resistance movement in Belgium was the Independence Front (Front de l'Indépendance–Onafhankelijkheidsfront). Mostly members of the Belgian Communist Party (BCP), founded in 1941, constituted the Independence Front. Still, a number of non-communist affiliates were also included. The Belgian Armed Partisans (Partisans Armés–Gewapende Partizanen) was officially the armed branch of the BCP.

---

[1]Winston S. Churchill *The Hinge of Fate*, *The Second World War*, vol. IV, (London: Houghton Mifflin, 1951), 294.

[2]The organisations were known by their French and Dutch names. Belgium is, for the most part, divided in two official language regions; Flanders (Dutch-speaking) in the north and Wallonia (French-speaking) in the south of the country.

In reality, however, the Armed Partisans (PA) was a section of the Independence Front. The Front operated throughout the country and was recognised as the leading civilian resistance organisation in 1943. It was given the task of coordinating civil resistance and had more than 35,000 as members. The term 'partisan' was often generally, though incorrectly, used for any Resistance worker.

One of the most successful organisations in terms of material destruction was Group 'G', whose numbers never exceeded 4,000. Group 'G', until 1943 known as either Group Gérard or General Sabotage Group, was founded in late 1941 or early 1942. This politically neutral movement originated in the Free University of Brussels, but later it extended its activities into the areas of Flanders (Antwerp) and Wallonia (Liège, Namur). On January 15, 1944, this group instigated the destruction of all the high voltage electrical lines in Belgium simultaneously. The PA assisted in this venture. Factories came to a standstill and it is estimated that this one action alone cost the Germans the equivalent of ten million man-hours of work.

Another organisation, the National Royalist Movement (Mouvement National Royaliste–Nationaal Koningsgezinde Beweging), was an ultraconservative group that advocated for an authoritarian kingdom to be headed by King Leopold III. Formed for the protection of their king against Flemish nationalists and communists, this group of royalists developed into an independent Resistance movement. The NKB ultimately gained some support amongst Catholic organisations, the military and the nobility. The movement operated mainly in Flanders and had 8,500 members.

The liberal White Brigade–Fidelio (Fidelio–Witte Brigade) was founded in 1940. It was the only major movement whose leadership was Flemish; the others were Francophone in makeup. It was a relatively small movement, although 'Whites' ('Witten') soon became the popular name given to all Resistance factions, as opposed to 'Blacks' ('Zwarten'), the name commonly given to collaborators. The White Brigade played a very active role in the liberation of the main seaport of Antwerp in September 1944.

Other organisations, the Belgian National Movement and the Liberation Army of Belgium, counted 15,000 and 7,200 members respectively. In addition, there were a number of other smaller organisations, with memberships ranging between 200 and 2,000. In 1944, the Belgian National Movement, the Group 'G', the Independence Front, the Liberation Army of Belgium and the Secret Army agreed to coordinate their activities.

As far as concerns the intelligence and action services, one of their key functions was to assist in the hiding and evacuation of escaped POW and downed airmen. Aside from the purely personal aversion of spending the remainder of the war behind barbed wire, escaping was a legitimate method of waging war. Many of them returned with crucial data or information, not the least was the information about how and why certain aircraft had been shot down. Other information included the state of affairs in occupied Europe, data about potential targets for air attack, and about the morale of both German troops and the Resistance groups. Furthermore, returning airmen gave a morale boost to others, who now realised that being shot down over Europe did not necessarily mean imprisonment. The training of aircrew was both a long and costly process, and the return of those shot down reduced the need to train replacements. Although many did not return to operations, the Germans desperately tried to stop their escape. A less obvious benefit was the need for the enemy to commit thousands of men to counter organisations structured to assist in escape and evasion.

The two most successful and best-known Second World War escape lines ran through France, and the names of Pat O'Leary and Andrée De Jongh will always be remembered. Pat established the Pat Line and Andrée, the Belgian Comète Line. There were, however, many other smaller lines that achieved considerable success. Also, many aircrew successfully evaded capture without ever making contact with an established line and attributed their success to the support and courage of individuals acting on their own volition.

The criteria for a successful evasion were many and varied, depending upon the airman's personality, the time of year, luck and, above all, the help of thousands of civilians in the occupied countries. Several escape lines came to light in Western Europe, such as the Tartan Pimpernel Line, the Burgundy Line, Luc-Marc, Zéro, Benoît, Eva, Sabot, Phénix and Greyhound. 'Eva', short for Evasion, was active from July 1943 until the liberation. This organisation specifically specialised in sheltering, feeding and clothing downed airmen. Assisted by a young Belgian woman, Anne Brusselmans, known by the rescued as 'Madame Anne', the evading airmen were handed over to Comète. Anne Brusselmans was credited with helping 130 airmen.[1]

Comète was perhaps the most remarkable lifeline for downed Allied aircrew and was the creation of Andrée 'Dédée' De Jongh, another young Belgian woman. She was one of several heroines within the Belgian Resistance, and her story serves as an example of many others.

Pugna Quin per Cutias (fight without arms), the motto of Comète, looks at first glance to be an oxymoron. But there is nothing contradictory about the achievements of this Belgian-run organisation that assisted 770 individuals – some say more – to return to Britain to fight another day. Dédée lived with her parents at 73 Avenue Emile Verhaeren in Brussels. She was inspired by the heroism of nurse Edith Cavell during the First World

---

[1]Yvonne Daley-Brusselmans, *Rendez-Vous 127 Revisited* (Manhattan KS: Sunflower UP, 2001), 127.

War and started working as an ambulance driver in a military hospital in Bruges in 1940. Dédée's father, Frédéric, was a schoolmaster. After Dédée successfully started the Lifeline organisation, his school office was temporarily used as the Line's headquarters.

The first intention of Comète was to help any Belgians wishing to reach Britain, to join the British army or the RAF, but it soon became obvious that Allied soldiers could also escape using this system. In August 1941, Dédée made her first of 24 trips across the Pyrenees. She went to the British Consul in Bilbao, Spain, and succeeded in convincing skeptical officials she could and would organise the safe houses, recruit the helpers, secure false identity papers, and provide food, clothing and all the necessary items for a successful escape operation. All she required from the British was money to pay the Basque guides for the dangerous trips across the Pyrenees. At the same time, however, she and her fellow organisers in Comète insisted on running the line their own way with no interference from the British.

The preferred and quickest method of escape would have been a Channel crossing or an air pick-up. But, this was far too complicated for the civilian-run Comète Line to organise. The next best option was by land through France, over the Pyrenees and into neutral Spain, a distance of well over 1,000 kilometres. Having been shot down over Luxembourg, Holland, Belgium and France, the airmen were brought by bicycle, tram and train to collection points like The Hague, Amsterdam, Brussels and Liège, and from there sent to Paris. From Paris they were escorted down one of the major escape routes through Toulouse to Marseille or St-Jean-de-Luz, a small fishing port in the shadow of the Pyrenees. It was here that Comète had secured the services of a tough Basque smuggler called Florentino Goicoechea, who became their most trusted and resourceful Pyrenees guide. Overnight, without any lights or hiking equipment, only espadrilles on their feet, Florentino took Dédée and her companions up and down the French side of the Pyrenees, guiding them by wading across the freezing cold River Bidassoa into neutral Spain. Then up another steep climb before descending to a safe farmhouse where they collapsed, exhausted after a ten-hour hike. After a hand-over to the British Embassy representative at Madrid, they were then taken on to Gibraltar, a British territory and naval base on the south coast of Spain. From there, they boarded ships back to England.

Comète soon blossomed – from July to October 1942 they brought out 54 airmen – but its success did not last and the Luftwaffe police infiltrated Comète shortly after its creation. Word had reached German Air Force chief Hermann Göring, who knew only too well the value of returned airmen, and in November 1942, numerous arrests were made. Dédée herself was arrested by the Gestapo in January 1943 and sent to concentration camps at Mezum, Essen, Kraizburg, Ravensbruck and Mauthausen. She was freed on April 22, 1945. Her father was arrested in

June 1943 and was executed on Mount Valérien, Paris, on March 29, 1944. But, despite the arrest of 800 of the approximately 1,000 Comète volunteers during a three-year period, the line still functioned. In total, Comète saved over 800 Allied airmen. More than 300 of these were concealed in secret forest camps and other hideouts throughout Belgium and France, while 75 were handed over to other organisations. An amazing 288 evading airmen were escorted to Spain by Comète helpers. The last one crossed the French-Spanish border in early June 1944. Recorded total Comète losses during the war were 23 people executed, while another 193 died from torture or did not return from German concentration camps. A fairer estimate, perhaps, is that for every successful evader, a Dutch, Belgian, French, or Basque helper gave his or her life. The British government awarded the George Cross to Dédée De Jongh, Elvire de Greef and Michou Dumon. It is the highest decoration given to a foreign national for bravery, and in so doing, recognised the courage of the women of the Comète Line.[1]

Shortly after the war started, the British needed an intelligence desk to facilitate the many civilians in enemy-occupied countries that were helping evaders. By December 1939, the War Office had established MI 9 (Military Intelligence section 9). Initially, it had a limited staff. As the war progressed and numbers of evaders multiplied, the organisation expanded. MI 9 had a number of missions. One was to provide the necessary training to airmen on how to avoid capture. Another was to organise and finance escape lines run by civilians in occupied countries. Radio communication links became very important. These contacts were established either through two-way radio contact with trained operators dropped into Europe or through coded messages embedded in the nightly broadcasts of the BBC. A third mission was the collection and dissemination of post-evasion information. When escapers and evaders successfully made their way back to Britain, they were a valuable resource for MI 9 and underwent a gruelling interrogation. Contrary to what many perceived, normally the airmen who had travelled the underground railways rarely flew operational missions again and were reassigned to other duties. This tradition, general throughout the Allied air forces, was not so much for their own protection but for those who had helped them. If the Germans knew they had a man who had passed through the escape line once, there were ways of making him talk.

MI 9 initiated two major European escape lines. As previously

[1]The author had the honour to meet Dédée in Mechelen in May 2005, during a big celebration honouring several extraordinary women of the Belgian Resistance that survived to that day. Dédée remained a charming and inspiring personality throughout her entire life. In 1985, she was ennobled countess by the Belgian King and received many Belgian and foreign awards, including the George Medal, the Croix de Guerre Française avec Palme and the Medal of Freedom with Golden Palm. After the war, Dédée continued to serve the needy, becoming a sister in leper colonies in the Belgian Congo. She died peacefully on October 13, 2007.

mentioned, the Pat Line or O'Leary Line, going through Biarritz, helped over 600 Allied servicemen evade capture. Pat O'Leary was known as its leader. His real name was Dr Albert Guérisse, a Belgian army surgeon. He had escaped from Dunkirk to England, where he joined the SOE, who gave him his alias as a French Canadian and commissioned him in the Royal Navy. On his first assignment aboard a Royal Navy vessel in mid-1941, they put him ashore on the south coast of France and tasked him to carry out clandestine operations. He was soon captured and interned but escaped and arrived in Marseille, where he helped organise the escape line bearing his alias. In early 1943, the Germans had completely penetrated that network, and Pat O'Leary himself was betrayed and arrested in March 1943. His arrest effectively spelled the end of the Pat Line, the first of the escape lines. Over 100 brave helpers of the line paid the ultimate price. O'Leary survived severe torture by the Gestapo and was liberated from Dachau in April 1945. He was one of the truly remarkable and gallant characters to emerge from the Second World War.[1]

In November 1943, MI 9 dropped two French Canadian soldiers into occupied France to organise the Shelburne Line. Following the disasters that had beset the Pat and Comète lines, their task was to establish a network of new safe houses in Paris, and create an escape line to link with the Brittany coast, where Royal Navy vessels would land secret agents to assist with the evacuation of evading airmen. By the summer of 1944, Lucien Dumais and Ray La Brosse had organised this line, which eventually rescued 128 evading airmen and seven agents. They had also arranged the safe passage of 98 men from France to Spain, and another group of 74 were hidden in the French countryside until liberated by the Allies. Prior to the liberation of France, Shelburne had rescued 365 airmen.[2]

The majority of civilians in the occupied countries usually had only a single opportunity to help an airman escape. Hundreds of aircrew that jumped from stricken aircraft ended up in the hands of ordinary people, some of whom had only remote contact with Resistance groups, while others only acted independently on the spur of the moment. It is also important to note that Resistance groups did not start out with a global plan to help evaders but rather the plans evolved from the natural links that were forged in thousands of communities, large and small. As well, the participants were, by and large, very young and inexperienced. Countless women, many still in their teens or early 20s, helped Allied servicemen

---

[1]King George VI invested Lieutenant Commander Pat O'Leary with the George Cross. Dr Albert Guérisse returned to the Belgian army and retired as a major-general, having won gallantry awards during the Korean War. He was later awarded an honorary knighthood by the British government, and ennobled to count by the King of Belgium. He died in 1989.

[2]Graham Pitchfork, *Shot Down and on the Run: The RAF and Commonwealth Aircrews Who Got Home from Behind Enemy Lines, 1940-1945* (Richmond UK: The National Archives, 2003), 87.

evade capture. Several of them became well-known leaders of escape organisations and, as previously discussed, were highly decorated after the war. These women regarded themselves as just ordinary people and discounted their extraordinary achievements. Their courage reached heights that few of us could either attain or fully appreciate.

A Deadly Business

While work on the escape apparatus lacked the drama of sabotage or espionage, it was no less dangerous. Despite the eventual emergence of a well-organised Resistance movement and while the attitude amongst the population was generally sympathetic, the odds were still very much against the evader. He was in a strange country and, more often than not, unable to speak the language, amid a population fearful and occasionally hostile. The Geneva and The Hague conventions spelled out the rights and responsibilities of prisoners of war and their captors. Under the increasing bombardment of the Allied air offensive against the Third Reich, however, the rules of 'civilized' warfare became subordinated to vengeance. More than one airman survived a crash only to be shot 'while attempting to escape'. A Führer order decreed death for all commandos and parachutists captured.[1] Spies were the chief targets, but there were instances of a literal application of that order towards any airmen found in civilian clothes. In the occupied countries, an airman on the loose became a sign of defiance to the German authority, but to the nationals of that country, these men were a symbol of eventual liberation. Except where greater gains were to be made, as in the efforts of the German Abwehr and Gestapo to infiltrate Underground activities, the manhunt for stranded airmen was conducted with ever-increasing viciousness. In March 1944, the Chief of the Sicherheitspolizei (SIPO) and Sicherheitsdienst (SD), Hitler's dreaded security services, forwarded an order to his regional offices. This Kugel Erlass (Bullet Decree) stated that every escaped officer and nonworking NCO prisoner of war, on recapture, with the exception of British and American prisoners of war, were to be handed over for 'special treatment' to the SIPO and SD. Whether escaped British and American officers and nonworking NCOs, upon recapture, should be handed over to the SIPO and SD was a question to be decided only by the Army's High Command. While the Abwehr had no official powers of arrest and their mandate was to make investigations only, the SD now had the authorisation to deal with cases where acts of 'terrorism' – like sabotage or other forms of resistance – were implicated. The involvement of the SD in the handling of captured Allied airmen would soon prove to be bad news for the Allied flyers.

The Nürnberg trials provided a glimpse of what special treatment meant. One witness, a French ex-prisoner, gave the tribunal an account of the

---

[1]Führer Order OKW/ WFst No. 003830/42 g. Kdos.

brutal murder of 47 British, American and Dutch fliers by the SD. At Mauthausen, three months after D-Day, the airmen, barefoot, were led into a deep stone quarry. They were loaded with huge rocks, weighing about 60lbs each, and forced to carry this burden on their backs to the top of the quarry. SD-men lined the route, lashing out at the captives with clubs and jackboots. On the second trip, the load was increased with larger stones. Those who fell were kicked to their feet. By evening the bodies of 21 airmen were strewn along the path. The remaining 26 died on the following day.

The same ruthless fate awaited anyone caught working for the Resistance. In many ways, it was even more hazardous, because German agents of the Abwehr or the Gestapo, speaking fluent English and posing as downed airmen or as helpers, were often planted in a network. These agents diligently delivered downed airmen to safety in order to gain information about the operation of the lifelines. This generally resulted in an entire chain of helpers being betrayed.

In January 1944, as the Allied invasion approached and bombardment missions increased, a growing number of airmen were downed over Belgium. Safe houses were in crisis mode as there was no way to move the evading pilots south in an expeditious way, but the evaders still had to be fed and kept safe from the Germans. In March 1944, word reached Brussels of a new escape route, called KLM, in Antwerp. As the Resistance organisations could not know, however, KLM was completely German-controlled. During a short period of time, the Eva organisation sent 32 airmen up to KLM, where they were all arrested.[1] Airmen were also being sent from Holland to the KLM line. Double agent René Van Muylem, in charge of KLM, was eventually responsible for the arrest of 177 airmen. Meanwhile, the Abwehr continued collecting intelligence on the escape lines. Often they simply put down surveillance on a safe house to observe who was coming and going.

As a result of Brussels' saturation with downed airmen and the incessant bombing of the railways, the normal mode of transportation used by airmen and helpers, Allied headquarters in England decided something had to be done. Fearing a protracted siege of Brussels could disrupt the major Belgian escape lines, the British MI 9 executed Mission Marathon, which had been pre-approved in mid-1943. Hundreds of evading airmen were secretly moved to camps established deep in the Ardennes Forest of south-east Belgium and in northern France, to await their liberators. Special agents were parachuted into Europe from England to help the local Underground movements organise these camps. Setting up the camps proved a very difficult task. Large quantities of tents, blankets and other equipment had to be found, in a country already suffering from scarcity.

[1]Fernand Strubbe, *Geheime Oorlog* (Tielt: Lannoo, 1992), 138 (translated by the author).

For weeks, on a daily basis, Resistance workers delivered food and messages, under the ever-present danger of an encounter with a German patrol. Luckily, German troops were not too anxious to venture deep into the wooded areas where these camps were located, as each camp was heavily guarded. Several German patrols were decimated in ambushes. Unfortunately, this often caused retaliation against innocent people, who were taken as hostages and executed.[1]

However, Mission Marathon could not provide for all the downed airmen, and hundreds of other evaders had to remain in their hiding places in the towns and cities until they could be reached by the advancing liberation armies in the summer and fall of 1944. Of all occupied European cities, Brussels harboured the largest number of downed airmen. In 1944, a staggering 800 evaders were tucked away in the Belgian capital. For example, in the final weeks of the German occupation, the intrepid Anne Brusselmans alone sheltered 54 airmen in various houses in Brussels and the vicinity.

The number of casualties incurred by the Underground demonstrated the effectiveness of infiltrating double agents. When the Comète Line was betrayed, two-thirds of its members became prisoners of the Germans.[2] At least 500 Underground escape workers from France, Belgium and Holland were arrested and shot or died in concentration camps. It is hard to ascertain overall figures for actual losses in the Belgian Underground movement, but some statistics are known. One source states 4,076 members of the Belgian Resistance disappeared or died whilst prisoners of the Nazis.[3] It is known for certain that 44,000 Belgian citizens were arrested as political prisoners or for opposing the German regime in a variety of ways. A staggering 14,000 of these people never returned. Add to these figures the many others that succumbed as a result of their treatment after they were released, and it becomes apparent that Resistance was not a job for the timid.

It will probably never be possible to count the total number of victims of the infamous Nacht und Nebel Erlass, the Night and Fog Decree, issued on December 7, 1941, by Field Marshal Keitel over the signature of Adolf Hitler. This order by the Führer set the policy for treatment of people who committed offences against the Reich or its occupation forces, except where a death sentence was a certainty. Under Nacht und Nebel, people suspected of opposing Nazi rule were arrested by the Gestapo in the dead of night and simply vanished from the face of the earth. In reality, they were

---

[1]A number of crewmembers shot down during the Montzen raid on April 27-28 1944, ended up in Mission Marathon camps.

[2]One of the double agents who infiltrated and betrayed Comète was Harold Cole, an ex-sergeant of the British Expeditionary Forces, who had narrowly escaped from the Dunkirk beaches in June 1940.

[3]'Ik lag tussen de doden,' *Het Nieuwsblad*, Nov. 12, 1990: 7 (translated by the author).

taken secretly to Germany and surrendered to the SIPO and SD for trial or punishment. Even when they died awaiting trial, their families never learnt their fate, for as stated by Keitel in an explanatory note that accompanied the decree: 'If these offences [against German authority] are punished by imprisonment, even with hard labour for life, this will be looked upon as a sign of weakness. Efficient intimidation can only be achieved either by capital punishment or by measures by which the relatives of the criminals and the population do not know of his fate.'

Even the Nürnberg trials failed to determine precisely how many people vanished under Nacht und Nebel. Few ever emerged from under its darken shadow alive.

Going Underground

We know in the spring of 1944 safe houses for evading airmen were more difficult to find. They obviously could not be near an airfield, a military camp, or a railway junction. A childless host family was preferable, as children might talk at school. However, people without children often did not want to get involved: there was the jealous husband who did not want other men in his home, an old maid who was concerned about her reputation and the younger women who thought too little of theirs. This often did not leave many choices. Food remained scarce and men's clothing difficult to obtain.

Fortunately, Hilaire Gemoets had quite a few links with Resistance helpers around the city of Diest. One of them was farmer Frans Van Dyck in the town of Waanrode, about four kilometres south of Assent. Frans was a member of the Service Evasion Verbiest, named after José Verbiest of nearby Budingen. José was a local chief in the PA and he had set up a lifeline for airmen that were downed in the neighbourhood. He eventually placed about 15 flyers in the summer of 1944.

In the evening of May 1, 1944, Hilaire took Teddy to a rendezvous point. There, Resistance workers August Schepers and Theofiel Willems appeared on the scene and took custody of the Canadian pilot. They had an extra bicycle with them, and together the threesome rode off. The Resistance men had hung some spools of electric wire around the bicycle handlebars, so people would think they were electricians on the road doing repairs. They soon arrived at the house of Frans and Maria Van Dyck in the Tolkamerstraat in Waanrode, who promptly took Teddy inside. The couple instantly became very fond of their new guest. Teddy was accommodated in the master bedroom, while Frans and Maria slept on a straw-filled mattress in the living room. He was kept inside during the day, Maria bringing meals to the shaded bedroom. Many years later, she maintained a clear memory of those nerve-racking days:

> Teddy was very undemanding and ate well. I still remember his peculiar eating habits – he first finished his vegetables, then his meat,

> and then his potatoes. During the day, he killed time carving wood. He skilfully carved a destroyer, which I have kept until this day.
>
> Every time when he heard aircraft, he rushed to the window and uttered, 'They are ours'. He was all fired up and ready to go back to England and continue to fight the Germans. He said he would fly over Waanrode then to drop coffee and chocolate. However, his painful shoulder still bothered him.
>
> During the evenings, he sat with us in the living room and talked about various subjects – in French and using sign language. He told us he had flown nearly 40 operational missions. He also listened to the BBC on the radio. At night he occasionally would go in the backyard for a breather, accompanied by one or several of the resistance men, who acted as bodyguards. We were extremely careful. The Germans sometimes came knocking on our door, which always terrified me, but it was usually to ask for eggs.
>
> The resistance came over one day to make a photograph of Teddy. He wrote his name and address on the backside and I still have it.
>
> After about 12 to 14 days, he left our house to go and stay with other people. That changing of places was necessary to avoid suspicion. They never left a hiding airman at the same place for longer than two weeks. I now wish they would have left him here with us.[1]

As per the universal Resistance rule, Teddy was moved after no more than two weeks in any one location. Hilaire Gemoets arrived to fetch him, and the pair cycled to a remote little town called Meensel, about six kilometres west of Waanrode. This had seemed a good choice to Hilaire, as news had reached his organisation that certain escape lines had been compromised by infiltration. Hilaire and his cohorts realised that it was becoming increasingly difficult to get Teddy back to England. Besides, both he and Teddy understood that the invasion of Western Europe was about to begin at any moment, and this fact fed their hopes of a quick liberation. All this led to the decision to tuck Teddy carefully away, at least until the situation became more certain. In Meensel, Teddy was taken over by Isidore Bruers and Albert Loddewijckx, both members of the Group 'G'. They took Teddy to an abandoned farmhouse, but after a day or two it became obvious he couldn't stay there, so Albert Loddewijckx took Teddy home with him, where he was hidden in the attic of their barn. Albert brought Teddy food twice a day and generally saw to his needs.[2] However, the Loddewijckx family was quite involved with Resistance work, which made it a dicey spot to hide an evader. Hence, some eight days later, it was

---

[1]Interview with Maria Van Dyck-Simons, August 24, 1989 (translated by the author). Her husband Frans died in 1951. Frans never got over the loss of his brother, who had been ruthlessly shot by Germans and Belgian collaborators.

[2]Both Albert Loddewijckx and Isidore Bruers were killed in December 1944, when the house where they were hiding was hit by a German V-1 'buzz bomb'.

decided to move Teddy again. He was relocated to the home of Jules Schotsmans, a 36-year-old socially isolated farmer living alone in a remote smallholding. The date was now around May 20, 1944. Back in England a few days before, Aunt Lucy finished writing a moving letter to Teddy's parents:

> My dear Winsome,
> I hesitate to write to you and Toby when I have no news for you, for fear you should hope for some on seeing a letter. Max showed me yesterday the letter from Teddy's CO in response to his enquiry, saying that nothing so far had been heard of any of his crew, but I expect he has written fully to Toby about this.
>
> I don't know about you, but I feel sometimes as if I would sooner know for certain and learn to bear what there is to bear. The boy is never out of my thoughts and I long to be able to do something for him and for you both. If we do get news, we shall, of course, cable it at once. So little we were able to do for him, but his wants seemed few and simple.
>
> I suppose we have to be grateful for the spirit of these young boys, but it always seems to me the most cruel aspect of war that it is just the very best of them who go; and the old sit simply at home and send them out to face the danger created by their folly.
>
> I know that you must, like me, be hoping and fearing in turns; but, my dear, do at least say to yourself you may always be proud of what he has done and been, whatever happens; and, too, you may be certain that he was completely happy – indeed, I have a letter from him written on the day itself which shows his content. And you did not hamper him in any way, however much you must have longed to urge him to stick to the safe routine jobs he could have had for the asking. It was fairly certain this would come to us in our turn, but I didn't find myself prepared. My love, Lucy.

Meensel was a very small farming community that merged with the comparable neighbouring town of Kiezegem. Together, Meensel-Kiezegem formed a rural but independent village in the middle of a quiet fruit cultivation area in the Province of Brabant, Belgium. The fused town's population was approximately 900 inhabitants. The nearby wooded area offered the inhabitants a natural hideout. The people lived in quiet isolation from the world, without highways, and were mostly occupied with farming. Meensel was on the light interurban railway from Tienen to Aarschot, which was virtually the only connection with the outside world. The nearest cities were Tienen, ten kilometres to the south, and the well-known university city of Leuven, 18 kilometres to the west.[1]

[1]Today, Meensel-Kiezegem is part of a cluster of rural villages, which all merged into a new town called Tielt-Winge in the 1980s. Tielt-Winge is situated some 40 kilometres east of Brussels, in the east of the province of Flemish-Brabant.

After the occupation, the villagers of Meensel-Kiezegem subverted the Germans in every way possible. The initial period of passive and unorganised insubordination of 1942-1943 soon evolved into a more robust form of resistance. Early in 1942, the Germans introduced forced labour, and many young men received notification to report to various labour sites supporting the German war effort. These labourers filled the vacancies left by millions of German men who had been transferred from the factories to the frontlines. Only a handful of young men in Meensel-Kiezegem obeyed the German summons. Most of the families, however, concealed their young men between the ages of 18 and 45 so that they would not be forced to work for the Germans. These dissidents constantly had to be on their guard against the frequent German police search parties.[1] This constant threat of arrest in their own homes fuelled their desire to more actively resist the Germans. The result was the birth of several local factions of the national Resistance movement.

A number of villagers of Meensel joined the NKB during the period 1942-1943. Their leader was a locally renowned notary Victor Mertens, who purposely remained in the background. Other core members were Maurice Vuchelen, Adolf Hendrickx, Prosper Natens, Jules Cauwberghs and Oscar Beddegenoodts. The latter owned the local café near the tram station. He and his daughter Jeanne soon gravitated towards the Armed Partisans who were more active in their resistance. Oscar, who was a very capable man, became a section leader in the PA, while his daughter Jeanne was very active as a liaison courier for the PA, mainly around Leuven. PA leadership soon established a centre of operations at Meensel-Kiezegem. Here, several members of the PA section of nearby Leuven found a sanctuary in the houses of Prosper and August Pasteyns, Frans Coeckelberghs, Leonie Bruyninckx, among others.

A number of inhabitants of Kiezegem also signed up for the Resistance. Here, a small group was formed around Constant Wittemans and his sons Joost and Jules. The group was subordinate to the Independence Front and included, amongst others, Petrus Vander Meeren and Jean Pypen. And so the peaceful town of Meensel-Kiezegem became more than just a refuge for disobedient forced labourers. The new members of the three national Resistance movements now formed a small but active group, which mainly operated around Meensel. Jules Cauwberghs became the local NKB leader. He worked for notary Mertens, who owned large woodland areas that thankfully could be used to hide fugitives and firearms. But, in late 1943, the NKB section of Meensel began to show cracks in their relationships. Adolf Hendrickx, age 21, and Prosper Natens, age 28, changed affiliation to now become associated with Resistance groups like the PA or the

[1]Etienne Stas, great-grandfather of the author, was arrested on July 26, 1943, because one of his sons had disappeared after being summoned for forced labour. Etienne was released from St. Gilles Prison in Brussels on August 3, 1943, but only after his son Alfons had turned up again.

Independence Front. Prosper Natens and his right-hand man, Adolf Hendrickx, ultimately regarded themselves as overall leaders of the Meensel-Kiezegem Resistance movement, boasting they were the favoured disciples of the covert notary Victor Mertens.

The Resistance factions at Meensel-Kiezegem experienced a difficult period of growth. Members of diverse ideologies had differing opinions, basically because there was not an instructional manual on how to organise Resistance movements. Also, Resistance members from outside Meensel-Kiezegem arrived to seek a hideout and interfered with local activities.

Escaped Polish and Russian prisoners of war, who had been put to work by the Germans in the Belgian coalmines, also sought shelter in this remote rural and forested area of East-Brabant. Influenced by all these outsiders, some Resistance groups at Meensel-Kiezegem lost their 'boy-scout' character and developed into aggressive Underground hit squads. They were involved in the disruption of the railway system between Aarschot and Wezemaal and derailed an ammunitions train. Some were present when the town hall of Tielt was raided to steal ration stamps, an action that resulted in three casualties. Others ensured the rape crop would not ripen so that the Germans could not extract the valuable oil from the ripe coleseed. Several town halls in the area were set on fire in order to destroy the local registry and communal archives. This action alone hindered the German hunt for fugitives. On June 25, 1944, Armed Partisans of Meensel and Leuven murdered a known collaborator in his home in Attenrode. This attack was planned in Prosper Pasteyns' home in Meensel. All this was done in full knowledge that there were collaborators and traitors residing in the village. If discovered by them, retaliation against the Resistance members would be swift and merciless. While most members of the Underground were very cautious and discreet, greater risks were taken by Resistance members as the war developed. In mid-1944, the normally peaceful commune of Meensel was transformed into a Resistance hotbed. Some villagers manifestly supported the Underground, while others looked on in silence or were forcibly persuaded to provide support, food and shelter.

It appears that on one occasion, while staying at the Schotsmans farm, Teddy was asked to join the Natens-Hendrickx clan on an armed Resistance action in the nearby town of St.-Joris-Winghe. Apparently some local risk-takers wanted to show this Allied officer what they were capable of doing. And so they coaxed Teddy to join them one night in June 1944. A group of about 20 emboldened men from Meensel, Werchter and St.-Joris-Winghe crept up on their target, the home of a notorious collaborator, named Glazemaekers. Led by Jules Cauwberghs and Hilaire Gemoets, a TNT device was positioned to blow up the house, but the explosives failed, at which point the group decided to open fire with their rifles and pistols. Windows were shattered and doors punctured, before the men retreated.

This action on the part of Teddy to join with these Resistance men that night was to be a costly mistake and likely determined his fate.[1]

Jules Schotsmans was not an active Resistance member, but the local NKB knew they could count on him when in need for a safe haven. Jules was neither educated nor wealthy, and he lived in rather miserable circumstances. His derelict home offered shelter to refugees and outlaws of all sorts, as it seemed unlikely the German police would come and look for anyone there. Teddy, having been placed there, did not care much for his paltry lodgings and felt quite isolated. He often thought about Helen and his parents and wondered how they were doing. Far away from him in Italy, Uncle Cyril wrote a moving letter to his sister, Teddy's mother, Winsome on June 8:

> Dear Winsome,
> I was so proud to hear of Teddy's decoration then so sad to hear that he is 'missing'.
>
> I know that nothing I can say will help much. But, I, like Teddy, have faced death, almost daily. We who fight where the bullets are do no longer fear death. Our fear is the pain and sorrow that our passing will cause to wives, mothers and sweethearts. If we can be sure that when our turn comes we can leave behind a trail of happy memories rather than grief, sorrow and heartache, then the passing on will be light and happy.
>
> 'Missing' I know is so uncertain, so hard on those left behind. All I can say is take that little spark of hope, hide it deep within your heart, keep it secret to yourself, and it will help that great healer time, ease the pain whilst He heals the wound within.
>
> We here, with the help of the Desert Air Force, have defeated the German. His retreat is a disorganized rout. If revenge is sweet to you, dear sister, I have already taken it, personally, tenfold.
>
> Ever your loving brother, Cyril.

Despite everything, Jules Schotsmans did his best to treat Teddy as his own brother and would not hear about moving his companion to another hiding place. Local Resistance deputy Adolf Hendrickx and his sister Lea brought Teddy food. On June 6, Adolf, who spoke a little English, told him the news about the Allied landings in Normandy. Teddy was elated and reckoned it would be a matter of months before he would be back in 'merry olde England'. Jeanne Beddegenoodts recounted the risks associated with Adolf's frequent visits to Teddy's hideout:

---

[1]Independent statements by Maurice Vuchelen, Octave Stas and Teophile Cauwberghs, November 1989-March 1990. Maurice Vuchelen admitted to the author that it had been a foolish mistake to take Teddy along and expose him during this action, even though he only passively observed the events.

> It quickly transpired that an Allied airman was hiding at the farm of Jules Schotsmans. Apparently Adolf Hendrickx' little brother Robert had discovered about Adolf's daily food runs to the Canadian. In his childish innocence, Robert and his brother Willy had bragged about this at school. My own little brother Maurice had heard this and told us after coming home from school. My father reacted very nervously to this news and told Maurice to not tell anybody else about this. Especially after our Maurice confirmed that young Ernest Merckx, son of a known collaborating family, had also overheard the tell-tale. Dad then summoned Prosper Natens, and furiously asked him what was going on. He asked him if they were trying to get Meensel destroyed. He told Natens that he was going to take care of the pilot himself, since clearly they weren't capable of handling the situation. He then contacted Miss Bruyninckx, who immediately agreed something had to be done.[1]

Emma Bruyninckx, an intrepid 42-year-old elementary school teacher from the nearby town of Glabbeek, was an important member of the Service Evasion Verbiest. Affectionately called Miss Bruynke, she personally organised the sheltering of several evading airmen during the war and chaperoned some to Leuven or Brussels. Most of her 'boys' successfully reached England again.[2] According to several testimonies, she wanted Teddy out of Meensel and put on an escape line to connect with the advancing liberation armies in France, or at least have him in a safer place. Although another Allied airman had recently arrived at her home, she was ready and willing to take the risk to shelter Teddy as well. To start with, she wanted him out of the Schotsmans farm quickly and communicated this request to the Natens-Hendrickx group in Meensel. She also sent regional NKB leader Jan Crab to Meensel, to recover Teddy from the local group. But his efforts were in vain.

So, about six weeks after arriving at the Schotsmans farm, local Resistance leadership finally convinced Jules that Teddy couldn't stay there any longer. Initially, Jan Crab arranged for Teddy to be taken to the house of Constant Dereze, who owned a small business in Meensel. He remained there a couple of days, and then he was moved again. On July 6, 'the Canadian pilot' was placed in the family home of Herman Pypen. It was a secluded farmhouse at Creftelbos Nr. 6 on the outskirts of Meensel, and bordered a large wooded area, called the Vrijbos (Free Woods). The Pypens were small farmers, but quite prosperous in their way of life. They had two cows, a horse and a pig. There were nine children of which one son had

---

[1]Interviews with Jeanne Beddegenoodts, September 1989-July 1990 (translated by the author).
[2]From May 7, 1944, until the liberation four months later, Emma Bruyninckx lodged Sergeant William Weare, the flight engineer of a Halifax shot down on April 26-27, 1944, in her own home – the 'schoolhouse'. She received no aid or money whatsoever, except from her 18-year-old cousin Charles and the local priest, Father Van Maegdenbergh.

died at the age of 14. The two eldest daughters were married. Teddy was presented to the younger children as the French-speaking boyfriend of their 18-year-old sister, Paula. This was so the children would not question his presence or raise suspicions at school. Teddy and Paula, a clever and active young lady, immediately bonded. He spoke French well enough to be able to communicate with her. Paula, in her teenage innocence, developed a soft spot for Teddy and was very proud of her handsome 'boyfriend'. More than four decades later, she emotionally revoked those poignant times. Some parts of the story she had never before disclosed:

> Eddy, as we used to call him, arrived at our home at 10 o'clock at night, I will never forget that. He had lived a miserable life at the Schotsmans farm, and he was very dirty and covered all over his upper body with fleabites. Nobody had taken care of him over there. His hair had turned grey and he was clothed in filthy rags. As he stood there, he felt very ashamed to arrive in a state like that in a young family home. Mother and I immediately heated water on the stove and filled the bath tub. I left the room not to embarrass him, and Mother washed him and washed him again, over and over. She then showed him the ground-floor bedroom in the back of the house, from where he could easily escape through the window should the need arise.
>
> In the morning, Mother went to his room to wake him, and was appalled to find him crying on his bed. He had been up all night, still bothered by lice in his clothes and by the pain of his inflamed fleabites. We immediately disinfected his room, and Mother attended to his wounds. For ten days, she worked hard to make him decent again. All this time, he stayed in his room. He didn't want the kids to be infected with his lice and fleas. Mother cared for him as if he was her own child. She had lost a son, our Louis, who was from the same year of birth as Eddy. She often said: 'He's my son'.
>
> Eddy was much taller than we were, so I borrowed a suit and shirt from Teophile Nijs, who was a tall man. I told him it was for my new boy friend.
>
> After his recovery, he looked so much better. He then became one of us and quickly felt at home. He ate and drank with us, and was accepted and loved by all of us. He was very handsome and so full of life. He played with the little children in the orchard – it was summer recess. He taught us all kinds of tricks – how to immobilize someone around a tree, how to tie someone's thumb to his big toe, etcetera. He was a great dancer; Mother really got a kick out of that. We had an old gramophone, and at nights he danced with Mother. He was a very polite and sweet boy. I spoke French with him, and he taught me some English. He told me lots of things. He didn't talk about home a lot, except that he was an only child. He always spoke about 'Mary'. It

> sometimes annoyed me a little bit and I was convinced he had a girlfriend called Mary somewhere, but I didn't dare to ask him. One day I did ask him, and he stood up and started walking arm-in-arm with Mother. Finally we understood that he was going to get married after the war.
>
> Eddy carried two small passport photographs in his breast pocket. He gave them to me, and I hid them and his escape compass under the roof in the barn.[1]

Paula had recently returned home from Brussels, where she had been hiding out after receiving instructions to report for work in Germany. She had returned hoping that the Germans would not still be looking for her and thinking she would be relatively safe at the remote Pypen farm. Her father Herman was an active Resistance worker and often out the door, but he could count on a network of informers should danger threaten his family. Paula's brother Jos, who also refused forced labour, often hid on the family farm as well.

From Paula's testimony, it appears that Teddy never obtained his forged papers that would have allowed him to pass as a Belgian national. His purpose-made photographs were never used. As a standard procedure, Resistance organisations always provided evaders with false identity papers, using the snapshots carried by those crews flying missions over the Continent. For the NKB in the district around Meensel-Kiezegem, this was the responsibility of regional leader Jan Crab, of Leuven. It is uncertain why this was overlooked in Teddy's case, but the poor relationship between Miss Bruynke and Jan Crab on one side, and the Natens-Hendrickx group on the other, might explain how this could have happened. In any case, Prosper Natens told the Pypen folks that their farm was the safest place to hide out in the entire area, and that Teddy could remain there until liberated. He probably did not see the need to provide Teddy with forged identity papers. As per usual, Prosper Natens underestimated potential danger, and possible consequences of his imaginary infallibility and invulnerability.

Teddy, although anxious to get on with the war, was well taken care of at the Pypen home. He reconciled himself to the idea of spending the rest of the war there and was quite content with it. He told the Pypens that he was happy there, and grateful for all that they had done for him. In return, he would ensure the family was compensated after the war. He stayed around the property most of the day, but in the evening he sometimes would wander off into the nearby woods. To pass the time away, Teddy carved wood, a hobby his grandfather had taught him as a child. While doing that, his thoughts were with Helen, his parents and the Skipper and Granny. He hoped that somehow they had received word he was alive. The

---

[1]Interviews with Paula Pypen, April 1989–May 1993 (translated by the author).

Pypen family had a radio, so Teddy had a source for receiving news from the outside world. He listened intently to broadcasts from the BBC and translated for Paula what he heard.

Germany's outlook was far bleaker in July 1944 than it had been during July 1918, when her last grand offensive had barely been halted. Even Adolf Hitler seemed to feel that dark days had arrived. The Reich's nightmare of a two-front war now had a third, with new fronts to follow if the Allies were to launch additional amphibious landing on adjacent parts of the Continent. The Allied breakthrough of the Atlantic Wall had been followed by an even greater disaster on their Eastern front. From the beginning of the new Russian counteroffensive, Germany had found nothing but disaster. This was the front where the Germans had hoped to hold the line while they dealt with the invaders on their Western front. The measure of their declining strength was evident in the crucial summer of 1944. The Russians, from the first day of the new offensive, had shattered the German defences in one of their worst defeats since Stalingrad.

In the south the Germans were still bleeding from the series of defeats that had begun in North Africa. The town of Monte Cassino in Italy fell to the Allies on May 18. With the fall of Monte Cassino, the whole Gustav Line crumbled, and the road to Rome was opened to the Fifth US Army and the British Eighth Army that included the First Canadian Corps. On June 4, American forces, under the command of General Mark Clark, entered Rome, from where the Nazis were quickly retreating northward. The capture of Rome marked the first of the Axis capitals to be captured by Allied forces.

German forces on all fronts were exhausted. The troops they faced were well trained, superbly equipped and by now formed a very competent fighting machine. Hovering over every German soldier was the crushing weight of Allied strategic and tactical air power, which knocked out railroads and highway bridges, chewed up communications, interdicted retreating columns and smashed industries vital to the war effort. Prudent Allied military men could only speculate on what the Luftwaffe was going to do to stop the advance. The German soldier on the ground, not bound by such caution, could come to only one conclusion: the Luftwaffe was just about out of business.

Still, the defeat of Germany was a long way off. D-Day accomplished the first phase of the invasion. By July 1, 1944, Allied ground troops had broken through the German coastal defences and had established a continental abutment for an eventual sea bridge that was to carry men and supplies from the United Kingdom to France. At the beginning of July, the Allies executed the second stage of the invasion, expanding their continental foothold to a size that could support an assault on Germany. Before the Allies could launch their definitive attack, they had to assemble enough men and material on the Continent to assure success. To expand their foothold, the Allied forces had to overcome a tenacious enemy and adapt to the stubborn terrain. Germany fought on, desperately and skilfully; Allied casualty lists continued to grow.

So, as July 1944 entered its final weeks, the Allied forces in Normandy faced, at least on the surface, a most discouraging situation. A large British armoured offensive west of Caen failed on July 18 and 19, and the US First Army conducted a bitter battle of attrition around Saint-Lô. American troops were bogged down in the Norman bocage landscape, massive square walls of earth, five feet high and topped by hedges. Local farmers had used these hedges over the centuries to divide their fields and protect their crops and cattle from strong ocean winds. The Germans had turned these embankments into fortresses, canalising the American advance into narrow channels, which were easily covered by anti-tank weapons and machine guns. The stubborn defenders were also aided by some of the worst weather seen in Normandy since the turn of the century. Incessant downpours turned country lanes into rivers of mud. By July 20, the size of the Allied beachhead had not even come close to the dimensions that the D-Day planners had anticipated. The slow progress revived fears in the Allied camp of a return to the static warfare of the First World War. Few believed that, in the space of a month and a half, Allied armies would stand triumphant at the German border.

The village of Meensel-Kiezegem might have come through the war unscathed, if it had not been for a most unfortunate incident on July 30, 1944.

CHAPTER TWELVE

The Tragedy of Meensel-Kiezegem

When morning broke on that Sunday of July 30, 1944, the day seemed to smile on the people of Meensel-Kiezegem. It was going to be hot and sunny, and the news of the recent Allied successes in Normandy produced contentment.

By July 25, 1944, with most of the German tanks now deployed against the British in the offensive near Caen, the Americans faced a battlefront almost denuded of armour. Reinforcement finally gave the Allies a clear superiority in armour and infantry. The American Operation Cobra, scheduled for July 25, commenced with a devastating air attack. Through the open gap, the First US Army advanced toward Avranches, which it took in five days. At this juncture, George S. Patton's newly formed Third Army joined in the advance. A massive American spearhead broke out and threatened to drive into Brittany but turned east to encircle the Germans from the south before Patton raced east past Paris. Meanwhile, an attack by the British Second Army commenced their drive on July 30, 1944. Operation Bluecoat drew substantial German forces away from their projected counterattack at Avranches, and contributed largely to the ultimate encirclement of the German forces at what is known today as the Falaise Pocket.

Besides the weather and the prospects of a forthcoming liberation, the citizens of Meensel-Kiezegem had another reason to be joyful. The annual summer fair was to take place in the neighbouring parish of Attenrode-Wever, and many looked forward to spending a Sunday afternoon at that social event.

By now, there appeared to be a natural balance between the Resistance workers of Meensel-Kiezegem, and the known Blackshirts. Meensel-Kiezegem being a small town, everybody knew each other well. The prominent and outwardly haughty Remi Merckx and Felix Broos families of Kiezegem had always openly expressed their sympathies for the German political cause. They were convinced that Nazi Germany would win the war and that this would result in their families gaining more power in the region. Up to this point, they had been left alone and unharmed by the local

Resistance groups. While the Resistance workers felt a strong contempt for those who collaborated with the enemy for personal reasons, they more or less respected those who were in league with the enemy for whatever ideological reasons they might harbour. Still, during the summer of 1944 more and more resentment began to be voiced against the Merckx and Broos families. Pamphlets and wall posters began appearing calling for action against them, but nothing ever happened, much to the relief of most of the villagers, who were only interested in a quiet and peaceful existence as their liberation approached.

Conversely, both the Merckx and Broos families were well aware of the identity of several of the leading Resistance figures, but they also did not interfere with them to any great extent. This virtual truce gave both parties confidence, even after the arrests of key Resistance members such as Prosper Janssens and Frans Coeckelberghs earlier in 1944. Their unexpected early release by the Gestapo even led people to suppose that the Merckx family had intervened on their behalf. Others, however, believed that their lives had been spared in return for sensitive information they provided about the Resistance activities in Meensel-Kiezegem. Had they talked during the intensive Gestapo interrogations? No one will ever know for sure.

In spite of everything, the relative peace at Meensel-Kiezegem was to be suddenly shattered on that Sunday afternoon of July 30. At around 02:00 p.m., 24-year-old Gaston Merckx left his parents' farm with three of his friends to walk to the fair at Attenrode. They were in high spirits, with the prospect of having a few beers and some fun with the young and vivacious local beauties. Gaston carried a concealed firearm, which he figured might come in handy if he was to threaten a challenger in a quarrel over a girl, or defy some over-confident Resistance members with the nerve to pester him. With the Allied liberation armies getting nearer, more and more youthful and immature Resistance followers surfaced wanting to make a name for themselves before the war came to a close.

When the foursome arrived at a crossroads called Boekhout, three plain-clothed youngsters coming from the direction of Meensel approached them, two men and a girl. Merckx and his companions were taken by surprise and came to a standstill, their eyes fixed upon the strangers. One of the three then stepped forward and shouted 'Gestapo, passport control!' Totally dumbfounded, Gaston and his companions reluctantly produced their requested document. Suddenly, however, Marcel Peeters, one of Gaston's friends took to his heels and disappeared behind a road bank. Gaston immediately followed his friend's example, but the three antagonists came after him in hot pursuit. They found him nervously hiding behind a haystack and, without further ado, shot him in cold blood. Gaston's two other friends had watched the whole incident completely stupefied. While the three strangers took to their bicycles and disappeared, both men ran back to the village of Kiezegem to report what they had witnessed.

The three aggressors were not locals. It took many years of post-war investigation to determine their identity and motive. They were members of the Armed Partisans section of Leuven, and known by their aliases 'Léon', 'René' and 'Gilberte'. It is believed that another PA member had picked up a conversation between Gaston Merckx and his friends after Sunday mass as they were discussing their afternoon trip to the fair. This bit of local news was quickly passed on to the PA leaders in Leuven. It seems that 'Léon' and his two cohorts were sent out with a warrant to assassinate a known Blackshirt. Or perhaps they acted on their own initiative, hoping to achieve the status of a 'true' PA member by their violent action. After cycling to Meensel around midday, the three assailants then reconnoitered the area, bought an ice cream from the local street trader and waited patiently at the crossroads just outside the village. When Merckx and his friends arrived on the scene, the passport inspection scheme exposed the identity of the person they were after and, confirmed their targeted man. Like his partners, Gaston Merckx quickly sensed there was something wrong, and decided to run. He did not go far.[1]

Shortly after the fatal shots had been fired, Gaston's friends rushed to the Merckx property bringing with them the shocking news. Immediately, Mother Clementine Merckx and other family members joined them and returned to the crime scene. There, Mother Merckx came upon the lifeless body of her son. While the corpse was loaded on a cart to be brought back home, Gaston's weeping mother swore revenge. At that very moment, dark clouds appeared over Meensel-Kiezegem – both literally and figuratively – and a heavy thunderstorm broke overhead. The news about the shooting quickly reached the village centres of both Meensel and Kiezegem, where people came into the streets to discuss the shooting. While local teenagers were excited by the neighbourhood homicide, their parents realised this sudden turn of events could only bring great misery to their town. An atmosphere of tension and discontent descended over the town.

That night, the Merckx clan and some of their Blackshirts friends assembled at the family farm in Kiezegem. Gaston had been a member of the infamous Flemish Guard (Vlaamsche Wacht), a Belgian military organisation collaborating with the Nazis.[2] His three elder brothers, Maurice, a schoolteacher, and Marcel together with Albert, were all

[1]In the mid-1980s, renowned journalist Maurice De Wilde made a TV series about resistance and collaboration in Belgium. Despite an oath of secrecy amongst former PA members, he managed to reveal the identity of the three assailants of Gaston Merckx, but he never succeeded in having them testify about their actions on television. Further research by the author exposed a document of 1947, in which former PA member Frans Vranckx from Kessel-Lo claimed to have liquidated Gaston Merckx (Dossier SRA for Frans Vranckx – SOMA, Brussels).

[2]The Vlaamsche Wacht was initially tasked with police functions on Belgian territory. In 1942, it became a section of the Wehrmacht, and in July 1944 the majority of all its members swore loyalty to Hitler.

members of the Flemish fascist movement VNV.[1] They were conceited and aggressive men who often openly carried guns and were feared by many of their fellow villagers. Gaston's stuck-up sister Maria also had strong Nazi ties, while his 14-year-old brother Ernest was a proud member of the National Socialistic Youth Flanders. Mother Merckx, an arrogant and obstinate woman, was the matriarch and the ruler of the family. Her wish was everyone's command. She insisted that her son's death be avenged, even *before* he was buried. According to a wide variety of sources, she demanded 100 hostages be taken to expose the true conspirators of the homicide. In addition, she and her husband Remi, together with their three eldest sons, compiled a list of names of fellow-villagers whom they knew – or suspected – to be members of the Resistance. Payback time had arrived.

Even though some contended that the victim had provoked the assault, and although the evidence was very contradictory, the German Security Police decided immediately on retaliatory measures. The unusual request by Mother Merckx gave them the incentive to take firm action in Meensel-Kiezegem. The acts of sabotage, harassments and numerous delinquent forced labour conscripts had repeatedly irritated the Gestapo and Security Police. Meensel-Kiezegem had been on their black list for a long time. It was decided they were going to use this death as an excuse to punish the town for its transgressions. Some of the known and more prominent Resistance offenders were to be taught a lesson, thereby intimidating the rest of the population.

Shortly after daybreak on Tuesday, August 1, 1944, the entire town of Meensel-Kiezegem found itself in a state of distress. Gunshots sounded, waking up frightened children who asked their nervous parents what was happening. Flemish Guard and SS members, accompanied by German field police officers, brutally and noisily invaded the town. Maurice, Marcel and Albert Merckx, who were masked to avoid being recognised by their fellow villagers, were guiding the intruders. SS Sturmbannführer Frans Packet from Antwerp was in charge of the entire operation. It immediately became apparent that they were looking for Resistance hideouts. They received help from a certain man called Andries, a Resistance worker from out of town who had been hiding at various addresses in Meensel-Kiezegem during the summer of 1944. Andries had been arrested shortly before and had succumbed to the intense interrogations. He was led along handcuffed, and it appeared he was giving some indications to the SS, obviously with

[1]This Vlaamsch Nationaal Verbond (Flemish National Union) was tied to the idea of creating a pan-Dutch state, called Dietsland, to include both Flanders and the Netherlands. Its slogan was 'Authority, Discipline and Dietsland'. Along the way, the new party became more and more authoritarian in doctrine, and it quickly became a Fascist movement. When Nazi Germany invaded Belgium in 1940, the VNV immediately sided with it. Hitler and SS-leader Heinrich Himmler profited from the situation and increased competition between various groups by founding some more extreme collaborationist groups like DeVlag, the German-Flemish Workers' Community. After the war, the VNV was outlawed and its leaders were put in prison.

the hope of being granted some mercy. Almost simultaneously, three groups of raiders banged on the front doors of three family homes in the centre of Meensel, those of Oscar Beddegenoodts, Ferdinand Duerinckx and August Craeninckx.

Twenty-four-year-old August Craeninckx was unmercifully dragged out of his home. He was ushered into his farmyard at gunpoint, and ordered to show where he was sheltering Resistance members. Nobody was found, but this didn't restrain the violent intruders. While his wife Germaine was watching in horror from behind a window, they led a begging August to the church path opposite his home. About ten metres from the church entrance, they shot him in cold blood. The town physician, Dr Goyens, and his son-in-law, Paul Martens, were ordered to carry the lifeless body back to the doctor's house, where SS troops had assembled other villagers.

A second group of assailants had simultaneously harassed those in a house adjacent to the Craeninckx home. This was the home of the local schoolmaster Ferdinand Duerinckx who, although not a very active member of the NKB, had supported the Resistance by doing occasional clerical matters when asked. His pregnant wife Maria was opening her shutters when a German and a Blackshirt approached her. They pointed a machine gun at her and demanded the whereabouts of Ferdinand. When she could not answer the question quickly enough, she was brutally slapped and pushed to the ground. Ferdinand, who had been reassuring his children in the kitchen, immediately jumped forward to protect her, only to be knocked to the floor with a rifle butt. Under the tearful eyes of his wife and their four little children, he received a battering which rendered him unconscious. He was subsequently dragged to the doctor's courtyard, where his fellow villagers could not recognise his disfigured face.

In the meantime another mob invaded the café of Oscar Beddegenoodts. They were looking in particular for his daughter Jeanne but, though terrified, she stayed put in her night hideout in another part of the house and was never found. The home of Oscar and his wife Pauline was searched inside out, while Oscar was severely abused by Flemish SS Untersturmbannführer Jozef Bachot. He interrogated Oscar about the location of the ammunition supplies used by his Resistance group. Meanwhile, Pauline and their 12-year-old son Maurice were threatened with guns while being questioned about the whereabouts of Jeanne. After venting their frustrations with the total destruction of the furnishings, the SS men took Oscar, Pauline and Maurice to the collection point at the doctor's place.

While the terrorised hostages were being assembled on the doctor's driveway and courtyard, four other homes were raided at the Vrankenberg, a neighbourhood a few hundred metres outside the village centre. There also doors were kicked in at 05:30 a.m. and residents were dragged onto the street. It was obvious that the raiders were well briefed, as they went straight to a number of hiding places virtually unknown to anyone but the property owners. Some of these hideouts were vacant, but two sought-after Resistance members were discovered at the home of 26-year-old Jozef Claes. This enraged the marauders even further, who believed they had now come across an important Resistance nest. All their neighbours were arrested and put against the wall of the Claes residence. One of them, Frans Bastijns, saw his chance to escape and did. He survived a salvo of gunfire and successfully got away. One by one, the 16 villagers were ordered into the Claes home. They were subjected to an intense and brutal interrogation concerning the whereabouts of other Resistance members on the 'black list', but no one divulged any information. Jozef Claes was manhandled to the extent that he lost consciousness on several occasions. He was dragged to the backyard of his property where the SS put a gun to his head while asking him where the weapons were hidden. Jozef never talked. His wife Melanie received a thrashing with a sword-belt on her naked body while her crying toddler was watching. At the nearby home of Jozef Boesmans, Frans Packet applied the whip to several people. Women were ordered to strip naked and viciously abused.[1]

Unaware of what was happening in and around the Claes residence, Petrus Vander Meeren, a farmer from Kiezegem, cycled by the home. An SS officer and a masked cohort stopped him. After investigation of his identity papers, the cloaked man nodded, and Petrus was ordered to join the others against the wall. Petrus' relationship with the Merckx and Broos families had not been exactly convivial recently. As he was a member of the Independence Front, he feared this might soon be revealed.

Shortly after Petrus' detention, several German soldiers departed the Vrankenberg and proceeded to the village centre to fetch Oscar Beddegenoodts at Dr Goyens' house. After Oscar's arrival at the farm of Jozef Claes, he and the other detainees were sent into a nearby wood, supposedly to point out shelters and weapons. Shortly after entering the woods, around 08:00 a.m., gunshots were heard. Oscar and Petrus had both been executed. The other villagers were ordered to carry their bodies to the doctor's residence where they were put alongside that of August Craeninckx. Then the SS marched the detainees to the tram station, where they confiscated a lorry and ordered the frightened driver, Antoine Edouard, to unload his goods and transport the hostages to the SD Headquarters, at 27 Vital Decosterstraat in Leuven. There, 15-year-old Madeleine Janssens was set free, but 14 others, 11 men and three women, were thrown in the state prison of Leuven. Among them were Resistance leader Prosper Natens, Oscar Beddegenoodts's wife Paulina Bollen, still unaware of the execution of her husband, Jozef Claes and schoolmaster Ferdinand Duerinckx. Paul Martens was released the following day, at the

---

[1]Maurice De Wilde, *De Tijd Der Vergelding, Het Drama van Meensel-Kiezegem*, BRT TV 1, May 1988.

same time as his father-in-law, Dr Goyens, was being arrested and placed with the other assembled prisoners. Four days later, most of the detainees were transferred to the St. Gilles prison near Brussels.[1]

After the events of August 1, the villagers of Meensel-Kiezegem were in total distress. In only a few hours, wives had lost husbands, children had lost fathers and mothers had lost sons. Everybody wondered if more was to come. Many tears were shed for the ones who were arrested, while others were relieved that they had escaped unscathed. When the initial shock wore off, people lived in hope that their loved ones would someday return. This hope would increasingly be put to a greater test. More than a month after the arrests, Maria Duerinckx-Janssens received a note that had been hurriedly scribbled by her husband on a piece of tin wrapping and thrown from a train transporting him to a German concentration camp on August 31: 'To Mrs Duerinckx-Janssens, Wersbeekstraat 2, Meensel-Kiezegem. Dear All, enroute to Germany. Unknown destination, everyone healthy. We hope to return soon. Pray for a good and quick homecoming. Ferdinand.'

The note was found and sent to Maria and her five little children. She had given birth to her youngest child only three weeks after Ferdinand was brutally snatched away from his young family, a family that would never see their father and husband again.[2]

Teddy Blenkinsop's host Herman Pypen became alarmed early that August 1 morning and decided everyone had to run. They had to go into hiding elsewhere until the situation in Meensel was deemed safe again. He took Paula, Jos, Teddy and some others through the woods to Kapellen, a village some two kilometres east of Meensel. Paula returned home that same night, but the others stayed in hiding at Kapellen until August 3. Returning home, Herman realised Jos and Teddy could no longer spend the night inside the house, so he designed an ingenious hiding place on the farm premises. To the casual observer, it was a haystack, but inside and underneath a room was dug out, where a handful of men could be hidden. Teddy and Jos Pypen became the first guests. Soon afterwards, Maurice Vuchelen arrived to take up a spot in the hideout. He had joined the PA and was a prominent member of the Natens-Hendrickx group, and the Germans wanted him. The fourth man to use the new shelter was Staf Broos, a smuggler. The foursome stayed there during the night – the preferred time for German roundups – or any other time danger loomed. During the day, Teddy always stayed in the vicinity of the farmyard. He attempted to whittle a wooden model of a Lancaster to pass the time, just as his grandfather had taught him in bygone days.

Meanwhile, Miss Bruynke was making new arrangements to get Teddy

---

[1]See appendix B for details about all the victims of Meensel-Kiezegem.

[2]Maria Janssens was a niece of the author's grandfather Albert Stas. Her son Freddy, who was born on August 25, 1944, was in fact her sixth child. She and Ferdinand had lost a baby girl shortly after birth in 1943.

out of Meensel without further delay. There was the risk of another German roundup, so he simply could not remain there anymore. She intended to bring him to the city of Leuven. There he could disappear into one of the countless dormitories or apartments used by the University of Leuven students and await liberation. On two occasions, she dispatched her confidant, Jan Crab, to take custody of Teddy. The first time, several days after Teddy's return from Kapellen, messenger Jeanne Beddegenoodts informed the Pypens about the place and time of the rendezvous. Jeanne's perseverance was even intensified after her father's assassination and mother's arrest. Teddy was expected at a wooded location on the Nevelberg, at midnight sharp. With Herman Pypen observing from a distance, Teddy and Paula cautiously hiked to the meeting point. Hidden behind some bushes, they waited for several hours, but much to Teddy's disappointment, nobody showed up.

The next day, on returning to the Pypen farm, Jeanne told Paula there definitely would be a rendezvous the following night. So, at midnight and with newfound courage, Paula and Teddy walked again to the spot within the darkened forest, and they waited in silence. Their hearts were in their throats. Again nobody turned up. On returning home, Teddy felt dejected and told Paula he would not repeat this rendezvous again. He realised that someone was playing games and said he would rather take his chances staying with the Pypens until the war's end. The Pypens were very irritated about the letdown, and asked Jeanne whom they were trying to fool. But Jeanne was mystified herself. It was obvious that someone had misled either her or Jan Crab. Finally, Miss Bruynke gave in, but not before Adolf Hendrickx assured her that the Canadian would be well taken care of and would be kept in maximum concealment. It later transpired that Prosper Natens and Adolf Hendrickx continuously refused to hand over Teddy to Miss Bruynke, allegedly because they wanted him as their trophy at the forthcoming liberation of Belgium.[1] Perhaps they were aware that other escape networks were keeping hundreds of their evaders in hiding places throughout the towns and cities all over Belgium, until the advancing armies could liberate them. With Natens now arrested, his deputy Hendrickx had no intention of changing that plan. It is not unthinkable that his co-worker Maurice Vuchelen, who was in Teddy's hideout at the time of the failed transfer, played a role to support his leader's objective.

And so it was that there continued to be two sides to this story. The Natens-Hendrickx clan definitely intended to keep Teddy in Meensel until the war was over. Several others, headed by Miss Bruynke, Jules Cauwberghs and Oscar Beddegenoodts, had always wanted him out of the village and put on an escape line to be repatriated by the Allies in France. This had led to heated arguments between Cauwberghs and his NKB

---

[1]Independent statements by Jeanne Beddegenoodts, Paula Pypen and Jan Crab, September 1989–March 1990 (translated by the author).

subordinate Natens, but following numerous Gestapo arrests in towns around Meensel during the summer of 1944, Jules had been forced to run for his own safety and go into hiding. Prosper Natens – now arrested – had replaced him as the head of the local NKB section. Still, it was obvious that envy and suspicion had caused cracks in the relationships inside the Meensel Resistance movement. It is not unimaginable that this gave rise to feelings of reprisal in some people's mind.

Paula was sick of it all. She told her parents that she would take Teddy to Brussels herself. Her godmother lived there, and Paula was convinced she could count on her until the liberation. But, the Meensel Resistance heads refused to allow her to leave town with their 'trophy'.

The Second Roundup

Gaston Merckx was buried on Thursday, August 3, 1944. Standing near the open grave, some of Gaston's family and Flemish Guard friends, while giving a Hitler salute, vowed they would avenge the death of their brother and fellow member. This uttered threat caused considerable discomfort among the few villagers present.

The funeral services of August Craeninckx, Petrus Vander Meeren and Oscar Beddegenoodts passed rather unnoticed. Many locals did not find it easy to conceal their uneasiness, nor did they want to risk being noticed by the wrong people while paying their respects to the three martyrs. Each villager stayed in or around his house trying to carry on with his or her normal life. A false and ominous tranquillity descended over Meensel-Kiezegem. Resistance members who got off scot free on August 1 had absconded. Even the town's notary, Victor Mertens, the actual mentor of the local Resistance, seemed to have disappeared. The panic amongst the population died down as the days passed, and people began to think no further incidents would transpire.

However, the Merckx clan were still vengeful. Three murders and 14 hostages failed to satisfy their feelings of grief, bitterness and rage. They were still intent on reprisal. Gaston's mother and his sister Maria voiced their indignation to infamous Flemish SD-members François Janssens and Fernand Faignaert about the perpetrators still walking around freely. They insisted that money was no object in the hunt for the murderers or their accomplices. Finally, instigated by his assertive mother, Marcel Merckx travelled to Brussels, where he offered a large sum of money to Robert Verbelen, a very influential Belgian Nazi. As a result, a second raid on Meensel-Kiezegem was meticulously prepared. It was believed that, by seeking out the 'criminals' of Meensel-Kiezegem – Resistance members, deserting forced labourers and saboteurs – the excessive demands of Mother Merckx could more or less be justified.

Following the arrests of August 1, the 14 prisoners were kept in quarantine in the Leuven prison. There, they were incessantly interrogated and flogged ruthlessly in order to make them divulge information. The Merckx brothers were often present to play an active part in the physical and psychological abuse of their fellow-townsmen. Little by little, the Gestapo was able to form a fairly complete picture of the rebellious activities in Meensel-Kiezegem. They had obtained additional information from local collaborators who had attended a meeting the day prior to the initial raid. Little by little, the plan for a second raid was completed, and the Merckx's list of names of those to be taken hostage finalised. Resistance foreman Prosper Natens was also viciously interrogated, while his chum Adolf Hendrickx, who had not been found on August 1, was hiding at his Uncle Pierre's home in Tienen. His name was at the top of the Gestapo's list. On August 10, Hendrickx made a costly mistake. Curious about the situation in Meensel-Kiezegem, he secretly returned home to visit his parents. When he went back to his hideout in Tienen, he was taken by surprise and arrested by the Gestapo, and brought to Leuven. There he received appalling treatment and an extensive cross-examination throughout the night until the following morning, when he and Natens were unknowingly going to play an important role in the Gestapo's plans.

The actual instruction for a second police action in Meensel-Kiezegem was promulgated on August 7. The Security Corps of the Higher Command and Police in Belgium and Northern France (Sicherheitskorps des Höheren und Polizeiführers in Belgien und Nordfrankreich) issued the action order. The document, classified 'Secret', was titled 'Order for Purge Action on Friday August 11, 1944', and stipulated:

1) The Place: Terrorists and forced labour deserters have found refuge in Meensel-Kiezegem and Kiezegem. Over the past months, several assaults and hold-ups have been committed in the area.
2) The Enemy: A gang of approximately 80 active members and co-workers. A number of these Partisans stay at their homes, others are hiding at local farms. Take into account that they can be armed. Research by the Secret Police has revealed most of the hiding places.
3) Our Assignment: Surround and besiege the village and arrest the known terrorists, as well as discovered illegals.
4) Composition of Our Group: The Security Corps with two storm troop sections of Germanic Flemish SS troops, reinforced by 50 Field Policemen and a group of the Flemish Guard. Altogether about 350 troops divided in three Battle Units of 100 men each, and one Command Cell of 50 men making the arrests. This Command Cell will be headed by Obersturmbannführer R. Verbelen.

The whole action resorts under the command of SS Stumbannführer Höfle.

5) Troop Assembly: At 03:00 a.m. in the Artillery Camp in Leuven. The troops will carry revolvers and rifles, and three machine guns will be at their disposal. At 04:00 a.m., they will besiege the village from

three directions and simultaneously advance towards the centre in line abreast with 50 metres spacing. The command cell will lead the way and order all arrests. They dispose of special weaponry predetermined by Verbelen.
6) Prisoners: Will be assembled in Meensel. Their deportation is the responsibility of Obersturmbannführer R. Verbelen.

The Command Post for this action will be established at St.-Joris-Winghe, where there will also be a field hospital. The end of the action will be announced by five rifle shots with one-second interval.[1]

Once again, a large part of the assault force consisted of Flemish nationalists, Belgians who had chosen to actively support the Nazi cause for ideological, political or self-centred motives. The foursome assigned to lead the mission in the field all had a history of unscrupulous cruelty, especially against members of the Resistance or anyone who opposed the German regime. Flemish SS Untersturmbannführers Tony Van Dijck, Jozef Bachot and Jef De Meyer headed the three battle units. All three were confirmed believers in National Socialism, and had joined the 'General SS Flanders' at a very early stage in the war. They were well matched in terms of cruelty. The command cell came under the leadership of Robert Verbelen, who had already made quite a name for himself. As Obersturmbannführer der Germanische SS, he was one of the best-known and most vicious Belgian collaborators. He organised the elimination of several Resistance groups in Belgium and was the 'staff leader' of the DeVlag (Deutsch-Vlämische arbeitsgemeinschaft).[2]

In the early morning of Friday, August 11, 1944, a column of army trucks filled with SS troops and their accomplices approached the sleeping town of Meensel-Kiezegem. Shortly before 04:00 a.m., the three battle units were dropped off at their respective starting points, where they quickly arranged themselves into the required formation. The first gunshots sounded, waking up the terrified villagers. The town was soon surrounded by heavily armed troops, and whoever was still inside the perimeter had little chance of escape. Some of those who had gone

---

[1]Summary of original report in S. Van Laere and F. Craeninckx, *Een Klein Dorp, Een Zware Tol* (Brussels: Manteau, 2004), 85 (translated from German).

[2]Robert Jan Verbelen, aka Alfred Heinrich Gustav Schwab, Herbert Schwab, Peter Mayer, Herbert Charpentier, Josef Pollack, Alfred Kluger and Herbert Lehmann, Belgian (Flemish) SS volunteer, went into hiding in Vienna after the war, put on trial in absentia by a Belgian court on 67 war crimes charges, including the torture of downed US pilots Lieutenants Nuntio Street and Eugene Dingledine at Buchenwald concentration camp. Convicted and sentenced in absentia to death by a bullet in 1947, he was allegedly employed by US Intelligence from 1947 to 1955, under the name Alfred H. Schwab. He became an Austrian citizen in 1959, and was arrested and put on trial by a Viennese court on November 29, 1965, on charges of being an accomplice in the murders of seven members of the Belgian Resistance. He was acquitted, the acquittal was overturned but no retrial was held. Robert Verbelen died in 1990.

'underground' and remained awake all night were alerted and able to escape just in time. While the three advancing companies completed their cordon, Verbelen's command cell went into action at 04:30 a.m.

Farmers and factory workers about to leave for an early work shift were stopped and told to turn back. Again, homes were brutally invaded by SS troops nervously clenching pistols and rifles. Peaceful citizens, not expecting any trouble, were routed from their beds. Unlike the previous raid, this time not only suspected Resistance workers were arrested, but others as well. Marcel and Albert Merckx again were actively involved. Despite their disguise, several villagers easily recognised them. All men between the ages of 16 and 65 were apprehended and ushered into the local girls' school opposite Meensel's church 'for identity control'. In nearby Kiezegem, their fellow townsmen were initially assembled in the communal boys' school there. They were lined up facing against the wall. A machine gun was strategically placed in the middle of the schoolyard. Once all were gathered, the Kiezegem detainees were collectively marched to the other school in Meensel. 'He who tries to run, will be shot at once!' a guard shouted.

Nearly all the houses in the central part of town were searched, but few villagers were mistreated or beaten during the initial arrests. However, fruitless attempts to establish the whereabouts of known Resistance workers infuriated the invaders. Farmer Constant Wittemans, his wife and daughter suffered dearly when their sons Joost and Jules, both active members of the Independence Front, could not be located. As a result, Constant, his wife and daughter were taken into custody.

Some individuals tried to break the siege and escape through the woods and fields. None succeeded. At the Herman Pypen farm, young Hermine Natens arrived in tears at 06:00 a.m., with tales of the SS actions in the village. Jos Pypen, Maurice Vuchelen and Teddy scented danger and didn't feel safe in their hideout. After conferring with each other, they decided to take their chance to make a getaway through the Vrijbos woods. Staf Broos did not agree with that plan and decided to stay put in the underground shelter. Maurice Vuchelen related what happened next:

> We started running, me first, then Teddy and then came Jos. Suddenly we heard rifle shots at the other side of the woods. Teddy fell down and I thought he had been hit. I crawled towards him, and saw that he had fallen owing to a loose shoe. He looked very worried and told me he wanted to keep his head down. I convinced him to continue running, so all three of us took off again. Suddenly I spotted two adversaries in the distance. Turning to the others behind me, I hollered 'Blackshirts!', and fired my pistol in the air. I then immediately ducked away in a ditch with some high grass. Jos and Teddy continued running, I thought they were about to duck away elsewhere. But, to my astonishment, they continued running, and ran right away into the

arms of the adversary.[1]

Jos Pypen later had this to add:

> The reason why Teddy and I continued running was that we had not seen that Maurice had ducked away. We were in a state of stress and confusion, and thought we were still running in the best direction behind Maurice, when suddenly two SS riflemen appeared in front of us with their arms pointed at us.[2]

Teddy and Jos were arrested, and were taken to the girls' school via separate routes. Maurice Vuchelen was not found by the SS and spent the rest of the war in hiding in Leuven. He had been very lucky. Herman Pypen decided to run in another direction in an attempt to break the siege. Despite being fired at he managed to get away to nearby Kapellen.

Paula witnessed the hasty departure of Teddy and Jos, but she was not aware of their subsequent arrest and detention. She stayed around the farmyard anxiously awaiting news, when suddenly Alfons Cauwberghs arrived. He told Paula that he had heard Flemish SS troops say 'And now it's time to go and get Paula Pypen', and insisted that she leave right away. He gave her 100 Francs, and Paula managed to catch a train that was leaving Meensel for the town of Tielt. Departing in haste she had not informed her parents. They heard of her escape later from Alfons. During the trip on the train she stayed hidden under a seat, scared to death. She travelled on to Brussels, where she stayed until August 15. Upon her return, she was shocked to learn that the SS had captured Teddy and her brother.

At the same time as Teddy's arrest, around 08:00 a.m., loud explosions were heard in the village of Meensel. SS soldiers set on fire the farm of Jules Schotsmans, one of Teddy's earlier hosts, using incendiary grenades. Verbelen and his cohorts had the Schotsmans farm on the list of known safe havens for Resistance workers, saboteurs and the like. They even had information that an Allied flyer was hiding in Meensel, allegedly at the Schotsmans farm. Jules refused to emerge, which infuriated the SS to the point where they decided to smoke him out. Jules succumbed in the inferno. His charred remains were discovered in the ruins of his home but no Allied airman was found. It seemed that the Verbelen group relied on somewhat outdated intelligence, which had Teddy still hiding at the Schotsmans property. They would soon learn that the aviator had been arrested elsewhere in the village.

When the detainees stepped through the gate of the Meensel community girls' school, they entered hell. A couple of hundred villagers were brought together within the school walls. Two masked men were present in the schoolyard, and apparently they were the ones who decided the prisoner's

[1]Interview with Maurice Vuchelen, November 14, 1989 (translated by the author).
[2]Interview with Jos Pypen, November 22, 1989 (translated by the author).

fate. Known Nazi sympathizers were immediately released and allowed to leave the school gate. The others, one by one, were led into a classroom for identity control. Verbelen and his cohorts had the infamous 'Merckx list' in their hands. This led to a selection process. The majority of the hostages were placed in the schoolyard after the scrutiny of their papers. They were instructed to squat down near the weapons and ammunitions cache and ordered to remain stock still. The remainder of the captives were the 'dangerous suspects' whose names were on the list, alleged Resistance helpers, forced labour deserters or relatives of untraceable Resistance members. They were then led, one by one, into another classroom, from where screams of torment were heard. The hallway leading toward that classroom was covered with blood. This obviously caused great distress among those waiting. In the room, the frightened villagers appeared before an improvised tribunal and were intensively questioned about their background or the whereabouts of untraceable individuals. When questioning was completed, the SS took them into custody.

Outside in the schoolyard, the final ordeal took place for those who 'passed' the first identity control. This large group of people squatting down were anxiously waiting for what was to come next, when suddenly Prosper Natens and Adolf Hendrickx were brought onto the scene, accompanied by heavily armed guards. They were handcuffed to the two masked men. They showed signs of terrible abuse. All prisoners in the schoolyard were ordered to stand up and form one row. One by one they were called forward, whereupon one of the cloaked brutes asked Natens and Hendrickx whether or not the detainee had supported the Whites. A slight head nod by Natens or Hendrickx indicated that a detainee was recognised as 'guilty' of aiding the Resistance. Sometimes, when Natens and Hendrickx shook their head trying to deny the involvement of the person brought before, they were insolently overruled by one of the Merckx brothers. The 'convict' was then taken aside by the SS guards and forced to kneel facing the wall. Those found 'innocent' were sent home. In this cynical way, the two shattered former Resistance leaders were forced to pronounce judgement on their fellow-villagers. Obviously, the entire performance was aimed at scaring everyone to death. People were kicked, beaten and threatened. Everyone was convinced that his or her last hour had arrived. Those present never forgot that morning in the girls' school of Meensel.[1]

At some point during this calamity, Teddy was brought into the schoolyard. He was handcuffed and his face showed signs of abuse. In one of the classrooms, he was questioned by one of the SS leaders about his own identity and those of his helpers. Following standard RAF procedure, he only disclosed his name, rank and serial number. This did not please the

[1]The two masked men were, as might be expected, Albert and Marcel Merckx, brothers of Gaston.

questioning SS, who threatened to use other methods to make him talk. Upon learning he was an Allied airman, hot-tempered Blackshirts and some Flemish SS men immediately began to harass him. Fortunately, one of the few decent German officers present intervened and offered him a cigarette.

In contrast, Jos Pypen after being seized was badly treated. He was separated from the others and placed under a stairwell, where he received a severe thrashing. Brought back together, he and Teddy were confronted, but neither one flinched. They acted as if they had never seen each other before, which undoubtedly saved Jos's life. Then both men were told to join the queue outside. When Jos appeared before Natens and Hendrickx, they nodded. Then it was Teddy's turn. He stepped forward. One of the masked men asked the two in judgement if the airman had been involved in their activities. Again, one or both nodded, and Teddy was added to the group.

This whole performance lasted until noon. Then, 73 men and three women were loaded onto trucks and driven to Leuven under heavy guard. All were hardworking country folks who, apart from a few exceptions, had nothing to do with the Resistance. Heedless of the potential consequences and imbued with patriotism, most had merely agreed to hide fellow villagers who were on a German wanted list.

In Leuven, the hostages were taken to the Gestapo HQ at the Vital Decosterstraat. Upon arrival there, their identity was confirmed and a sequence of photos taken and they were subjected to a series of humiliating remarks and intimidations. Then the detainees were taken to the ancient Central Prison of Leuven, and locked away in cramped cells, eight persons apiece. Three days later, the group was split up. Six of the Meensel-Kiezegem prisoners, mainly forced labour deserters and persons with invalid exemption or identity papers, were left in their original cell. Jos Pypen was one of them. He and the five others were subjected to severe thrashings and interrogations during the days thereafter. The remainder of the Meensel-Kiezegem prisoners, the suspected Resistance helpers and other 'dangerous terrorists', were ordered to board a number of enclosed trucks. Teddy was with the last group. They had to kneel down on the truck floor, whereupon the vehicles and their armed escorts drove to Brussels. It was a very hot day, and the journey was one of real agony. No one was allowed to speak. In Brussels, the trucks stopped at the central SIPO HQ at 347 Avenue Louise, before continuing their journey to the larger State Prison at the Avenue Ducpétiaux in St. Gilles.

It seemed Teddy's luck had finally run out. After the miraculous escape from his Lancaster and the several months of successful clandestine survival, he ended up as a prisoner of the Germans after all and not under the protection that an Allied airman would normally expect to receive. The Allied armies were so close, and on the verge of a major breakthrough out of Normandy and an advance in the direction of Belgium.

CHAPTER THIRTEEN

In Prison

Upon arriving at the St. Gilles prison lobby, the inmates' few possessions were confiscated. Teddy's valuables consisted of one watch, one family signet ring, one broken compass, 11 money coins, 1,000 French francs, 350 Belgian francs and 20 Dutch guilders. This was obviously the money from his escape kit, which he had carefully kept stashed away in case he would have to depart his hiding place in a hurry. He had always figured it would come in handy during the next stage of his evasion expedition. All his valuables were meticulously inventoried – in German – on a piece of paper dated August 12, 1944. Teddy signed the document, including his rank, squadron leader.

The St. Gilles prison was a large, bleak building of greyish-black stone, surrounded by high walls. It was a foreboding place, which looked like a medieval citadel of some sinister lord and master. The Germans called it the Wehrmachtuntersuchungsgefängnis (the Military Investigation Prison), but it was nothing more than their central assembly point from where all transports departed for the German detention camps. For some prisoners, including Belgians accused of working for the Resistance, this prison was their last stop. One section of the prison wall was deeply scarred by the impact of steel-jacketed slugs that had sealed many a patriot's fate, while others were left to die in the special basement cells.

The people from Meensel-Kiezegem were separated and locked away in cells with other prisoners, unknown to them, four to a cell. Small, typed cards on each cell door recorded personal data of each prisoner. The cellblock sections radiated out from what was called the building's central 'chapel', like the spokes of a wheel. There were five separate tiers of cells, each designated by a letter. One held women prisoners, mostly underground agents captured in a wave of arrest in 1943 and early 1944. Captured airmen were lodged in the military section, along with German soldiers who had run afoul of military law. Other cellblocks held captured Resistance members together with common criminals. The prison regulations forbade the inmates from sleeping during the day, to use blankets as pillows, to look through windows, to knock on doors, walls or windows, to contaminate the cell walls, to sing, whistle or make noise, to communicate with other prisoners in any way or to exchange anything with the other prisoners. Of course, all these injunctions were ignored whenever possible by all internees. They communicated from cell to cell, section to section and wing to wing. In times of alarm, everyone was kept informed by the inmates hammering on the heating pipes that ran through the cells. On June 6, the day of the Allied landings in Normandy, the news had filtered through this jungle network to the prisoners. For the rest of the day, the whole establishment echoed with patriotic songs emanating from the nearly 2,000 inmates.[1]

Still, an utter feeling of loneliness took hold of these unfortunate people from Meensel-Kiezegem. Every link with their fellow sufferers was severed as they often shared a cell with those who didn't speak their language. When they did spot a familiar face during the daily airing in the prison's inner courtyard, talking was strictly prohibited. Nearly everyone lost any sense of time. The days were long and meaningless, only interrupted by irregular meals pushed through a slit in their cell door, meals that were frugal and tasteless. Served twice a day, they consisted of black bread, watered-down soup and some equally diluted coffee. The cells were filthy, with insects everywhere, and the only bedding was an old straw mattress laid out on a wooden floor. Everyone caught body lice.

Shortly after his arrival at St. Gilles, Teddy met another airman. He even spent a couple of days in the same cell with him. He told Pilot Officer Roy C. Brown about his narrow escape from his Lancaster and about his stay with the Resistance. He also explained that the Germans knew he was an RCAF officer, but that things looked bad for him on account of his affiliation with the Resistance. Then Teddy was removed from that cell and Roy never saw him again.[2]

From St. Gilles, most of the Meensel-Kiezegem folks were taken to the SIPO HQ on Avenue Louise on a repeated basis. In the cellars of this office block, they were exposed to harsh interrogations and torture. On occasion, Albert and Marcel Merckx, who were unmasked this time, were present in the room and took part in the mistreatment. Still, it struck many that the subject of the interrogations was not the murder of Gaston Merckx, but the functioning and organisation of the Resistance movement in and around Meensel-Kiezegem. This only confirmed what many thought, that the Gestapo had used the Gaston Merckx assassination, and his mother's incessant demands, as an incentive to clean up the irritating Resistance cell located in Meensel-Kiezegem. Many of the prisoners gave in to the cruel cross-examination methods used by the SIPO and Gestapo agents. They signed a written statement in which they pleaded guilty of Resistance

---

[1]*Golden Book of the Belgian Resistance* (Brussels: Leclercq 1947), 347.

[2]In late 1944, Roy Brown met Winsome at the RCAF Western Air Command HQ in Vancouver, and she asked him to write a formal statement down about his meeting with Ted in St. Gilles.

support. That signature immediately put their names on a list for that long train ride into Germany.

The perpetual question, which one could never answer, was why Natens and Hendrickx had nodded when Teddy was presented before them at the girls' school of Meensel. It was obvious that both young men were under tremendous strain, both physically and emotionally. During interrogation, SD agents had put a gun to Natens' head several times and his face showed the scuffmarks. He had been deprived of food and water for several days and looked extremely pale and exhausted. Hendrickx's hair had been pulled out and his face and clothes showed signs of serious abuse. When ushered onto the schoolyard, both men clearly realised that their captors already knew everything there was to know about the Resistance movement in Meensel-Kiezegem, and subconsciously they likely did not want to rekindle any more German wrath than absolutely necessary. In addition, Teddy had been physically present during the Resistance action against the infamous collaborator Glazemaekers of St.-Joris-Winghe. Furthermore, witnesses later stated that Teddy's knowledge of explosives had been solicited. More evidence of Teddy's direct involvement in Resistance activities was later exposed in a secret report compiled by MI 9, the British Intelligence service that normally questioned Allied evaders upon their return to England. One of these reports contains a formal statement made right after the war by Flight Sergeant Joseph Murphy, a wireless operator from 75 Squadron who was shot down over Belgium on July 19, 1944. It turned out to be an invaluable testimony by Teddy himself:

> During my imprisonment at St. Gilles prison in Brussels, I met a Canadian Squadron Leader Blenkinsop. I was lined up with mostly German prisoners to take a shower. I was on the end of the line and this fellow on the end of the other line asked me if I was an airman. I said 'yes' and he switched into my line. He said if I ever got back to England would I please tell his story as he ran his finger across his throat and said 'I am in for this tomorrow'. He said that while evading capture in Belgium he was helping the White Army. One day he was with a group of them on the way to blow up a house occupied by the Germans [sic]. He was captured when they ran into 200 Gestapo men armed with machine guns. He fled into a wood, being unarmed, and was captured. Immediately after his arrest, he was threatened with torture, but refused to speak. Two of the Belgians, after torture, said Blenkinsop had been implicated. On this evidence the Germans said they would shoot him. Whether this was done or not, I could not say, but he was not with us when we were evacuated from St. Gilles with 40-odd British and Americans at the beginning of September 1944.[1]

In St. Gilles prison in late August 1944, there were 52 other Allied airmen

[1]WO 208/3298-3327 – MI 9 Evasion Reports, Public Records Office, London.

who had been captured wearing civilian clothes. Some carried a forged Belgian passport. They were under continual interrogation. The Germans told the airmen that, if they would tell where they received their clothing and passports, they would be given a service uniform and allowed all the privileges of a POW under the Geneva Convention. If they refused, they could be treated as spies and shot.

During preventive escape and evasion training lectures given to the RAF aircrews, a number of key principles were given special emphasis. Security was an absolute essential. If arrested, while in the custody of the Underground, under no account were they to divulge the names or addresses of their helpers, even if the helpers were arrested at the same time. These instructions were of the utmost importance. Treatment of those caught sheltering evaders was brutal to say the least. Those individuals considered expendable after Gestapo enquiries into the makeup of the wider organisation were normally executed, sometimes together with their families. If the real organisers and principal characters were captured, all were submitted to severe torture and extended incarceration in a concentration camp, where many died.[1]

Teddy was driven several times to the SIPO HQ on Avenue Louise. There he was under continuous interrogation by Gestapo agents who told him of their infiltration into the Underground escape network and particularly that they knew the details of the Belgian Resistance organisations. This was part of an elaborate psychological ruse designed to break his confidence and make him more amenable to answering their questions. Underlying the entire procedure was the unspoken but implied threat that Ted had been captured in civilian clothing and was subject therefore to a quick and final solution, customary for all spies. During other interrogation sessions the gloves were off, and Teddy was berated, beaten and put at risk of being shot. Lieutenant Jack Terzian, an American Thunderbolt pilot who had been shot down over Belgium on May 22, 1944, and also incarcerated in St. Gilles, later described the Gestapo cross-examinations:

> The Gestapo took me to their HQ and started questioning me. I refused to talk and they questioned me again later in the St. Gilles prison. An NCO dragged me around while an officer beat me up. I was locked away in complete darkness for four days, and then put in solitary confinement for three weeks. I wasn't allowed to wash or shave. Then they put me in a cell with three other airmen, an American sergeant, a Canadian flying officer and the New Zealander Joseph Murphy. One week later, I was put in a cell with a few Germans that were convicted for theft.[2]

---

[1]Graham Pitchfork, *Shot Down and on the Run: The RAF and Commonwealth Aircrews Who Got Home from Behind Enemy Lines*, 1940-1945 (Richmond UK, The National Archives, 2003) 23-38.

[2]Letter from Jack Terzian to the author, March 27, 1991.

Despite the degrading methods the Germans had imposed on Teddy, he told Joe Murphy he had flatly refused to give any names of those who helped him and was now condemned to death. He said that he had spent several days in solitary confinement in one of St. Gilles's punishment cells, described as a tiny, airless box without lights or bedding. Joe surmised Teddy appeared to be awaiting this fate with complete serenity. Joe also stated he looked to be in poor physical condition with the mildew on his clothes, the worst Joe had ever seen.

An interesting testimony about the interactions between prisoners at St. Gilles came from Fred Davies, who was the set operator of Ted Blenkinsop's former 'C' Flight commander's crew in 405 Squadron, Squadron Leader Gordon Bennett. The Blenkinsop crew had participated in several raids together with the Bennett crew and they knew each other well. Fred also spent a month in St. Gilles and wrote:

> We used to tap out Morse code messages on the heating pipes to find out just who was in the prison, and it used to drive the Jerries wild. Mostly because we did it at night in the dark when they couldn't see who it was and also when they were trying to sleep. The sound would go through the whole prison and it was a big place.[1]

Although a condemned man, it appears Teddy never gave up the fight. One day, he again saw his chance to communicate his situation to the outside world. Flying Officer Stuart M. Leslie, a Canadian pilot with 429 Squadron, and who had been shot down over Belgium on May 2, 1944, recalled:

> While in St-Gilles in late August 1944 to the best of my remembrance, during one of the very infrequent group shower baths, an American flyer who was also in prison name unknown, stood next to me. He whispered that, as I was a Canadian, to remember the name Squadron Leader Blenkinsop. He had communicated with Ted, who was in solitary confinement in a dark cell, via the steam heating pipes that ran through the cells. Ted was in St-Gilles prison for a short time and was being transported into Germany after having been apprehended operating with a Maquis Resistance Group in Belgium, and was condemned to death, as it was told to me in the very short space of time in the prison shower room.[2]

---

[1]Letter from Fred Davies to the author, December 4, 1989. Gordon Bennett's Lancaster was shot down by a night fighter during a raid to Aachen on May 24-25, 1944. Squadron Leader Bennett, DSO, DFC and his flight engineer, Flight Sergeant Rees, both perished at the aircraft controls, giving the crew a chance to bail out. One of 405 Squadron's leading figures, Gordon Bennett is buried at the Bergen-op-Zoom War Cemetery in the Netherlands.

[2]Letter from Stuart Leslie, now a retired Air Canada flight dispatcher, to the author dated November 29, 1988. Flying Officer Leslie was the only survivor of his crew, which had been shot down by a night fighter during a raid to St-Ghislain, Belgium. He ended up with the Resistance, but was arrested when on his way to a Mission Marathon camp in southern Belgium.

This particular US airman communicated with Teddy by tapping on the heating pipes in Morse code. Contact between Teddy and him was interrupted in the middle of a message and although the American tried to re-establish contact later, he was never able to do so. The reason for this appears to have been that Teddy had been abruptly moved from St. Gilles prison. This American officer escaped and returned to England in September 1944, where he reported to authorities that the Germans used to march Teddy in the courtyard, blindfolded and threatened to shoot him for not disclosing the names of Underground people who helped him. Stuart Leslie for his part reported the information to the RAF in London in October 1944, and it reached Teddy's parents in November 1944.[1]

The German security service was well aware Teddy was a ranking RCAF officer. The question that comes to mind is why Teddy and the other airmen had not been treated as prisoners of war, as stipulated in the Geneva Convention. Generally speaking, the German and Italian authorities adhered to the convention and accorded a prisoner his proper rights if he could establish his true identity. However, Allied soldiers captured in civilian clothes or carrying a forged passport could be regarded as spies and were not protected by that convention. Furthermore, the German Kugel Erlass (Bullet Decree) stated that prisoners of war were to be removed from POW status and transferred to the Gestapo if they were guilty of 'crimes'. This order would apply if they had escaped and been recaptured, were screened out by the SIPO or SD, or were guilty of sabotage. No reports on transfers were required. Prisoners of war sent to a concentration camp under this decree were regarded as dead to the outside world and usually ended in execution. Teddy was probably charged with sabotage activities, and certainly screened out by the SD, for withholding information about the Meensel-Kiezegem Resistance. As he was wearing civilian clothes at the time of his arrest, the odds were really stacked against him. The only way out would have been for him to name the people who had given him assistance. This option would never have entered Teddy's mind and so it appears there was no way for Teddy to escape his predicament.

It appeared the majority of the 52 Allied airmen being held in St. Gilles also refused to cooperate with the Germans. Joe Murphy:

> Seeing the torture and treatment of Belgian civilians who had been arrested, many said to have been betrayed by their own compatriots but some by captured airmen, and being under interrogation with these people, the chance of being shot was the only option for us. The Germans were desperate to break into the Resistance movement. I think most loyal airmen would have rather died than let this happen. Some apparently broke but Squadron Leader Blenkinsop never did.

---

[1]In a letter by Squadron Leader W.R. Gunn, RCAF Casualties Officer, to Hubert Blenkinsop, dated November 17, 1944.

> He certainly was an inspiration to myself.[1]

All but a few of the 52 flyers were put on a collective list for transport to a German concentration camp. Oddly enough, although the Germans knew his true background, Teddy was registered as being from Meensel-Kiezegem. To the Germans, his fate was never associated with the Allied cause but remained indelibly connected to the village that sheltered him.

In late August 1944, the Allied liberation armies were on the verge of crossing the French-Belgian border. The Germans feared a prisoners' revolt would rise up against them as they started their retreat. Berlin ordered that all Belgian prisons and internment camps be evacuated. They were to transport all prisoners – as hostages – to Germany where the execution of death sentences were to be carried out. On the night of August 30, 1944, the evacuation of St. Gilles commenced. At 02:30 a.m., Teddy and 70 citizens from Meensel-Kiezegem were among the 400 inmates of St. Gilles who were awakened and told to prepare for their departure. Three hours later, they were released from their cells and pushed into formation lines. The building echoed with confusion, noise, shouting and scurrying feet. The prisoners were given back their personal effects. Then the guards ordered them to make two parcels, one to take with them containing food, cigarettes and toiletries, and the other was to be labelled with their name. It was to be sent on at a later date. While being repeatedly shouted at by armed SS troops who were charged with the evacuation, the prisoners were ordered to board the lorries waiting in the prison square. Half an hour later, the column left St. Gilles and drove to the rail station at Schaerbeek, a suburb of Brussels. There, the hostages were loaded in cattle cars, 60 to 70 of them per wagon. When the train was loaded, SS guards doled out small Red Cross parcels, three per person. At that moment, the inmates realised they were in for a long train ride ahead. At 10:00 a.m., the train started moving. Victor Malbecq, one of the prisoners, continues:

> The train had covered about 500 metres when it stopped again, and pulled back to the station. There we stayed during the whole day. The heat almost suffocated us, and everybody was sweating heavily. There was no opening in the wagon. Around 7:00 p.m. that Thursday 31 August, the train started moving again. We were all very saddened and many were crying. We realised that the English troops were very close and the thought of just missing them was heart-breaking. We tried to keep courage, hoping that the Allies would intercept us somewhere. The train drove slowly. With nails and a few pocket knives, we succeeded in making small holes in the wagon floor and sides. This way we could see us arriving in Antwerp at nightfall. Many of us were asleep. After a while in Antwerp station, the train

[1]Letter from Joseph Murphy to the author, September 25, 1990.

> continued and we crossed the Dutch border around midnight. Some tried to find a way to escape, but most of us realised the danger of this. What was the use of escaping and being killed by a bullet, when most of us thought we would be home again in a month or so? Via Roosendaal and Breda we passed through Arnhem and Deventer. Then the train turned east into Germany, which we entered late on that Friday September 1. At midnight, the SS guards left the train at a border post at Bentheim. Much to our relief, they were replaced by elderly men and regular policemen. We continued our journey along Rheine and Osnabrück. Our new guards gave us water at every stop. They even apologised if not everyone had seen chance to have a drink before the train left again. When night fell, we arrived in the vicinity of Hamburg. We tried to sleep but there wasn't enough room to lie down. I kept standing up and watched the activity at the port of Hamburg. Suddenly air raid sirens sounded. The train stopped and the guards took cover. The search lights lit the sky while the anti-aircraft batteries opened fire. In the morning of Sunday, September 3, we arrived near the camp. At 2:00 or 3:00 a.m., we started looking in the darkness for our scarce belongings, and waited for the train to stop. The train slowly moved on, and then stopped at the camp of Neuengamme. This was a dreadful sight for everyone. Huge spotlights lit the barracks and a long concrete road lined with heavily armed SS soldiers holding police dogs. Then the wagon doors opened and we heard loud shouts: 'Loss! Loss!' We were counted and groups of 50 prisoners were then marched in five rows to the entrance of the camp, under a shower of blows and insults by the SS men.[1]

During the terrible train journey to Neuengamme, the passengers sat one on top of the other. Teddy was sitting against a French-speaking Belgian called Octave Honoré and they started a conversation that took their minds off their ordeal. He told Octave of Helen and his plans to marry her after the war. During the night, Octave allowed Teddy to lean against him to get some sleep. After arriving at KZ Neuengamme, Teddy gave Honoré his address, by writing it in the dirt. Shortly after that they were split up, never to see each other again.[2]

After entering the camp, the prisoners were led in groups into the cellar of a brick building. There, Russian prisoners shaved the prisoner's heads bald. They were then marched to wooden barracks while the SS held everyone in serried ranks with loud shouts and rifle butt blows. All orders were given in German. In the barracks, everyone was stripped naked and his or her complete body was shaved. They were then pushed into showers,

[1]S. Van Laere and F Craeninckx, *Een Klein Dorp, Een Zware Tol* (Brussels: Manteau, 2004), 117-22.

[2]Octave Honoré from Boussu, Belgium, returned from Neuengamme on July 1, 1945. He remembered Teddy's address and wrote him a letter on July 11, 1945, to find out how he was.

which first delivered hot and then ice-cold water. After that, everyone received a prison outfit and a metal plate with a number. Teddy's number was 44388. This would be his identity from then on. While the people from Meensel-Kiezegem tried to remain together as much as possible, Teddy hardly recognised anyone. He had arrived in hell and, not knowing anyone, was all alone.

The next batch of St. Gilles prisoners, 1,500 in total, was abruptly aroused in the very early morning of September 2, 1944. The group included close to 50 Allied airmen, numerous Resistance workers arrested in different parts of Belgium, and 13 hostages from Meensel-Kiezegem. At 6:00 a.m., they were driven by truck to a marshalling yard called La Petite Ile at Brussels' South Station (Gare du Midi). Overnight, the Germans, unbeknown to the stationmaster, had assembled a train consisting of 32 cattle cars and a few passenger coaches. However, in the early morning hours, an unidentified patriot gave prior warning to the stationmaster of the imminent evacuation of St. Gilles Prison. The news spread rapidly amongst the railway station employees and, when the special train was exposed, they put two and two together. The Belgian Railways had many Resistance workers and patriots in their midst, and they promptly agreed that something had to be done.

Immediately upon the arrival of the truck convoy, nervous German soldiers started cramming the prisoners into the cattle cars of this special train. The heavily armed Germans were extremely edgy as they knew the British 30 Corps was rapidly approaching Brussels.[1] All they could think of was getting the job done as quickly as possible, before the general evacuation of the Belgian capital commenced. The railway station was bedlam. News about the evacuation of St. Gilles had travelled throughout Brussels. Onlookers, filled with rage and indignation, hurled curses at the German guards. Groups of distraught and cursing prisoners reacted to their German guards who were using rifle butts and bayonets to herd them into the cattle cars. The prisoners may have known how close they were to liberation and freedom, yet for them it appeared such an unfortunate event. Little did they realise this was to be their lucky day. The railway personnel knew an open confrontation with the German soldiers was impossible, but instinctively they knew other forms of retaliation were possible. Several railway workers risked their lives trying to keep the trains from leaving Belgium. As a start, they did not divulge the fact that a serviceable locomotive and driver were really available. The appointed engineer

---

[1]After crossing the Somme River, the charismatic Lieutenant General Sir Brian Horrocks, commander of 30 Corps, realised the importance of liberating Brussels and the seaport of Antwerp quickly. He succeeded in motivating his men to cover 600 kilometres in only seven days. The advanced units of the Grenadier Guards of the 30 Corps, Second British Army, reached Brussels before dusk on September 3, 1944. Their armour had covered 120 kilometres in ten hours. The next day, the Belgian Brigade Piron and the Guards Armoured Division marched through a delirious Brussels city centre.

suddenly became 'very ill' and was released from duty. His replacement faked a serious fall and was carried away 'injured'. Several hours later, a third one was placed on the daily roster. This engineer named Louis Verheggen delayed the coupling of the engine and the freight cars. Late in the day, the train finally started moving at 4:50 p.m. Despite the threatening presence of SS troops, Verheggen used all kinds of excuses to slow down the journey. He was determined not to take the train across the Belgian border. With the help of several signalmen accomplices along the route, the train was stopped at many stations out of Brussels. This scheme continued during the rest of the day and night, until the train mysteriously arrived back at its departure station. Rail lines to the north, south, east and west were now all under the control of the Resistance, who had blown up the tracks in a series of engagements with the German rear guard. Finally, on September 3 at around 2:00 p.m., the rail car doors were thrown open, and the assembled prisoners jumped off. Those Germans and Blackshirts left in the railway station, whose only objective now was to find a train that would repatriate them to Germany, had the good sense to ignore the escapees. Utterly relieved, the prisoners from Meensel-Kiezegem united together, and proceeded to walk home. Brussels was crowded with retreating Germans, many who were plundering the shops as they departed the city. In the distance, the Palace of Justice was seen burning, set afire by the Nazis as a means of destroying their meticulous but incriminating records.

It was later discovered that diplomatic correspondence had been taking place during the last few days between the Swiss, Finnish and Spanish consuls, the Swedish ambassador, the German leadership in Belgium and the International Red Cross for the purpose of accelerating the liberation of all political prisoners in Belgium. Finally, in the early hours of September 3, German Ambassador Mayr-Falkenberg and the more humane German doctor, General Werner Wachsmuth convinced the SS General Richard Jungclaus to free all prisoners and Jews in Belgium.[1] These instructions were brought to the Gare du Midi by a delegation of diplomats. There was still some disagreement between the delegation and a very stubborn German officer, but the stoic demeanour of the diplomats ultimately resulted in the release of the 1,500 prisoners. A small group of patriots had kept their promise that the train would never leave Belgian soil. At least these prisoners would never have to experience the horror of a Nazi concentration camp.[2]

---

[1]In April 1942, SS officer Richard Jungclaus had been ordered by Himmler to deal with 'ethnical issues' in Belgium. The 'Service Jungclaus' quickly became a parallel occupation government in Belgium. In July 1944, Hitler ordered the military hierarchy in Belgium to be replaced by a civil one, and Jungclaus was put in charge of all police services in Belgium, becoming SS Gruppenführer und Generalmajor der Polizei Belgien-Nordfrankreich (SS Group Leader and General Major of the Police in Belgium and Northern France).

[2]In January 2000, The History Channel (USA) broadcasted an episode about this miraculous escape of the last group of St. Gilles prisoners, called *The Nazi Ghost Train*. This episode is available on DVD.

CHAPTER FOURTEEN

Extermination through Labour

Neuengamme Concentration Camp was situated about 20 kilometres east of Hamburg, a major city in northern Germany. The SS had established the camp there in 1938 to incarcerate dissident German citizens who had openly opposed Hitler's Nazi policies. For the next five years, the camp accommodated a total of 106,000 inmates, spread over the main camp and 96 outposts situated across northern Germany. Inmates were composed of 28 nationalities (34,350 Russians, 16,900 Poles, 11,500 Frenchmen, 9,200 Germans, 6,950 Dutchmen, 4,800 Belgians, 4,800 Danes, etc) in addition to those from the local Jewish community. But the camp also detained communists, homosexuals, prostitutes, gypsies, Jehovah's Witnesses, a few prisoners of war and many other groups. Work at the mother camp was primarily involved with the production of bricks. In addition, its prisoners assisted in the construction of a canal to transport the bricks to and from the site. Inmates had to excavate the heavy, peat-like soil using inadequate tools, with no regard for the weather conditions or the state of their health. In late 1944, as the labour shortage in Germany worsened, the SS expanded the use of the camp prisoners to include the production of armaments. More than 3,000 male prisoners from Neuengamme camp were forced to work in factories manufacturing ammunitions and bombs for Germany's armed forces. By January 1945, there were about 50,000 prisoners in the Neuengamme concentration camp system. This figure included almost 10,000 women.

Teddy was held in Neuengamme as a Belgian political prisoner and treated as such. Four survivors returned to Meensel-Kiezegem after the war and gave an official and signed statement to their mayor, which was translated and sent to Ottawa. It read:

> We undersigned, Loddewijckx Marcel, Trompet Frans, Pittomvils Petrus and Van Gilbergen Frans, all four political prisoners, declare upon our honour that Blenkinsop Edward, a Canadian Squadron Leader, was with us in Germany at Neuengamme and that he was treated there like us. He had to work with us, was starved and was tortured almost more than we were ourselves.

Frans Trompet later added:

> Unfortunately, few of the Meensel-Kiezegem folks spoke French or English, so nobody could converse with the Canadian. Upon our arrival in the camp, we had not lost all hope, as we thought that we were going to have a better life once we started working in the camp or in one of the satellite camps. They promised us that good labourers would get extras. We were all strong farming people, so we were used to working hard. We thought we would get a lot more food soon, and this made us a bit more optimistic. About a week after our arrival in Neuengamme, I saw the Canadian go 'on transport' out of the camp, probably to a forced labour site.[1]

Contrary to the prisoners' initial expectations, life in the concentration camp proved to be beyond difficult; one could only describe conditions as horrendous. Teddy and his fellow inmates suffered through starvation, hard labour, physical abuse, unsanitary conditions, and insufficient medical care. Death and disease was omnipresent. Many prisoners found rest only in death brought on by the most severe mistreatment and torture imaginable. Prisoners who were injured, sick or weakened were of no further use to the Germans and were disposed of. By April 1942, the SS had completed construction of the initial crematorium at Neuengamme Concentration Camp. From that period on, the bodies of prisoners who died were cremated and their ashes spread on the local fields as fertilizer. As the prisoner population increased, their death rate also rose, resulting in the SS constructing a second crematorium.

Typhus was an ongoing problem because of the primitive sanitary conditions and chronic overcrowding in the camp. Over 1,000 prisoners died during an outbreak of typhus that began in December 1941. Prisoners in the Neuengamme camp were also subjected to medical experiments. As an example, Dr Ludwig-Werner Haase tested a new water filter by adding 100 times the safe dose of arsenic to the prisoners' drinking water. He then filtered the water using this new device, and gave it to more than 150 prisoners over a 13-day period. The heavy doses involved in the test no doubt caused long-term illness to the detainees. SS doctors also subjected some Neuengamme prisoners, including children, to medical experiments involving tuberculosis.

In the dormitories 40 to 50 men had to sleep in a space adequate for only ten people. They had to sleep on wooden boards sometimes with, and sometimes without straw bedding, and with insufficient blankets. The majority of the Meensel-Kiezegem folks were employed in the backbreaking clay pits used in the brick production. This proved to be extremely hard physical labour. Only a few were sent to manufacturing

---

[1]Interview with Frans Trompet, June 1989 (translated by the author).

sites outside Neuengamme. One of the Meensel-Kiezegem detainees, Marcel Loddewijckx, recognised Teddy in Neuengamme and later joined him on a train to one of the work camps. He related:

> In Neuengamme, we received 80 grams brown bread each day, plus some watery beet soup. You could only drink boiled water, all the rest was contaminated. There were 7-8,000 deaths per month.
>
> At one time, there wasn't enough room for new prisoners anymore in our barracks. The German guards ordered us to take an icy cold shower, followed by a hot one. Then we had to stand in line outside the whole night, fully naked. I caught pneumonia that night. Not many survived that night, and the survivors were put together in one shed. Our shed was then empty for a load of new prisoners. The deceased were thrown in the crematorium ovens.
>
> Eight days after our arrival at Neuengamme, they transported us to Hamburg to work in a war factory there. This group counted 6-700 men and several men from Meensel-Kiezegem went there with us, including the Canadian. When Hamburg was bombed by the Allied air forces on October 17, we were returned to Neuengamme. There, I spent a long time in the sick bay, but I still had to perform labour near the canal they were digging. One day I saw Vital Craeninckx, totally exhausted, being stuck in the clay. When he couldn't move rapidly enough, he was shot dead from a short distance by one of the guards. A week or so later I saw a guard beating August Mathues to death with a cane.[1]

Hamburg was the main refining centre for petroleum products in Germany. In Hamburg's New Petroleum Harbour, Teddy was forced to work at the Eurotank Oil Refinery, which produced and stored synthetic oils of various types. It was ironic that Teddy was now assisting in the German war effort, the very one he had been trying to destroy only six months earlier. Not surprisingly, and just like hundreds of his fellow prisoners, he kept his productivity to a minimum. He met a Frenchman from Biarritz by the name of Noël Berchoux, and the two of them became instant friends. As luck would have it, Noël had been brought up on the banks of Lake Ontario in Toronto and he acted as the interpreter for Teddy, who spoke only limited French. This kept the two of them always together. They promised each other that the one who returned home first would let the other family know what had happened in the camp. Through Noël, Teddy met other Frenchmen. One of them, Marcel Pouher of Hermeray, worked in the prisoners' kitchen. He often took extreme risks when he slipped Teddy extra food behind the backs of the SS guards. It was the difference between life and death to have good friends supporting one another in a

[1]Interview with Marcel Loddewijckx, August 11, 1989 (translated by the author).

nightmare situation like they were now all living through.[1]

While Teddy was trying to survive the hardships in the camp, his parents were still anxiously hoping for any sign he was still alive. In late October 1944, much to their surprise, they finally received the first factual report about their son since he had gone missing nearly six months earlier. Ernest Betts, a driver with the Royal Army Signals Corps of the British Liberation Army, wrote them a letter on October 6, 1944:

> Dear Mr or Mrs Blenkinsop,
> First I had better tell you who I am and why I am writing. I am one of the sons from England. I landed in Normandy soon after D-Day. I guess you know the news from there.
>
> We went through France into Belgium; it was in Belgium that we stopped one night. I went to a small country home to try and get some eggs. The people made me very welcome, and asked me in. Over the fire-place I saw a photo of a young fellow. I asked who it was; they told me it was a photo of an RAF man. As best as they could, they told me it was about April 28 that his plane got shot down near their home. I don't know what happened to the rest of the crew but Squadron Leader Blenkinsop was not hurt much.
>
> These people took him in and hid him until August 11 away from the Jerry. It was on August 11 that they came and found him, and took him away to Germany, I guess. That is about all I can tell you, but I made sure of this, when he left their home, he was very well. The people thought the world of him, and they were very lucky not to have been shot for hiding him.
>
> I hope you do not mind me writing to you about this, but I thought any little news will help. They gave me a small book, which he had been writing in. He tried to teach the three young girls English. I have a page of the book in my kit. I will try and find it and enclose it, and then you will know it is his writing.
>
> I must close now. May God Bless Squadron Leader Blenkinsop. Without the RAF we could have done nothing, hope I have been some little help. Ernest Betts.
>
> PS: I was lucky enough to go back the other day. I called in to see the folks and told them I had written a letter to the address they gave me. The mother said she had a photo she could let me have, so I have enclosed it. Once again I must say cheerio. Keep smiling as this war will soon be over. Ernie.

Teddy's parents received Ernie's letter on October 28, 1944. Needless to say, the message gave Hubert and Winsome a tremendous lift. Naturally,

---

[1]In addition to the physical deprivations, the prisoners had to undergo severe bombing attacks on Hamburg by the Allied air forces – RAF Bomber Command on October 12-13 and 14-15, 1944, and the US Eighth Air Force on October 25 and 30, 1944.

they immediately sent a telegram to Helen and Uncle Max, telling them the encouraging news. Everybody was overjoyed. Helen's return telegram of November 3 to Winsome read: 'Wonderful Wonderful news Darling – I was right after all – Love Woodcroft.'

Driver Ernie received very warm letters of gratitude for his unselfish and caring act. Winsome wrote to a friend that deep in her heart she always knew Teddy was alive. Ernie had enclosed the address of the Herman Pypen family, so now Ted's parents knew exactly where he had been sheltered after being shot down. And more importantly, their son had survived the crash and was still alive and well just two months prior. The fact the Germans had arrested him did cause them considerable concern, but both Hubert and Winsome had high hopes based on the belief in the international conventions on treatment of prisoners of war. Uncle Max's letter to Hubert on November 16 clearly showed everybody's optimism:

> I am writing to Driver Betts thanking him. It was really splendid of him to take all that trouble. So many, I fear, would not have done it.
>
> I will also write to the Belgian as soon as it is possible to communicate with his country, which at present cannot be done from here. How the debt to him and his family can ever be repaid, I do not in the least know, as they must, of course, have risked their lives in looking after Teddy. The whole story is rather like a fairy tale, in one sense. It seems too good to be true.

Winsome, meanwhile stationed as a section officer at RCAF Station Comox, British Columbia, tried everything in her power to obtain more information concerning Teddy's whereabouts via official channels. At the same time, Hubert worked on it from their home at 1212 Broad Street, Victoria, while his brother Max used each and every one of his contacts in England in an attempt to get any further news concerning his nephew.

Two weeks after receiving Ernie Betts's message, Hubert had another interesting piece of correspondence in the mail. A Mr Labyt from Glabbeek, a neighbouring town of Meensel-Kiezegem, wrote Hubert a letter informing him of Teddy's stay in Meensel-Kiezegem and his arrest 'by the Gestapo' on August 11. Labyt, an acquaintance of Miss Bruyninckx, had handed the letter to Sergeant William Weare on September 10, with the request it be posted once back in England. Evader William Weare, who had been hiding at Miss Bruyninckx' home for four months until Belgium's liberation in early September 1944, duly complied.

The news of Teddy's status as a prisoner filtered through to the Victoria's *Daily Colonist* newspaper. Relatives of Teddy's ill-fated crewmembers immediately wrote letters full of fresh hope to Teddy's parents after seeing the news item. Some of these relatives had already received telegrams from Ottawa in July 1944, which stated that their beloved one had lost his life. Others had heard nothing. The uncertainty and lack of knowledge for such a long period of time was emotionally draining all of them. George Smith's young wife Audrey wrote: 'It was very encouraging to hear that one member of the crew is alive, so probably the other boys are hiding in Belgium. I haven't had any information regarding my husband. It would seem that we should hear something now that the war seems to be centred in Belgium.'[1]

Unfortunately, the anticlimax came only three weeks after Ernie Betts's letter arrived. On November 20, 1944, Hubert received a letter from the RCAF casualties officer, Squadron Leader W.R. Gunn, containing the testimony by the American airman who had communicated with Ted in St. Gilles. The American had been among the 50 or so fortunate airmen on the Ghost Train and had finally reached English shores in September 1944. His statement about Teddy's death sentence disturbed Hubert and Winsome immensely, but they did not suspend their efforts to find out more particulars about their son's situation. Max even went so far as to write Anthony Eden, Member of Parliament. Besides asking Mr Eden for his support in locating Teddy, he suggested that a record should be made of Teddy's possible execution for refusing to give information about those who gave him assistance. This documentation would be a necessity, he continued, in order that those responsible may eventually be brought to justice for their war crimes.[2]

Around Christmas 1944, an anxious Hubert received a welcome present. Lea Gemoets, sister of Teddy's intrepid helper Hilaire, sent a few snapshots that were taken at the time of Teddy's clandestine stay in the woods behind the Gemoets family home. It was uplifting to see Teddy with a smile on his face, surrounded by people who obviously treated him kindly. Shortly after receiving the photos, Hubert wrote his sister Lucy telling her he was still convinced that although Teddy was a prisoner, he would hear from him again one of these days. Without knowing that his son was living his last days at the time of his writing, Hubert continued: 'I hate to think of him being cold and hungry though, the only thing is that his brain is so active always that it will help him to put up with the privations which no doubt he is suffering.'

A few days after Christmas, the families of Teddy's crewmembers received word from the RCAF that their son or husband had been buried in the communal cemetery of Webbekom in Belgium. The RCAF Overseas

---

[1]Letter from Audrey Smith to Hubert Blenkinsop, November 30, 1944.

[2]Robert Anthony Eden was a British politician who was Foreign Secretary for three periods between 1935 and 1955, and prime minister of the UK from 1955 to 1957. At the outbreak of the Second World War, Winston Churchill appointed Eden Secretary of State for War. Later in 1940 he returned to the Foreign Office, and in this role became a member of the executive committee of the Political Warfare Executive in 1941. Although he was one of Churchill's closest confidants, his role in wartime was restricted because Churchill conducted the most important negotiations with Roosevelt and Stalin himself, but Eden served loyally as Churchill's lieutenant. In 1942 he was given the additional job of Leader of the House of Commons.

Missing Research and Enquiry Service, advancing through Belgium in the wake of the liberation armies, had stumbled upon their graves. This unit, which advanced behind friendly lines, had been established for the purpose of securing and collating information on missing RCAF personnel. They were making enquiries in liberated territories in an endeavour to obtain additional specifics to supplement known information, which had already been received. By a twist of fate, Teddy was living his last days during the very same period that this additional information was collected.

After the bombing of Hamburg's harbour refineries in mid-October 1944, the forced labourers were returned to Neuengamme. However, before long, 400 prisoners had been put to work in another Kommando in Hamburg, the Deutsche Werft shipyards. Teddy was one of them and he became friends there with François Fernand of Châtenois en Vosges, France. In June 1945, François reported to Hubert about the harsh conditions at the dockyards. He stated that prisoners had to rise during the night and go to work without eating a thing. They were badly shod with only a pair of wooden sandals held on the feet by a piece of rag and dressed in a simple papery costume which became soaked with moisture at the least drop of rain. At noon, they received a soup consisting of mostly water with a few potatoes or beetroots, 200 grams of black bread and ten grams of margarine – that was it. There were no Sunday breaks, and no one cared whether the workers fell ill or not. Teddy slept near François on a palliasse placed on a plank with one blanket, which they shared.

In November 1944, Teddy became very ill. The lack of food, water, proper clothing and medical attention rapidly accelerated the decline of his health. In addition, the weather in November and December 1944 was exceptionally cold and wet, accompanied by ice-cold winds that swept in from the Baltic Sea. Between Christmas 1944 and New Year 1945, it was brought to light that Teddy had developed tuberculosis. Months later, François Fernand was the first to report what had happened to Teddy in a letter he sent to Hubert:

> We took care of him as well as we could and tried by all means to find some decent food. But without medicine it is difficult to fight illness. He worked until his death. He died of congestion of the lungs caused by a chill. As many another, he died of exhaustion without realising he was going. In spite of all he did not undergo torture, being a Canadian. The few rare objects that we had gathered together belonging to our dead comrades were stolen by the Germans. Please Sir, believe I much regret having to give you all this sad information; your son has always been a very good friend to me. Yours Very Truly, François.[1]

It took several more months before Hubert was officially informed about

[1]Letter from François Fernand to Hubert Blenkinsop, undated (probably June 1945). Translated by one of Hubert's associates.

Teddy's death. In late September 1945, a letter arrived from the RCAF casualty officer stating that Teddy had died in Neuengamme. More confirmation about his demise came through a less formal channel. In her letter of October 1, 1945, to Hubert, Christine Pypen explained how her sister-in-law went every day to a Red Cross office in Brussels, where updated lists of deceased prisoners were frequently posted. Apart from her brother, the woman noticed the name of Teddy Blenkinsop on that list. The entry read: 'Blenkinsop, Edward Weiman – Meensel-Kiezegem – Born 08/10/1920 – Died on 23/01/1945 at Neuengamme.'

Winsome and Hubert were devastated, as were the Skipper and Granny. Their worst fears had become a reality. It was not until December 1945 that the RCAF Casualty Office indirectly provided them with the full details about Teddy's end, including evidence about the place of death. Wing Commander Gunn reported the specifics to Wing Commander F.K. Belton, the Chaplain of Winsome's air force unit, with the instruction to convey this information personally to Teddy's parents. Through the RCAF Overseas Missing Research and Enquiry Service, a detailed statement was secured from Noël Berchoux, Teddy's friend and interpreter. He testified that Teddy had been bedridden in the sick quarters for 15 days in November after becoming too ill to work at the shipyard. A Russian doctor who was also a prisoner there attended him. He then returned to work but ultimately became stricken again. After an air attack on December 31, 1944, during which bombs hit the factory, the sick and wounded were transferred by rail to Neuengamme. Before leaving Hamburg, the Russian doctor told Noël that Teddy had contracted tuberculosis. Noël next saw Teddy in the Bergen-Belsen Camp around January 15 to 20, 1945. He was in the tuberculosis section and died there somewhere between January 28 and February 3, 1945.

Following the statement by Noël Berchoux, an RCAF casualty investigator visited the concentration camp at Bergen-Belsen, about 100 kilometres south of Hamburg. The former camp commandant of Bergen-Belsen assured him that they had destroyed all records prior to the liberation of the camp in April 1945. Captain Palme of the Allied Displaced Persons Service confirmed this. When the investigator looked into the German records preserved at Neuengamme, it was stated there that Squadron Leader Blenkinsop died of 'heart failure' at 'Meensel-Kiezegem "Q" Camp' in Neuengamme on January 23, 1945. This report was most likely erroneous as to location of death. No further information could be obtained at Neuengamme.[1]

Noël Berchoux's dates were reasonably close to the ones written in the

[1]Letters from Wing Commander W.R. Gunn, RCAF casualty officer, to Wing Commander F.K. Belton, Command chaplain of RCAF Western Air Command, dated September 21 and December 4, 1945. The first letter wrongly stated that Teddy had died on February 14-15, 1945. Noël Berchoux corrected this in a second interview, reflected in the second letter.

German records at Neuengamme. It was obvious that, under the conditions in which Noël Berchoux and his friends were living, it was extremely difficult to recollect exact times and dates. While the true date of Teddy's death will probably never be known, the RCAF officially presumed it to have occurred on January 23, 1945. It is further assumed that his body was cremated at the concentration camp of Bergen-Belsen with a number of other bodies, and the ashes spread over the camp gardens, but, again, this theory cannot be confirmed as, shortly before the arrival of the Allies, the Germans had most of their records destroyed.[1]

After his return to France, Noël Berchoux wrote a long letter to Hubert and Winsome. He assured them that Teddy had not suffered and died a brave man. He shared the grief of both parents, as he had regarded Teddy not only as a comrade in their mutual agony but as a brother. One of Noël's compatriots, Mr Noël Charles from Jarville, also met Teddy while working as a prisoner in the Eurotank refinery. On June 13, 1945, while in a Swiss sanatorium where he was recovering from his life in the camps, he wrote a similar letter to Hubert, including: 'Your son was much loved by all Frenchmen, as he spoke our language, and I can tell you also that he could be relied upon in any circumstance.'

On February 27, 1946, the Belgian Commission for Repatriation sent Teddy's official death certificate to the mayor of Meensel-Kiezegem, with a request to forward it to his family. The Pypens duly sent it on. Some time later, Mrs Pypen also went to the Ministry of Reconstruction in Brussels, to collect Teddy's signet ring and escape compass, which had been found in the Neuengamme camp by Belgian Army investigation officers. She accepted the compass, but asked the official to return the signet ring to Teddy's parents. The request was duly noted, and a few weeks later the ring arrived in Victoria through the Canadian Embassy in Brussels. Teddy's other effects had been sent back home from his unit in England some time earlier.

On Wednesday, April 10, 1946, a formal service for the rest of Teddy's soul was performed in the Church of Meensel at 11:00 a.m. The RCAF made up an official casualty notification on June 14, 1946, which stated that various conflicting dates of the death of Squadron Leader Edward W Blenkinsop were received. It further declared conclusively his death, for official purposes, was to have occurred on January 23, 1945.

---

[1]Bergen-Belsen was an infamous Nazi camp initially set up as a detention camp for prisoners who held foreign passports and were thus eligible to be traded for German citizens being held in Allied internment camps. Later Bergen-Belsen became a concentration camp under the command of Josef Kramer, the former commandant of the Auschwitz II camp Birkenau. A section for sick prisoners, who could no longer work in the forced labour camps, was set up in March 1944. Bergen-Belsen was liberated by units of the British-Canadian 21st Army Group on April 15, 1945. They discovered 10,000 unburied bodies there, while another 13,000 prisoners died after the liberation, partly due to a typhus epidemic. The camp was located about a mile from the tiny village of Belsen and a few more miles from Bergen, a town with a population of 13,000.

Teddy Blenkinsop was awarded posthumously the Croix de Guerre avec Palme by the Belgian government, for distinguished service rendered to Belgium during the liberation of its territory. The decoration was forwarded to Teddy's parents through the Belgian embassy in Ottawa in 1948 and published in the *Canada Gazette* on July 17, 1948.

Teddy's other decoration and medals awarded include the Distinguished Flying Cross, the 1939-45 Star, the Air Crew Europe Star, the Defence Medal, the Canadian Volunteer Service Medal with Clasp, and the War Medal 1939-45. This courageous Canadian airman is commemorated in perpetuity on the Air Forces Memorial to the Missing at Runnymede, England, having no known grave.

Another token of respect came on April 6, 1950, when the people of Canada, through the Government Geographical Names Board of Canada, approved the name Blenkinsop for a tiny island, in his honour and in recognition of his exceptional services during the war. Blenkinsop Islet is situated in a wild and beautiful area of the British Columbia coastline at the junction of the Grenville and Douglas channels, position N53°17′ W129°19′.[1]

---

[1]Five members of Teddy's Lancaster crew were also remembered with geographical features: David Ramsay with Ramsay Creek in BC (N49°28′ W125°08′) and David Street in Port Alberni BC, Larry Allen with Allen Lake in NWT (N60°56’ W103°48’), George Smith with Smith Lake in Saskatchewan (N55°57′ W106°45′), Bob Booth with Booth Lake in Manitoba (N59°23’ W99°36’), Hugh Clifford with Clifford Lake in Ontario (N48°19′ W79°52′). There is no feature named after Leslie Foster.

CHAPTER FIFTEEN

Epilogue

Teddy Blenkinsop was certainly not the only Allied airman who did not receive humane and proper treatment as directed under the Convention Relative to the Treatment of Prisoners of War, signed in Geneva July 27, 1929. Until April 1944, it was highly unusual for German authorities to send Allied prisoners of war to concentration camps and not to a POW detention facility. As discussed earlier in Chapter Eleven, things started to change when the dreaded Security Service SD – commonly referred to as the Gestapo – in reality took over escape line matters from the Abwehr.

During the so-called 'Dachau trials' held from 1945 to 1948, US Army courts in Germany tried 1,672 individuals in 489 proceedings. These 489 encompassed more than 200 cases of which some 600 persons, mostly German civilians, were prosecuted for the killing of some 1,200 US nationals, mostly airmen.[1] However, this attitude towards the violation of international law towards enemy airmen did not meet the approval of the armed forces, especially that of Reichsmarshall Göring or his subordinates in the Luftwaffe. Göring condemned to the utmost the incessant Allied bombing attacks on Germany, which he stated were primarily directed against a defenceless civilian population. He and his staff nevertheless opposed the handing over of downed and defenceless aviators to an aroused and angry mob to carry out 'lynch law'.

Still, the so-called Bullet Decree of March 1944, went one step further. It became some sort of official state policy to kill downed airmen upon capture. But the German Foreign Office soon expressed concern about shooting prisoners of war and suggested that only enemy airmen suspected of evading capture with the help of local Resistance networks should be denied legal POW status. Acting on this subtle difference, certain Gestapo and security police divisions on interrogation informed captured Allied evaders that they were considered criminals, not POWs. Using this justification, the Gestapo and security police sent hundreds of Allied airmen to concentration camps. An excuse for treating an Allied flyer as a criminal

[1]Institute of Criminal Law of the University of Amsterdam; Records of the trials of German major war criminals, vol.18.

was justified in their minds because of the attire a captured airman wore at the time of his arrest – civilian clothing was regarded as the outfit of a spy.

An example of the ruthless application of the new policy by some Gestapo branches is found in the story of Flight Lieutenant Walker from 83 Squadron, RAF. Walker was among the airmen who had flown alongside Teddy on the Nürnberg raid on March 30-31, 1944. This pathfinder pilot was subsequently shot down on a raid over Wesseling, bailed out over Holland and managed to contact the Dutch section of the escape route. He was in a safe house in Tilburg when the Germans raided it. Walker and two other RAF men, all wearing civilian clothes, were shot dead in cold blood.

Chapter Eleven also relates the story of the 47 unfortunate airmen who died in Mauthausen concentration camp. Likewise, on August 20, 1944, the concentration camp of Buchenwald received a group of 168 aviators. This group consisted of 26 Canadians, 82 Americans and 60 from the United Kingdom, Australia and New Zealand. All these airmen had been shot down over occupied Europe and made contact with the French Resistance in an effort to escape from the Germans. They had been issued false papers and were dressed as civilians to help in their escape. A treacherous member of the Resistance betrayed them and they were all arrested as spies. They were questioned, beaten and subjected to other forms of cruelty. When the advancing Allied armies came within reach of the Fresnes prison in Paris, the Germans hurriedly placed these inmates in cattle cars destined for Germany on August 15, 1944. On reaching Buchenwald in Germany, they were subjected to the same inhumane treatment and abuse as other prisoners, including starvation, disease and the constant threats by cruel guards. One Canadian pilot lost more than 29.5 kg there during his six weeks in captivity. The men witnessed horrific beatings, hangings and torture. Thanks to the strong intervention of two high-ranking Luftwaffe officers, 156 of the 168 airmen were transferred from Buchenwald to POW camp Stalag Luft III on the night of October 18, 1944. Too sick to travel, 12 airmen remained at Buchenwald. Two of them died, including one Englishman and an American fighter pilot, Lieutenant Beck, who succumbed to pneumonia. The other ten were later transported to the POW camp. The two months in the concentration camp left many of the men permanently scarred, physically and psychologically. The informer, who was responsible for the capture of these airmen, and the capture of many others, was himself arrested by the Americans in 1947 while in Germany and was turned over to the French government. The state of France tried him for crimes he had perpetrated against the French people. He was executed in 1949.[1]

[1]H. Onderwater, *Reis Naar de Horizon* (Amsterdam: Hollandia, 1985), 152-53; L. C. Beck, *Fighter Pilot* (Los Angeles: Wetzel Publishing, 1946). The latter book is based on letters written by Lieutenant Beck to his parents from prison; article by Jim Hastin of the 361st Fighter Group, USAAF, in the 361st FG Association *Newsletter*, February 1993.

It is obvious that the approximately 50 Allied airmen who were held in St. Gilles in August 1944 – and subsequently rescued from the Ghost Train – were destined to end up in a German death camp such as Buchenwald. We will never ascertain why Teddy was treated as one of the Meensel-Kiezegem political prisoners and not despatched with the other airmen in St. Gilles. Basically though, it became clear to many that his sentence was because of the fact he was accused of being actively involved in Resistance actions of the Meensel-Kiezegem clique. His selfless nature and his ethos to always fight on, in essence, cost him his life.

After the liberation of Brussels in early September 1944, the Belgians celebrated for over a week. It was only at the insistence of the government that they finally returned to work. Life was slowly returning to normal. While some were mourning the death of their loved ones in German prisons in Belgium, others rejoiced at the sight of the returning detainees. Many of them needed intensive medical care after their ordeal, but the elation of being home again seemed to do wonders for their recovery.

Jos Pypen returned home from prison in Leuven in early September 1944 and right away volunteered to join the Third Infantry Brigade of the Belgian army in Great Britain. Meanwhile, his parents – and Paula – were anxious for news of Teddy. In April 1945, the Pypen family wrote their first letter to Teddy's relatives. Civilian mail between Belgium and England was again re-established, and their letter inquired of Uncle Max if they had received any news of Teddy's whereabouts. They explained to him how they were looking for any news that Teddy might have survived. As of yet, none of their fellow citizens arrested in August 1944 had returned home. Three weeks later, they replied to a letter received from Hubert. They gave Hubert a full account of the five weeks Teddy had spent with them, and expressed their great esteem and affection their entire family had for Teddy. It was the start of a period of intense correspondence between the two families.[1]

Indeed, for the majority of the concentration camp survivors, the war was not over in April 1945. At the start of 1945 Germany decreed that no concentration camp prisoner should fall into Allied hands. SS-leader Heinrich Himmler, while trying to save his own life by attempting to leave the country anonymously, had long ago decided that all incarcerated prisoners would be disposed of in case of a retreat. These people were considered 'undesirables' but more importantly, had witnessed the Nazi's 'Final Solution'. Himmler charged the Verdammten (Damned) section of the SS, with the elimination and disposal of all concentration camp victims. The sheer number of victims and the unanticipated rapid advance of the Allies ultimately compromised the fulfilment of this order.

As British forces approached the Hamburg area in mid-April 1945, the SS began the forcible evacuation of the Neuengamme concentration camp,

[1]Letters by the Pypen-Vander Meeren family, dated April 26 and May 14, 1945. They were translated from Dutch into English by a friend of the Pypens.

burning all records as they departed. A considerable number of detainees lost their lives during these last few weeks, while others were rejoicing the welcoming sounds of the Allied guns. Thousands of ill or weakened prisoners had already been transferred to the nearby Bergen-Belsen concentration camp, when Camp Commandant Max Pauly ordered the Neuengamme prisoners to be divided into three groups. A first group of prisoners were sent to the satellite camp of Sandbostel. The second was ordered eastbound in the direction of the Russian front, while a third batch of 14,000 captives were forced marched or herded onto trains for the north. They would ultimately live out their darkest nightmare at Lübeck Bay.

Contrary to general belief the world's greatest ship disaster did not occur in the Atlantic Ocean and the ship was not the *Titanic*. The greatest ship disaster occurred on May 3, 1945 in Lübeck Bay in the Baltic Sea and the ship was the *Cap Arcona*. Two other ships were involved in the catastrophe: the *Thielbek* and the *Athen*. The Germans had assembled ships in the Baltic Sea as troop transports for the defeated German army fleeing westward from the advancing Russian army. But, as the prisoner migration advanced northward and flooded the area with captives, Hamburg's regional commander, Karl Kaufmann, sought ships to accommodate the concentration camp inmates at sea. The first of 11,000 Neuengamme prisoners arrived in cattle cars at Lübeck harbour on April 19, 1945. Between April 19 and 26 more railway transports arrived. Roughly 50 per cent of all prisoners did not survive the journey from the camps to the port. The *Cap Arcona* and *Thielbek* were already in position and anchored offshore in Lübeck Bay close to the city of Neustadt. The *Athen*, fortunately, as it would appear later, was actually tied up in the Neustadt harbour.

On the morning of April 20, 1945, Camp Commandant Max Pauly sent SS Sturmbannführer Christoph-Heinz Gehrig, head of administration at Neuengamme, to Lübeck. Gehrig had been responsible for the murder of 20 Jewish children at the Janusz-Korczak School in the Hamburg district of Rothenburgsort. These children had been subjected to tuberculosis experiments at Neuengamme. Gehrig was instructed to escort the prisoners aboard the *Cap Arcona* and, needless to say, it appears to their deaths.

This slender, three-funnelled luxury liner was the former flagship of the Hamburg-Süd Line. In the face of advancing Russian troops, this recent arrival in Neustadt harbour had just transported German civilians, Nazi officials and military personnel from East Prussia to northern Germany. Her turbines needed repair after her latest journey. When she dropped anchor in Lübeck Bay on April 14, 1945, she was no longer manoeuvrable and of little future use to the navy. She was being returned to the Hamburg-Süd line, her original owners. Nicknamed the *Queen of the South Atlantic*, the ship had seaward-facing cabins for the viewing pleasure of its peacetime passengers, but these cabins, which were designed to accommodate maybe one or two, now held some 20 emaciated prisoners.

Gehrig ordered Captain Nobmann of the *Athen* to take 2,300 prisoners and their 280 SS guards on board and to ferry them to the *Cap Arcona*. Captain Nobmann initially refused but obeyed when threatened with a drumhead court martial whose outcome would be certain death. The SS herded the prisoners on board with yells and blows. The prisoners had to climb down rope ladders into the ship's deepest cargo holds. In the haste many prisoners fell and were seriously injured. There was barely room to move in the dark, cold and damp holds. There were no toilets or water. After some hours the fully laden ship left the harbour for the *Cap Arcona* that was anchored off Neustadt. Captain Bertram at first refused to allow this human cargo aboard his *Cap Arcona*, but an SS unit soon arrived. Bertram and Captain Nobmann were given the ultimatum: either immediately give permission for the *Athen* to moor alongside and transfer its prisoners to the *Cap Arcona* or be shot without a court martial. Bertram capitulated. Before the *Athen* could come alongside, a launch brought SS men under SS-Untersturmbannführer Kirstein on board. He had all life belts and jackets, all benches that could be used as rafts, locked away in storage. It was now obvious to everyone that these ships were commandeered to take the camp prisoners on board with the intention of drowning them when the ship was sunk.

Antagonism between the crew and the 500 SS guards on board is recorded, as is Captain Bertram's petition to have his ship painted with a large red cross, or at least illuminated, so that it might be recognised as a hospital ship. These requests were denied. On May 2, more prisoners arrived to be crammed into the 27,500-ton *Cap Arcona*. Ultimately, there were 6,500 prisoners and 600 SS guards on board this luxury liner. There was hardly anything to eat or drink and as a consequence many prisoners succumbed. The Russian prisoners aboard received the worst treatment as they were billeted at the bottom of the cargo holds without sufficient air, light or food. The number of dead grew larger by the day. The *Athen* made its last journey to the *Cap Arcona* on April 30 but this time to take prisoners off as the *Cap Arcona* was so overcrowded that even the SS could no longer endure the starvation or the stench of the dead. There were now 2,800 prisoners on board the *Thielbek*, and 1,998 prisoners on the *Athen*.

On the morning of May 3, 1945, some British fighter-bombers flew over Lübeck Bay and observed the *Cap Arcona* and *Thielbek*. The prisoners waved, believing they were about to be saved. The planes flew at 10,000 feet to avoid the flak and the prisoners were apparently not seen because of the height at which the planes were flying and because the low-hanging broken cloud obscured their vision. The ships were subsequently strafed and bombed by Royal Air Force Typhoons of 263, 197 and 198 Squadron. The pilots had been briefed about German troops attempting to escape to Norway via the sea and were unaware that the SS had concentration camp prisoners on board. They found Neustadt Bay teeming with 'military' targets of opportunity. The pilots could never have guessed at the carnage they were wreaking. If the prisoners in the crammed, exposed cabins did not die in the attack, they were soon burning or drowning in a capsized floating prison. But incredibly, a few hundred men and women made it into the water and swam the mile or so onto the beaches. Unfortunately for them, the Verdammten SS were there first, and machine-gunned them down as they crawled out of the surf. Of the 4,750 prisoners aboard the *Cap Arcona*, only 350 were reported to have survived, most of these picked up by local trawlers. Sixty-four of the ship's 80 crew died, but only 100 SS guards perished. All the 1,998 prisoners from the *Athen* survived and 50 were rescued from the *Thielbek*. Frans Van Gilbergen and Alfons Van Wanghe from Meensel-Kiezegem were aboard the *Cap Arcona*. Frans was transferred to the *Athen* before the air raid, and survived. Alfons perished aboard the *Cap Arcona*.

Overall, during the Neustadt Bay air raid at least 7,500 people of 24 nationalities were killed, 23 vessels were sunk and a further 113 were damaged. Among these craft were open-topped barges crammed with yet more concentration camp prisoners, who had just recently arrived from Poland. An hour after this air raid the German forces surrendered without a fight at Neustadt. In another 44 hours all hostilities had ceased. It is to be noted, that no British government has ever made reference to the deaths of the 7,500 people in Lübeck Bay. There has never been a wreath laid or a speech made in their memory. Today, there is a memorial for those who perished in the *Cap Arcona* at the cemetery in Grömitz. Not one of the many Germans, guilty of the murder of the prisoners on board the *Cap Arcona* or the *Thielbek*, has ever been tried or sentenced.

Jozef Claes and Frans Trompet were forcibly put on a train in an effort to keep the 'hostages' out of the hands of the advancing Allies. Despite atrocious conditions and total exhaustion, they were among the few prisoners still strong enough to survive the ordeal. They were liberated by a British Army unit in May 1945, and returned home in June 1945 only to spend months in hospital. Another group of Neuengamme prisoners, including several from Meensel-Kiezegem, were quickly transferred to Brünswick as the Allied troops advanced toward Neuengamme. From Brünswick, they were again moved further east to Ravensbrück and Malkow. They were 'liberated' by the Russians, who took them to a camp at Elrich, on May 17, 1945. About 18 prisoners escaped during a closed ranks forced march, and were able to reach the Allied lines. The only citizen of Meensel-Kiezegem in this group of 18 escapees was Marcel Loddewijckx. He was the only one of this entire group that was 'liberated' by the Russians and who returned home to Meensel-Kiezegem after the war.

Thousands of other Neuengamme prisoners were marched or transported to other camps. Those who could not keep up during these appalling death marches were left behind to die or were shot. The marchers arrived, starved and exhausted, in satellite camps such as Sandbostel or Wöbbelin. There, they were abandoned in conditions beyond description. Exhausted and ravaged by famine, the prisoners fought for the last piece of bread or ate the grass that lined the footpaths. Many died from diseases or starvation.

On May 4, 1945, the British forces liberated a totally abandoned camp at Neuengamme. The death register at Neuengamme indicates approximately 40,000 prisoners had perished at this camp by April 10, 1945. Thousands more died before the liberation of the camp on May 4. In total, 55,000 succumbed to the subhuman conditions found in the camp. Today the site of the Neuengamme concentration camp is a protected memorial site containing cenotaphs, restored buildings, which accommodate a documentation and research centre.

By late June 1945, eight emaciated villagers of Meensel-Kiezegem had returned home from Germany. To a man, they bore the marks of torture, psychological abuse, starvation and disease. These men all were fearful and dysfunctional the rest of their lives but, needless to say, their wives and families were overjoyed to see them.

Immediately after the liberation of Meensel-Kiezegem, a wave of repression descended over the village. Collaborators were seized and left to the peoples' rage. A second spontaneous outbreak of repression followed the return of the eight emaciated survivors from the death camps. Resistance fighters from outside the town arrested the Merckx and Broos families. Albert, Maurice and Marcel remained untraceable. They escaped abroad and went into hiding, probably in South America. Maurice Merckx was known to have lived in Cologne, West Germany, at one time. The court proceedings took place in a turbulent atmosphere, with many spectators hoping for a severe sentence. In May 1946, the three eldest Merckx sons were sentenced to death in absentia by the Court Martial of Leuven. The father, Remi Merckx, mother Clementine, daughter Maria and son Jozef were sentenced to life imprisonment, while the youngest son Ernest, received ten years. Collaborator Felix Broos, who replaced the arrested mayor, Romain Morren, after the roundup on August 11, was also sentenced to life imprisonment.

None of the death sentences was ever carried out, nor were any of the pronounced life sentences ever fully served. All the former Blackshirt families, needless to say, departed Meensel-Kiezegem to reside elsewhere.

SS Obersturmbannführer Verbelen, leader of the command cell during the roundups at Meensel-Kiezegem, never spent a day behind bars. He lived out his life in comfort and was employed with the American secret services in Germany and Austria, and died peacefully in 1990. The Antwerp Court Martial sentenced Flemish SS Untersturmbannführer Tony Van Dijck, leader of one of the three battle units during the raid of August 11, to death in April 1947. His sentence was commuted to 17 years imprisonment, of which he served 16 years. His cohorts, Jozef Bachot and

Jef De Meyer, were never charged, tried or convicted of any crime that anyone can ascertain.

Finally, Max Pauly, camp commandant of Neuengamme between 1942 and 1945, and 13 of his accomplices were tried in Hamburg in 1946. Pauly was accused of crimes against humanity and executed in October 1946.

The fate of Teddy's closest helpers in the Belgian Underground gives an illustration of the risks those in the Resistance undertook when helping downed airmen. Charles Jonckers and his brothers were left alone by the German oppressor but had to go into permanent hiding by mid-1944. Their leader Hilaire Gemoets paid the highest price when he was killed in a gunfight with the retreating Germans on September 3, 1944. His father, Charles Gemoets, who had been the first Belgian to open his home to Teddy, was arrested on July 16, 1944. He was a leader in the local Group 'G' section and was taken into custody because the Germans wanted his son Hilaire. Charles Gemoets was incarcerated in the notorious Buchenwald and Dora concentration camps, where he barely survived. He was liberated on April 13, 1945, but spent the rest of his life disabled. Jules Schotsmans, one of Teddy's first helpers in Meensel-Kiezegem, died during the roundup of August 11. Finally, Herman Pypen was shot at by the SS while successfully evading capture during the siege of the village. His son Jos, arrested together with Teddy, was among the fortunate prisoners abandoned at a prison in Leuven during the German retreat. He was released on September 4 and walked home.

Perhaps the saddest example of the hazards involved in being (even if only allegedly) associated with airmen's lifelines was the story of Ferdinand Alen. Ferdinand just happened to live near the field where Teddy had been hiding the night and day following his miraculous escape from the exploding Lancaster. A woman sympathizer couldn't resist blathering about it in the presence of Germans or collaborators, with the foreseeable result. Ferdinand was arrested and died a horrible death in the Dora concentration camp. He was a widower and father of four children, the eldest being 24 years old at the time of his father's death. His orphaned children never knew why their father was arrested. They assumed he might have given flour to the Resistance, but they never knew for sure. After the war, the four children tried to make the best of the situation and keep their heads above water. When they applied for government support in 1946, they were allowed a state pension. But, much to their shock, they discovered in 1963 that their father had never been recognised as a political prisoner by the Belgian government. As a result, they had no rights to bring a claim for damages as orphans of a political prisoner. When they demanded a rectification, this seemed impossible, as the requests for recognition of political prisoners had to be processed by 1956.[1]

The quiet town of Meensel-Kiezegem paid an immense price for the SS roundups triggered by the demands of a vengeful woman and her family.

Three men had been murdered in their hometown on August 1, and a fourth one burned alive on August 11. An incredible 91 villagers were arrested; 20 were liberated from the Ghost Train or a prison in Leuven, but 71 ended up in concentration camps in Germany, mainly Neuengamme. From there, only eight men ever returned home alive after the war. Only one-fifth of all those arrested were members of the Resistance. Some families were virtually decimated, and the town deprived of 7 per cent of its inhabitants. Former Mayor Natens lost four sons and a son-in-law. The men from Meensel-Kiezegem who never returned left behind 32 widows and 95 orphans. For decades to come, Meensel-Kiezegem would be a 'silent' town, where people disliked talking about the war, but where the post-war generation vowed never to forget. A composite photograph made of the victims is displayed in many family homes in Meensel-Kiezegem and included in this picture is Teddy Blenkinsop, considered by all the villagers to be one of them.

On Sunday August 10, 1947, a memorial park was inaugurated at Meensel-Kiezegem for the victims of the raids in August 1944. There, an individual headstone was erected, which bears personal details and a photograph of 55 villagers of Meensel-Kiezegem who perished. Although Teddy Blenkinsop is not buried in this little graveyard behind the commemorative chapel, a headstone was erected there in his memory. The Pypen family supplied his photo. Hubert Blenkinsop made a donation to the town to defray the costs of his memorial. On that Sunday in 1947, and each year thereafter, the people of Meensel-Kiezegem hold a commemoration ceremony to remember their heroes. This service always takes place on a Sunday between August 1 and 11 and continues to this day. In 1984, His Majesty King Baudouin visited the town for the 40th anniversary of the brutalities to honour those fallen, while in 1989 Brigadier General John Neroutsos and his wife Mary were the first members of Teddy's immediate family to participate in this very moving annual event. For the first time in 2004, wounds had healed enough to extend an invitation to a German representative to attend the 60th anniversary of the tragedy. The German ambassador, the Belgian chairman of Parliament and the Canadian military attaché sat side by side on the VIP stand.

The story of Teddy Blenkinsop is just one of many thousands of tales of the valour of Canadian service men and women in the Second World War. There were 42,090 Canadian soldiers killed in the war, approximately 2,000 from the navy, 22,000 from the army and 17,100 from the air force. RAF Bomber Command alone lost some 55,573 airmen, of whom 9,919 were Canadian. This figure does not include approximately 12,000 who parachuted from stricken aircraft and were captured to become POWs, or those lost in accidents and crashes and the nearly 20,000 wounded in

[1]The Belgian government did approve, under exceptional circumstances, additional claims from recognised political prisoners of the Second World War during the year 1999 only.

action. This would be an inconceivable amount of blood spilled from any nation at war, but it was young Canadian and Belgian blood that was spilled in Belgium – and from its true wealth, its human resource.

The Belgian armed forces – including those who valiantly served in Britain's army, air force and navy – lost 10,000 men killed or missing, while 90,000 Belgian civilians were killed during the war. With two world wars having been fought on its 'neutral' territory over only 30 years, the country was in shambles, but, thanks to the Marshall Plan, signed by US President Truman on April 3, 1948, Belgium and its sister-state Luxemburg received a total of $777 million. Together with the typical Belgian diligence, this American plan for rebuilding and creating a stronger foundation for the Allied countries of Europe brought on quick recovery. The years 1948 to 1952 saw the fastest period of growth in European history.

In conclusion, while Belgium's war casualties were many, the scale of the calamity in that small and tranquil village of Meensel-Kiezegem where so many Belgians needlessly perished has to be considered among the great tragedies of that brutal war. One can only assume, because so few facts were ever officially uncovered, history passed by the recording of these events and the players who performed so admirably upon that stage.

On June 2, 1947, Frans Van Dyck, with the help of a local teacher, wrote a moving letter to Teddy's parents:

> Dear Mr Blenkinsop,
> Be so kind and let me have the latest news you possess about your son Edward Blenkinsop, late Squadron Leader in the RAF.
>
> I knew your son very well. He came to my place in Waanrode on the 1st of May. My wife and I and got very fond of him. In our imagination, we still see him moving about the house – his civilian clothes were somewhat large for him. At night he would go out for a breather accompanied by one or several of the resistance men, they acted as body-guards.
>
> The place of his concealment in my house will remind me for ever of this gallant boy who gave everything a man of heart can give a people for whom he has taken up the fight of his life. The thing we did for him is only a tiny atom compared with what he did for our country. His conduct will serve us as a symbol of courage and decency in our further life.
>
> I know how you must feel as my own brother was shot in a brutal way by those damned Germans. Let us remain true to the motto 'Union makes Force'. We shall feel much obliged if you will forward to us a few lines. In the mean time we remain, dear Mr Blenkinsop, your sincere friends, (signed) Frans Van Dyck.

In July 1990, Teddy's former bomb aimer in Africa, Wing Commander Donald Wilson, wrote this moving tribute:

> It was with mixed emotions that I received your saga of Ted Blenkinsop DFC. The first was that of shock. Shock that he died of tuberculosis, exhaustion, and, no doubt, malnutrition and other deprivations in that most infamous of concentration camps – Bergen Belsen. The second was of regret, regret that, in the course of my own rehabilitation, I had not found the time to determine his ultimate fate. Finally, the third was pride, pride that I had the good fortune to have known such a man for the one short month that we flew together on operations from Tunisia in 1943.
>
> Please convey to your grandparents my feelings of profound respect for those patriots of their village – Meensel-Kiezegem – who fought and died alongside Ted against the Nazi tyranny. It is through people like them that many Allied airmen were able to evade capture to return to their bases.
>
> I am sure Ted lies alongside his fellow patriots, content in the knowledge that they had died together in the cause of freedom.

Lieutenant General Reg Lane, DSO, DFC, CD, who grew up in Victoria with Teddy and was right behind him the night they were shot down, added: 'Ted Blenkinsop was never recognised by his own country for his great unselfish determination and final sacrifice. His story should be added to the many others of gallantry that, for whatever reason, did not come to light and hence went unrecognised.'

Finally, Yvonne Jukes, undoubtedly someone who loved him dearly, wrote in 1989 about Teddy: 'We were all so young and so unprepared to face what was before us. I knew a boy who became a very great man – or at least in my estimation.'

Teddy's fiancée, Helen Woodcroft, returned to Canada after the war and in due course married an Alcan executive, taking on the name of Vair. She lived in Mandeville, Jamaica, and latterly in Montreal, Quebec. She kept in touch with Teddy's extended family until her generation was no longer.

Teddy's parents never found the strength of heart to accept the Pypens' recurring warm invitations to visit them in Meensel-Kiezegem. They did, however, send the Pypens a variety of presents, ranging from food parcels to baby clothes for Paula and Jos's children. Paula married on May 10, 1947. Florence Neroutsos, the Skipper's older sister, then approaching 90, came from London to attend the wedding and brought presents from the family. Paula continued to correspond with Teddy's parents until 1967.

Hubert and Winsome never got over the loss of their only child. The fact that they never really knew what had happened to him and where he was actually buried increased their sorrow. Although both accepted Teddy had fought a 'just war', they had great difficulty coming to terms with the loss, and their grief was such that the subject was seldom raised during the course of their life. Correspondence with the relatives of Teddy's crewmembers obviously dwindled with time, and they both tried to get on with their lives in their own way. Hubert died in November 1973 at the age of 83. He spent his last years at the Gorge Road Hospital's extended care facility in Victoria. Winsome received Canada's Memorial Cross Order – best known as the Mother's Silver Cross. In later years, she was chosen to represent all mothers who had lost a child at a Remembrance Day ceremony at the monument in front of British Columbia's Parliament buildings in Victoria. She was now an elderly woman and found this function an extremely difficult one for her to perform, but she did it for all the mothers, knowing the grief they all shared in common.

Winsome never talked to anyone about her feelings surrounding the loss of her only child, not even to her mother. After Winsome's death on June 10, 1986, while closing her affairs, her nephews found a personal diary in which she poured out her grief and anger concerning the circumstances under which she had lost her darling son. She had been a devout person, but her entire faith was now shattered. She could not find the answers to why a Higher being allowed torture and slow death from lack of food, clothing and medical attention while exposing her son to all the elements.

Teddy's grandmother, being a serene and mystical person, found her emotional outlet in a poem she dedicated to her beloved, Edward Weyman Blenkinsop, in which she called him her 'trusted knight'.

The Trusted Knight

When the Cosmic Host decided
To cleanse the human mind,
They called together a chosen few
To probe and delve and find.
One trusted knight of the Most High
Was allotted the hardest fight.
To feel and know how cruel could be
The Minds that lost the Lights.
Our hero gaily took the Path
And clasping to his breast,
The lamp of God which glowed and glowed
In the darkness of his quest.
And when one day the Cosmic Host
Gave the signal from above.
He was wafted up the golden stairs
To Light and Life and Love.

Ada Sarah Neroutsos, December 1945

Appendix A

27/28 April 1944 – Montzen Marshalling Yards – Aircraft Losses[1]

Squadron	Type	Serial Nr	Captain	Crash Site	Attribution
51	Halifax III	LW479 (E)	F/L R. Rothwell, DFC	Maastricht-Caberg (Nl)	Lt Potthast
51	Halifax III	LV783 (Z)	Sgt P. Keenan	Moelingen (B)	Oblt Hager
51	Halifax III	MZ565 (O)	F/S J.H.P. O'Neill	Kemexhe (B)	Heavy Flak
419	Halifax II	JN954 (R)	P/O R.A. McIvor	Heer (Nl)	Oblt Augenstein
431	Halifax III	LK842 (N)	1st Lt J.H. Earman	Zwartberg (Genk) (B)	Oblt Greiner
431	Halifax III	MZ529 (E)	P/O W.E. Woodrow	Herselt-Blauberg (B)	Oblt Henseler or Lt Hoevermann
431	Halifax III	MZ536 (F)	W/O J. Gilson	Trognée (B)	Oblt Greiner or Lt Hittler
431	Halifax III	MZ522 (U)	F/L J.M. Hill	Boutershoven (B)	Oblt Henseler or Oblt Thörl
432	Halifax III	MZ588 (W)	F/O L.D. Deloughry	Verviers (B)	Oblt Schnaufer
432	Halifax III	LW592 (A)	P/O H.H. Whaley	Engis (B)	Oblt Hager
432	Halifax III	LK807 (J)	F/S G. Millar	Hannêche (B)	Heavy Flak
434	Halifax III	LL243 (U)	F/O G.F. Maffre	Wittem (Nl)	Lt Fengler
434	Halifax III	LL258 (W)	P/O E.A. Vigor	8 km N of Aubel (B)	Oblt Schnaufer
640	Halifax III	LW506 (X)	P/O R. Earnshaw	Heijningen (Nl)	Hptm Thomeschat
405	Lancaster III	JA976 (S)	S/L E.W. Blenkinsop, DFC	Webbekom (B)	Oblt Hager (Maj Jabs?)

[1]This table is based on the official Missing Aircraft Register (AIR 14/2791) held at the Public Records Office, London, crash records held at MoD Air Historical Branch, London, and additional findings of fellow researchers Wim Govaerts, Marcel Hogenhuis, Theo Boiten, Ron Pütz and Hans Ring. Close comparison of these data with the original Raid Plots (AIR 14/3222) of 27/28 April 1944, which contain accurate plots of each individual aircraft loss, resulted in the required correlation. Additionally, the author had correspondence with three of the involved Luftwaffe night fighter crews and conducted field research at some of the crash sites.

Appendix B

1 and 11 August 1944 – Victims at Meensel-Kiezegem

Victims of the raid on August 1, 1944

August Craeninckx	Executed	Buried at Meensel.
Oscar Beddegenoodts	Executed	Buried at Meensel.
Petrus Vander Meeren	Executed	Buried at Meensel.
Jozef Boesmans	Arrested	Died in CC Blumenthal-Schützenhof.
Maria Boesmans	Arrested	Liberated from Ghost Train in Brussels.
Paulina Bollen	Arrested	Liberated from Ghost Train in Brussels.
Stefanie Brams	Arrested	Liberated from Ghost Train in Brussels.
Jozef Claes	Arrested	Returned from CC.
Ferdinand Duerinckx	Arrested	Died in CC Neuengamme.
Madeleine Janssens	Arrested	Released same night.
René Janssens	Arrested	Died in Bremen.
Paul Martens	Arrested	Released August 2, 1944.
August Mathues	Arrested	Murdered by a guard in CC Neuengamme.
Léon Natens	Arrested	Died in CC Neuengamme.
Prosper Natens	Arrested	Died in CC Sandbostel.
Alfons Vangoidsenhoven	Arrested	Died during 'death march' near Neustadt.
Alfons Van Wanghe	Arrested	Died aboard the *Cap Arcona* during RAF air attack.
Frans Wauters	Arrested	Died in CC Neuengamme. Age 65.
Dr Hendrik Goyens	Arrested	Liberated from Ghost Train in Brussels. Arrested on Aug 2, 1944.

Victims of the raid on August 11th, 1944

Jules Schotsmans	Executed	Died when his farm was burned down.
Jozef Bastijns	Arrested	Died in CC Blumenthal-Schützenhof
Edward Blenkinsop, DFC	Arrested	Died in CC Bergen-Belsen.
Justin Bollen	Arrested	Died in CC Wolfenbüttel. From nearby town Attenrode.
Theofiel Bruers	Arrested	Died in CC Neuengamme.
Leontine Bruers	Arrested	Liberated from Ghost Train in Brussels.
Honorine Bruyninckx	Arrested	Liberated from Ghost Train in Brussels.
Evrard Cauwberghs	Arrested	Died in CC Neuengamme.
Louis Claes	Arrested	Died in CC Neuengamme.
Frans Clinckx	Arrested	Returned from CC. From nearby town O.L.V. Tielt.
Jozef Coeckelberghs	Arrested	Died in CC Neuengamme.
Frans Coeckelberghs	Arrested	Died during 'death march' near Lübeck.
Vital Craeninckx	Arrested	Murdered by a guard in CC Neuengamme.
Frans Craeninckx	Arrested	Liberated from Ghost Train in Brussels.
Jozef Craeninckx	Arrested	Liberated from Ghost Train in Brussels.
René-Vital Craeninckx	Arrested	Died in Neuengamme. Also reported among the *Cap Arcona* victims.
Daniël De Brier	Arrested	Died in satellite camp Meppen-Viersen.
Jozef De Bruyn	Arrested	Died in CC Neuengamme.
Marcel De Bruyn	Arrested	Died in CC Blumenthal-Schützenhof.
Louis De Cock	Arrested	Died in CC Blumenthal-Schützenhof.
Gustaaf Dereze	Arrested	Died in CC Neuengamme. From nearby town Wersbeek.
Evrard Devroey	Arrested	Died in CC Schandelah.
Godfried Goedhuys	Arrested	Died during 'death march' near Brünswick.
Adolf Hendrickx	Arrested	Died in CC Sandbostel.
Louis Hendrickx	Arrested	Died in CC Bergen-Belsen. Father of Adolf Hendrickx.
Richard Hendrickx	Arrested	Died in CC Blumenthal-Schützenhof.
Theofiel Hendrickx	Arrested	Died in CC Sandbostel. From nearby town Binkom.
Octaaf Janssens	Arrested	Died in satellite camp Meppen-Viersen.

Ferdinand Laevers	Arrested	Died in CC Dora. From nearby town Wersbeek.
Frans Lemmens	Arrested	Died in CC Neuengamme.
Frans Loddewijckx	Arrested	Liberated from Ghost Train in Brussels.
Marcel Loddewijckx	Arrested	Returned from CC.
Emile Lowies	Arrested	Died in CC Neuengamme.
Remi Morren	Arrested	Died in CC Neuengamme. Mayor of Meensel-Kiezegem.
Romain Morren	Arrested	Died at Meppen-Viersen or Bergen-Belsen.
René Natens	Arrested	Died in CC Blumenthal-Schützenhof.
Octaaf Natens	Arrested	Died in satellite camp Meppen-Viersen.
Joseph Natens	Arrested	Died in satellite camp Meppen-Viersen.
Emile Pasteyns	Arrested	Died in CC Neuengamme or satellite camp Meppen-Viersen.
Jozef-August Pasteyns	Arrested	Died in CC Neuengamme.
Frans Pasteyns	Arrested	Died aboard the *Cap Arcona* during RAF air attack.
Cordelie Pens	Arrested	Liberated from Ghost Train in Brussels.
Jules Pittomvils	Arrested	Liberated from Leuven prison early September 1944.
Petrus Pittomvils	Arrested	Returned from CC.
Jozef Pittomvils	Arrested	Died in CC Bergen-Belsen.
Denis Puttevils	Arrested	Returned from CC.
Jos Pypen	Arrested	Liberated from Leuven prison early September 1944.
Jean Pypen	Arrested	Liberated from Leuven prison early September 1944.
Jozef Pypen	Arrested	Died in CC Neuengamme. From Brussels.
Roger Pypen	Arrested	Died in CC Neuengamme. From Brussels.
Jules Pypen	Arrested	Died in CC Neuengamme.
René Rasschaert	Arrested	Liberated from Leuven prison early September 1944.
Jozef Rasschaert	Arrested	Died in CC Neuengamme.
Maria Rentiers	Arrested	Liberated from Ghost Train in Brussels.
Emile Reynders	Arrested	Died in CC Blumenthal-Schützenhof.
Kamiel Robeyns	Arrested	Died in CC Neuengamme.
Georges Swinnen	Arrested	Died in Blumenthal-Schützenhof. From nearby town St.-Joris-Winghe.
Georges-Jozef Thielens	Arrested	Died in CC Ravensbrück. From nearby town Kessel-Lo.
Adolf Timmermans	Arrested	Died in CC Neuengamme.
Louis Timmermans	Arrested	Returned from CC.
Marcel Trompet	Arrested	Died in CC Neuengamme.
Frans Trompet	Arrested	Returned from CC.
Herman Vandegaer	Arrested	Died in CC Blumenthal-Schützenhof.
Jozef Vandegaer	Arrested	Died during 'death march' in Ravensbrück.
Theofiel Vandermotte	Arrested	Died in CC Blumenthal-Schützenhof.
Frans Vangilbergen	Arrested	Returned from CC.
Louis Vangoidsenhoven	Arrested	Died in CC Neuengamme-Schandelah.
Edward Vangoidsenhoven	Arrested	Died in CC Blumenthal-Schützenhof.
Evrard Vangoidsenhoven	Arrested	Died during 'death march' near Ludwiglust-Wöbbelin.
August Vanhellemont	Arrested	Died in CC Neuengamme. From nearby town Attenrode.
Guillaume Vanhellemont	Arrested	Died in CC Blumenthal-Schützenhof.
Jozef Van Kerkhoven	Arrested	Died in CC Neuengamme. From nearby town St-Joris-Winghe.
Jozef Veugelen	Arrested	Died in CC Neuengamme. From nearby town St-Joris-Winghe.
Leon Vuchelen	Arrested	Released from Leuven prison a few days after his arrest.
Désiré Vuerinckx	Arrested	Liberated from Leuven prison early September 1944.
Constant Wittemans	Arrested	Liberated from Ghost Train in Brussels.
Germaine Wittemans	Arrested	Liberated from Ghost Train in Brussels.

CC – Concentration Camp

Concise Bibliography & Sources

Personal Research Helpers

In Canada

Les Allison, Les Anderson (431 Sqn), Leslie Arkley (née Foster), Stan Armstrong (405 Sqn), Ross Baroni (405 Sqn), Dave Birrell (Director Nanton Lancaster Air Museum), G. Harry Booth, Paul Bourdages (425 Sqn), Denny Boyd (*Vancouver Sun*), Herbert Brown, Bill Chorley, Harry Clarke, Mowatt Christie, Rolland Cright (Sqn Historian 405 MP Sqn), Fred Davies (405 Sqn), Robert C. Dickson, PhD, MD, W.A.B. Douglas (DND), Glenmore Ellwood (405 Sqn), Ruth Evans (née Blenkinsop), W. Farrell (Canadian Forces Photographic Unit), Leslie W. Foster, Julius Goldman, Paul Gribbons, Alex Guise-Bagley (405 Sqn), Mrs Florence Gust, Patricia Hamill (*Islander Magazine*), Lorna Hayes (405 Sqn), Art Hazle, Theodor Howlett (425 Sqn), Bus Imrie, Joyce Inkster, Jerry Jenkinson, Peter Koch (405 Sqn), Fergus Kyle, Michael M. Leblanc, Stuart Leslie (429 Sqn), Albert J. MacDonald (425 Sqn), John MacDonald, PhD, Gloria MacKenzie (Library and Archives Canada), Scotty MacKay (425 Sqn), Ken Maclure, Henri-Bernard Marceau (425 Sqn), Frances Martin, Ella Matthes-Smith, Ken McMillan (425 Sqn), Glen Merrifield (405 Sqn), Mrs Lee Miskae, Carl Morgan (*The Windsor Star*), Don Morrison (RCAF ex-POW Assn), Donald Munro, Len O'Hanlon (405 Sqn), Jacques Page (425 Sqn), Colin Pattle, Murray Peden, Mrs June Peters, BGen Peter F. Ramsay, John B. Rutherford, Faye Sage (née Blenkinsop), Jim Scannell (405 Sqn), Stanley Scislowski (*The Windsor Star*), Mrs Audrey Smith, Mrs Florence Smith, Herman & Olga Smith, Raymond & Waldtrout Smith, Louise Smith (*Medicine Hat News*), Cec Southward, T.J. Stephens (425 Sqn), Rob Tardif & Jo-Ann Gingras-Stewart (*The Assiniboia Times*), Gabriel Taschereau (425 Sqn), Les Wainwright (425 Sqn), MGen David Wightman, Donald C. Wilson (425 Sqn), Mrs Eileen Woods, John Uhthoff, The British Columbia Provincial Archives and Records Service, The National Archives of Canada, The National Defence Headquarters – Directorate of History, The National Personnel Records Centre, The Victoria City Archives.

In Belgium

Ward Adriaens (Director Jewish Museum of Deportation and Resistance), Jeanne Beddegenoodts, Jozef Bussels, Theofiel Cauwberghs, Jozef Claes, Theodore Claes, Jan Crab, Frans Craeninckx, Marc Deboeck, Régis Decobeck, Cynrik De Decker, Achiel De Ruyter, Jacques De Vos, Maurice De Wilde, Anna Gemoets, Lea Gemoets, Wim Govaerts, Charles Jonckers, Marc Lennarts (Administration Communale de Montzen-Plombières), Marcel Loddewijckx, François Michiels, Jan Pypen, Jos Pypen, Paula Pypen, Leon Raemaeckers, Jos Roovers, Valère and Mrs Seys-Cauberghs, August Schellens, Maria Simons, Albert Stas, Octave Stas, Albert Steennot, Louis Timmermans, Frans Trompet, Louis Valgaerens, Gie van den Berghe (SOMA), Sylvie Vander Elst (Federale Dienst Oorlogsslachtoffers), Theofiel Willems, Maurice Vuchelen, Marcel

Weckx, Centre for Historical Documentation of the Belgian Armed Forces.

In the United Kingdom
Chris Ashworth, Gerald Blenkinsop, Chaz Bowyer, Michael J.F. Bowyer, Tom Cranston (405 Sqn), Ann Gillett (née Blenkinsop), Brian Goulding, Peter Green, James A. Johnson, Francis K. Mason, Tom Messham, Martin Middlebrook, Edward Munday (Ministry of Defence – Air Historical Branch), Michael S.J. Parker, Dennis 'Ren' Renvoizé (425 Sqn), Ray Sturtivant, Andy Thomas, Jimmy Trilsbach (405 Sqn), Simon Watson, Geoff Wood.

In the United States of America
Yvonne Daley-Brusselmans, Phil Shannon, Jack Terzian.

In New Zealand
Barbara Coulter (Ministry of Defence), Joseph Murphy (75 Sqn), W.J. Simpson (NZ Bomber Command Assn).

In France
Mme. Andrée Berchoux, Pierre Frois.

In Germany
Bundesarchiv, Freiburg, Horst Diener, George-Hermann Greiner, Hans-Joachim Jabs, Fritz Rumpelhardt (all NJG 1).

In The Netherlands
Theo Boiten, Marcel Hogenhuis, Ron Pütz, Wim Vermeulen (Vriendenkring Neuengamme).

Selected Bibliography

Aders, G. *Geschichte der Deutschen Nachtjagd*. Stuttgart: Motorbuch Verlag, 1978.
Anderson, L. *Days of Laughter, Nights of Fear*. Winnipeg: Les Anderson, 2001.
Beck, L.C. *Fighter Pilot*. Los Angeles: Wetzel Publishing, 1946.
Bernard, H. *Totale Oorlog en Revolutionaire Oorlog*, vol. III. Brussels: KMS, 1975.
Bowman, M. *Wellington, the Geodetic Giant*. Shrewsbury UK: Airlife, 1989.
Bowyer, C. *Pathfinders at War*. Shepperton UK: Ian Allan, 1987.
Chorley, W.R. *RAF Bomber Command Losses – 1944*. Leicester UK: Midland Counties, 1997.
Churchill, W. *The Hinge of Fate, The Second World War*, vol. IV. New York: Collins, 1951.
Cosgrove, E. *The Evaders*. Markham ON: Simon and Schuster of Canada. 1976.
Crab, J. *Resistere*. Leuven: NKB Vlaams-Brabant, 1984.
Daley-Brusselmans, Y. *Belgium, RendezVous Nr. 127*. Manhattan KS: Sunflower UP, 2001.
D'Udekem d'Acoz, M-P. *Voor Koning & Vaderland*. Tielt: Lannoo, 2003.
Duerinckx, O. *Meensel-Kiezegem 1&11-8-'4 – Getuigenissen*. O. Duerinckx, 1984.
Golden Book of the Belgian Resistance. Brussels: Leclercq, 1947(?).
Harris, A. *Bomber Offensive*. London: Greenhill Books, 1990.
Hick-Lhomme, M.-J. *Montzen-Gare se souvient*. Montzen, 1985.
Jefford, C.G. *RAF Squadrons*. Shrewsbury UK: Airlife, 2001.
Jouan, C. *Comète, Histoire d'une Ligne d'Evasion*. Furnes: Editions Beffroi, 1948.
Keen, G.F. *My 56 Months in the RCAF*. Langton: George Keen, 2003.
Lavender E. and N. Sheffe. *The Evaders*. Whitby ON: McGraw-Hill Ryerson, 1992.

Lemarec. *45e Anniversaire de la 425e Escadrille Alouette*, 425 Sqn RCAF, Bagotville, 1988.

Mahaddie, T.G. *Hamish: The Memoirs of a Pathfinder*. Shepperton UK: Ian Allan, 1989.

Mason, F. *The Avro Lancaster*. Bourne End UK: Aston, 1989.

Middlebrook, M. *The Bomber Command War Diaries*. Harmondsworth: Viking, 1987.

Middlebrook, M. *The Berlin Raids*. London: Viking, 1988.

Musgrove, G. *Pathfinder Force: A History of 8 Group*. London: MacDonald and Jane's, 1976.

Nixon, R. *405 Squadron History*. Winnipeg: Craig Kelman & Associates, 1990.

Onderwater, H. *Reis Naar De Horizon*. Baarn: Hollandia, 1985.

Peden, M. *A Thousand Shall Fall*. Toronto: Stoddart, 1988.

Pitchfork, G. *Shot Down and on the Run: The RAF and Commonwealth Aircrews Who Got Home from Behind Enemy Lines, 1940-1945*. Richmond UK: The National Archives, 2003.

Price, A. *Pictorial History of the Luftwaffe*. Shepperton UK: Ian Allan, 1969.

Strubbe, F. *Geheime Oorlog*. Tielt: Lannoo, 1992.

Van Laere S. and F. Craeninckx. *Een Klein Dorp, Een Zware Tol*. Antwerp: Manteau, 2004.

Other Sources

Microfilm Add. MSS. 0447. Personal Files, Correspondence, Photographs and Miscellaneous Family Papers, 1920-1945 – Edward Weyman Blenkinsop, British Columbia Archives and Record Service, Victoria, B.C.

Family letters to and from Edward W. Blenkinsop, 1934-1944.

Family letters to and from Hubert W. Blenkinsop, 1919-1948.

Family letters to and from Winsome Neroutsos-Blenkinsop, 1919-1950.

Dossiers Agents de Service de Renseignements et d'Action (SRA), SOMA, Brussels – Dossiers of Charles Jonckers, Hilaire Gemoets, Charles Gemoets, Frans Van Dyck, Jules Schotsmans, Emma Bruyninckx, Herman Pypen and Frans Vranckx.

Catalogue of Concentration Camps, Ministerie van Wederopbouw – Algemene Directie voor Schade aan Personen, SOMA, Brussels.

Federal Service Social Security – Archives of the Service for War Victims (FOD Sociale Zekerheid – Dienst voor Oorlogsslachtoffers), Brussels – Dossiers DDO of Ferdinand Alen (SVG-d148829), Edward Blenkinsop (SVG-d172419), Adolf Hendrickx (SVG-d069214) and Prosper Natens (SVG-d110475).

RCAF Record of Service Airmen for Edward W. Blenkinsop, Frank Darling, Lawrence Allen, David Ramsay, Robert A. Booth, George J. Smith, Nicholas H. Clifford and Leslie A. Foster – The National Personnel Records Centre, Ottawa, Canada.

Operations Record Books Nos. 420, 424, 425 and 405 Squadrons, RCAF, and of No. 331 Wing, RCAF – Public Records Office, Kew, London, UK and Gribbons Enterprises, Ottawa, Canada.

Raid Plot and Missing Aircraft Register Montzen Raid, 27/28 April 1944 – Public Records Office, Kew, London, UK.

Flying Log-Book Squadron Leader Edward W. Blenkinsop, DFC, CdeG.

Flying Log-Book Pilot Officer Robert A. Booth, CdeG.

Flying Log-Book Pilot Officer Leslie A. Foster, CdeG.

Flying Log-Book Pilot Officer Scotty MacKay.

Flying Log-Book Pilot Officer Johnnie Miskae.

Flying Log-Book Flight Lieutenant Les Wainwright, DFC.

Photo Albums and Records of 405 Maritime Patrol Squadron RCAF, Greenwood, Nova Scotia, and 425 Fighter Squadron RCAF, Bagotville, Québec.

Index of Personnel Names